Human Resource Management in the Hospitality Industry

Now in its ninth edition, *Human Resource Management in the Hospitality Industry* is fully updated with new legal information, data, statistics and examples. Taking a 'process' approach, it provides the reader with an essential understanding of the purpose, policies and processes concerned with managing an enterprise's workforce within the current business and social environment.

Since the eighth edition of this book there have been many important developments in this field and this ninth edition has been completely revised and updated in the following ways:

- Extensively updated content to reflect recent issues and trends including: labour markets and industry structure, impacts of IT and social media, growth of international multi-unit brands, role of employer branding, talent management, equal opportunities and managing diversity. All explored specifically within the hospitality industry.
- The text explores key issues and shows real-life applications of HRM in the hospitality industry and is informed through the authors' research projects within Mitchells & Butlers plc, Pizza Express, Marriott Hotels and Café Rouge.
- An extended case study drawing from the authors' experience working with Forte and Co., Centre Hotels, Choice Hotels and Bass, Price Waterhouse and Grant Thornton.
- Supported with new lecturer and student online resources at http://www.routledge.com/books/details/9780415632546/.

Written in a user-friendly style and with strong support from the Institute of Hospitality, each chapter includes international examples, bulleted lists, guides to further reading and exercises to test knowledge.

Michael J. Boella is Faculty Fellow at the University of Brighton and specializes in teaching human resource management and law.

Steven Goss-Turner is Head of Operations of the School of Sport and Service Management at the University of Brighton.

Contents

Contents

Figures

Appendices

About the authors

Dr Steven Goss-Turner is Head of Operations for the School of Sport and Service Management at the University of Brighton. He has degrees from both Strathclyde and Portsmouth Universities and was awarded a PhD from the University of Brighton in 2010 for a programme of study entitled, "The Relationship between Organisational Culture and Labour Turnover", which included substantial field research within the hospitality industry.

Before joining the University of Brighton in 1992, he spent 16 years with the then Trusthouse Forte Hotels, including Regional Human Resources Director for the London and International Division. He is the author of a number of books and articles, focussing particularly on aspects of the service industries connected to workplace cultures, labour turnover and human resource strategy in multi-site businesses.

Michael J. Boella has a Master's degree in employment studies from Sussex University. He is a Faculty Fellow at the University of Brighton and specialises in teaching human resource management and law. He was a visiting professor at the University of Perpignan in France and teaches regularly at the University of Applied Sciences in Bonn and at the Angell Business School in Freiburg. He also taught regularly at the Ecole Hotelière de Lausanne. Mike worked for Forte and Co Ltd and Bass as a Human Resource Manager and for Price Waterhouse as a management consultant. Mike has been editor of a number of Croner publications for over twenty years and is joint author of Principles of Hospitality Law.

Mike has received several awards for his work: the Special Achievement Award of the Hotel and Catering Personnel and Training Association, Honorary Faculty Fellowship of Brighton University, the Award for Excellence from the University of Applied Sciences in Bonn and admission to the Confrérie du Sabre d'Or.

Foreword

Philippe Rossiter, MBA, FIH, FCMI, FTS, FRGS, FRSA, AIL
Chief Executive
Institute of Hospitality
January 2013

It says much for the quality and value of this publication that it has now reached its ninth edition. To have maintained its place as an essential text for so many years *Human Resource Management in the Hospitality Industry* has had to remain relevant to its broad audience. That it has done so through successive reviews is a tribute to the scholarly work of its authors, Michael Boella and Steven Goss-Turner, and this latest edition, once again, bears witness to their assiduous attention to detail and careful evaluation of the topic in the context of today's environment.

Full of informative examples and pertinent guidance, this ninth edition has updated the subject in a timely and appropriate fashion. Whilst the fundamental principles governing the sound management of people remain constant, the circumstances in which they operate continue to evolve at an ever-accelerating rate. For example, the rapid advances in technology since the previous edition have witnessed the advent of social media as a powerful force in our lives. This phenomenon alone is now requiring managers and businesses to re-assess their relationships with employees, many of whom have 'grown up' with these technological advances. Furthermore, these new entrants to our industry often approach the world of work with a very different set of cultural norms to those held by their managers, presenting a new set of challenges for both parties.

For these reasons, *Human Resources Management in the Hospitality Industry* remains a vital text for all who aspire to a leadership role within the sector. As the industry's professional body, the Institute of Hospitality's prime objects are: the promotion of best practice and the advancement of education in hospitality management. This is why I am delighted to see these twin missions so amply supported in this latest edition, and the authors are to be congratulated on maintaining the freshness, relevance and breadth of coverage in a book that should be a key component in the skills armoury of all managers and aspiring managers across the hospitality industry.

Foreword

Michael Hirst, OBE
Former Chairman and Chief Executive
Hilton International
January 2013

This book, now in its ninth edition, offers an in-depth description of sound human resource management practices, in the hospitality industry. Managing the workforce effectively is perhaps the single most important issue in delivering first-class service which underpins a hotel's performance, reputation and profitability.

For more than 40 years, I have persisted in the international hotel industry. First as a hotel school graduate, then as a trainee in almost every department, before rising through the management ranks of UK domestic hotel companies to assume the most senior job with one of the leading international hotel brands, Hilton Hotels. Throughout this journey the importance of good, well-skilled and enthused people was paramount in helping me achieve corporate objectives.

In retrospect I don't think the principles of sound people management or the challenges of developing a committed labour force in the hotel industry have really changed since I first started in the industry. Of course labour laws and regulations have increased as policymakers and employee representatives have sought to offer greater employment safeguards and benefits.

At the international level, the countries of origin of hotel staff, particularly management and supervisors, have changed dramatically. In the past, companies, in order to preserve their brand integrity in new countries, tended to post skilled staff from their own already successful properties. In many countries, however, immigration rules have changed in order to protect local employment, ensuring that home-grown employees have employment priority. In addition, more international companies can now rely on a more abundant source of local trained labour in domestic markets, as a result of local education and training initiatives. Even so, restrictions on importing senior management and skilled supervisors present companies with challenges as they work to protect the integrity of their brand.

Outsourcing too has changed the management of many properties. Initially services such as laundries were outsourced. This was extended to housekeeping and some food and beverage operations. Now restaurants are being run by celebrity chefs, all adding to the variety of operational and employment arrangements and challenges both within a single property and within a whole company.

I have always felt that good hotel management requires a hands-on approach and strong communications and leadership skills. However, we now see an almost never-ending supply of new branded hotels, operating on an almost formulaic basis, setting out in countless manuals and checklists the dos and don'ts of human resource management, removing much of a hotel manager's accountability, responsibility and discretion.

There's no denying that hotel brands, operated under management contracts or by franchise have become the way in which hotel companies are growing across all continents of the world, and consistency of operation is critical. Getting the balance right, however, is vital. Local culture and employment regulations play a big part in how employees are deployed, just as local culture impacts upon guests in the experience they expect and receive.

The real risk for general managers is that some remote Head Office function removes the discretion of local management to organize and inspire their workforce according to the particular circumstances and market position of each hotel. This removes the one most critical attribute of the General Manager and his or her Department Heads, i.e. his or her ability to exercise judgement, to make decisions. Granted that employment law is a minefield and pre-scribed arrangements need to be in place and understood, it is my view the human resource function should be at the service of General Management and not the other way round.

It is a much-used statement to say 'Hotels are a People Business', but it is a truism. Having a clear understanding of the overarching principles of HR planning, recruitment, selection, induc-tion, training, performance management and people development (now talent management), reward and remuneration and regulation is a necessary part of running a people business.

In Michael Boella and Steven Goss-Turner's book, both authors with years of experience in some of the world's largest hotel and hospitality companies, you'll find all of this and a lot more.

Preface

This book has always presented a particular challenge, knowing that its long-term success has been largely because it has been written to be very readable and accessible to a wide range of readers. This book has never been addressed solely to the academic community – instead it is addressed to practising managers and to students intending to be managers, and to their teachers. More than anything else we aim to indicate 'best practice'. What constitutes 'best practice' is a question of opinion but we are basing what we consider 'best practice' on a wide range of sources including publications and research and discussions with many managers from many companies and countries.

We have avoided straying into the related sector of 'tourism', because the various different hospitality sectors represent over 60 per cent of the hospitality, leisure, travel and tourism businesses (People 1st, *State of the Nation Report*, 2011) and, whilst there are considerable overlaps between the various sectors, we believe that the hospitality sectors have distinctive characteristics.

As we wrote in the eighth edition of this book, the original edition was written when *personnel* management in the hospitality industry was practised by a handful of employers and even in these cases it was confined to a few functions of personnel management such as recruitment and training. Today, forty years later, we can say that human resource management (HRM) in the hospitality industry has grown in its impact and status, with an increasing number of HR Directors being appointed at executive board member level. However, it is clear that in such a fragmented industry, with the vast majority of businesses employing five or fewer staff, there is still much to do, in order to develop a positive image of the sector as a first choice for long-term career employment.

Each new edition has been prompted by a variety of changes that have affected the hospitality industry, including political, legal, economic, social and technological changes, and this edition is no different. Many of these changes have had considerable influence on the management of the industry's human resources.

One key issue, developed even since the last edition, is the impact of the Internet – in the case of staff recruitment most major companies have largely abandoned the print media for the Internet. Furthermore, various web-based media, such as TripAdvisor, have very significant impacts on marketing, which in turn impacts on staff recruitment and training. There is now also an increasing concern for the environment and sustainability, in many cases a genuine concern, in other cases mere 'green-washing'.

A key economic element has been the growth in the reach and the scale of hospitality companies, many now global actors. Such growth has an almost insatiable appetite for human resources at all levels and one consequence is the multicultural nature of the workforce – today it is reported that nearly 40 per cent of staff in UK restaurants were not born in the UK and over 30 per cent of managers were born overseas. Similar patterns can be observed in many other countries.

The issues of HRM across multi-site companies and in an international context have been developed to a greater extent in this edition, largely due to Steven Goss-Turner's PhD research into the field.

Together with the globalization trend, the need to meet shareholder expectations creates other pressures which often result in changes to the management of an enterprise's human resources. Such changes may include more flexible but often polarized and distanced work-forces, outsourcing of large sections of a business activity, reliance on agency staff and short-term contracts. In the UK it is reported that 70 per cent of businesses rely upon part-time workers. All of which creates a purely economic relationship with little room for loyalty. Another consequence of such economic pressures is flatter organization structures with more empowered or enabled workers, but often with fewer internal promotion and personal development prospects.

At the same time, many employers, some conscious of these trends, are improving their human resource management practices through participating in a range of schemes such as Investors in People, the British Hospitality Association's Excellence through People, and the Institute of Hospitality's Hospitality Assured schemes.

Such trends and developments create tremendous paradoxes for contemporary hospitality managers. Whilst many companies wish to recognize the needs of all their stakeholders, they also have to remain competitive in a global market.

We are grateful to all those who have made this latest edition and earlier editions possible, including the many companies and associations that have allowed us to use their material. These include: the British Hospitality Association, the Chartered Institute of Personnel and Development, Janine Mills of the Institute of Hospitality and Matthew Ruck of Marriott Hotels.

Finally, we are very grateful to Philippe Rossiter of the Institute of Hospitality, and Michael Hirst, previously CEO of Hilton International.

Thanks also to Juliet Boella for all her work on this ninth edition, having worked also on every edition since the first edition.

Michael J. Boella, MA, FIH, Charter member CIPD
Steven Goss-Turner, Ph.D., MSc, FIH, Charter member CIPD
January 2013

Part 1

The hospitality industry HRM context

Chapter 1

Background to the industry's workforce

A proliferation of competing brands, shorter business and product life cycles together with many different business models all make the world's business environment more complex and challenging.

The hospitality industry is no exception. Even in periods of recession such as those experienced since 2008 the hospitality industry has seen significant changes with some sectors growing such as restaurants, coffee houses and the budget hotels sectors, whilst others have seen an equally dramatic decline such as the public house (licensed bar) sector.

Within hotels we have seen the continuing growth of the budget hotels sector and we have seen the steady growth of boutique hotels, once the preserve of enthusiastic private hotel operators, into significant chains within larger multinational chains. At the international level we also see rapid expansion of international hotel brands, such as Hilton, as the middle classes grow in many countries including the BRIC countries (Brazil, Russia, India, China) to which are added some African economies.

Hotels and hotel companies are constantly changing hands so that we see what some may describe as 'churning' of many hotel properties. Some iconic brands have been bought and sold several times in a few years. Many have disappeared.

Various different forms of business models are now common. Apart from simple owner-operated properties other forms of operation include management contracts (or agreements), franchising, voluntary chains (or consortia), joint ventures, branded reservation services and combinations of two or more of these. In addition, subcontracting, outsourcing and offshoring alter significantly the traditional business models.

At the social level we are witnessing important developments. On the negative side we are witnessing significant increases in obesity- and alcohol-related problems. On the positive side there are increased concerns for the environment, sustainability, animal welfare, health and healthy eating and drinking. These all impact directly or indirectly on the industry. At the technological level there has been a dramatic transformation in how customers access these services.

In the past, customers may have relied upon classification systems and brands for 'promises' of quality. Today, social media has entered the business environment, with sites such as TripAdvisor playing a significant part in customer behaviour. A report published in Ehotelier.com (December 2011) stated that '60% of guests use one or more social networking platforms during their search, shop and buy process'. And whilst brands play a vital role they are seriously challenged to deliver on their 'promises' by the social media.

In addition, whilst hospitality operators have operated basic forms of 'yield management' for many years, the adoption and development of computerized hospitality-specific yield management systems have led to the need for new skills and, in many cases, modified organization structures.

All these developments have significant impact on the human resourcing of businesses. Shorter business and product life cycles, flatter organization structures and the 'churning' of properties means that lifelong careers, or even moderately long careers with one employer are harder to encounter, being replaced by 'portfolio' careers and even portfolio jobs (i.e. two or more part-time jobs at the same time).

From the hospitality industry's perspective, there are many accompanying societal changes with great significance for the industry's operators. These include easier and cheaper travel and, as a consequence of improved lifestyles and medical services, increased longevity, resulting in increasing populations and demographic restructuring. Alongside this, the media in their many different forms are informing and shaping people's behaviour as never before.

The contributions made by the hospitality industry to this general rise in standard of living are considerable and varied, providing essential products and services, leisure services, large-scale employment and wealth creation. Tourism, of which the hospitality industry is a principal element, is now claimed to be the world's fastest growing industry and also one of the leading earners of foreign currency.

The total value of tourism to the UK in 2009 was estimated to be £86 billion, with overseas visitors spending close to £12 billion of that figure in foreign currency (People 1st, 2011). The value to the nation's 2009 gross domestic product (GDP) of specific hospitality sector and related services was estimated at 4.9 per cent.

The UK hospitality industry, with its ever-developing range of products and services, has seen considerable growth in recent years. In 2010 and 2011 alone, according to the British Hospitality Association, 276 new hotels were built adding 35,000 rooms to the hotel stock. The high streets of towns are now as much a forum of branded restaurants and coffee houses as they are for general retailers. Whilst there have been substantial technical improvements, and conditions in the industry may have improved over what they were in the past, the relative status of the industry as an employer, compared with other employers, has not improved significantly. Admittedly at the top of the scale, some highly skilled workers such as chefs, who are in short supply, can command very high incomes, but at the other end of the scale, kitchen porters and cleaners, for example, would earn considerably higher wages for broadly similar work in other employment sectors. This is in spite of efforts being made by some of the larger companies in the industry to improve conditions.

Among the reasons must be the fact that most employees only generate between £42 and £81 per hour for their employer compared with many other industries in which employees may generate many times that for their employer. Of this between 10 and 40 per cent will be taken up by labour costs, the remainder going towards material costs, property costs, fixed costs and profit. In contrast, the gambling sector generates around £120 per hour per employee (People 1st, 2011). With few exceptions, catering services do not lend themselves easily to significant mechanization. As a result, the industry is heavily labour-intensive and labour costs dominate many profit-and-loss accounts.

The reasons for the relatively slow rate of improvement in the industry's conditions of employment are considerable, including an understandable reluctance on the part of many proprietors and managers to be among the first to charge higher prices for their services, particularly when the UK is reported to be among the most expensive of tourist destinations. Second, the industry also consists of many small employers (46 per cent with fewer than ten employees). A third reason, linked to the former reason, is that there are few barriers to entry and limited capital requirement. One consequence is that many entering the industry lack knowledge and experience and so the failure rate is relatively high. A fourth reason is that the trade union movement exerts no influence in most sectors of the industry, which contrasts with some other countries. A fifth reason is that the industry's workforce consists largely of people drawn from the secondary labour market, i.e. those not committed to the industry on a long-term basis (such as students, school leavers, housewives). For these reasons, the industry has its own less obvious but costly labour problems including such phenomena as a high labour turnover rate, institutionalized pilfering and low service standards in many establishments.

Because of the nature of the hospitality industry (i.e. many small businesses taking cash) the industry is host to a significant 'black or shadow' economy. This is discussed in more detail in Chapter 16, Employment Law. However, the black or shadow economy was estimated, at the European level in 2005, to be in the region of 15 per cent of the industry's total revenue (Schneider, 2005). In the UK the tax authorities (HMRC) suggests that the UK's black economy is of the order of 6 to 8 per cent of GDP and probably higher in the hospitality industry.

It is, of course, to be expected that some aspects of working in the hospitality industry may be unattractive when considered alongside other sectors. There are intrinsic and largely unavoidable challenges such as having to work evenings, weekends and bank holidays. Other problems, however, can certainly be reduced or eliminated by determined management action. These problems include split-shift working, unpredictable working hours, staff reliance on tips, ignorance of methods of calculating pay and distributing service charges, and management's reluctance to involve staff in matters that affect their working lives. A number of reports have highlighted these difficulties which, together with some management attitudes and practices, undoubtedly cause much of the industry's human resourcing problems. Even today, for example, many employers and managers expect all employees, whatever their position and wage rate, to be dedicated to their jobs, to have a vocational fervour towards their work and to sacrifice leisure time for pay that is not high by general economic standards. These same employers and managers fail to recognize that their own motivation to work is usually completely different from that of their staff, and that many work people throughout the community are becoming less work-oriented for various reasons. Employers in industry must reconcile themselves rapidly to the fact that the majority of potential staff are less likely to be singularly and vocationally committed unless ways and means are found to harness what some researchers claim is a natural motivation to work.

At the International Hotel and Restaurants Association Human Resource Think Tank in the Netherlands (1999) this issue was discussed and it was concluded that a distinction has to be made between 'loyalty' and 'commitment', loyalty being a two-way long-term attitude of trust and reliance between employer and employee, whereas commitment is perceived as a shorter-term professional/economic relationship which endures so long as each is dependent upon the other (see Chapter 2). A similar issue has been addressed in the UK government's MacLeod report which was concerned with employee engagement, with examples from the hospitality industry (MacLeod and Clarke, 2010).

The British hospitality industry, its workforce and the British economy

The value of the hospitality and tourism sectors to the UK economy has been emphasized earlier, and has encouraged the government to take increasing heed of the issues faced by the industry, such as during the foot-and-mouth disease outbreaks in 2001 and 2007, which had devastating impacts on many tourism and hospitality businesses.

The British Labour Force Survey 2010 reported that the hospitality, leisure, travel and tourist industries' workforce numbered around 2,150,000, an increase of 14 per cent over 2005. The workforce represents around 7.2 per cent of the UK workforce as a whole.

Tourism and travel

The increased demand for tourism and international travel services is a worldwide development and a consequence is the internationalization of many of the leading hospitality companies. A result of this for the British hospitality industry's employers is that many potential employees now look overseas for employment. At the same time many foreigners come to the UK, in many cases to learn English.

Social and demographic changes

The industry is, of course, responding to major changes in the demand side of the industry, i.e. the consumer side. Demographic changes alone, such as the increased proportion and number of older people, have created demands for more products catering for their needs, and the reduced number of young people is creating both demand and labour market problems. Among the younger population, changes in eating habits – a shift to 'grazing', for example – have created opportunities for many different types of fast food outlets, some blamed for the worldwide increase in obesity. The move to healthy eating too is responsible for a range of new products and a related growth in vegetarianism to be contrasted with the growth of obesity within many populations.

A breakdown in the traditional socio-economic usage of different hospitality products is probably of significance. No longer are some products used exclusively by particular socio-economic groups. Instead, the use of catering products, such as fine-dining, is to a greater extent than previously determined by the occasion (behaviourally determined) rather than by the socio-economic group.

Business continuity

One of the crucial features of modern life is that businesses and organizations are subject to events outside of their control, including natural disasters such as storms and flooding, and man-made events such as terrorism. One thing that modern organizations need to do therefore, because of the potential impact of such events on the organization itself and upon its employees, is to have business continuity plans in place. (See Appendix 2, the Institute of Hospitality's 'Business Continuity' guidance notes.)

The changing hospitality industry

Within the hospitality industry itself there are important developments that have long-term implications for the industry. First, as many hospitality businesses became larger (i.e. operating more establishments) and as individual establishments have become larger and more complex, there was in the 1980s an expansion of numbers in junior and middle management, particularly in the non-line functions. In the late 1980s and the 1990s, however, economic pressures have led to a reduction, a 'delayering', of such roles. This is discussed later in this book.

One of the biggest developments in business has been the emergence and development of a multitude of brands ranging from global brands with many thousands of outlets through to small local brands with as little as a handful of outlets. At the same time hospitality organizations have become more market-oriented. This has led to increased market segmentation and to many of the larger companies establishing specialist subsidiary companies which are concerned with a range of highly specialized products such as boutique hotels and aparthotels.

This proliferation of brands has developed because of the variety of business models including the simple owner-operated business, management agreements or contracts, consortia (voluntary chains), marketing groups, joint ventures, licensing agreements and, probably most importantly, franchising.

Franchising has been around for many years although the word 'franchising' was rarely used. Breweries offering tenancies was one major form enabling individuals to go into business at relatively little cost, with the support of a major brand, leaving tenants (the franchisee) to operate their pubs, in many cases within a relatively loose 'tied house' arrangement, with most pubs being different, i.e. a 'soft brand'.

Other hospitality sector brands, however, were developing. In the UK one of the earliest fast food brands to develop was the Wimpy bar, to be followed years later by the entry and domination of US brands including McDonald's, KFC and Burger King. These brands really heralded the emergence of what we now refer to as 'hard' brands, offering consistency and reliability which many other brands failed to deliver. For many years these 'hard' brands imposed their perception of customer demand on customers. Such fast food operations constitute a relatively easy and inexpensive field to enter but success demands expertise and promotional effort, which are increasingly beyond the resources of the independent. The franchise side of the hospitality industry, as a result, is growing along with franchising generally.

In the hotel sector, similar developments are evident in the growth of the consortium movement, such as Best Western, by which individual hotel businesses can collaborate with other similar establishments in order to compete effectively against the large national and multinational companies, especially in the areas of marketing and global distribution and reservation systems.

While the industry has established its importance from an economic point of view, it could be hoped that those employed in the industry would be reaping rewards that echo this increased importance. In many cases this may well be so, with key people such as chefs and waiters at leading restaurants and good managers earning high rewards.

However, as reported above, the industry does still have a reputation for low pay, which is also discussed later in the book, because it is not as simple a matter as outside observers appear to think. The value of tips, food, accommodation, laundry and savings on fuel and fares all have to be taken into account: anyone 'living in' avoids some of the heavy daily transport and accommodation costs. Also it must be borne in mind that a very large proportion of the industry's workforce is drawn from a secondary labour market. Because of this, many work people may not have high-value skills to offer, or alternatively their motives to work may put a premium on the convenience of their work (location, hours, family), for which they will sacrifice higher incomes.

In fact, earlier research from Bath University, published in 1999, found that 'catering workers are in the half of the population most happy with their jobs despite poor pay and image':

Job	Satisfaction rating (%)
Restaurant and catering managers	55
Bar staff	50
Chefs and cooks	47
Catering assistants and counterhands	44
Waiters and waitresses	40
Kitchen porters and hands	40
Publicans, innkeepers, licensees	40

Figure 1.1 Job satisfaction rating
Source: Bath University, 1999.

The most satisfied workers were child-carers, with a satisfaction rating of 60 per cent. The lowest were metal workers, with a rating of 20 per cent. Professor Michael Rose of Bath University concluded 'that part-time women were more satisfied than full-timers and men in similar positions … and staff satisfaction tended to drop with improved skills and greater access to alternative jobs' (*Caterer and Hotelkeeper*, 16 September 1999). Lucas (2004) supports the general tone of the Bath findings, utilizing evidence from the 1998 Workplace Employment Relations Survey, declaring that many hospitality employees are more positive about their jobs than many in better-paid sectors.

Undoubtedly, low pay in the industry exists, but it is not something that can be put right overnight. Britain's hotels and restaurants are already reported to be among the most expensive in the world, so increases to tariffs are not the answer. Instead, a thorough reappraisal of the services offered and the consequent manning levels and staff training may lead to greater productivity. In this field, strides have been made; capital investment is made to replace the most menial or repetitive tasks, and efforts are made to improve the standard of training. However, increased productivity in service industries is not as easy to achieve as in many other industries without making radical changes to the nature of the service itself. To some extent this is happening, particularly through increasing the amount of customer participation, whether this is by buffet-style breakfasts or by automated check-in and check-out procedures such as those developed by Formule 1, the budget division of the French Accor group.

Most improvements and efforts seem to be made at the tip of the iceberg, mainly among the larger companies. Much the greater numerical proportion of the industry is made up of smaller employers who each employ a few staff only and who for a variety of reasons are not able or prepared to evaluate their own business methods as rigorously as is required in today's aggressive business climate. One consequence is the growth of the larger companies at the expense of smaller companies, which is a phenomenon not confined to the hospitality industries, but is a general phenomenon of consolidating industrialized societies.

In essence, therefore, major structural changes are taking place in the workforce, and in methods and organization of work. These can be summarized as follows:

1 Employment in manufacturing is declining as productivity is improved through automation and outsourced to other (lower wage) countries.
2 Employment in personal services is increasing.
3 There will be growth in the secondary labour market and a decline in the primary labour market.
4 There will be an increase in white-collar employment.
5 There will be a decline in manual employment.
6 There will be a decline in long-term, full-time work, with more people doing more than one job, including professionals pursuing a so-called 'portfolio' career and a growth in 'interim' management.
7 There will be a reduction in job security.
8 Technological change and economic pressures cause redistribution and reorganization of work as evidenced by the outsourcing to other countries such as India of much routine information processing and call-centre work.

These trends were anticipated some years ago by Charles Handy (see Chapter 2) who wrote that the full-employment society was becoming the part-employment society, that the one-organization career was becoming rarer and that sexual stereotyping at work was no longer so rigid.

It is worth adding that such changes in working patterns are not all imposed by employers. In many cases it is the supply side of the labour market, the employees, who demand conditions such as more flexible working practices and family-friendly policies of the employer, caused largely by societal changes such as the increase in the number of single-parent families. This is evidenced today by employers asking when potential employees would be available for work, rather than insisting on traditional shift patterns. The trend towards fewer full-time jobs was supported by the *Labour Market Review 2003* (Hospitality Training Foundation, 2004), which reported that only 48.1 per cent of the hospitality workforce is full-time. In 2011 63 per cent of employers offered flexible working which included job-share, condensed hours working and flexi-time (People 1st, 2011).

Labour turnover and employment

The industry has, for many years, had a reputation for a very high level of labour turnover. Twenty years ago the Hotel and Catering Industry Training Board (HCITB) published its report *Manpower Flows in the Hotel and Catering Industry*. It found the following gross turnover rates: managers 19 per cent;

pubs, bars and nightclubs; 31%
restaurants; 26%
hotels; 25%
food and service management; 9%
events; 31%
visitor attractions; 29%
gambling; 11%
travel and tourist services; 16%
self-catering, holiday parks and hostels; 12%

Figure 1.2 Labour turnover rates by sector
Source: People 1st, 2011.

supervisors 94 per cent; craftspeople 55 per cent; and operatives 65 per cent. Cafés and public houses had the highest rates of losses, caused largely by young people using the industry as an interlude between school or college and a full-time career. Figures for 2011 are shown in Figure 1.2.

Although labour turnover can appear to be relatively high among some sectors and some employers, it is vital that proper comparisons are made and also to recognize that not all labour turnover is the consequence of poor employment practices. Many smaller employers cannot offer careers or career progression, so employees will naturally move from one employer to the other, but they remain in the industry. These can be described as 'transient workers'. Transient workers are most common within customer service staff (13–14 per cent of workers) and front-line staff (16–19 per cent of workers) (People 1st, 2011). Some refer to this as 'circulation' as opposed to 'turnover', because the employees concerned are not lost to the industry.

In other cases many employers recruit directly from the secondary labour market, i.e. workers who are not committed to a particular industry. Many workers such as school leavers, students and 'long-term tourists' are seeking short-term employment, sometimes just to earn holiday money or to learn the language, before starting their studies or returning home. Among some employers, particularly in the fast food sector, there is a very high level of labour turnover, often attracting candidates experiencing their first entry into the job market, but labour turnover is anticipated and can be properly managed.

Some key features of the hospitality industry workforce include (People 1st, 2011):

- High proportion of part-time working; 67 per cent of hospitality businesses rely on part-time working to manage demand fluctuations.
- High proportion of women; ranging from 65 per cent in sales and customer services to 44 per cent in management.
- High proportion of younger people; 44 per cent of the workforce is under 30 (UK overall figure is 24 per cent).
- High proportion of transient workers; up to 19 per cent for some front-line staff.

Pay

While there are many instances of high rates of pay in the industry – top executives are in the six-figure bracket – the image overall is not good in this respect. Reliance, in some sectors, on tipping still exists to a greater extent than some consider desirable. The practice of paying employees the basic or near basic wage and also putting notices on menus and price lists that service charges are included has had the effect of diverting customers' tips into company revenue. In many cases this practice has an adverse effect on net earnings. First, all of the service charge may not be distributed to the staff, and second, income from such a source is taxed (VAT and income tax), which was not done previously.

In these circumstances, where low pay and distrust of the employer's wage practices exist, it is to be expected that pilfering on a significant scale takes place. A report based upon an Open University case study, 'Room for Reform', claimed that pilfering appeared to be an institutionalized part of wage bargaining in hotels. Management often recognized it as a way to boost inadequate pay (see Mars and Mitchell, 1979).

Today, 'fiddles' (theft) range from straightforward short-measuring and short-changing of customers to supplying one's own household with cleaning materials, toilet paper, light bulbs, crockery, cutlery and even towels and other linen. Some fiddles are quite sophisticated and operate at quite high levels. It has been known for managers to redecorate their own homes at their employer's expense, or for a manager to deduct 'the cost of grass cutting' from the hotel's petty cash and to arrange for a farmer to pay the manager for hay taken from the same land. In regular spot surveys, not one industrial release student questioned had not witnessed pilfering.

Such practices, however, must be seen in proper perspective, bearing in mind that some other industries, trades and professions provide vastly more lucrative opportunities than those provided in the hospitality industry.

Human resource management in the hospitality industry

(This section needs to be read in conjunction with Chapter 2.) Until the early 1960s, personnel management as a specialist function in the hotel and catering industry was almost non-existent. Where it did exist, it was devoted to small elements of personnel management, such as recruitment and training. It was not until the introduction of employment legislation, such as the Contracts of Employment Act 1964 and the establishment of the Hotel and Catering Industry Training Board in the 1960s, that personnel managers began to appear in the industry in any numbers. Today all of the larger companies now employ human resource (HR) specialists, with a range of different titles including Personnel Manager, Human Resource Manager or Director, Director of People, Talent Acquisition Manager. There is still, however, too little regard paid to it by many employers. HR managers are frequently junior managers learning the ropes at the staff's expense. The fact that many of the sector's businesses are sole traders or micro-businesses is also a critical factor in determining the extent to which Human Resource Management (HRM) can be professionalized across the industry.

- 24 per cent are sole traders
- 46 per cent of businesses employ fewer than five people
- 74 per cent of the establishments in the sector employ fewer than 49 staff (People 1st, 2011).

Within larger hospitality companies HRM appears to be taken more seriously. Even so, the determining factor appears to be one more of attitude to human resource issues rather than the size of business in itself. Where human resource or personnel professionals are employed, HR management has become more sophisticated.

Evidence of the increasing sophistication of the human resource may be found in some academic research (see Chapter 2). Furthermore other evidence was to be found in the Hotel and Catering Personnel and Training Association's (HCPTA) annual awards for excellence in human resource management. Each year hospitality companies submit human resource activities for consideration for these awards. Many of the ideas submitted show considerable concern for the employers' human resources. These range from the distinctive branding of the HR function as a separate activity (or 'product') within the company through a range of training initiatives to schemes concerned with the care of company pensioners. Further encouraging evidence about the increasing professionalism of HRM in the hospitality sector was evidenced in the research and writings of Kelliher and Johnson (1997), Hoque (2000) and Lucas (2004).

Two of the industry's most influential bodies set in motion a number of significant initiatives that should have long term effects on the industry's labour force.

Excellence through People – British Hospitality Association

In 1998 the British Hospitality Association started their Excellence through People scheme. This was partly a response to the Department of National Heritage's report (1996) which listed a familiar range of complaints about the industry's employment practices, including poor wages, long hours and high labour turnover. The report went on to state that 'the tourism and hospitality industry faces the threat of a self-perpetuating vicious circle that is harmful to profitability and competitiveness … The negative image of many jobs in the industry – low pay, low skill, low status – discourages many people from joining the industry, thus taking us back to the beginning of the vicious circle.' Figure 1.3 shows the BHA's Excellence through People 'Ten-Point Code'.

Hospitality Assured – Institute of Hospitality (IoH)

The Institute of Hospitality operates the Hospitality Assured scheme, supported by the BHA. This sets out to recognize and reward high standards of customer service in the hospitality industry. The process for achieving Hospitality Assured consists of customer research and feedback and assesses a business's performance in standards of service and business excellence, with prominence given to aspects

---

Excellence through People is based on a ten-point code of good employment practice. It commits employers to:

Recruit and select with care
(so that you can promote a positive image and attract quality staff)
1 Equal opportunities
2 Recruitment
A good employer attracts, selects and employs quality staff, whether full-time or part-time or casual, who are legally entitled to work in the UK.

Offer a competitive employment package
(so that the staff you take on know what to expect and are well cared for)
3 Contract of employment
4 Health and safety
A good employer ensures that staff are fully aware, in writing, of their terms and conditions of employment and provides a healthy and safe work environment for them.

Develop skills and performance
(so that standards of customer service and productivity can be enhanced)
5 Job design
6 Training and development
A good employer constantly seeks to increase productivity, business efficiency and customer service by improving staff competence, motivation, effectiveness and job satisfaction.

Communicate effectively
(so that you and your staff are working towards the same goals)
7 Communications
8 Grievances and discipline
A good employer ensures that staff know what is expected of them, keeps them informed of performance and has arrangements for dealing with discipline and grievances.

Recognise and reward
(so that you can retain highly motivated staff)
9 Performance review
10 Rewards and recognition
A good employer takes steps to keep and motivate quality staff by rewarding them equitably by means of a well-understood remuneration package.

Figure 1.3 Ten-point code
Source: British Hospitality Association.

such as the customer promise, business planning, standards of performance, service delivery, training and development. See Appendix 1.

Investors in People

Investors in People (IiP) was launched to 'improve business performance and secure competitive advantage'. The scheme has four main principles:

- Commitment – to invest in people to achieve business goals.
- Planning – how individuals and teams are to be developed to achieve these goals.
- Action – to develop and use the necessary skills in a programme directly tied to business objectives.
- Evaluation – measuring progress towards goals.

Further reading and references

Department of National Heritage (1996) *Competing with the Best: People Working in Tourism and Hospitality*, London: Department of National Heritage.

Ernst and Young (2012) *Global Hospitality Insights, Top Thoughts for 2012*, London: Ernst and Young.

HCITB (1978) *Manpower in the Hotel and Catering Industry*, London: HCITB.

HCITB (1984) *Manpower Flows in the Hotel and Catering Industry*, London: HCITB.

Hoque, K. (1999) 'New approaches to HRM in the UK hotel industry', *Human Resource Management Journal*, 9(2): 64–76.

Hoque, K. (2000) *Human Resource Management in the Hotel Industry*, London: Routledge.

Hospitality Industry Congress (1996) *Hospitality into the 21st Century*, Henley: Henley Centre.

Hospitality Training Foundation (2004) *Labour Market Review (Hospitality) 2003*, London: HTF and VT Plus Training.

Hotel and Catering Training Company (1994) *Catering and Hospitality Industry 1994*, London: HCTC.

Hotel and Catering Training Company (1994) *Employment Flows in the Catering and Hospitality Industry*, London: HCTC.

Kelliher, C. and Johnson, K. (1987) 'Personnel management in hotels – some empirical observations', *International Journal of Hospitality Management*, 6(2): 103–108.

Kelliher, C. and Johnson, K. (1997) 'Personnel management in hotels – an update', *Progress in Hospitality and Tourism Research*, 3(4): 321–331.

Kelliher, C. and Perrett, G. (2001), 'Business strategy and approaches to HRM – a case study of new developments in the United Kingdom restaurant industry', *Personnel Review*, 30(4): 421–437.

Lucas, R. (2004) *Employment Relations in the Hospitality and Tourism Industries*, London: Routledge.

MacLeod, D. and Clarke, N. (2010) *Engaging for Success: Enhancing Performance through Employee Engagement*, London: Department for Business, Innovation and Skills.

Mars, G. and Mitchell, P. (1979) *Manpower Problems in the Hotel and Catering Industry*, London: Heinemann.

People 1st (2011) *State of the Nation Report 2011, Analysis of labour market trends, skills, education and training within the UK hospitality, leisure, travel and tourism industries*, London: People 1st.

PricewaterhouseCoopers (2010) *UK Hotels Forecast 2010*, London: PricewaterhouseCoopers.

PricewaterhouseCoopers (2011) *European Cities Hotels Forecast 2011 and 2012*, London: PricewaterhouseCoopers.

Schneider, Friedrich (2005) 'A. T. Kearney analysis', Johannes Kepler University of Linz, Austria.

For those interested in earlier reports on the industry, previous editions of this book contain some details.

Members of the UK's Institute of Hospitality can access publications including Management Guides which summarize key information of relevance to hospitality operations (www.instituteofhospitality.org).

Members of the UK's Chartered Institute of Personnel and Development (CIPD) can access a range of materials including Fact Sheets and articles from over 300 online journal titles relevant to HR. CIPD members and *People Management* subscribers can see articles on the People Management website (www.peoplemanagement.co.uk).

Questions

These questions have been designed so that the first question in every case can be answered from material in the accompanying chapter. Subsequent questions may need reference to material contained in the reading list and maybe to other sources as well. The last question, in most cases, requires knowledge and experience of the industry, acquired, for example, through normal employment, holiday work or industrial placement.

1 The hospitality industry consists of several different and distinct sectors. Discuss these sectors, identifying the key features of selected sectors (such as casual dining, fine-dining, fast food, hotels) and how these features influence the nature of the workforce of the selected sectors.

2 What factors are likely to influence the hospitality industry's workforce in the future?

3 Discuss the key features of the workforce of an employer with whom you are familiar and the factors which influence the make-up of the workforce.

Chapter 2

Human resource management (HRM)

Introduction

The great importance of the workforce, the human resources (HR), in ensuring the commercial success of the hospitality industry and its many thousands of outlets may be succinctly summarized. At a financial level, the hospitality workforce payroll is frequently the single largest cost item, measured as a percentage of wage costs to sales. From a perspective of a service sector, the human resources are usually the first point of interpersonal contact between a hospitality enterprise and its customers. Herein lies the source of the most critical dilemmas and challenges that face the industry: to contain and control the costs of labour whilst maximizing the quality of service to the customer, the principal focus of the business. The effective management of these human resources is therefore vital to the prosperity of the enterprise, whether undertaken by the line managers and owner-managers of smaller businesses or as part of the responsibility of specialist HR managers in the larger chains.

This hospitality industry, of such national and international economic significance as outlined in Chapter 1, is highly competitive and labour-intensive. It is not surprising that in recent years both practitioners and academics have increasingly sought to tackle the key challenges facing the sector with a range of HRM initiatives and research-based proposals. Many hospitality companies have launched extensive recruitment campaigns utilizing all current means of gaining attention from potential employees, including the Internet and social media. There have been examples of major training programmes across international boundaries and the setting up of central training academies as focal points for management development. From mainstream HRM literature, for example, Storey (2007: 4) notes that as with other service organizations, hospitality has been the subject of an increasing number of industry-specific human resource studies and publications. There has certainly been a steady output of publications dealing with the hospitality industry and its frequently documented workforce issues (e.g. Brotherton, 2000; Hoque, 2000; Lucas, 2004; Nickson, 2007). Although greatly dependent on the performance, commitment and interpersonal behaviour of its employees, the hospitality industry has been regularly criticized for inadequate people management practices (Price, 1994; Ogbonna and Harris, 2002; Ritzer, 2007). In particular, the industry and its image is characterized by its detrimentally high labour turnover rates (Deery and Shaw, 1999; Lashley and Rowson, 2000), the causes often put down to poor management and training of the all-important workforce, and the negative implications being increased employee costs and variable customer service (Davidson *et al.*, 2010).

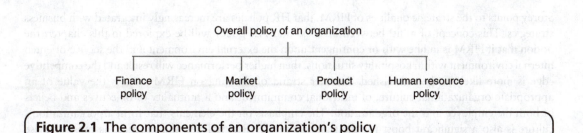

Figure 2.1 The components of an organization's policy

In the modern era of competition and of service industry dominance, human resource policies feature prominently as part of a contemporary organization's overall business policy and planning, as virtually every management decision affects, to a lesser or greater extent, the people working within the enterprise. Most strategic decisions are made within an organization's policy framework (see Figure 2.1), representing the aims (mission), purposes, principles and intentions of the organization. These stated policies provide management with the strategic framework within which they make their decisions, and HR strategy and practice have increasingly become crucial components of this framework for labour-intensive service businesses in the globally competitive environment of the past few decades. The hospitality industry, with its high dependence on a workforce that is capable of delivering the promise of a quality product and service, must embrace the principles that underpin the concept of human resource management.

HRM: a contemporary phenomenon

Over the past three decades the term 'human resource management' (HRM) has gradually entered the language and discourse of everyday business life. Employees refer to their 'HR' department when needing to resolve an employment issue; many organizations have renamed their previously entitled 'Personnel' office to fall in line with the trend to use the HR label, and job titles have also been radically overhauled to reflect the contemporary approach (Legge, 2005; Storey, 2007).

A review of the appointments pages in the past 15 editions of *People Management* (a publication of the CIPD – the Chartered Institute of Personnel and Development) reveals the increasing movement towards specialist roles within the discipline, including senior HR positions where the job holder is required to be a significant expert in fields such as reward and recognition, employment relations, learning and development, training, and the management of cultural change. The spread of the influence of HRM into more strategic business policy matters and overall organizational performance is typified by the 'business partnering' model developed by Ulrich and Brockbank (2005). Consequently contemporary HRM is conceptualized by some in terms of organizationally 'embedded' HR managers working alongside line managers, supported by an array of highly specialized services closely aligned to business strategy and planning, far removed from the purely administrative role expected of the personnel management department of the past.

A definition of HRM that encapsulates many of the component factors that come together in a contemporary interpretation of the meaning of HRM is offered by John Storey:

> A distinctive approach to employment management which seeks to achieve competitive advantage through the strategic deployment of a highly committed and capable workforce, using an array of cultural, structural and personnel techniques.
>
> (Storey, 2001: 6)

Storey points to the strategic qualities of HRM, that HR policies are increasingly integrated with business strategies. This concept of a 'fit' between business and HR policy will be explored in this chapter: the notion that if HRM is in line with or contingent upon the external environment and the service-oriented internal environment within hospitality situations, then higher performance will result and the competitive edge is more likely to be established. Another strand of thinking on HRM stresses the value of an appropriate organizational culture, of individual commitment and a mutuality of objectives and beliefs of both the employee and the organization. The emphasis on the elements that form an organization's culture is also a significant boost for the significance of HRM policies and practice, as most of these elements, from worker behaviour and workplace 'rituals' to communications and reward systems, may be influenced by the people management of the business especially in service sectors such as hospitality. It should also be recognized that the interpretation of HRM as outlined above, an all-encompassing approach to managing people, is not just a role for HRM specialists, but is a role for all line managers and supervisors, as an integral part of their everyday operational management of employees.

Storey's definition also recognizes that within HRM there is still a requirement for a set of specialist and essentially administrative personnel practices and techniques; these may include the technical aspects of job design, job and person specifications, recruitment and selection processes, training plans, job evaluation exercises and payroll management, employee records, grievance and disciplinary procedures and so on. The HR department is also responsible in many firms for advice and guidance to line managers in order to ensure compliance with employment legislation, and for staff welfare matters, and HRM specialists may be required to assist managers in finding solutions to a range of issues related to people at work (see Figure 2.2). In connection with the recognition that part of the concept of HRM

absenteeism	harassment
alcohol abuse	health and safety
annual hours contracts	information technology
	internationalism
benchmarking	
bullying	law of employment
change management	organization structures – business process
communications	re-engineering
competencies	outplacement
continuous professional development	outsourcing
culture and cultural changes	
delayering	part-time working
discipline	performance-related pay
distancing	psychological tests
drug abuse	
	quality and human resource management
employer branding	
empowerment	racial discrimination
equal opportunities – discrimination	re-engineering
on grounds of gender, race,	
age, disability	sexual discrimination
ethics	smoking at work
	succession planning
'family-friendly' policies	
flexible pay systems	talent management
	trade unions
grievances	
	violence at work

Figure 2.2 Some issues in human resource management

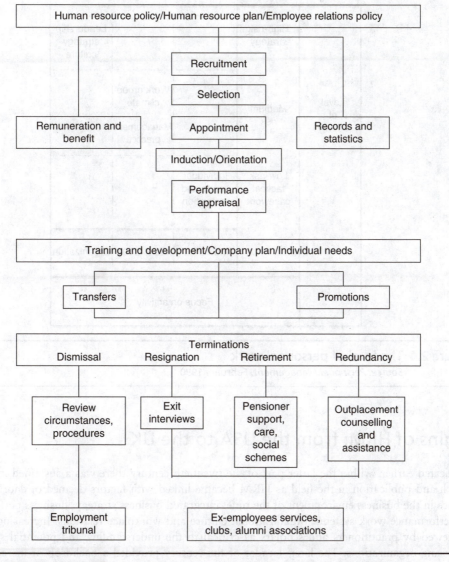

Figure 2.3 Elements of the specialist personnel management function

retains the application of more operational personnel practices and techniques, Figure 2.3 outlines the main functions and responsibilities normally covered under the specialist personnel management function.

Human resource policies and practice do not develop in a vacuum. They are an expression also of the style and culture of the organization, an expression of its values. Human resource approaches need to be dynamic, both changing and shaping the behaviour of the workforce within the organizational culture and framework. The standing and influence of the HR department is therefore a critical factor. Its importance can be estimated and demonstrated by considering the levels of risk with which the function is involved. The different levels of risk range from leadership and strategy to work group morale and atmosphere (or 'climate'), to the individual's motivation at work, as illustrated in Figure 2.4.

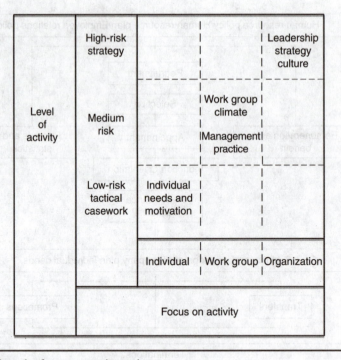

Figure 2.4 The level of personnel work
Source: *Personnel Management*, February 1990.

Origins of HRM: from the USA to the UK

As indicated earlier, within the latter part of the twentieth century there was a sustained increase in research and publication in the field as HRM became linked with factors deemed of enormous significance in the business environment of the time: integrated business strategy, business performance, high-performance work systems, organizational culture and workplace relations. Increasingly HRM was viewed by practitioners and scholars as critical to the understanding and potential success of enterprising organizations. The later decades of the century provided a backdrop of incredibly fast and significant change, driven by economic and technological developments, changing product and labour markets, global markets and competition, and, in the developed economies, the increasing dominance of the service industries (Redman and Mathews, 1998; Korczynski, 2002; Legge, 2005; Noon and Blyton, 2007). The economic dominance of service industries, including hospitality and tourism, in developed nations focused attention on the qualities and competitive potential of employees and their behaviour and competencies in those all-important customer contact situations.

Debate over the meaning and implications of the emerging HRM concept has been energetic in outlining the contradictions and changing perspectives of the theory and the practice, examining just how much of the concept is rhetoric and how much is reality (Purcell, 1999; Storey, 2007; Boxall and Purcell, 2011). Key areas of concern to both academics and practitioners have been the links between HRM and strategy, between HRM and high-performance work systems, between HRM and high-commitment employee management, and of the key role of HRM in connection with organizational culture. The development of HRM as a strategic and influential aspect of management practice derives especially from the integration of corporate strategy and of organizational culture (notably its 'corporate' culture interpretation), and the goals of high commitment and performance (Guest, 1987; Appelbaum *et al.*, 2000; Paauwe, 2008).

A critical factor in the achievement of the frequently stated HRM goals of attaining high commitment and high performance from employees is a stable workforce of well-trained and motivated people. Workforce stability, as in effective work groups unfragmented by constantly high labour turnover, provides the conditions for the building of a cohesive and capable team, and for the employees within those teams to optimize their performance levels. The hospitality industry has invariably topped the CIPD national 'league tables' for labour turnover (CIPD, 2009; People 1st, 2011) and this has been the statistical outcome of a range of HRM issues and challenges faced by the hospitality industry which require analysis and addressing for its future success.

An exploration of the origins and development of models of human resource management necessitates an initial review of writers and industrialists based in the United States (see Schuler and Jackson, 2005). Managers and scholars in the USA were significantly influenced by the work of leading theorists such as McGregor (1960) and Maslow (1943/1970). These important studies of motivation and people at work fall within the province of the social sciences which are concerned with studying the relationships between individuals, groups of individuals and their environment. The knowledge obtained can be used in two principal ways, namely to understand and predict changes (i.e. to focus on 'content'), and to bring about change (i.e. to focus on 'process'). These classical and fundamental approaches, a number of which are summarized in Figure 2.5, help our understanding of the basic and higher needs of humans, from biological satisfaction to social fulfilment. This latter state manifests itself in the human pursuit of status, security, power and other outward signs of success. Many people may not be conscious of these higher needs that drive or motivate them. If, however, management can recognize them, they can take appropriate steps to ensure that these driving forces can be used to the advantage of both the individual and the organization. There is clearly a major role here for HR management and its underlying concepts of assisting employees in reaching high performance through high commitment, and this vital link was first developed within the United States.

The rapid development of the US economy after the Second World War was accompanied by this rapid development in the study of organizations and management with much attention given to organizational behaviour and workforce motivation, summarized and critiqued effectively by Beaumont (1992). Legge (2005: 101) concurs that the term HRM, 'may be charted first in the writings of US academics and managers'. As an early example of this influence, Sampson (1995) refers to statements by the Chief Executive of the oil company Esso in the 1950s and 1960s, who insisted that the organization made long-term staff development plans because the staff were as important a physical asset as the oil reserves drilled from the earth. Sampson (1995: 99) comments that this was 'part of the trend towards calling people "human resources"'.

One of the pre-eminent theorists of the post-war period whose influence can be detected in the modern models of HRM was Douglas McGregor, whose publication *The Human Side of Enterprise* (1960) can be seen to have had a major impact on later approaches to the academic study of HRM as an emerging discipline. The concepts of Theory X and Theory Y bridged the divide between the concepts of the earlier scientific management (see Frederick Taylor in Figure 2.5) and human relations schools (see Elton Mayo in Figure 2.5). Theory X, with its prescription for tightly controlled workers, their effort motivated by extrinsic, monetary rewards pre-empted the so-called 'hard' approach of HRM. Theory Y, with its emphasis on intrinsic, social motivational aspects such as group work, self-development and fulfilment, provided the foundation for HRM approaches referred to as 'soft'. Indeed, as HRM became a focus for research and scholarship in US business schools, the 'hard', Theory X-based approach became more associated with the University of Michigan (Fombrun *et al.*, 1984), whilst the 'soft', Theory Y-based model became known also as the Harvard approach (Beer *et al.*, 1985).

1841–1925	Henri Fayol (France)	Claimed to be the earliest proponent of a theoretical analysis of managerial activities. Defined management as five functions: • to forecast • to organize • to command • to coordinate • to control.
1864–1920	Max Weber (Germany)	Responsible for defining three types of legitimate elements or criteria, including a clearly defined hierarchy, and objective selection.
1856–1915	Frederick W. Taylor (USA)	The founder of the movement known as 'scientific management'. He proposed four great underlying principles: • the development of a true science of work • the scientific selection and progressive development of the workman • the bringing together of the science of work and the scientifically selected and trained man • the constant and intimate cooperation of management and men.
1880–1949	Elton Mayo (USA)	Often referred to as the founder of the Human Relations movement. His work demonstrated the importance of groups in affecting the behaviour of individuals at work. He is most famous for the Hawthorn investigations which led to a fuller understanding of the human factor at work.
1903–1981	Rensis Likert (USA)	Showed that effective supervisors and managers tended to be employee-centred rather than job-centred. Likert distinguished four systems of management: • exploitive/authoritative • benevolent/authoritative • consultative • participative.
1906–1964	Douglas McGregor (USA)	Famous for theories X and Y. In Theory X, people are assumed to dislike work and need direction and control. In Theory Y, people are assumed to enjoy work and external control is not necessary. Managers' assumptions about their subordinates shape their behaviour.
1923–2000	Frederick Herzberg (Germany/USA)	Famous for demonstrating that factors that lead to dissatisfaction (hygiene factors) are quite different from those that lead to satisfaction (motivators). Determinants of job satisfaction are: • achievement and recognition • work characteristics • responsibility and advancement • company policy and administration • salary and working conditions • supervision and interpersonal relations.
1908–1970	Abraham Maslow (USA)	Maslow saw human needs in the form of hierarchy: as one set of needs is satisfied another emerges. Their order is: • physiological needs • security and safety needs • affiliation or acceptance needs • esteem needs • self-actualization.
1909–2005	Peter Drucker (Germany/USA)	Famous for developing the concept of 'management by objectives' (MbO). He believed in five basic principles of management: • set objectives • organize • motivate and communicate • measure performance • develop people.
1928–	Edgar Schein (Switzerland/USA)	Known for his work on motivation, introducing the concepts of psychological contract and the career anchor. His work has also included the study of corporate culture, an organization's set of artefacts, beliefs, values and assumptions.
1929–	Amitai Etzioni (Germany/USA)	Developed the classification of managers' power and workers' involvement: **Managers' power** — **Workers' involvement** Coercive — Alimentative Utilitarian — Calculative Normative — Moral

Figure 2.5 Eleven theorists who have contributed to management thinking

The 'hard' and 'soft' models have several key differences in approach in terms of impact on the development of the concept and ideas of HRM, summarized by Walton (1985) as a shift from management control to employee commitment. The Michigan approach had developed a preoccupation with the strategic focus of HRM, a demand for high performance by a highly controlled human resource inextricably bound to the goals of the organization as it responds to market conditions. The Harvard model emphasizes human relations at work, the mutually beneficial integration of organizational and individual commitment and mutual attainment of organizational and individual goals. This 'soft' model of HRM can be seen to have connection with the development of the concept of corporate culture, emphasizing such components as commitment, sharing values and achieving mutually beneficial goals. The two approaches are fundamentally different, but are essentially directed towards the same goal, that of high performance and high commitment within the workplace. In a critically analytical review of US literature in the HRM domain, Beaumont (1992) suggests that the two leading themes to dominate the US output of the time were corporate culture and the alignment of HRM strategy with business strategy.

Contrasting with the US experience, the UK's post-war concern with the development of HRM was set in a context of industrial unrest as the traditional manufacturing and heavy industry sectors fought for survival in a globalized market alongside a national economy more and more focused on the service sector. The 1970s in particular experienced turbulent industrial relations against a background of the oil crisis of 1973, increasing global competition and rapidly developing, modern technologies, resulting in successive stand-offs between trade unions and government as well as management and employees. Those involved with HRM at that time mainly fulfilled 'go-between' roles, mediating, negotiating terms and conditions between management and unions, and ensuring organizational compliance with an ever-increasing raft of employment and industrial relations legislation (Lucas, 2004). The amount of employment legislation rose sharply following Britain's entry into the European Economic Community, now the European Union, in 1972.

The 1980s experienced further industrial unrest but also a UK government, led by Margaret Thatcher, committed to deregulation in the labour market and the gradual dismantling of the voluntary industrial relations processes and institutions (Lucas, 2004). Managers found new strength in an environment of change and trade union reform, as information technology-based industries (sometimes termed knowledge organizations) and service firms flourished, employing non-standard employees. These service sector workers, particularly in the hospitality industry, were increasingly female, often part-time or on temporary contracts, and without any tradition of trade union membership and activity. Trade union membership fell sharply as the traditional manufacturing and male-dominated industries declined. Millward (1994) notes the new power and confidence that these events gave back to management, re-empowered to take decisions on how the firm was to be organized and structured, and how jobs were to be designed for flexibility. The latter factor was also supported by the deregulation of pay frameworks (such as the Wages Councils), and the casualization of an increasingly female-dominated, part-time and essentially fragmented service sector workforce.

The impact of these changes on the development of people management practices within a UK context was subtle but long-lasting. Personnel Managers, their job titles gradually changed into Human Resource Managers, had to reappraise their role in a new workplace and service-oriented economy. They had to consider how their activities would integrate and align with corporate strategy and objectives, and with employee relations (rather than industrial relations) in the post-industrialization era (Lucas, 2004). Guest and Hoque (1996) suggested that four different scenarios developed in the 1980s as a result of this new era. In their typology of 'good', 'ugly', 'fad' and 'bad', they describe four types of organization in this predominantly non-union economy. The 'good' type of firm increasingly adopted enterprising HRM strategies and policies, aimed at 'high-involvement management' and a high-commitment workforce. The 'ugly' type took full advantage of the lack of employee union representation, became 'efficiency-driven', with a ruthless focus on the bottom line, offering minimum pay rates and minimizing the effects of costly employment rights. The 'fad' type of business had little coherent strategy but replicated and applied the latest HRM fashion without any real analysis, likely to drop the initiative with the same level of speed and integrity. Finally, the 'bad' face of non-unionism surfaced in a business that failed to adopt any meaningful HRM strategy, and rejected the positive HRM practices available, managing without concern for HRM.

In response to the themes of US writers and practitioners in terms of an HRM concept focused on strategic alignment and corporate culture, some early UK commentaries suggested that there was little more substance than a relabelling, a superficial renaming of personnel management to human resources management. This view can be compared with the 'fad' type of company described above, and is supported by Guest (1987: 506) who notes the number of departments that have been merely renamed as HR departments, even academic textbooks retitled without significant change to content.

However, for his part, Guest (1987: 507) proceeds to argue persuasively concerning a set of conceptual differences between traditional personnel management and contemporary HRM. His premise is based on the four key factors of: strategic integration, on employee commitment rather than compliance, on flexibility and on quality. In a later summary of his research in the 1990s, Guest (2001) considers that HRM and its emphasis on commitment had changed the nature of the psychological contract, the often unwritten, implicit set of expectations and obligations between employee and employer. He links the experience of more HRM practices with a more positive psychological contract and an improved level of trust and commitment. A psychological contract based on compliance indicates a cowering workforce, fearing the consequences of not following management directives due to the coercive power being enforced (see Etzioni in Figure 2.5). A psychological contract based on commitment offers employees the hope of a moral involvement and engagement, a committed workforce valuing its role in fulfilling the organization's purpose, and less likely to leave their employment. As Guest notes:

> Finally, intention to quit is higher among those with a poor psychological contract, who report poor employment relations and who also have a lower level of commitment.
>
> (Guest, 2001: 108)

Faced by increasing national and international competition, many organizations, including major hospitality, retail and tourism firms, placed increasing emphasis on the customers' needs and customer service. In the increasingly competitive service sector of the late twentieth century, personified by the globally branded hospitality industry (represented by the Holiday Inn chain, the Accor group's many brands and Intercontinental Hotels), the customer assumed a new power, demanding better service quality in a marketplace of alternatives and choice. Managers of hospitality businesses needed to ensure that their strategic decisions were made with a sharp focus on the customer, as service receiver, and the employee as service provider (Redman and Mathews, 1998).

By the year 2003 service industry growth reached the level of 80 per cent of all employment in the UK (Lucas, 2004). Within service firms the aim of increased employee commitment through HRM initiatives was also impacted upon by distinctive features of service work and customer-oriented service encounters that differentiate service work from manufacturing work. These characteristics include the challenge of simultaneous production and consumption of the product and service, requiring staff to possess a commitment to both the organization and the customer (Redman and Mathews, 1998; Korczynski, 2002; MacDonald and Korczynski, 2009). This is particularly pertinent for the hospitality industry, where managers seek to achieve high efficiency as well as high customer satisfaction through quality service. As an example, the hotel receptionist has the simultaneous challenge of ensuring efficient check-in and registration of the arriving guest through accurate usage of the front office computer system; but must also be a welcoming host who possesses a wide range of human skills and product knowledge, from empathetic interpersonal behaviour and display of appropriate emotions through to the deployment of advanced selling skills that aim to maximize the customer's purchases of hotel services.

Before turning to the specific HRM issues that face the hospitality industry, it is important to note a very contemporary HR and leadership issue regarding payments and remuneration packages for senior executives. In the early years of this century, and particularly following the financial and economic crises of the credit crunch and banking collapses in 2008, serious concern was expressed about excessive pay in boardrooms (see High Pay Commission report in Chapter 10). Shareholders began to criticize and sometimes reject the remuneration proposals and bonus amounts for Chief Executives in sectors such as banking, in some cases the top salaries being 100 times that of the average earnings of employees. There was concern in the UK and other countries around the world, such as France, where the government proposed that the most senior managers of public sector organizations should not earn more than 20 times the average wage of their lower-paid employees (see the Drucker rule also in Chapter 10). This really posed the question as to who senior managers served; themselves or the wide range of stakeholders in their business.

These issues bring to prominence the body of work by Robert Greenleaf and his concept of the leader as servant (2004). His view of leadership largely reflects the views of those leaders who see themselves as serving their various communities. Greenleaf defined a management philosophy in terms of its all-embracing approach to the quality of people, the work itself and the community spirit. He stressed the need for a 'servant leader', one who looks to the needs of employees, their issues and their development, as only people who are motivated and fulfilled will meet their expectations.

HRM and the hospitality industry

The demographics of the diverse and essentially non-standard hospitality workforce, as outlined in Chapter 1, warrant an in-depth understanding of the sector and its HRM characteristics such as occupational skill shortages and volatile labour turnover patterns (McGunnigle and Jameson, 2000; Hoque, 2000). As an example, the personal profiles of food service employees may consist of full-time, skilled professionals; unskilled part-time and temporary staff; transient 'tourist workers' and university students; and housewives supplementing the family income (Pratten, 2003: 829). The importance of recognizing the different demographic features of the hospitality workforce are particularly important when linked to an individual's need for job satisfaction, or the extent of their motivation and commitment and their degree of loyalty to the organization.

There are also implications for such a diverse and non-standard workforce in terms of the industry's need for effective work teams, often organized and rostered to work together on regular shifts. The resulting impact of group dynamics and social interaction becomes a potentially significant factor in efficiency and effectiveness in delivering high quality customer service. Preece *et al.* (1999) stress the importance of team spirit, or a team culture within the licensed retailing sector of the hospitality industry. They found that the team or work group in pubs is critical in accepting and in socializing a new team member and in conditioning that new colleague into the group's way of behaving and interacting with each other, and thence with the customer. Employee induction programmes in hospitality businesses become critical as new staff will be greatly influenced by the prevailing attitudes of existing teams and supervisors (Lashley and Rowson, 2000; Seymour and Sandiford, 2005; Yang, 2008).

Employee induction is also a regular and significant activity in the hospitality industry, in part because of the high turnover rates associated with a plentiful numerical supply of labour, such as students and seekers of part-time and temporary work. Service sector firms such as hotels and retail operations rely a lot on external supply of labour but often suffer from an underdeveloped internal labour market and a lack of training and development and career development planning. The inference is that many hospitality firms employ a workforce that is easily replaceable and easily trained due to the low skill levels. These factors affect the managerial approach and attitude towards an acceptance of high labour turnover rates. In a study of multi-divisional companies, Purcell and Ahlstrand (1994: 194) refer to a 'traditional style' of management in sectors like the hotel and catering industry. Their study of multi-unit firms is of significance to the hospitality industry as so many large chains, national and international, typify the branded and high-profile sections of the business. Yet they still found 'traditional styles' at work in hotels, restaurants and fast food outlets, where labour was perceived as a cost alone, and all efforts made to minimize that cost, resulting in a command-and-control managerial style, a 'hard' HRM approach. In their words:

> Firms with a traditional style are most often found in labour-intensive, low technology industries where the level of skill required is so low that labour can easily be replaced without much training … typically the case in hotel and catering firms.
>
> (Purcell and Ahlstrand, 1994: 194)

The underlying factors and characteristics discussed above have had significant impact on the perception and image of the hospitality industry as an employer that has consistently failed to tackle effectively its human resource management challenges.

HRM issues in the hospitality industry

Analysis of recent literature concerned with managing the hospitality workforce reveals a preoccupation with a set of perceptions about working in the industry that warrants some consideration in laying the foundations of this book. These perceptions consist of elements such as low pay, long and unsocial hours, poor employment terms and conditions, an autocratic management style unrestrained by trade union activity, high labour turnover, a lack of training, and little emphasis on contemporary human resource management practices (Hoque, 2000; Kelliher and Perrett, 2001; Lucas, 2004; Baum, 2006; Nickson, 2007).

Recently, there has been a lively debate as to whether or not the dominant perception of the industry is in fact a true reflection of reality. Research and commentaries within hospitality trade journals in the 1980s and early 1990s tended to paint a rather depressing picture of the extent of the development of forward-thinking HRM policies and practices, with Lucas (1995: 14) describing an industry, 'characterised by ad hoc management, a lack of trade unions, and high, possibly unavoidable labour turnover'. Lucas also comments that there has been a lack of empirical research into the HRM practices within the industry. She later concludes that the hospitality industry workforce is 'vulnerable' and that as a result, gaining employee commitment is elusive:

> The labour force is highly mobile, often with a short-term orientation to the (industry), generating high labour turnover and leaver rates. Recruitment and retention is particularly problematic, particularly for managers where a lack of professionalism may impede business success.
>
> (Lucas, 2004: 225)

The industry's continuing challenges of skill shortages, recruitment and retention issues are also highlighted in an *Employers Skill Survey* (Department for Education and Employment, 2000). McGunnigle and Jameson (2000) considered that there was certainly an awareness that hospitality management should seek to gain more commitment from its workforce, but 'little evidence is found of contemporary recruitment and selection methods commensurate with this aim' (2000: 1). However, this study found some examples of HRM innovation, particularly training schemes, though such examples were sporadic and placed somewhat awkwardly alongside very traditional 'personnel management'.

McGunnigle and Jameson (2000) also found in their research, undertaken within the hotel sector of the industry, that there was a consuming effort regarding recruitment and selection, especially in terms of the mechanics of personnel administration. Managers were preoccupied with tasks such as the updating of job descriptions and health and safety records, rather than a move towards a more strategically driven HRM policy approach. Kelliher and Johnson's follow-up study in 1997, a decade after their first inquiry, revealed only minor developments, and concluded significantly that, 'because of the high levels of labour turnover experienced by the hotel industry, recruitment was found to be the dominant activity' (1997: 321). In a later study of the alignment of business strategy and HRM in the restaurant sector, Kelliher and Perrett (2001) again found some evidence of HRM practices being developed, but that there was a lack of a strategic linkage between business and HRM activities, the lack of a consistent approach. The major emphasis was once again on recruitment and retention, though there were examples of more sophisticated approaches to selection and to training programmes. Citing the work of Redman and Mathews (1998), Kelliher and Perrett conclude that the 'strategic fit' of business policy and HRM policy and procedure is clearly a difficult goal to achieve within the service sector in general and the hospitality sector specifically.

The scholastic debate concerning the hospitality industry and its stage of HRM development was particularly enlivened by the publications of Hoque (1999, 2000), following an in-depth study of HRM practices in the UK hotel sector. Hoque's conclusions appeared in contrast to much of the previous research output in that it painted a substantially brighter picture of a sector embracing the policies and practices of contemporary HRM, declaring that such approaches were developing rapidly in the sector due to the competitive environment and to the service culture and service quality demands. Hoque's assertions inspired critical responses from some hospitality management academics, notably Nickson and Wood (2000: 88–90). They criticized aspects of Hoque's research methods, the wider relevance of a study confined only to large hotels, and to Hoque's apparent disregard for the 'dominant critical tradition' of the previous studies referred to above. These comments were particularly aimed at the 1999 article, and in his later book publication in 2000, Hoque does point to the fact that many studies have revealed little interest in HRM (p. 25), but also seeks out some of the more positive aspects of studies regarding HRM and the hospitality industry. He points to HRM and service quality initiatives, to a more consultative management style, and to empowerment and career planning through more focus on the internal labour market within the multi-unit chains (Hoque, 2000: 49).

Much of the criticism of the industry can be understood by reference to the simultaneous developments of the organizational culture and HRM concepts. In particular, it is relevant to draw comparison with the 'hard' and 'soft' models, discussed earlier in this chapter, and the perceived move towards more concern with integrative, 'soft' approaches stressing commitment, as opposed to the 'hard' approaches stressing control and compliance. For customer-service oriented activities such as the highly competitive hospitality industry, workplace tension and stress are constant possibilities as management seeks to create a 'service culture' in which staff are required to be committed to both customer service and organizational efficiency, as exemplified by the hotel receptionist earlier. Lashley's research within one national pub/restaurant chain in the late 1990s uncovered practices and approaches that concurrently displayed 'hard' and 'soft' approaches. Lashley exemplifies it as follows: 'a preparedness to apply the hard perspective in controlling the labour cost, and exercise care in the management of the human resource' (Lashley, 1997: 171).

Legge (2005: 126) refers to this application of 'hard' and 'soft' approaches in parallel in connection with the employment model of core and peripheral workers. The hospitality industry staffing strategy has long been predicated on a group of key or core workers (e.g. the restaurant manager or head housekeeper), supplemented as required by a group of peripheral or 'casual', temporary workers (e.g. casual room attendants or banqueting staff) engaged only when required. Legge proposes the situation where the 'soft' version of HRM might well be applied to the core workers, the permanent resource that needs to be committed, loyal, developed and valued in a mutually beneficial relationship with the employer. However, the 'hard' version might well be applied to the temporary, peripheral worker whose labour is required only when necessary and is therefore seen much more as a cost to be controlled.

There remains the task of unlocking potential solutions to these fundamental issues inherent within the everyday activity of the hospitality industry, a task identified by the work of Korczynski (2002). He proposes that the HRM role is connected with trying to understand and facilitate the effective management of staff who are required to have a dual focus on efficiency and on customer orientation. He comments that service encounters such as those within the hospitality industry are combinations of a rational drive for efficiency whilst needing to provide service to a customer who is both rational and irrational: rational in requiring the purchase (e.g. a drink at the bar) to fulfil and satisfy a physical need for refreshment, and often irrational in wishing to derive pleasure and self-esteem from the situation (e.g. recognition by name and awareness and deference of status as the 'customer is king'). In this way, Korczynski (2002) refers to the HRM and wider management challenge of controlling the business at the same time as allowing employees a degree of discretion over their dealings with customers. Solutions to this dilemma require understanding of the emotional tensions and stress felt by staff, often referred to as 'emotional labour', and developing strategies to help staff cope with such stress, including the pressure to be welcoming and courteous at all times, despite tiredness, fatigue and the inevitable problems associated with difficult customers.

In these situations, staff need strong and mutual support from their managers and work group colleagues, as well as effective training in the skills of how to deal with emotions and stress at work and how to gain pleasure and satisfaction in successfully managing the emotions of themselves and sometimes their customers as well. The solidarity of the work group is vital in providing a strong mutual support mechanism, an empathy and sense of belonging amongst their closest colleagues. Managers also need to ensure that they display their personal awareness of the emotional stresses of hospitality service encounters, allowing staff to take sufficient breaks, perhaps to have comfortable relaxation areas, even places to let off steam and vent frustrations (Noon and Blyton, 2007). Seymour and Sandiford (2005) noted that larger hospitality companies were more likely to give formal, planned training to staff in such matters as interpersonal skills and customer care. However, all these approaches to tackling a fundamental issue for hospitality workers are dependent on HRM policies and procedures that are designed to be relevant and professional in the recruitment, training and retention of employees, and the subject so often at the heart of many hospitality employment issues, namely unacceptably high labour turnover, will be further explored in Chapter 14 of this book.

HRM and leadership styles

From the preceding section regarding a managerial approach to helping hospitality employees deal with the pressures of service work, it follows that the leadership style of hospitality managers, whether HR specialists or the all-important line managers and supervisors, is extremely influential in terms of achieving high commitment and performance from the workforce. Within the hospitality industry, there are many different types and sizes of operation, many being small and often owner-managed. All such circumstances are factors within which to analyse the most appropriate style of leadership to adopt. In Guest's typology of HR models (1989), it can be seen that some hospitality firms are likely to emphasize a particular approach. The paternalistic/welfare model seeks to look after employees as if part of a wider 'family', trusting that if the employees are well treated, they will in turn treat the customers well: this model may well apply to the smaller, owner-managed operation but has also been associated with the philosophy of larger organizations dominated by the original founder, such as the former Trusthouse Forte Hotels founded by the late Lord Charles Forte. Guest's production model of HRM may have its roots in manufacturing but could also be applied to large-scale catering within more unionized environments, perhaps food production assembly plants but also airline contract catering. The professional model certainly exists in many large-scale and multinational companies where, for example, there are fully staffed HRM departments providing policies and procedures for global, company-wide training programmes. The human resource model in this typology is a fully people-oriented organization with a consistent and thematic stream of HR policies and procedures that link closely to business policy, and emphasize the mutuality of individual and organization. Finally, the 'Modern-Day Taylorism' model – perhaps now it might be termed 'McDonaldization' after the work of Ritzer (1996) – is a variant of the production model and is firmly based on scientific management principles, clearly adapted to the needs of some service businesses such as fast food operations.

Within the overarching model of HRM, the relationship between employee and manager is a dynamic one: there are expectations on both sides, and these expectations need to be well matched in an organization because this determines to a large extent whether employees obtain satisfaction from their jobs and whether managers will achieve their business objectives and goals. Traditionally, leadership styles have been summarized into several simplistic but relevant approaches: autocratic or authoritarian style has been often attributed to hospitality bosses, an approach that relies on issuing orders without need for explanation or discussion; democratic managers see themselves more as one part of the team and thus attempt to involve members of the team in decisions and plans, a variation being a pluralist approach, recognizing the aspirations and value of all sections of the workforce; more recently there has been much written about the style known as 'empowerment', giving clear lines of authority/ discretion to employees within the parameters of their jobs, a style with resonance to some views on the contemporary HRM concept within service work; and there still may be value in recognizing a management style known as laissez-faire, an abdication of management responsibility, such as when the duty manager disappears when the receptionist has to deal with the most serious and emotionally charged of customer complaints!

The attitudes of managers towards their staff may also be exemplified by the work of Etzioni (1980), a useful classification of the power used by managers to ensure compliance by their staff. The three principal orientations are: coercive power, in which fear of the consequences is the main motivator; second, there is utilitarian use of power, manipulating rewards such as wages in order to achieve production levels; third, there is normative power, adopting status, esteem and social acceptance as a means of motivating employees, as with impressive job titles, stratified benefits packages and the like. Again, there are clearly points of reference here with the earlier discussion about the prevailing HRM approaches; some styles and their corresponding attitudes are more in tune with the 'hard' HRM concept than the 'soft', some more underpinned by the elements of Theory X than Theory Y. There is a general move away from the traditional HR styles based on a more authoritarian/coercive means of achieving employee compliance to a more pluralistic, empowered means of achieving employee commitment. An example of one international hotel company's strategic document regarding employee commitment is given in Figure 2.6, a clear statement of the organization's philosophy and stance with regard to people management and culture, aiming for commitment to and from the employee and demonstrating a wider concern for the environment and the communities it serves.

Having given these brief outlines of some important contributions to our understanding of the behaviour of people at work in hospitality, it must be emphasized that there are many other important contributions which may be explored by reference to the reading and reference list at the end of this chapter. This chapter has in the main attempted to outline recent, developing and current perceptions regarding the meaning and role of contemporary HRM policy and practice and to identify how important this subject has become within the highly competitive, international world of hospitality. However, it must also be recognized that in an industry of so many thousands of different types and sizes of businesses, from global brands with over 4,000 hotels to owner-managed bed and breakfast properties, attaining consistent and progressive HRM policies and practices will remain a constant challenge.

Our People

Pan Pacific Hotels Group is an international hotel management company with a global portfolio that spans over 30 hotels, resorts and serviced suites in Asia, Oceania and North America.

With our hotels employing over 10,000 associates and serving over a million guests and customers each year, we believe that corporate responsibility involves doing what is right for its stakeholders.

As a business, this entails balancing financial priorities while ensuring sustainable relationships with the environment and communities where we operate, as well as with our own associates.

This belief is woven into our business fabric – it extends beyond our Business Code of Conduct and Ethics; it is a part of our Values, and the 'global mind-set' we instil in all our associates.

- Our Culture
- Our Diverse Workforce
- Our Code of Business Conduct
- Our Commitment to the Environment
- Our Commitment to the Community

Our Culture

In furthering Pan Pacific Hotels Group's Purpose of 'Great Brands, Great Hotels, Great People and Great Relationships', and fulfilling our Vision of 'Creating Memorable Hotel Experiences', it is a business imperative that our associates embrace diversity – in cultures, value systems, opinions, experiences and skills.

Our Values, set the 'rules of engagement' for our team members and how we connect with guests, business partners, owners, suppliers and community.

"Collaborating, communicating openly, recognising and valuing diversity" are key aspects of Pan Pacific Hotels Group's Values and help direct our behaviour at all times.

Our Diverse Workforce

The Group believes in providing equal employment opportunities and rewarding associates based on merit, qualifications, competence and performance without discrimination. Given our global presence, our talent needs are shaped by a diversified team boasting different nationalities, age groups, backgrounds and skill-sets that bring forth broader and more enriching perspectives to the workplace.

In building our leadership teams and talent platform, we are conscious and focused on mixing talent. We do not stack leadership teams with individuals from similar backgrounds, be it in corporate experience or country of origin. We seek out different talents and opinions and ensure individual viewpoints are not crowded out.

As Pan Pacific Hotels Group grows and expands with new properties, locations, and associates, the more important it will be for us to embrace and encourage diversity.

"Having leaders who help create global mind-sets who embrace Diversity and Inclusion is critical in the hospitality industry … having a global perspective is a key aspect in the selection of the management team since it has an important impact on the employees and customers alike." – A. Patrick Imbardelli, President and Chief Executive Officer Pan Pacific Hotels Group

Our Code of Business Conduct

Under our Code of Business Conduct and Ethics, Pan Pacific Hotels Group is committed to provide equal employment opportunity and reward our associates based on merit, qualifications, competence and performance. Regardless of race, colour, age, religion, sex, national origin, disability, genetic information, and sexual orientation or any condition or status as protected by law.

A policy of non-discrimination prevails throughout all aspects of the employment relationship including recruitment, selection, placement, transfer, promotion, layoff, termination, training, working conditions, benefits and compensation.

All associates and job applicants are guaranteed equality of employment opportunity. This means that Pan Pacific Hotels Group will not discriminate against any worker or applicant on the basis of any condition as stipulated by law. All recruitment selection, placement and training made by Pan Pacific Hotels Group management will be based on candidates' job-related abilities and match for the position.

Our Commitment to the Environment

With 22 global destinations in its portfolio, the Group is deeply mindful of its ecological footprint and is committed to responsible environmental practices. Green Committees comprising representatives from the facilities, operations, procurement, IT and finance teams have been formed at our hotels to champion and enhance the Group's sustainability efforts.

PanEarth

In North America, Pan Pacific Seattle's PanEarth sustainability programme continues to lead our conservation efforts. Its zero-impact policy offers guests the option of carbon-neutral stays by purchasing credits for the generation of clean wind energy. The hotel matches, dollar-for-dollar, all guest donations towards renewable energy credits, with 10% of total proceeds going to beneficiaries at Food Lifeline, a local non-profit organisation for hunger relief.

Figure 2.6 Mission, vision and values of Pan Pacific Hotels Group
Source: Reproduced by courtesy of Pan Pacific Hotels Group.

The benefits resulting from the PanEarth sustainability programme have been immense. While setting benchmarks for environmental efforts, PanEarth also works closely with several community organisations and contributes to social causes ranging from hunger relief and muscular dystrophy, to autism and AIDS. Moreover, it supports programmes for the elderly and disadvantaged children through fund-raising and volunteer activities. Our ambition is to globalise PanEarth and to spread its initiatives to our other hotels, resorts and services suites worldwide.

PARKROYAL on Pickering

The highly anticipated PARKROYAL on Pickering, scheduled to open in 2012, highlights the Group's efforts in sustainability. The development incorporates environmentally sustainable features such as rainwater harvesting, automatic sensors to regulate energy and water usage, and solar cells for powering landscape lighting. Lush foliage is a prominent feature, with impressive sky gardens, green walls, waterfalls and a wide variety of plants adding to the biodiversity of its tropical hotel-in-a-garden concept.

Prior to being operational, PARKROYAL on Pickering was awarded a Green Mark Platinum certification – the highest in its category from Singapore's Building and Construction Authority. With award-winning architects WOHA behind it, the development has set new benchmarks for the amount of landscaping and greenery created in a high-density urban environment.

PARKROYAL on Pickering also bagged the Solar Pioneer Award – a recognition conferred by the Energy Innovation Programme Office, which is led by Singapore's Economic Development Board and Energy Market Authority. In its third year, the Solar Pioneer Award honours pioneering solar installations in Singapore that are innovative in system design, size and installation techniques. Notably, the hotel was commended for its energy-efficient air-conditioning system; use of sustainable LED lighting, and high-performance laminated double-glazed low-E glass that cuts out exterior heat and noise.

Our Commitment to the Community

Through charitable missions, volunteer work and donation drives, Pan Pacific Hotels Group and its hotels put our values into practice by encouraging caring and sharing within the wider community, instilling greater compassion towards the plight of society's less fortunate.

The Group has undertaken numerous initiatives focused on youth development, as well as families and children – one of which is its Youth Career Development Programme (YCDP). Launched in Thailand in cooperation with United Nations Children's Fund, the YCDP is designed to provide innovative educational and vocational training to disadvantaged youths who may otherwise be engulfed in crime, prostitution, drugs, exploitation, abuse, and deprivation.

Over the past decade, the programme has successfully facilitated access to training and employment opportunities in the hospitality industry to hundreds of young men and women from underprivileged families – beneficiaries of the Rajaprajanukrow Foundation – mainly from the Northern and Northeastern provinces of Thailand.

Figure 2.6 Mission, vision and values of Pan Pacific Hotels Group (contd.)

Further reading and references

Appelbaum, E., Bailey, T., Berg, P. and Kalleberg, A. L. (2000) *Manufacturing Advantage*, Ithaca, NY: Cornell University Press.

Armstrong, M. (2012) *Handbook of Human Resource Management Practice*, 12th edn, London: Kogan Page.

Baum, T. (2006) *Human Resource Management for Tourism, Hospitality and Leisure*, London: Thomson Learning.

Beaumont, P. B. (1992) 'The US human resource management literature', pp. 20–37, in Salaman, G. (ed.) *Human Resource Strategies*, London: Sage Publications.

Beer, M., Spector, B., Lawrence, P., Quinn Mills, D. and Walton, R. (1985) *Human Resource Management: A General Manager's Perspective*, Glencoe, IL: Free Press.

Boxall, P. and Purcell, J. (2011) *Strategy and Human Resource Management*, 2nd edn, Basingstoke: Palgrave Macmillan.

Brotherton, B. (2000) *An Introduction to the UK Hospitality Industry*, Oxford: Butterworth-Heinemann.

Chartered Institute of Personnel and Development (2009) *Annual Survey of Employee Turnover and Retention 2008*, London: CIPD Publications.

D'Annunzio-Green, N., Maxwell, G. A. and Watson, S. (eds) (2002) *Human Resource Management: International Perspectives in Hospitality and Tourism*, London: Continuum.

Davidson, M., Timo, N. and Wang, Y. (2010) 'How much does labour turnover cost?', *International Journal of Contemporary Hospitality Management*, 22(4): 451–466.

Deery, M. A. and Shaw, R. N. (1999) 'An investigation of the relationship between employee turnover and organizational culture', *Journal of Hospitality and Tourism Research*, 23(4): 387–400.

Department for Education and Employment (2000) *Employers Skill Survey: Case Study – Hospitality Sector*, London: DfEE Publications.

Etzioni, A. (1980) *Modern Organization*, Englewood Cliffs, NJ: Prentice Hall.

Fombrun, C., Tichy, N. M. and Devanna, M. A. (eds) (1984) *Strategic Human Resource Management*, New York: Wiley.

Greenleaf, R. K. (2004) *The Servant Leader Within: A Transformative Path*, Mahwah, NJ: Paulist Press International.

Guest, D. (1987) 'Human resource management and industrial relations', *Journal of Management Studies*, 24(5): 503–521.

Guest, D. (1989) *Personnel Management*, January, London: CIPD Publications.

Guest, D. (2001) 'Industrial relations and human resource management', pp. 96–113, in Storey, J. (ed.) *Human Resource Management – A Critical Text*, 2nd edn, London: Thomson Learning.

Guest, D. and Hoque, K. (1996) 'The impact of national ownership on human resource management practices and outcomes in UK greenfield sites', *Human Resource Management Journal*, 6(4): 50–74.

Hoque, K. (1999) 'New approaches to HRM in the UK hotel industry', *Human Resource Management Journal*, 9(2): 64–76.

Hoque, K. (2000) *Human Resource Management in the Hotel Industry*, London: Routledge.

Kelliher, C. and Johnson, K. (1997) 'Personnel management in hotels – an update', *Progress in Hospitality and Tourism Research*, 3(4): 321–331.

Kelliher, C. and Perrett, G. (2001) 'Business strategy and approaches to HRM – a case study of new developments in the United Kingdom restaurant industry', *Personnel Review*, 30(4): 421–437.

Korczynski, M. (2002) *Human Resource Management in Service Work*, Basingstoke: Palgrave Macmillan.

Lashley, C. (1997) *Empowering Service Excellence: Beyond the Quick Fix*, London: Cassell.

Lashley, C. and Rowson, B. (2000) 'Wasted millions: staff turnover in licensed retailing', paper presented to the 9th Annual Research Conference of the Council for Hospitality Management Educators, University of Huddersfield.

Legge, K. (2005) *Human Resource Management: Rhetorics and Realities*, 2nd edn, Basingstoke: Palgrave Macmillan.

Lucas, R. (1995) *Managing Employee Relations in the Hotel and Catering Industry*, London: Cassell.

Lucas, R. (2004) *Employment Relations in the Hospitality and Tourism Industries*, London: Routledge.

MacDonald, C. and Korczynski, M. (eds) (2009) *Service Work: Critical Perspectives*, Abingdon: Routledge.

McGregor, D. (1960) *The Human Side of Enterprise*, New York: McGraw-Hill.

McGunnigle, P. J. and Jameson, S. M. (2000) 'HRM in UK hotels: a focus on commitment', *Employee Relations*, 22(4): 403–422.

Maslow, A. (1970) *Motivation and Personality*, 2nd edn, New York: Harper Row.

Millward, N. (1994) *The New Industrial Relations*, London: Policy Studies Institute.

Nickson, D. (2007) *Human Resource Management for the Hospitality and Tourism Industries*, Oxford: Butterworth-Heinemann.

Nickson, D. and Wood, R. C. (2000) 'HRM in the UK hotel industry: a comment and response', *Human Resource Management Journal*, 10(4): 88–90.

Noon, M. and Blyton, P. (2007) *The Realities of Work*, 3rd edn, Basingstoke: Palgrave Macmillan.

Ogbonna, E. and Harris, L. C. (2002) 'Managing organisational culture: insights from the hospitality industry', *Human Resource Management Journal*, 12(1): 33–53.

Paauwe, J. (2008) 'HRM and performance: achievements, methodological issues and prospects', *Journal of Management Studies*, 46(1): 129–142.

People 1st (2011) *State of the Nation Report 2011, Analysis of labour market trends, skills, education and training within the UK hospitality, leisure, travel and tourism industries*, London: People 1st.

Pratten, J. D. (2003) 'The importance of waiting staff in restaurant service', *British Food Journal*, 105(11): 826–834.

Preece, D., Steven, G. and Steven, V. (1999) *Work, Change and Competition: Managing for Bass*, London: Routledge.

Price, L. (1994) 'Poor personnel practice in the hotel and catering industry: does it matter?', *Human Resource Management Journal*, 4(4): 44–62.

Purcell, J. (1999) 'Best practice and best fit: chimera or cul de sac?', *Human Resource Management Review*, 9(3): 26–41.

Purcell, J. and Ahlstrand, B. (1994) *Human Resource Management in the Multi-Divisional Company*, Oxford: Oxford University Press.

Redman, T. and Mathews, B. P. (1998) 'Service quality and human resource management', *Personnel Review*, 27(1): 57–77.

Redman, T. and Wilkinson, A. (2006) *Contemporary Human Resource Management*, 2nd edn, Harlow: Pearson Education.

Ritzer, G. (1996) *The McDonaldization of Society: An Investigation into the Changing Character of Contemporary Life*, Newbury Park, CA: Pine Forge Press.

Ritzer, G. (2007) 'Inhospitable hospitality?', pp. 129–140, in Lashley, C., Lynch, P. and Morrison, A. (eds), *Hospitality: A Social Lens*, Oxford: Elsevier.

Sampson, A. (1995) *Company Man: The Rise and Fall of Corporate Life*, London: Harper Collins.

Schuler, R. S. and Jackson, S. E. (2005) 'A quarter-century review of human resource management in the US: the growth in importance of the international perspective', *Management Review*, 16(1): 1–23.

Seymour, D. and Sandiford, P. (2005) 'Learning emotion rules in service organizations: socialization and training in the UK public house sector', *Work, Employment & Society*, 19(3): 547–564.

Storey, J. (2001) 'Human resource management today – an assessment', pp. 3–20, in Storey, J. (ed.) *Human Resource Management: A Critical Text*, 2nd edn, London: Thomson Learning.

Storey, J. (ed.) (2007) *Human Resource Management: A Critical Text*, 3rd edn, London: Thomson Learning.

Torrington, D., Hall, L. and Taylor, S. (2008) *Human Resource Management*, 7th edn, Harlow: Financial Times Prentice-Hall.

Ulrich, D. and Brockbank, W. (2005) *The HR Value Proposition*, Boston, MA: Harvard University Press.

Walton, R. E. (1985) 'From control to commitment in the workplace', *Harvard Business Review*, March–April, 2: 98–106.

Yang, J-T. (2008) 'Effect of newcomer socialisation on organisational commitment, job satisfaction, and turnover intention in the hotel industry', *The Service Industries Journal*, 28(4): 429–443.

Members of the UK's Institute of Hospitality (IoH) can access publications including Management Guides which summarize key information of relevance to hospitality operations (www.instituteofhospitality.org).

Members of the UK's Chartered Institute of Personnel and Development (CIPD) can access a range of materials including Fact Sheets and articles from over 300 online journal titles relevant to HRM. CIPD members and *People Management* subscribers can see articles on the People Management website (www.peoplemanagement.co.uk).

Questions

1 What links McGregor's Theory X and Theory Y models with contemporary HRM approaches?

2 What are some critical elements which characterize the nature of the concept of HRM?

3 What are the most striking differences between manufacturing and service businesses in terms of people management?

4 What styles of leadership are most appropriate to a progressive policy on HRM?

5 What HR policies in terms of recruitment, selection and training would you consider appropriate for a hospitality firm? Consider a firm you know well and evaluate their approaches.

CASE STUDY QUESTION – see the Lux Hotels case study Appendix 5

What are the key factors which you believe will influence the development of a human resource management strategy?

Effectively resourcing the hospitality organization

Chapter 3

Job design

Although the term 'management' (in its abstract sense) has almost as many definitions as there are managers, it is generally understood to refer to the art or practice of achieving required results through the efforts of others. Drucker says that management is a practice rather than a science (*Professional Manager*, 1993). There is today, however, considerable debate about what precisely it is that motivates people to achieve the results required of them. At one extreme there are those of the scientific school of management (see Chapter 2) who believe that all that is necessary is to select the right people, give clear directions and enough money, and the required results will be achieved. On the other hand there are those from the human relations school (see Chapter 2) who believe that organizational objectives will only be achieved by recognizing to the full the needs and expectations of working people. Whichever view prevails, however, it is generally held that people produce their best performances when they know clearly what is expected of them. W. Edwards Deming, one of America's great management gurus stated, 'People need to know what their jobs are' (*Personnel Management*, June 1992). Consequently if an undertaking's objectives are to be achieved, it follows that all its managers and work people must know clearly the results they are expected to produce. Such a statement of an organization's expectations of its employees can be made either orally or in writing. There are many who believe that the written word is less likely to be misunderstood and that the need to think carefully before putting words to paper generally produces more logical and effective results than oral statements.

It is for such reasons that clear, precise job descriptions are given to people at work, because once a job is clearly described on paper there should be little room for subsequent misunderstandings. As a result the job should be performed more efficiently. Having said this, in the hospitality industry, with its large number of small establishments, there are many work people who do not have or need job descriptions. Furthermore there is a view that job descriptions and the related hierarchies merely serve to slow down effective communication. Tom Peters says that the only way to compete in an ever-faster world is for 'a revolution in structure to create a world with no barriers between functions' (*Financial Times*, 23 February 1990), see also Rosabeth Moss Kanter (1983).

However, before producing job descriptions it is essential to realize that the job description should be the result of a process referred to as job design (Figure 3.1). First, job design can be seen as the process by which the employer sets out to maximize the output of the workforce – a scientific-school-of-management approach. For many employers this remains the sole objective. Second, there is increasing

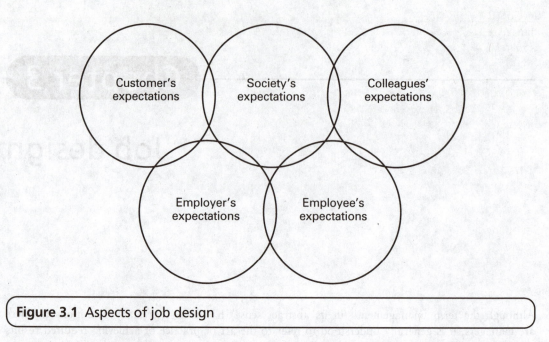

Figure 3.1 Aspects of job design

recognition that if job design is to be effective, the resulting jobs must satisfy a variety of stakeholder interests.

This second approach recognizes Drucker's view that it is important to distinguish between efficiency and effectiveness: 'Managers must in the end be measured by their economic performance, though this is not necessarily synonymous with maximum profits' (Kennedy, 2007). Designing jobs for short-term efficiency may result in alienation, resulting in, for example, absenteeism and high labour turnover with a drop in customer satisfaction and hence in long-term effectiveness.

Third, of course, job design must result in customer satisfaction. Fourth, most people work in teams or groups, so colleagues' expectations have to be considered. And, finally, the job must be designed in such a way that society's expectations (e.g. health and safety, pollution) are satisfied (see Figure 3.1).

Approaches to job design

In setting out to design any job, therefore, it is essential to recognize the expectations of all stakeholders involved. The actual approach adopted will depend on an amalgam of these sets of expectations; for example, where customers and employers want fast service with minimum personalized contact, such as in many fast food operations, the resultant job may emphasize speed at the cost of job satisfaction. The consequence may be high labour turnover, which may well be acceptable, even desirable, to the employer where there is a steady supply of replacement labour.

Job specialization

This approach to organizing work has been around for thousands of years and has led to civilization as we know it today. However, as an approach to organizing modern industrial production it was developed by a number of practitioners and theorists, including F. W. Taylor, the founder of scientific management (see Chapter 2). Major principles resulting from the scientific management approach are as follows.

Science of work

The need for scientific methods of observing, measuring and analysing work activities to replace unsystematic approaches.

Standardization

Using the resulting knowledge, efficient working methods and performance levels can be set for work.

Selection

Systematic and scientific approaches to selecting workers with relevant qualities and abilities, together with planned training for the work involved. Modern views are that work people should be selected for 'attitude' to the work. Training adds the necessary skills.

Specialization

Both management and workers should concentrate upon specific functional activities involving a limited range of tasks for which the individual's abilities and training enable expert performance.

There have been two main consequences of the application of these ideas. First, areas of expertise and responsibility have become much more specialized, particularly in the technical and management areas. There are now many more specialists in management than there were fifty years ago, even ten years ago. Second, and in contrast, particularly at an operative level, in many cases such as fast food restaurants job content is simplified through reduction of the number of tasks, with each operative performing a very limited number so that the need for skill and training is minimized.

The apparent economic benefits of job simplification, however, were accompanied by many problems, such as industrial strife and alienation, the causes being put down to that same job simplification. In contrast, the findings of behavioural scientists were showing that work people could not be treated as mere components of machines: instead they had a range of needs to be met by the work they performed. As a consequence other approaches to job design became necessary.

Job rotation

One reaction to job simplification was job rotation. This provides individuals with some variety in either the working conditions (i.e. where or when the basic job is done) or the actual tasks performed. The jobs, however, remain simple; they may provide little stimulation and may not satisfy self-esteem needs.

Job enlargement

Job enlargement, in contrast, extends the range of tasks performed and is aimed at reducing boredom, increasing interest in work and increasing self-esteem. Job enlargement, however, brings about the very problems that work simplification sets out to eliminate, such as the need for greater knowledge, skill and training.

Job enrichment

Job enlargement, as described above, extends horizontally the range of tasks to be performed by an individual by adding tasks of a similar nature. It does not, however, meet the more complex expectations such as the need for autonomy. Job enrichment instead extends vertically the range of tasks by increasing an individual's responsibility and autonomy through adding elements of the job which may have been the responsibility of supervisors or management, such as planning, organization and control. Such an approach has been adopted by a number of leading companies in the hospitality industry. For example, room attendants have been given additional responsibilities, resulting in a reduction in the number of supervisors.

Socio-technical systems

This approach to job design sets out to bring together an employer's technical system (e.g. buildings and equipment) and the social system comprising the work people. This is because the scientific school aimed to maximize the technical system, seeing the work people as components. In contrast, the human relations theorists concentrated on maximizing the satisfaction of human needs. These two approaches can be seen to be incompatible. It is necessary to look at an organization as a socio-technical system which compromises between technical efficiency and group needs.

In the socio-technical system of job design three major factors are considered. These are: first, a recognition of the needs that are met by formal and informal groups; second, work is allocated to groups that are able to identify clearly with the work; third, the group is given a high degree of autonomy over its work. Such an approach can be seen in the increased autonomy of many work groups (see the discussion of empowerment).

Quality circles

Quality circles (QCs) trace their origin to post-war Japan and the Japanese desire to change the image of Japanese products as cheap imitations of Western products. Quality circles evolved as a result of an increasingly literate workforce being able to participate in problem solving. The quality circles movement spread from Japan to the USA in the 1970s and to the UK in the late 1970s.

The principles of QCs are:

- QCs should be introduced in a totally voluntary way and should only grow as and when volunteers wish to join.
- QCs are based on a McGregor Theory Y (see Chapter 2) concept of working people; i.e. they are willing and able to participate in solving problems that affect them.
- QCs should be unbureaucratic and need only brief action notes following each meeting.
- QCs, as with any other crucial approach to management, need middle and senior management commitment.
- QCs focus problem solving at the point at which problems occur, and therefore release middle and senior management time.

Quality circles are based upon the working group. Groups of about four to ten volunteers who work for the same supervisor meet about once a week, for about an hour, to identify, analyse and solve their own work-related problems. Discussions should be free from hierarchical restraints. Members take ownership of departmental issues and no longer see problems as other people's problems. Quality circle members will need some training in appropriate techniques, such as brainstorming, used to identify and suggest solutions. In addition they will need to be trained in problem-solving techniques. In some cases smaller numbers of employees may be involved, in which case such groups may sometimes be referred to as 'quality bubbles'.

The benefits of QCs may be at least threefold: first, problems are solved; second, attitudes that identify with the organization's goals are developed; and third, the quality of supervision and communications is improved.

Obviously it can be seen that if QCs are developed and operated effectively their influence on job design can be very significant. In particular, job design becomes a dynamic process with the possibility that jobs could be constantly changing in detail.

A related approach is Kaizen (continuous improvement): a Japanese business philosophy of continuous improvement of working practices, personal efficiency consisting of constant small incremental changes in order to improve quality and/or efficiency. Kaizen may operate at the level of an individual, or through Kaizen groups or quality circles.

Job design, therefore, is the process that sets out to harness the energies of human resources in order to achieve an organization's objectives. In turn, job descriptions are the written results of the process of job design. In some cases, particularly in the industry's smallest establishments, written job descriptions are not used and may be too formal and rigid. In other situations brief descriptions only may be sufficient, whereas in yet others quite detailed and complex documents are called for. The degree of detail needed in describing the various elements of a job varies from job to job and from organization to organization. There are, however, two main documents: job descriptions and job specifications. They are described below. In addition a brief description of management by objectives is included in this chapter because it may be described as a methodical and systematic approach to the design and description of jobs and setting of objectives.

Empowerment

In the last few years the word 'empowerment' has entered the management vocabulary. Other words are sometimes used, such as 'enabling'. The French use the word *responsabiliser*: 'to make responsible'. The concept has had a mixed reception, partly because empowerment has been associated with reduction in the layers of management of many organizations.

This reduction in the number of layers of management is partly the result of recession, new technologies and also competitive pressures. An associated reason has been the development known by some as 'business process re-engineering' (BPR) by which many organizations have analysed closely the way they carry out their organizational functions. Consequences of BPR have included delayering, i.e. reducing the number of levels of management; empowerment, i.e. giving more responsibility lower down the hierarchy; and outsourcing, i.e. subcontracting non-core activities.

In its simplest form, empowerment is a management philosophy that allows work people to take on responsibilities that were once the prerogative of management. This might include making operative staff responsible for the quality of their own work or whole teams of staff responsible for organizing how they work as a team. Examples include major hotel chains eliminating assistant housekeepers and making the room attendants totally responsible for the quality of the work they do. In another company the restaurant teams were given the responsibility of organizing the whole of the restaurant service operations. Management roles change in such a situation; managers becoming coaches, counsellors and facilitators rather than supervisors (see Ashness and Lashley, 1995). As Lashley and McGoldrick (1995) wrote, 'an increasing number of firms are considering employee empowerment as part of their human resource strategy for competitive advantage'. They go on to point out, however, that it is not the only strategy open to employers, suggesting that some have taken a too simplistic view of empowerment as a business solution. In 2010 it became a major workforce initiative (People 1st, 2011; MacLeod and Clarke, 2010) with major hospitality companies, such as Malmaison and Hotel du Vin, embracing the concept.

Job descriptions

Job descriptions are a broad statement of the scope, purpose, duties and responsibilities involved in a job (see Figure 3.2). Their main purposes are to:

1 give employees an understanding of their jobs and standards of performance
2 clarify duties, responsibilities and authority in order to design the organization structure
3 assist in assessing employees' performance
4 assist in the recruitment and placement of employees
5 assist in the induction of new employees
6 evaluate jobs for grading and salary administration
7 provide information for training and management development
8 provide evidence of 'due diligence' in cases with legal implications.

There are two distinct but equally important parts to the full description of jobs. The first is the statement of conditions for which employees contract to do work; sixty years ago in the UK it was recognized that the definition of conditions was not generally adequate, with the result that the Contracts of Employment Act became law in 1963. Now the Employment Rights Act 1996 requires that certain minimal information about conditions of employment such as hours of work, job title and length of notice be given to employees. This subject, together with other legal reasons for producing and issuing comprehensive job descriptions, will be dealt with in subsequent chapters.

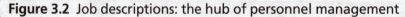

Figure 3.2 Job descriptions: the hub of personnel management

The second part of describing jobs requires the provision of information to employees, which specifies clearly what results are expected of them and indicates how their performance will be measured. Job descriptions should contain the following main elements:

Job identification
This section identifies the job by title, department and level in the hierarchy.

Scope of job
This section provides a brief description of the scope of the job.

Content
This section is a detailed statement and normally includes a list of duties and how these are performed, and what standard of performance is required.

Conditions
This section describes any particular conditions that make the job more, or less, difficult; for example, if a public house is situated in a rough area, this will need to be highlighted.

Authority
This section describes any limits to the employee's authority such as cash limits, authority to make contracts on behalf of the employer, and authority to engage or dismiss subordinates.

Figure 3.3 shows a typical job description for a chef. A major criticism of many job descriptions is that, by prescribing tasks and responsibilities, they can work against the overall objectives of the organization. This is particularly so in service organizations where staff need to understand that their role is to provide a service, even when it is not in their job description. People increasingly do not have a 'job'; they

Title	Chef
Department	Food and Beverage
Scope	All hotel food preparation operations
Responsible to	Food and Beverage Manager
Responsible for	1 *Personnel*: all kitchen staff including kitchen manual staff 2 *Equipment*: all kitchen fixed and removable equipment and kitchen utensils
Lateral communication	Restaurant Manager, Front Office Manager, Head Housekeeper
Main responsibilities	The planning, organization and supervision of food preparation in the hotel including:
	1 Menu compilation according to agreed costed recipes 2 Purchasing of foodstuffs, kitchen materials and equipment from nominated suppliers within agreed budget levels 3 Portion and waste control 4 Control of labour and other variable costs within budget levels 5 Arrangement of staff rosters 6 Training of new staff 7 Hygiene and cleanliness 8 Fire precautions 9 Security of all kitchen supplies, equipment, utensils and silverware
Limits of authority	Engagement and suspension of all subordinates until circumstances can be reported to the Food and Beverage Manager
Hours of work	As agreed with Food and Beverage Manager

Figure 3.3 Job description for a chef

have a 'role', and to keep up with this new industrial revolution it is necessary to turn away from job analysis towards role analysis. An example of role analysis might specify that members of staff have customer satisfaction as one of their roles. In this way staff might take on (or own) a customer's problems rather than decide that the problem is not in their job description and try to pass the problem and the customer on to someone else. A job description might not include the expectation that waiting staff pick up dropped items from the floor, but a role expectation is that they keep the restaurant clean and tidy.

Job specifications

In many cases more detail than is normally contained in a brief job description may be necessary for a job to be performed satisfactorily. A detailed statement of the job may be required, specifying the precise skills and knowledge needed to carry out the various component tasks of the job. This information may be contained in a document, often referred to as a job specification. Alternatively, the information may be contained in such documents as manuals of operation, operating instructions, standard operating procedures (SOPs) and the like. Extracts from a job specification for a waiter/waitress are shown in Figure 3.4.

Duties		Knowledge	Skill	Social skills
1	Preparation			
1.3	Preparation of butter, cruets and accompaniments	Correct accompaniments for the dishes on the day's menu	Operation of butter pat maker. Preparation of sauces, e.g. vinaigrette	
3	Service of customers			
3.3	Taking orders	1 Procedures for taking wine and food orders 2 Menu and dish composition 3 Procedure for taking requisitions to kitchen, bar dispense and cashier		1 Assisting customers with selection in order to maximize sales 2 Informing customers of composition of dishes
8	Wine dispense	Product knowledge 1 Suitable wines for dishes on the menu 2 Suitable glasses for different wines 3 Correct temperatures for red, white and rosé	1 Presenting bottle 2 Opening bottle 3 Pouring wine	1 Assisting customers with selection 2 Dealing with complaints
		Licensing law 1 Young persons 2 Drinking up time		1 Refusing service 2 Asking people to 'drink up'
11	Preparation for cleaners after last customers have left			
11.3	Stripping tables	1 Safe disposal of ash tray contents 2 Disposal of cutlery, crockery, linen, cruets		

Figure 3.4 Extracts from a job specification for a waiter/waitress

Within the last few years job descriptions and specifications have become much more highly developed in the hospitality industry. Many companies use training booklets, DVDs and online media which serve several important purposes, including the provision of:

- job descriptions
- trainers' programme
- trainees' *aides-mémoire*
- list of duties
- list of tasks
- standards of performance
- interviewer's checklist
- training checklist.

Not only are these aids very useful for selection, induction and training purposes, they may also be useful for discipline purposes and even for 'due diligence' in cases of prosecution or litigation. If someone has been trained to do something, and the fact is recorded, then certain standards can be expected.

Job analysis

This is sometimes considered to be a document describing a job in detail, but the term is more commonly used when referring to the technique of examining jobs in depth.

Preparation of job (or role) descriptions and job specifications

Some managers like to prepare job descriptions and other such documents with the employees concerned, and, generally speaking, this is by far the best approach. Frequently, however, this principle can apply only to supervisory and management grades, because the jobs of operative grades are often so clearly defined that discussion, apart from explanation, would only raise hopes that would be disappointed when it became apparent that no changes were forthcoming. Furthermore, it is not always possible to involve the employee concerned, because the need for job descriptions often does not make itself apparent until a person has to be recruited. Even so, with the increasing development of participative approaches such as empowerment, it is very likely that the involvement of operative staff in the design of their own jobs will increase in the hospitality industry as in other sectors.

The preparation of job specifications normally requires a more skilled approach than that needed for the preparation of job descriptions. The uses to which such documents are to be put should determine who prepares them; for example, if job specifications are to be used for training purposes, they should be prepared by training specialists and the line management concerned. On the other hand, if they are to be used as a basis for work measurement or job grading/evaluation, specialists should work with line management.

Whatever form the description of jobs takes, however, vague terms such as 'satisfactory gross profit' should be avoided and, instead, actual quantities or levels should be specified, such as 'a gross profit of 65% is to be obtained'.

It is good practice also to incorporate budgets and forecasts into job descriptions, since these set specific and quantified targets. Additionally, documents such as manuals of operation or training booklets may be directly related to job descriptions.

Because of the vital part played by job descriptions and specifications, particularly in such things as induction, training, job evaluation and performance appraisal, their preparation should be monitored by one person or department to ensure consistency. They should be regularly updated and a copy should be held by the job holder, by his or her superior, sometimes by the superior's boss as well and, of course, by the HR department (where one exists).

Some job-design tools

Job design, as indicated above, can involve a number of different skills and techniques. These can include the following:

Work study
This divides into method study and work measurement.

Method study
A part of work study concerned with recording and analysing methods and proposed methods of work, the purpose being to develop more effective ways of doing things.

Work measurement
A technique used to measure the time an experienced worker will take to perform a task or job to a predetermined standard. Measurement may be carried out by direct observation, by sampling or by using 'synthetic' values, i.e. times previously determined for particular movements.

Ergonomics
The study of the relationship between a worker and his or her work equipment and environment. In particular it is concerned with the application of anatomical, physiological and psychological knowledge to working situations such as design of work stations, chairs, etc. The aim of ergonomics is to produce safe and effective equipment and environments for working people, using physical and psychological knowledge.

Management by objectives (MbO)

Management by objectives (and various similar approaches) is an approach to management which, if operated effectively, influences all levels and activities of an organization (see Peter Drucker, Chapter 2). By concept it is typical of a democratic style of management, although, in practice, it is often introduced by other types of manager. It usually relies heavily on specially designed job descriptions and similar documents. It seeks to integrate all of an organization's principal targets with the individual manager's own aspirations.

Management by objectives requires the establishment of an undertaking's objectives and the development of plans to achieve these objectives and of methods for monitoring progress. At the same time each manager must be personally involved in the preparation of his or her own targets and in the means of achieving these targets. Objectives should not be handed down by superior to subordinate, but should be negotiated and agreed between the two after all factors have been considered.

Only the critical areas (key result areas) of each manager's job are defined, the objectives where possible are quantified and means of checking results, or identifying obstacles, and of achieving objectives are developed. Planning and improvement go on continuously through review meetings between superiors and subordinates held at regular intervals. The difference between target- or budget-driven management and MbO is that in MbO targets are freely negotiated between superior

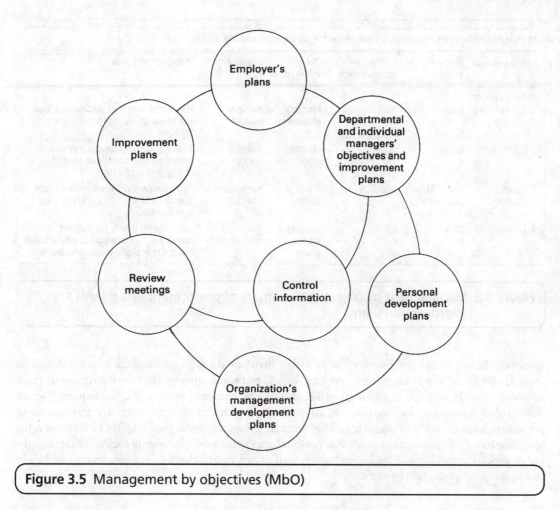

Figure 3.5 Management by objectives (MbO)

and subordinate. The procedure is illustrated in Figure 3.5 and an extract from an MbO job description is shown in Figure 3.6.

Where MbO concepts have been used in hospitality operations to set standards, it is generally found that the performance standards of operative staff are 'guest-centred', i.e. they are concerned with identifying the standards of service to be provided to the guest. The performance standards of heads of departments, on the other hand, are 'profit-centred', i.e. they identify the revenue and cost criteria for producing the services for the guest. Heads of departments are, however, directly responsible for ensuring that the operational performance standards are met by department staff, so their performance standards may incorporate quality management standards as well as profit-centred standards.

Current issues to be faced in job design

With the rapidly changing nature of the workforce and labour market, including skills shortages and the raised expectations of working people, job design now has to consider a wider range of factors than merely designing the task and work content of jobs. Job designers, i.e. most managers, will need to focus

Manager, White Hart Restaurant: Objectives for six months ending 30 June					
Key result area	Performance standard	Current level of achievement	Control information	Improvement target	Improvement plan
1 Gross profit					
(a) catering	63%	58%	Monthly stocktake	Achieve budget	Review selling and purchase prices, introduce more high-yield dishes, by 30 April.
(b) liquor	60%	58%	Monthly stocktake	Achieve budget	Alter sales mix, introduce premium-priced beer, discontinue sale of cheaper draught beer.
2 Sales volume	£60,000 per month	£66,000	Takings sheets	Increase to £84,000	Promote new private function room, spend £2,000 on promotion during first quarter.
3 Labour	23%	26%	Weekly wages sheet	Reduce to budget, 23%	Increase staff only for booked functions, no more staff to be recruited except to replace those who leave.

Figure 3.6 Management by objectives: example of performance standards and improvement plans

more than before on the conditions of work rather than just the job content. Such issues will include more family-friendly polices, flexible working hours, providing support for women returners, more autonomy, etc. in addition to eliminating menial tasks by mechanization, and tasks requiring scarce skills. Other dimensions include the need to ensure that forms of discrimination are not created or perpetuated, intentionally or unintentionally, through job design (see Figure 3.1). A crucial issue is the identification of repetitive tasks not needing personal interactions and eliminating such tasks through the use of various technologies. Hotel mini-bars as well as automated check-in processes are examples of tasks previously performed by staff.

Job design in hospitality operations

At one extreme, job design can simplify work so that little skill and training are needed. Trends in this direction are very apparent in the hospitality industry in several sectors including fast food operations and budget hotels. Another example is the use of cook–chill and cook–freeze in many different operations, including schools, hospitals, banqueting and flight catering, a process sometimes referred to as 'decoupling'. In such cases the production and service elements are totally separated – pre-prepared meals being produced away from the service point. Such systems are concerned mainly with the 'production elements' of many products. However, because of the significant 'customer contact' element, it is difficult to 'simplify out' many of the tasks that customers expect as part of the service and which employees themselves find rewarding, because of the social interaction, such as in fine-dining.

Hard and soft brands

The nature of a brand itself will have a significant impact on job design. Hard brands are those brands which are very strictly specified and controlled. Such brands aim to provide consistency, sometimes worldwide, but tend to leave little room for personal initiative at operative and even supervisory levels. Many of the fast food, coffee chains and budget hotel brands fall into this category of 'hard brand'; everything from recipes to service scripts (what to say, when) may be prescribed in standard operating procedures (SOPs). Soft brands, on the other hand, offer less consistency to the customer but may well leave more flexibility for owners and franchisees and their management and staff to operate within a looser format. Several consortia, such as Best Western and the French hotel chain, Logis de France, may be described as 'soft brand'.

Further reading and references

Armstrong, M. (2011) *How to Manage People*, London: Kogan Page.

Armstrong, M. (2012) *A Handbook of Human Resource Management*, 12th edn, London: Kogan Page.

Ashness, D. and Lashley, C. (1995) *Employee Empowerment in Harvester Restaurants*, Human Resource Management in the Hospitality Industry Conference Document, University of Brighton.

Beardwell, I., Holden, L. and Claydon, T. (2004) *Human Resource Management – A Contemporary Approach*, 4th edn, Harlow: Prentice Hall.

Foss, N. J., Minbaeva, D. B. and Pedersen, T. (2009) 'Encouraging knowledge sharing among employees: how job design matters', *Human Resource Management* 48(6): 871–893.

Goss-Turner, S. (2002) *Managing People in the Hospitality Industry*, 4th edn, Kingston-upon-Thames: Croner Publications.

Hackman, J. R. and Oldham, G. R. (1976) 'Motivation through the design of work: test of a theory', *Organizational Behavior and Human Performance*, 16(2): 250–279.

Herzberg, F. (1968) *Work and the Nature of Man*, London: Staples Press.

Institute of Hospitality (2011) *Performance Management in Hospitality Businesses*, London: Institute of Hospitality.

Kanter, R. M. (1983) *The Change Masters*, London: Simon and Schuster.

Kanter, R. M. (1989) *When Giants Learn to Dance*, London: Simon and Schuster.

Kennedy, C. (2007) *Guide to the Management Gurus*, 5th edn, London: Random House.

Lashley, C. and McGoldrick, J. (1995) *The Limits of Empowerment*, Human Resource Management in the Hospitality Industry Conference Document, University of Brighton.

MacLeod, D. and Clarke, N. (2010) *Engaging for Success: Enhancing Performance through Employee Engagement*, London: Department for Business, Innovation and Skills.

Mohr, R. D. and Zoghi, C. (2008) 'High-involvement work design and job satisfaction', *Industrial and Labour Relations Review*, 61(3): 275–296.

People 1st (2011) *State of the Nation Report 2011, Analysis of labour market trends, skills, education and training within the UK hospitality, leisure, travel and tourism industries*, London: People 1st.

Pugh, S. and Hickson, D. (2007) *Writers on Organizations*, 6th edn, London: Penguin Books.

Simons, R. (2005) 'Designing high-performance jobs', *Harvard Business Review*, 83(7): 55–62.

Taylor, F. W. (1911) *The Principles of Scientific Management*, New York: Harper and Brothers.

Torrington, D., Hall, L., Taylor, S. and Atkinson, C. (2011) *Human Resource Management*, 8th edn, Harlow: Pearson Education.

Members of the UK's Institute of Hospitality can access publications including Management Guides which summarize key information of relevance to hospitality operations (www.instituteofhospitality.org).

Members of the UK's Chartered Institute of Personnel and Development (CIPD) can access a range of materials including Fact Sheets and articles from over 300 online journal titles relevant to HR. CIPD members and *People Management* subscribers can see articles on the People Management website (www.peoplemanagement.co.uk).

Questions

1 Describe the different approaches to job design.

2 Discuss the various influences and stakeholders that need to be taken into account when designing jobs.

3 Discuss the impact of 'hard' and 'soft' brands on job design.

4 Discuss what future influences are likely to affect job design.

5 Discuss how job design may differ when applied to management and non-management jobs.

6 Evaluate the approach to job design used by an employer you know well.

CASE STUDY QUESTION – see the Lux Hotels case study Appendix 5

In this chapter several different approaches to job design have been described. Consider in particular if you think Lux Hotels to be a 'hard brand' or a 'soft brand'.

Now discuss which main approach or approaches, for the different levels of employee, would be most suited to Lux Hotels, giving reasons for your recommendation.

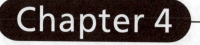

Chapter 4

Recruitment

The hospitality industry throughout much of the world appears to have recruitment problems associated with a poor image as an employer. At the international level, over many years, the issue has been highlighted at various international hospitality conferences such as the International Hotel and Restaurants Association in Israel in 1995 and in the Netherlands in 1999. This issue is further highlighted by recent reports such as the *State of the Nation Report 2011* (People 1st, 2011).

In the UK many reports over the years, some summarized in earlier editions of this book, have highlighted the persistent nature of many of the issues confronting employers and employees. Now, however, the hospitality industry in the UK, led largely by some major employers and by the British Hospitality Association, the Institute of Hospitality and by People 1st, appears to be attempting to tackle both the image and the recruitment problems, particularly through 'employee engagement'. This is a major issue now being addressed by companies and government. Employee engagement was addressed in 2009 at the UK national industry level by a report commissioned by the British government. The brief was 'to take an in-depth look at employee engagement and to report on its potential benefits for companies, organisations and individual employees'. The inquiry resulted in a major report: *Engaging for Success* (MacLeod and Clarke, 2010). Several leading hospitality companies participated.

This report defined 'employee engagement' as:

> A workplace approach designed to ensure that employees are committed to their organisation's goals and values, motivated to contribute to organisational success, and are able, at the same time, to enhance their own sense of well-being.

Recruitment advertising in the hospitality industry

The quality of recruitment advertising in the hospitality industry varies considerably. At one end of the scale, large companies such as Hilton, InterContinental, McDonald's and Whitbread are able to employ the best of expertise in designing recruitment media. At the other extreme are the small operators who, with no expertise and very limited resources, have to design advertisements which, not surprisingly in many cases, are ineffective. For example, media research has demonstrated that inclusion of earnings in a recruitment advertisement increases the effectiveness of the advertisement and yet a proportion of advertisements in the *Caterer and Hotelkeeper* do not include earnings levels, whilst most job advertisements in *People Management*, the magazine for HR professionals, do. It is of interest that in some other countries – France, for example – there is a reluctance to include earnings in recruitment advertisements because employers wish to negotiate with applicants rather than adhere to predetermined salary scales.

By itself, good recruitment cannot overcome the problem of high labour turnover. This has to be tackled by keeping all conditions of employment under constant review and by making appropriate improvements to conditions as circumstances dictate. The nature of the hospitality industry, however, with its large number of small employers, is such that most people holding management or supervisory positions are going to be faced frequently with the need to recruit people to fill vacancies.

Employers need to recognize that they recruit not just from their primary markets, but also from secondary labour markets. In addition recruitment needs to appeal to 'passive' job seekers, i.e. those not actively seeking a job change (and those who influence them, such as parents, friends and teachers) and not just the active job seekers.

Furthermore employers, even during recession, operate in a 'buyers' market (i.e. many potential employees have a range of opportunities, including social security). One only has to look at the application forms from some leading high-street employers to see that they ask their applicants for the times that they are available for work – a big contrast to a few years ago when employers dictated the hours of work, on a take it or leave it basis! A major restaurant operation in the USA, 'Lettuce Entertain You', reported that when they recruited staff one of the first things they did was to determine what hours the applicant could work and how much they wanted to earn. With this information, because earnings were largely through tips, they were then able to match actual shifts with the employee's availability and earnings expectations.

Labour markets

In order to recruit successfully, however, it is important to have an understanding of labour markets, in the same way as in promoting products and services it is essential to know the nature of the target markets.

Labour markets have a number of characteristics, including their size, technological complexity, elasticity, pay levels, geographical distribution and status (e.g. primary or secondary). For the purpose of this book the primary and secondary markets will be discussed in a little more detail.

Primary labour market

The primary labour market consists of those people who through education, training and experience are committed to an industry, sometimes even a sector of an industry. In the hospitality industry these include hotel managers, chefs, hotel receptionists, hall porters and cocktail bar staff. Such people intend to develop their careers in the industry and in many cases view their opportunities nationally, even internationally. As a consequence many of these people are mobile, both geographically and organizationally.

Secondary labour market

The secondary labour market consists of people, on the other hand, who have skills of use to an employer, but who may not be committed to a career in a particular industry. They probably attach more importance to a geographical area than to a career. Typically the secondary labour market contains women with family responsibilities, students and unskilled working people who choose to work in a particular industry in order to earn a living rather than because of a strong commitment to that industry. The secondary labour market also includes people with skills that may be common to many industries, such as secretaries, maintenance people, book-keepers and accountants.

International labour market

With the enlargement of the European Union in 2004 and the addition of the new member states' labour markets, the opportunities for employers to find employees from an enlarged labour market have widened considerably. The UK Office for National Statistics reported that in 2009–10 over 35 per cent of restaurant staff in the UK were migrant workers. In hotels the figure was 25 per cent (People 1st, 2011).

The competition for the best staff will be severe as many industries suffer from significant skills and numbers shortages and because there is a decline in the proportion of young people in the population. The hospitality industry is heavily reliant on young people; 77 per cent of waiting staff are under 30 years old. Overall, 44 per cent of the sector's workforce is under 30 (ibid.).

Discrimination

The hospitality industry in the UK has always had a very high proportion of migrant workers concentrated in certain sectors so the issue of discrimination can be significant. In 2011 around 12 per cent of the workforce were migrant workers. In restaurants this peaked at close to 40 per cent. Women represent 58 per cent of the workforce. Only 6 per cent of workers are over 60 years of age (ibid.). See Chapter 16 for the law concerned with discrimination. In essence discrimination in the workplace is illegal in many economies such as the European Union, the United States, Australia and New Zealand. However, in some countries discrimination is practised, either illegally or legally. For example in India recruitment advertisements may specify gender. On the other hand some companies insist upon treating everyone equally, irrespective of gender or culture. One company's 'values' statement is reproduced in Figure 4.1.

The recruitment process

Recruitment is the process used to attract suitable applicants from whom the most suitable person may be selected for a particular job. It depends upon having the proper information available, including a job or role description (see Chapter 3), a personnel specification and a knowledge of the labour market. The process starts with the production of a personnel specification, based on a job description or job specification, and ends with the appointment of a successful candidate.

Personnel specification

From the job description a 'personnel specification' (or person spec.) – a description of the type of person most likely to be able to carry out the job described by the job description – can be prepared. The precise nature of a personnel specification will depend upon the degree of sophistication or otherwise of an organization. Figure 4.2 is an example. From the job description in Figure 3.3, therefore, a personnel specification could be drawn up and might look something like Figure 4.3. If considered necessary or useful, distinctions could be made between 'essential' or 'desirable' attributes.

Extract from Code of Conduct, page 2

TEAM MEMBER STANDARDS OF CONDUCT

Below is a list of expected behaviors from Team Members, regardless of position. The examples below are not all-encompassing. Hilton reserves the right to determine whether particular conduct is inappropriate.

Personal Accountability

All Team Members are expected to behave in a way that is consistent with Hilton's "Values" of Hospitality, Integrity, Leadership, Teamwork, Ownership and Now. Every day, in every action they take, Team Members can have a direct impact on Hilton's reputation. Our continued success depends on every Team Member accepting personal responsibility for doing what's right, all the time, and for taking responsibility for the actions they take and for the consequences of those actions. Team Members must avoid and prevent actions that can hurt each other, our guests, our business partners, our communities and our reputation.

As global leaders in the hospitality business, we understand the importance of treating people well – all people and not simply our guests.

Personal accountability also means reporting issues and concerns. You are encouraged to call or walk through the open door of the office of your supervisor, your department manager or your local Human Resources Department, if you have any questions, concerns or problems. If you report concerns in good faith, then retaliation against you is prohibited and will not be tolerated.

We expect everyone throughout our system to be treated and to treat each other with respect and dignity at all times.

Respecting and Valuing Diversity

We encourage and value a diverse work environment and will achieve success by valuing and leveraging the diversity of our workforce, our guests, our suppliers, and our partners. Respecting the diverse cultures throughout our global organization, as corporate citizens, we will address the local needs of the communities in which we serve, live, and work around the world. Therefore, we will not tolerate any discrimination, harassment or retaliation against any individual or group on the basis of ethnic, gender, racial, religious or cultural factors or any other characteristic protected by applicable law. We will seek and employ the most qualified Team Members, and provide equal opportunities to all Team Members based on merit, skills, qualifications, experience, effort, and ability to perform the job responsibilities.

Maintaining a Harassment-Free Workplace

Hilton is committed to a work environment that does not tolerate any form of harassment based on any characteristic protected by applicable law. Any behavior that creates an intimidating, offensive, abusive or hostile work environment, or that otherwise interferes with any Team Member's ability to perform his or her job is unacceptable.

Harassment can take many forms including but not limited to:

- Written or verbal abuse or threats;
- Unwelcome remarks, jokes, slurs or taunting of a discriminatory nature;
- Practical jokes that embarrass or insult someone;
- Ignoring, isolating or segregating a person;
- Materials that are of a discriminatory nature that are displayed publicly, circulated in the workplace, etc.; or
- Unwanted physical contact.

If any Team Member feels that they are being harassed they should take immediate action by alerting a supervisor or their local Human Resources Department. All claims of harassment will be appropriately addressed. Hilton will conduct any investigations as confidentially as possible. All Team Members are required to cooperate with any investigations. Hilton prohibits retaliation against any Team Member who brings forward a harassment claim in good faith and cooperates with the investigation.

Figure 4.1 Hilton Worldwide 'values' statement
Source: Reproduced by courtesy of Hilton Worldwide.

PERSON SPECIFICATION

(To be completed with Job Description prior to recruitment)

JOB TITLE... .. LOCATION..

	Minimum Requirements	Desired Requirements	Undesirable Factors
Appearance & Health General Health Physical Capabilities Appearance/Image Speech Others			
Attainments Education Job Training Job Experience Others			
Special Aptitudes Manual Dexterity Numerical Dexterity Communication Skills Languages Others			
Disposition Self-reliance Maturity Confidence Assertive/Leadership Temperament Pleasant/Friendly Others			
Circumstances Family Commitments Accommodation Travel Mobility (Transfers) Others			

COMPLETED BY... DATE...

AUTHORIZED BY... DATE...

Figure 4.2 Example of person specification form

Job title	Chef de cuisine
ESSENTIAL Qualifications	
(a) educational	No formal requirements
(b) technical	City and Guilds of London 706/1/2 or
	formal apprenticeship, NVQ Level 3
Experience to include	(a) experience in all kitchen departments
	(b) experience of controlling a brigade of not less than five
	(c) recent experience of good quality à la carte service (up to 200 covers a day)
Personal qualities	(a) able to control mixed staff of English, Continental and Asian nationalities
	(b) stable employment record (e.g. no more than three jobs over the last ten years)
Personal circumstances	(a) able to work late (11 p.m.) about three nights a week
	(b) will have to live out
DESIRABLE Qualifications	Qualified skills trainer
Experience	Large-scale banqueting

Figure 4.3 Personnel specification for a chef

From the information in the job description and personnel specification subsequent recruitment steps can be decided upon.

Internal recruitment

The first step always in filling a position is to consider promoting or transferring existing employees. Considerable dissatisfaction can be caused by bringing newcomers in over the heads of present staff, which is often done with the intention of causing as little disturbance as possible to the organization. Unfortunately, because the hopes of some individuals in the organization may be frustrated, they may leave or behave in other unsatisfactory ways and the long-term effect is therefore far more damaging.

It is good management practice, therefore, for all vacancies in a company, and particularly those that may be seen by existing employees to be promotions, to be advertised internally on staff noticeboards, on the company's intranet or by circulars. Circulating details to supervisors only is generally not satisfactory, since some employees may, for various reasons, fear that their supervisors will not put them forward.

External recruitment

The next step, if no currently employed staff are suitable, is to go to the labour market. This is where most problems arise and where most money and effort can be wasted. The numerous and varied means of recruitment include:

1. the Internet, including recruitment/careers pages on a company's promotional website
2. online recruitment agencies, job boards
3. newspapers: national, local and trade
4. agencies, including the various government agencies
5. executive selection and management consultants

6   posters, leaflets and application forms, in one's own premises, postcards in local post-office windows
7   colleges and universities
8   the armed forces
9   existing employees; by offering introductory bonuses to existing staff
10 open days.

The choice of media is critical to success and always depends on the type and level of vacancy and whether prospective employees are part of a local, national or an industry labour market, i.e. a primary or secondary labour market. In recent years there has been a significant shift to use of the Internet as a major recruitment medium, some companies abandoning completely other forms of recruitment.

Advertising

The ability to use the right media is absolutely vital today particularly as major operators are now extremely sophisticated in their use of media. But it is no longer enough to choose one medium as opposed to another. Many employers are increasingly adopting 'multi-channel' recruitment often using their websites as the early steps in their selection process.

One of the recruitment needs, particularly for larger companies, is to develop a comprehensive interaction between the various media so that, for example, a press advertisement will lead a potential applicant to an interactive website. Many companies are now outsourcing such processes to specialist commercial 'job board' firms. Whilst the Internet, together with the social media, has grown significantly, some print media, particularly local newspapers, still remain a commonly used medium for recruitment of less senior staff.

The Web, whilst adding considerably to the recruiter's armoury, must not be seen as a replacement for older methods – instead it should be seen as just another weapon. Often a contemporary treatment of traditional methods may be used, such as specially printed table-top recruitment flyers in fast food outlets and pub-restaurants. Older, well-tried methods ranging from staff recruitment notices in premises windows, or sandwich boards outside, through to open days will continue to play a crucial role.

It is evident that a large part of any recruitment can be expected to rely on various forms of advertising and, therefore, apart from the choice of media, the drafting of advertisements is important. To recruit successfully these days, in the face of expert competition from other employers, it is no longer enough just to place an advertisement. It has to be an effective advertisement. Some suggested rules for creating an effective advertisement might include:

1   Do not mislead. Careless or misleading statements can lead to early resignations, resentment and consequent high labour turnover.
2   Catch likely candidates' attention with a suitable headline.
3   Hold their attention by giving clear, factual information including:

   (a) locality
   (b) job content
   (c) prospects
   (d) qualifications
   (e) experience
   (f) conditions of employment.

4   Keep the language simple, avoid jargon, if it is directed at unskilled applicants.
5   Stimulate interest in the employer and promote their image, but remember that the priority is to fill a vacancy, not to advertise the establishment.

6   Avoid meaningless statements such as 'attractive wage' or 'salary according to qualifications'.
7   Test the advertisement on others before finalizing it.
8   Describe what action has to be taken in order to apply.
9   If it is intended to close applications after a certain number have been received make this clear in the advertisement.
10 Stimulate readers to action by telling them to call in, write, telephone or complete an 'online' application.

Advertising a vacancy should be the method by which an employer communicates to potential employees that they are seeking to fill a vacancy. If the advertisement is vaguely worded, it may encourage too many unsuitable applicants or, worse still, it may not attract the most suitable people.

A well-designed advertisement will do more than just communicate basic information in words; it can, by its graphic design, say a lot about the employer and their style. There is an often-quoted law of recruitment advertising which states that the ideal advertisement attracts only one applicant and that this applicant will be successful. This is obviously overstating the case but it does illustrate the need to think carefully about the media selected and the message.

The chef's position described in Figure 3.3 could be advertised in the form shown in Figure 4.4. This illustrates an advertisement for a skilled person. Advertising for unskilled people needs a different approach; for example if advertising for a barman/barmaid it may well be that the person appointed will need no experience, but some personal qualities instead, such as 'good appearance and personality'.

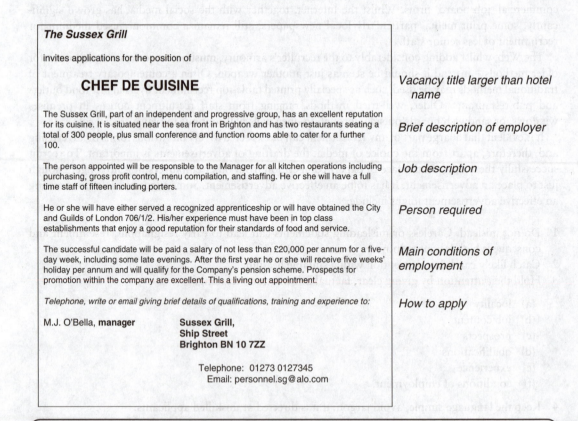

The Sussex Grill

invites applications for the position of

CHEF DE CUISINE

The Sussex Grill, part of an independent and progressive group, has an excellent reputation for its cuisine. It is situated near the sea front in Brighton and has two restaurants seating a total of 300 people, plus small conference and function rooms able to cater for a further 100.

The person appointed will be responsible to the Manager for all kitchen operations including purchasing, gross profit control, menu compilation, and staffing. He or she will have a full time staff of fifteen including porters.

He or she will have either served a recognized apprenticeship or will have obtained the City and Guilds of London 706/1/2. His/her experience must have been in top class establishments that enjoy a good reputation for their standards of food and service.

The successful candidate will be paid a salary of not less than £20,000 per annum for a five-day week, including some late evenings. After the first year he or she will receive five weeks' holiday per annum and will qualify for the Company's pension scheme. Prospects for promotion within the company are excellent. This a living out appointment.

Telephone, write or email giving brief details of qualifications, training and experience to:

M.J. O'Bella, **manager**   **Sussex Grill,
Ship Street
Brighton BN 10 7ZZ**

Telephone: 01273 0127345
Email: personnel.sg@alo.com

Vacancy title larger than hotel name

Brief description of employer

Job description

Person required

Main conditions of employment

How to apply

Figure 4.4 Display advertisement for a chef de cuisine

THE SPLENDIDE HOTEL

situated in the centre of Newtown and catering for a busy commercial trade requires

A SMART ENERGETIC PERSON

to work as a part-time assistant in the cocktail bar. The successful applicant will assist the cocktail barman on Tuesday to Saturday evenings each week. Once the person appointed is familiar with the work he or she will stand in for the cocktail barman on Sunday evenings. Hours will be 5.45 p.m. to 10.45 p.m. (The Hotel is on several convenient bus routes which run up to about 11.00 p.m.)

No previous experience in bar work is required as training will be given, but the ability to get on with people will be essential. A meal will be provided during the evening and the rate of pay is 50p above the National Minimum Wage.

Splendide Hotel
Newtown, Newtownshire
Telephone Newtown (0021) 12345

If you are interested telephone Mr A. Smith, Food and Beverage Manager.

Figure 4.5 Display advertisement for a barman or barmaid (local press)

For this reason the headline could be directed at unqualified but 'smart energetic' people, not experienced bar staff (Figure 4.5).

There are three main ways of inserting advertisements in newspapers: display, semi-display and classified. The examples in Figures 4.4 and 4.5 are display; because this form of advertisement takes up the most space and involves the most work, it is the most expensive.

The second method is semi-display, which gives the advertiser some prominence in the classified section. Often this is all that is required to attract applicants. An example of semi-display is shown in Figure 4.6.

Classified advertising is the least expensive but may be less effective. This is because a large number of job advertisements are grouped together and consequently are less likely to catch the reader's eye. This is most likely to be the case when trying to recruit unqualified part-timers, because these are often recruited from normal readers who are not looking for jobs and consequently they will not look up the classified columns. On the other hand, a good display advertisement may well attract their attention and prompt them to apply. Many people, after all, have never thought of themselves working in a bar or restaurant, but the advertisement in Figure 4.5 would probably prompt several to apply. Figure 4.7 shows a typical classified advertisement.

In preparing recruitment advertisements it is useful to draw from product-marketing techniques and to use the acronym AIDA which stands for:

ATTENTION
INTEREST
DESIRE
ACTION.

WORKING HEAD CHEF

required

for busy 60 room
Hotel.

100-cover restaurant and separate pub
food operation.

Banqueting suite for 120.

Ideal candidate will be required to manage a
team of five, including one trainee, plus part-time
staff as needed.

He/she will maintain strict food and labour cost
control and will be totally responsible for health
and safety.

Apply in writing to:
Managing Director
The Old Post House
Fairwarp, Sussex
TN00 100

or by email to md.oph@alo.com

Figure 4.6 Semi-display advertisement

COOK REQUIRED at Ashdown Woods
Nursing Home for alternate weekends, hours
8 a.m.–1 p.m. If you are a kind, capable person
interested in good home cooking then you may be
the person we are looking for. Telephone for an
informal chat on Cobham 12345

Figure 4.7 Classified advertisement

Recruitment agencies

In large organizations where recruitment costs run into many thousands of pounds a year, it is often normal to retain a recruitment agency. Their services may cost relatively little, since they receive a commission from the media owners. Smaller firms, on the other hand, will not be able to offer recruitment agencies enough business for them to be interested, but in this case the media themselves may give advice and guidance.

The Internet

In 2004 reasons employers gave for using the Web included:

Reducing cost per hire (85%)
Increasing speed to hire (85%)
Strengthening the employer brand (65%)
Greater flexibility and ease for candidates (59%)
Broaden applicant pool (56%).

(Changeworknow/Lisa Astbury, *People Management*, July 2004)

Such benefits are obvious and it is no surprise that in 2011 some major employers reported that they had decided to rely entirely on Internet recruitment, leaving completely the print media. One French publication reported that over 80 per cent of vacancies were now being filled likewise. Reasons would include immediacy, elimination of postal costs and delays, but probably more importantly preliminary stages of the selection process can also be managed through the Internet.

Word of mouth

One particular method of recruitment has been purposely left until last because of the unique and important part it plays in recruitment. People in the hospitality industry know well the value of word-of-mouth recommendation. Many highly successful hotels, restaurants and public houses do not need to spend a penny on attracting customers. Their reputation, broadcast by word of mouth, is enough. This applies equally to staff and there are many successful managers who never have to spend a penny to recruit new staff. Consciously or unconsciously, their existing employees recruit newcomers for them.

This method of recruitment is particularly good because of the two-way recommendation. An existing employee is recommending someone as a good employer and the applicant is being recommended as a suitable employee. Recognizing the value of this method of recruitment, some firms actually stimulate it by paying bonuses to employees who successfully introduce newcomers to the firm.

However, for large organizations there can be a risk of falling foul of race relations legislation, because word-of-mouth systems of recruitment have been found to be discriminatory.

Costs

Recruitment, like any other business activity, costs time and money. Most other business activities are measured in some way and standards or ratios are used to indicate the efficiency of the activity or otherwise.

This principle should apply equally to recruitment if it is a regular and substantial part of the running costs of the business. Where an agency is retained it will calculate the cost-effectiveness of various media, but if an agency is not used this should be calculated internally. Figure 4.8 shows a simple form for the

	Internet	Daily Globe	Evening Star	Evening Star	Blue Agency	Job Centre
Job		Chef	Receptionist	Waiter	Waiter	Porter
Cost(£)		240	80	80	140	
Number of applicants	Set up and	8	20	4	7	16
Number interviewed	maintenance	5	12	3	6	9
Cost per applicant (£)	costs*	30	4	20	20	
Number of successful applicants		1	4	2	2	2
Cost per successful applicant (£)		240	20	40	70	

Figure 4.8 Recruitment costs analysis for various jobs and media

Note: * The costs of setting up and maintaining a company's jobs website can be quite high but may be shared with the company's main site, including advertising and promotion. However, once set up the additional cost of advertising any job will be very limited. It is therefore more difficult to cost an additional job. In the case of other media each job will tend to carry its own costs, as indicated above.

analysis of such costs, which, however, excludes the employer's own internal costs such as the Human Resource staff costs. Calculating the cost of Internet recruitment might be even more difficult because a 'jobs' page may be part of a company's total Internet platform which will include fees for webpage design, maintenance and rentals.

Analyses can be much more complex, but something along the lines of the form shown in Figure 4.8 will prove sufficient for the average organization to recognize which means of recruitment is the most effective and which involves the least interviewing, correspondence and other administration.

Recruitment code

The Institute of Personnel Management (now the Chartered Institute of Personnel and Development) drew up the 'IPM Recruitment Code', the main points of which were as follows and can still serve as sound practice:

1 Job advertisements will state clearly the form of reply desired (e.g. curriculum vitae, completed application form) and any preference for handwritten applications.
2 An acknowledgement or reply will be made promptly to each applicant. Where consultants are acting mainly as forwarding agents for companies, the parties will agree who will acknowledge applications.
3 Candidates will be informed of the progress of the selection procedure, what this will be, the time likely to be involved and the policy regarding expenses.
4 Detailed personal information (e.g. religion, medical history, place of birth, family background) will not be called for unless and until it is relevant to the selection process.
5 Recruiters will not take up any reference without the candidate's specific approval.
6 Applications will be treated as confidential.

Some employers, in addition to indicating closing dates, now indicate that they will close applications once a certain number of applications have been received.

Traditional forms of recruitment and sourcing labour, it appears, are not going to be sufficient to provide the necessary number of people required by the hospitality industry over the next few years. With declining proportions of young people and many other countries developing large middle classes, demand for hospitality services and the necessary human resources is bound to become very competitive. Instead new methods and sources are going to be needed. For example, much more effort will be needed to create a positive awareness of the industry among young school children, not just those about to leave school, by schemes such as 'adopt a school' in which local hospitality businesses develop close working relationships with schools by, for example, giving cookery demonstrations and organizing visits. Another measure that can be developed is to recognize that, already, large numbers of young people work in the industry on a casual and part-time basis and more effort needs to be devoted to converting a proportion of these into permanent workers in the industry, by offering real career prospects involving training and personal development. Effort is also needed to develop more family-friendly policies in order to attract and retain more women returners and single parents, and to assist them through the provision of family-friendly arrangement, etc. Apart from these sources of labour, employers could also consider targeting the young unemployed by participating in schemes such as the UK government's Social Mobility Strategy schemes which are aimed at tackling youth unemployment. Several hospitality companies have signed up to support such schemes. Other sources of labour could include older people. Only 6 per cent of the industry's workforce is over 60.

Other sectors of the population include people who have been unemployed for a long period and various minority groups. These are in addition to the many millions of young people in continental Europe who are keen to work in Britain for a period to improve their English.

Further reading and references

ACAS (2010) *Recruitment and induction [online]*. Advisory booklet. London: ACAS. Available at: www.acas.org.uk

Armstrong, M. (2012) *A Handbook of Human Resource Management*, 12th edn, London: Kogan Page.

Astbury, L. (2004) *Changeworknow*, People Management.

Beardwell, J. and Claydon, L. (2010) *Human Resource Management*, 6th edn, Harlow: Prentice Hall.

D'Annunzio-Green, N., Maxwell, G. and Watson, S. (2002) *Human Resource Management – International Perspectives in Hospitality and Tourism*, London: Continuum.

Goss-Turner, S. (2002) *Managing People in the Hospitality Industry*, 4th edn, Kingston-upon-Thames: Croner Publications.

Government Equalities Office (2011) *Equality Act 2010: What do I need to know? A quick start guide to using positive action in recruitment and promotion*, London: GEO. Available at: www.homeoffice.gov.uk/publications/equalities/equality-act-publications/equality-act-guidance/positive-action-recruitment

Incomes Data Services (2011) *Recruitment*, HR Studies, London: IDS.

Institute of Hospitality (2009) *Career and Job Seeking Guide*, London: Institute of Hospitality.

Institute of Hospitality (2011) *The Case for Recruiting and Retaining Older Workers, A Business Imperative for the Hospitality Sector*, London: Institute of Hospitality.

MacLeod, D. and Clarke, N. (2010) *Engaging for Success: Enhancing Performance through Employee Engagement*, London: Department for Business, Innovation and Skills.

People 1st (2011) *State of the Nation Report 2011, Analysis of labour market trends, skills, education and training within the UK hospitality, leisure, travel and tourism industries*, London: People 1st.

Rankin, N. (2009) 'Using corporate websites for recruitment: the 2009 IRS survey', *IRS Employment Review*, 926, 3 August.

Storey, J. (ed.) (2007) *Human Resource Management – A Critical Text*, 3rd edn, London: Thomson Learning.

Taylor, S. (2010) *Resourcing and Talent Management*, 5th edn, London: Chartered Institute of Personnel and Development.

Torrington, D., Hall, L., Taylor, S. and Atkinson, C. (2011) *Human Resource Management*, 8th edn, Harlow: Pearson Education.

Members of the UK's Institute of Hospitality can access publications including Management Guides which summarize key information of relevance to hospitality operations (www.instituteofhospitality.org).

Members of the UK's Chartered Institute of Personnel and Development (CIPD) can access a range of materials including Fact Sheets and articles from over 300 online journal titles relevant to HR. CIPD members and *People Management* subscribers can see articles on the People Management website (www.peoplemanagement.co.uk).

Questions

1 Describe the objectives of recruitment and the various steps you would normally expect to find in a systematic recruitment procedure.

2 Discuss the differences between the primary and secondary labour markets and their significance to staffing hospitality businesses.

3 Discuss which you consider to be the most important steps in recruitment and why.

4 Discuss what changes are likely to be made in the future to improve recruitment.

5 Visit several hospitality recruitment websites and using some principles outlined in this chapter compare and contrast them, concluding which you consider to be the most effective.

6 Evaluate the approach to recruitment used by an employer you know well.

CASE STUDY QUESTION – see the Lux Hotels case study Appendix 5

In this chapter key approaches to recruitment have been described. Now discuss which main approach or approaches would be most suited to Lux Hotels. Consider the main different levels of employee giving reasons for your recommendation for each different level.

Chapter 5

Selection

In spite of recession and high unemployment, the hospitality industry labour market is an extremely competitive one. This is caused partly by the increase in number of hospitality outlets, rising 9 per cent between 2005 and 2010, the number of employees rising by 14 per cent between 2005 and 2010 (People 1st, 2011), curbs on immigration and competition from other service industries, such as supermarkets and call centres. Many other advanced economies, such as France, experience similar challenges.

One major consequence is that organizations have to put much more effort into designing attractive jobs and conditions, using effective recruitment methods and developing applicant-friendly selection techniques. These techniques will have to serve the dual-purpose of ensuring that the proper candidates are selected and also that the employing organization is sold effectively, maybe through positive employer-branding, remembering always that many candidates may also be customers of the enterprise.

Today, with the Internet, it is now common amongst larger organizations to combine the recruitment process (see previous chapter) with the first steps in selection, by including job application procedures on the employer's website. In some cases a selection program, using key words, will conduct an initial sorting of applications.

The selection process

Most business leaders and managers state that their employees are their major asset, so one of their major responsibilities is to recruit, select and motivate staff. In filling a vacancy a manager obtains information, sorts it, compares it, draws conclusions and implements action. This is illustrated in Figure 5.1.

A manager will use the selection procedure normally for three different occasions:

1 To choose the most suitable person from several applicants to fill one vacancy.
2 To choose the right job from several for an applicant or several applicants.
3 Where there is only one applicant for a vacancy, to decide whether to appoint that applicant and, if so, to know his or her strengths and weaknesses so that additional supervision or appropriate training can be given, or so that the job can be modified.

In order to do this the manager should go through the procedure (described in Chapters 3 and 4) of preparing a comprehensive job or role description and personnel specification. Effective advertising will attract candidates and it is then the manager's job to ensure that information is obtained from

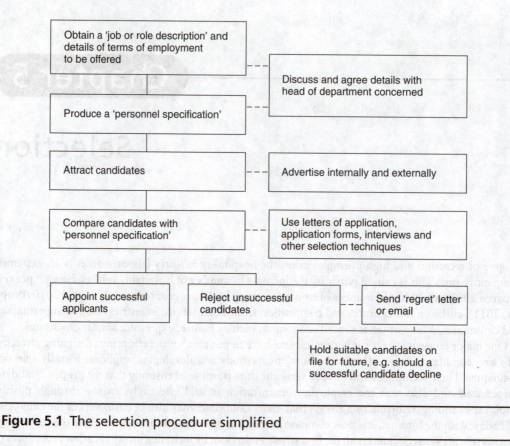

Figure 5.1 The selection procedure simplified

candidates in a way that enables a comparison to be made with the personnel specification. From this procedure the most suitable applicant will emerge.

To assist in selection a variety of tools are available to the manager or owner. The size of the organization will determine the methods used. Some 86 per cent of the industry's businesses employ nine or fewer workers (People 1st, 2011), so many employers will rely on basic methods such as telephone calls, letters of application, emails and interviews. Larger organizations will use application forms, which may be printed or Internet-based, structured interviews, group selection procedures, assessment centres and a range of tests sometimes referred to as psychometric tests.

Selection procedures attempt to predict, as accurately as possible, a person's likely performance in a particular job or, where there are several vacancies, the job in which he or she is most likely to be successful. Most selection methods are of a 'historical' nature, i.e. they base their predictions about future performance on a person's past performance.

Other methods, such as assessment centres and group selection procedures, set out to predict future performance by simulating the type of work the candidates will have to perform. However, most people accept that, economic and human considerations apart, the best method is to employ a person for a period of time and then, if they prove satisfactory, to offer them the job. In many cases this is obviously not a practical method, although trial periods are used both consciously and unconsciously in most industries. Selection procedures, however, need to be designed in order to elicit the most useful and appropriate information in the most economical way.

THE SEVEN-POINT PLAN (NIIP).

The seven-point plan covers:

1 Physical make-up—health, physique, appearance, bearing and speech.
2 Attainments—education, qualifications, experience.
3 General intelligence—fundamental intellectual capacity.
4 Special aptitudes—mechanical, manual dexterity, facility in the use of words or figures.
5 Interests—intellectual, practical: constructional, physically active, social, artistic.
6 Disposition—acceptability, influence over others, steadiness, dependability, self-reliance.
7 Circumstances—domestic circumstances, occupations of family.

THE FIVEFOLD GRADING SYSTEM (MUNRO FRASER).

The fivefold grading system covers:

1 Impact on others—physical make-up, appearance, speech and manner.
2 Acquired qualifications—education, vocational training, work experience.
3 Innate abilities—natural quickness of comprehension and aptitude for learning.
4 Motivation—the kinds of goals set by the individual, his consistency and determination in following them up, his success in achieving them.
5 Adjustment—emotional stability, ability to stand up to stress and ability to get on with people.

Figure 5.2 A summary of two approaches to staff selection

The personnel specification

In attempting to assess or measure a person's suitability for a job it is important to know what characteristics are to be measured. The range and description of these characteristics can be vast and in many cases almost meaningless to the uninitiated. Some interview assessment forms contain a long list of items including charm, punctuality, honesty, integrity, ability, etc. Many of these are supposed to be assessed (or guessed) at an interview.

Most characteristics or patterns of behaviour, however, can be grouped under several broad headings and two long-standing methods of assessment in particular are of interest. The National Institute of Industrial Psychology (NIIP) system uses seven broad headings and J. Munro Fraser's plan uses five (Figure 5.2). The fivefold system is a system for measuring to what degree an individual possesses each of five points or groups of characteristics. Most managers will not wish to use rigidly such systems, instead they may wish to develop their own. It is important, however, to be consistent and to ensure that such specifications are not discriminatory in any way.

In producing a personnel specification, therefore, inclusion of such aspects with indications of desirable characteristics or precise requirements creates a 'pen picture' of the person required. During the subsequent selection procedure, all candidates should be assessed or measured in the same way, making it a relatively simple task to identify the person with the assessment nearest to the personnel specification. He or she should be the most suitable of the candidates.

Forms of application

Generally, it is not advisable to use emails or letters of application as a selection method, any more than the telephone, without the support of interviews or other methods. However, well-designed advertisements can invite a potential applicant to visit the employer's website where they should be invited to give sufficient information from which candidates can be chosen for interview.

Telephone and Internet applications

Some employers have developed such methods for using the telephone and the Internet systematically as the first step in the selection procedures. When an applicant telephones he or she is interviewed via the telephone, the interviewer using a telephone interview questionnaire. The employer is able, as a consequence, to decide on the next step in the process. The Internet is used in a similar way. In some cases a 'selection program' may analyse responses and select or de-select an applicant.

Some employers might still direct applicants to send a covering letter with a CV to the employer. Some French employers, who still use 'graphology', will require a handwritten application.

The main occasion when selection will depend only upon a website application or letter is when applicants live at some distance, usually overseas. In such cases the cost of travel excludes the possibility of interviewing. However, tele-conferencing does make a 'distance' interview possible. Previous employers' references are, of course, extremely important.

Care has to be taken now as some unscrupulous people are intercepting website applications and inviting 'applicants' to pay moneys up-front to secure a (non-existent) job!

Application forms

The application form is the first step in the selection process. It is used primarily to gather together relevant details so that this information is at the fingertips of the selector who can then make fair comparisons with the personnel specification and with other candidates' applications (see Figure 5.3 as an example).

When designing an application form, whether print or electronic, it is important to remember that it may have to serve several purposes such as:

1 deciding whom to invite for an interview
2 being used as an interview assessment form
3 documenting employees and obtaining referees' names and addresses
4 providing a reserve list of potential employees
5 measuring the effectiveness of various recruitment media
6 analysing the labour market
7 obtaining agreement for medical examination, reference enquiries, etc.

The information required on an application form will, therefore, include some or all of the following:

1 position applied for
2 personal data – name, address, telephone number, email address, nationality
3 education – schools, subjects studied, exams passed and further education
4 professional qualifications
5 experience – jobs, duties, responsibilities, employers, earnings, reasons for leaving
6 skills – e.g. computer skills (which applications?), PBX, languages
7 military experience – branch of the service, rank attained, experience
8 personal circumstances – when available, prepared to travel or to move, current holiday plans
9 medical history
10 interests – hobbies, sports, other activities
11 record of offences. *Note*: This is subject to the Rehabilitation of Offenders Act.

Note: Questions relating to sex, marital status, sexual orientation, children, age may be discriminatory and have to be considered very carefully (usually after legal advice). If asked, the purpose should be for discrimination monitoring purposes, i.e. to demonstrate that no discrimination occurs.

The exact nature and extent of the information asked for will depend on the type of job and the employer's administrative requirements, but it should be confined to information necessary for sound

WHITBREAD
HOTEL COMPANY

CONFIDENTIAL APPLICATION FOR EMPLOYMENT

Please complete this form clearly in ink and in your own handwriting

Position applied for: Location:
Full time ☐   Part time ☐   Temporary ☐

Personal details
Forenames _____ Surname _____ Title _____
Address _____ Postcode _____
Age _____ Date and place of birth _____
Home telephone no. _____

Education

Schools	Dates (approx) From	To	Examinations (subjects/results)

Further education and training	Dates (approx) From	To	Examinations (subjects/results)

Britains favourite Hotel Company

MARRIOTT HOTELS • COURTYARD BY MARRIOTT • TRAVEL INN • THE BREWERY

Employment: 1
For school leavers and college leavers...
Please provide details of any paid employment you had while you were at school/college.
Please provide details of any Youth Training Scheme (YTS) courses you completed.

Employment: 2
Have you ever been employed by Whitbread PLC?
If Yes, please give details.

From/To	Whitbread Division	Position Held	Reference Contact	Reason for Leaving

Employment: 3
Please complete if you are currently in employment, or have previous work experience.
Please give details of your work history beginning with your most recent job.

From/To	Whitbread Division	Position Held	Reference Contact	Reason for Leaving

Which job have you enjoyed most and why?

Interests/hobbies (Give details of pastimes, sports etc.)

Offices held in social/sports clubs etc.

Have you ever been convicted of a criminal offence?   Yes ☐   No ☐
Details   (Declaration subject to the Rehabilitation of Offenders Act)

If offered the position will this be your only form of employment?   Yes ☐   No ☐ (if no, give details)

How will you get to work?

Please give the name of one work related referee from your last or current job and one personal referee (not a member of your family) who has known you for at least two years.
Name: _____ Address: _____
Occupation: _____
Telephone no: _____ Telephone no: _____

Please give details of next of kin who can be contacted in an emergency:
Name: _____ Relationship: _____
Address: _____ (business)
Telephone no: _____ (home)

Please state your National Insurance Number: _____

Figure 5.3 A typical extended application form
Source: Reproduced by courtesy of Marriot Hotels.

WHITBREAD
HOTEL COMPANY

	Yes	No			Yes	No	
Interview Comments	☐	☐	Reference taken up		☐	☐	
Reject letter sent	☐	☐	Reference OK		☐	☐	
Offer letter sent	☐	☐	Proof it details seen		☐	☐	
Job offered			Driving licence		Yes ☐	No ☐	N/A ☐
Start date _____			Other (specify) _____				
Pay _____			P45 or P60 provided		Yes ☐	No ☐	
Hours _____							
Job accepted	Yes ☐	No ☐					
Work permit seen	Yes ☐	N/A ☐	Yes ☐	No ☐			
Number _____			Expiry date _____				
Notes _____							

MARRIOTT HOTELS • COURTYARD BY MARRIOTT • TRAVEL INN • THE BREWERY

Managing Diversity

The Whitbread Hotel Company is committed to an equal opportunities policy in employment and will assess applicants for jobs without regard to sex, marital status, race, disability, age or sexuality. To enable the company to monitor this policy please indicate to which ethnic group you belong. These are the approved categories from the Commission of Racial Equalities.

Single ☐	Married ☐	Separated ☐	Divorced ☐	Widowed ☐

Number of children: _____ Male ☐ Female ☐ Ages _____

Nationality _____ Do you need a work permit to work in this country? Yes ☐ No ☐

White ☐	Indian ☐
Irish ☐	Pakistani ☐
Black African ☐	Bangladeshi ☐
Chinese ☐	Black Caribbean ☐
Black Other (Please specify) _____	
Other (Please specify) _____	

Are there any disabilities which may affect your application? Yes ☐ No ☐

Describe disabilities _____

Are you registered disabled? Yes ☐ No ☐ RDP No. _____

Declaration

The contents of this form are confidential. If you are successful it will form the basis of your records held by the Company. You should understand that if at a later date it is discovered false information has been given, this could lead to your dismissal.

I authorise the Company to obtain references to support this application once an offer has been made.

Declaration: I confirm that the information on this form is, to the best of my knowledge, true and complete. Any false statement may be sufficient cause for rejection or, if employed, dismissed.

Signature _____ Date _____

Figure 5.3 A typical extended application form (contd.)

assessments to be made. It is not appropriate, therefore, for one blanket-type form to be used for all job categories. The type of form used for senior executives, which asks about professional qualifications and total employment history, would not be suitable for an unskilled worker such as a cleaner, where the last five years' work history may be quite sufficient.

In the design of an application form, legal aspects also have to be considered, particularly discrimination legislation. See Figure 5.3, an example of a typical application form, which has an example of the company's approach to 'Managing Diversity'.

The interview

The next step after candidates have completed and submitted their applications, is to invite selected candidates in for interviews. The interview is the most commonly used method of selection. It is also considered by many to be one of the least effective, largely because it does not represent what a person is likely to be employed to do and also because few managers are properly trained in interview techniques.

In conducting an interview, however, it is important to keep to a plan (see Figure 5.4 for an example), and the simplest method is to follow chronological order – starting at a point in time, e.g. five years ago

Interview plan	
Part 1	
Introduction	Introduce oneself, describe position held and responsibilities, give brief description of unit, company, job, conditions, prospects, reasons for vacancy, hours of work, rate of pay. Format of interview.
Part 2	
Facts	What made applicant decide to come into the industry? Any connections with the industry, e.g. brought up in hotels?
Life	Where did applicant go to school, college, university? What qualifications did he or she attain? Special interests at school, college, both academic and non-academic. What was the first job after leaving school?
All jobs	Reasons for joining. Reason for leaving. Responsibility when first appointed and upon termination. Earnings when appointed and upon termination. What did applicant think of employer, manager? What was the most important lesson learnt there? What changes could be made? Main problems there. Main achievement there.
General	What is applicant's most important achievement? Hobbies and interests. What is ambition in life – next year, five years, ten years?
Technical expertise	A series of questions to test an applicant's technical knowledge should be asked.
Attitudes	Towards, e.g., recent legal changes. Unions, customers, work, management, college training/ informal training.
Achievements	Greatest personal achievement. Greatest work-related achievement.
Family	Any domestic responsibilities at home? When available to start? What hours/days prepared to work? Mobility.
At present	Working? Type of job, duties, progress made in that job. Prospects, wages, benefits, reason for leaving, reason for coming to this position. Health, personal and of family. Criminal convictions.
Part 3	
Close	Answer applicant's questions. Explain next step in selection procedure. Check on travelling expenses.

Figure 5.4 An example of what can be included in an interview plan

or ten years ago, even leaving school, college or university. This starting point will be dependent upon the nature of the employment and job requirements such as experience and motivation. Questions normally become more searching as one approaches current or more recent experiences, and these later questions must therefore be designed to test fully a person's claimed level of competence, motivation and likely level of achievement.

Main types of interview

The most common method is the individual interview, i.e. one interviewer interviews one candidate at a time. Although this method usually enables the candidate to relax more quickly, there is the risk of bias or preference – particularly if the interviewer's decision is made independently of other colleagues.

The second method is a series of interviews, maybe two or more, involving different managers, each bringing a different perspective.

The third method is a panel interview or selection board – very common in the public sector. This will usually consist at least of the line manager concerned and a personnel specialist. These last two approaches reduce the risk of bias, particularly as the panel increases in size. However, for many candidates a panel interview can be a daunting experience, particularly as some panels are constituted more for political reasons than for expertise.

There is one type of interview sometimes referred to as a 'stress' interview. The intention is to create a stress situation to see how an applicant reacts. It is only valid if a person is likely to encounter stress situations (e.g. difficult customers) regularly and such interviews should only be administered by trained interview specialists. Even so, there are serious doubts about the ethics of conducting such an interview without giving the candidate prior notice – in which case much of the effect of the stress interview will be lost. The methods of selection used by the armed services tend to create such situations but this is because the military are likely to be subjected to severe stress, and applicants are forewarned.

Some dos and don'ts

The following dos and don'ts should be useful.

Do

1 Have a clear job or role description, personnel specification, details of conditions, and an interview plan that contains prepared technical questions.
2 Use a quiet, comfortable room.
3 Suspend all phone calls and other interruptions.
4 Introduce yourself, be natural and put the candidate at ease.
5 Explain clearly the job, conditions of employment and prospects.
6 Ask questions that begin with when, where, why, who, what and how. This avoids receiving 'yes' and 'no' as an answer and encourages the candidate to talk.
7 Avoid asking unnecessary questions already answered on the application form.
8 Listen and let the candidate talk freely, but at the same time guide and control the interview.
9 Encourage the candidate to ask questions.
10 Close the interview firmly and explain the next step in the procedure.
11 Treat all candidates as though they are potential employees and customers.
12 Write up your assessment immediately after each interview (see Figure 5.5 for an example, and also Figure 5.3).

NAME .... AGE .... APPRAISED FOR ....

INTERVIEWED BY .... DATE ....

1 PRESENT CIRCUMSTANCES:

Firm .... business .... size ....

Position held .... location ....

Salary .... benefits .... pension .... holidays ....

Availability .... preferred location ....

Notice given/received .... other appointments pending ....

Salary expectation ....

Responsible to: ....

Responsible for: ....

a) no. and type of staff ....
b) duties ....

Prospects: ....
....

Reasons for leaving: ....
....

Reasons for wanting this appointment: ....
....

2 PERSONALITY AND APPEARANCE:

Appearance: ....

Dress: ....

Self-expression, accent, voice: ....

Manner: ....

Acceptability: ....

3 FAMILY BACKGROUND:

Origins .... married/single .... children ....

Views of candidate and his/her spouse on conditions of employment, including travel:
....

4 EDUCATION:

Type of education .... achievements ....

5 PROFESSIONAL QUALIFICATIONS:

Type .... place ....

Method of achievement; number of attempts:
....
....

Figure 5.5 Selection interview appraisal report (for a senior appointment)
Source: Croner's Personnel Records, with kind permission of Croner Publications.

```
6  EXPERIENCE:
   ..............................................................................................
   ..............................................................................................
   ..............................................................................................
   ..............................................................................................
   ..............................................................................................
   ..............................................................................................


7  APPRAISAL

   Intelligence and ability
   ..............................................................................................
   ..............................................................................................

   Knowledge and experience:
   (breadth and depth) ........................................................................
   ..............................................................................................

   Career development — salary progression:
   ..............................................................................................
   ..............................................................................................

   Motivation, personal relationships, adjustment, stability:
   ..............................................................................................
   ..............................................................................................

   Health, outside interests, etc.:
   ..............................................................................................
   ..............................................................................................
   ..............................................................................................

8  RECOMMENDATION:
   ..............................................................................................
   ..............................................................................................
   ..............................................................................................
   ..............................................................................................
   ..............................................................................................
```

Figure 5.5 Selection interview appraisal report (for a senior appointment) (contd.)

If necessary make notes during an interview, but do explain to the candidate that this is necessary so that nothing of importance will be forgotten.

Don't

1 Keep the candidate waiting.
2 Oversell the job.
3 Conceal unpleasant facts about the job.
4 Interrupt or rush the interview.
5 Preach to the candidate.
6 Read out to the candidate what is on the application form: he or she filled it in and knows it already.
7 Ask questions that indicate the answer.
8 Ask questions that only get 'yes' or 'no' for an answer.
9 Allow the first impression to influence the whole interview.

10 Ask unnecessary personal questions.

11 Raise hopes unnecessarily.

12 Leave candidates with a bad opinion of your organization; they may be potential customers in other contexts.

13 Wait until the end of the day or even till the following day to write up your assessments.

The three Cs – contact, content, control

There are many different approaches to developing and conducting interviews. One simple approach for the non-specialist HR or personnel manager to use as a guide is one referred to as the three Cs – contact, content, control.

'Contact' refers to the ability to make contact with the candidate, to relate to him or her, to develop a rapport. This is achieved by setting out to enable the candidate to relax so that the real person comes through. This is a difficult situation to achieve because for many candidates the interview can be very stressful. However, a number of techniques, usually combined, can help, such as those listed below:

- Interview in an informal setting, but where there are no risks of disturbances or of being overheard.
- Dependent upon the job applied for, avoid having a desk between the interviewee and the interviewer – a desk creates a psychological barrier.
- Maybe offer some refreshment, e.g. a cup of tea or coffee.
- Discuss common ground, e.g. a hotel, a company, a manager, a town, a football team, known to both of you (this information is easily found in a good application form).
- Use body language, e.g. move towards the candidate to emphasize that you are interested in what is being said.
- Use encouraging statements such as 'Tell me more about that'.

'Content' is concerned with the two most important issues of selection – competency and compatibility. Can the person do the job, i.e. will he or she be competent? Second, will he or she fit into the team, i.e. be compatible? Thus the interview must cover all the important ground, including a person's technical competence, ability to get on with others and maybe their ability to take on increased responsibilities. It is particularly difficult to judge a person's future potential but one useful piece of information can be provided by a person's perspective of what is challenging. The question 'What is the biggest work-related responsibility you have ever had?' can be very informative. One person may answer, 'To have catered for 5,000 at an agricultural show', whereas another candidate may answer, 'To have prepared a cold buffet for 200'. Such answers enable the interviewer, having checked the facts, to determine which of the applicants is more likely to fit in with the employer's scale of expectations.

Another important piece of information useful in predicting a candidate's growth potential is their career progression. From this, one can look for growth in responsibility, such as size of establishment, number of subordinates, standards (e.g. star rating), and earnings over a period of time. Figure 5.6 shows three hypothetical career paths.

Manager A (aged 33) has had an erratic career, manager B (aged 33) appears to be on a growth path and manager C (aged 40) has 'plateaued' out. If all three were applying for a position with, say, around 150–200 subordinates, everything else being equal, then manager B appears to be most likely to be suited for the position. Obviously, many other factors have to be considered such as the number of job changes or promotions in each person's career and the reasons for the changes.

Another important aspect of 'content' is to ensure that the interviewer communicates all the necessary information to the candidate, pleasant and unpleasant (e.g. unsocial hours). The interview is, after all, a two-way process.

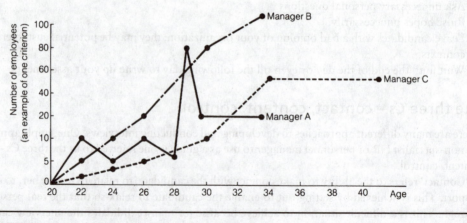

Figure 5.6 Comparative career progression chart

'**Control**' refers to the interviewer's ability to ensure that the interview plan is completed in the time allocated. This will require the skill to guide the candidate through the career and technical questions and to bring the candidate back if he or she begins to wander from the subject – without changing the 'contact' or rapport being built up.

One final rule and a useful one by which an interviewer's skill can be measured is to estimate the amount of time devoted by the interviewer to listening and to talking. Generally, the less the interviewer talks the better he or she is at formulating questions, listening and making the right assessment.

Assessment centres and group selection procedures

The main weakness of the interview is that it relies on one main technique only. This weakness can be compensated for to some extent by training and by involving a number of people in the process. One way of improving the reliability of a selection method, however, is to introduce more techniques so that the combination of techniques exposes more of a candidate's skills, personality traits, etc. to scrutiny. This is increasingly done through assessment centres or group selection procedures, which trace their roots back to methods used to select officers for the armed services.

These are specialized techniques and should always be conducted by people trained in their design, operation and interpretation. The purpose of an assessment centre is to observe candidates' behaviour in a situation or in a variety of situations similar to those they would have to face in the organization. Such a procedure could include:

1 analysis of problems with reports and presentations
2 group discussions and debates
3 business games and in-tray exercises
4 individual interviews
5 tests – aptitude, personality, interest
6 informal drinks and dinner aimed at determining social skills
7 simulating an element of the job for which the candidate is applying, e.g. selling conference facilities.

Assessment centres are normally used to identify personality traits, skills, etc. and to predict behaviour that is difficult to assess in an interview or from personal history. These traits may include leadership ability, persuasiveness, self-confidence, ability to stand up to pressure, and mental flexibility. Such procedures may be used both for recruiting new employees (usually senior) and for assessing the promotion potential of existing employees.

Psychometric tests

The testing of individuals in education, at work and in other aspects of life has been going on in various forms for hundreds of years. Its main purpose in employment is to help predict future performance in particular fields by understanding individual and group behaviour. As with other selection procedures, testing assists in identifying the most suitable person for a job and in identifying the most suitable jobs for individuals. Most recognized tests can normally be administered only under the supervision of a qualified person. The five main groups of tests are as follows.

Intelligence (IQ) tests

These measure the stage of development of intelligence in children and the intelligence of adults relative to the general population. The mean score is 100. Such tests are commonly used to determine whether a person will be able to cope with certain intellectual tasks.

Attainment tests

These measure the degree to which a person has acquired knowledge or skill. Applicants for jobs such as cashier, book-keeper or other clerical positions could be given simple attainment tests which could easily be devised by supervisors along with a personnel or training specialist. But it is important, in designing such tests, to recognize that failure to do the test may not indicate total unsuitability, but only a need for training. Many more skill or attainment tests, including those shown in Figure 5.7, could be used in this industry.

Aptitude tests

This group of tests identifies an individual's innate suitability for particular types of work and can indicate whether a person would be more suited to one type of work rather than another.

Example of category of employee	Nature of test
Chefs and cooks	Demonstrate knowledge of recipes and practical skill in making up certain dishes
Waiters and waitresses	Demonstrate knowledge of recipes, the accompaniments for certain dishes, and the service of some complex dishes
Barmen and barmaids	Demonstrate knowledge of and ability to prepare certain of the more popular drinks Demonstrate the ability to compute the cost of rounds of drinks
Cashiers and receptionists	Demonstrate knowledge of some common reception routines, the ability to operate appropriate office machines and to compute typical cash transactions

Figure 5.7 Attainment tests – examples of uses

Interest tests

These tests indicate broadly which type of work an individual would prefer, such as: indoor, outdoor, computational, gregarious, individual, routine, creative. It is important to stress that an interest in, or preference for, particular work need not indicate an aptitude for that work. However, where an aptitude for a certain type of work is supported by an interest in the same type of work, the chances of that individual being suitable are likely to be higher.

Personality tests

These tests determine an individual's reactions to different situations, from which general conclusions can be drawn about likely future behaviour. They are concerned mainly with measuring non-intellectual characteristics. In particular most personality tests attempt to measure how a person relates to the world around him or her and they do this by measuring the degree to which the person possesses certain personality traits, such as drive, stability, persuasiveness, self-confidence, introversion and extroversion. Some personality tests, such as Raymond Cattell's 16PF (Sixteen Personality Factor Questionnaire), are claimed to be extremely comprehensive, covering most aspects of personality encountered in normal individuals.

In some countries, France for example, graphology is used. Graphology is the study of handwriting in order to determine personality. In the UK and many other countries, however, it is not considered to be a reliable method of testing for employment purposes.

Test batteries

It will be clear that each of the groups of tests mentioned above, with one or two possible exceptions such as the Cattell 16PF, attempts to measure specific but limited aspects of an individual. These are intelligence, attainment, aptitude, interests and personality. Each individual employed, however, needs levels or aspects of each of these characteristics and using one type of test only may not do the person justice. As a result some selection specialists use a battery or variety of tests that measure several of those aspects of a person that may be considered of importance. Additionally, a test battery may be only part of an overall procedure incorporated, for example, in an assessment centre.

There is concern that some tests may have a disparate impact, i.e. their use may result in discriminating against, or in favour of, one or more social groups. Codes of practice concerning the use of tests have been produced by the Institute of Personnel and Development and by the Commission on Racial Equality.

References

It is important to remember that references are only as reliable as the judgement of the person giving them, and because of the fear some employers have of the legal consequences of putting a bad or indifferent reference in writing, many written references are of little value. The best procedure for obtaining references, therefore, is to telephone referees and to discuss a candidate's application on the telephone. This discussion should be written up afterwards so that it can be put into a person's file (remember that under the Data Protection Act the subject may have the right to see this). Alternatively, a standard letter or questionnaire asking previous employers to confirm certain details can be used.

References must only be sought after candidates have been offered an appointment 'subject to references', since they may not have informed their current employer of their plans to move – unless, of course, they have given specific permission for references to be applied for before an offer of appointment is made (which is common in the public sector).

Successful selection is vital to the prosperity of an organization. It is argued by many senior managers that their greater responsibility is 'talent management', i.e. to have the right people in the right place, at the right time, at the right price.

Selection can only be successful if it is carried out methodically, and this requires a clear job description and personnel specification, plus a system that ensures that the most suitable candidates are attracted and identified. This will require well-designed recruitment and selection procedures that elicit appropriate information. Interviews and other selection techniques, as outlined above, will then have to be conducted enabling the assessor to predict, as accurately as possible, a candidate's performance if he or she were to be appointed. This will involve knowing which characteristics are desirable and it will also involve using techniques that identify or measure those same characteristics.

Careful selection should be an investment in team building which should result in having the right people in the right place at the right time. It should also result in a reduction in labour turnover together with the consequent improvement in efficiency and customer satisfaction.

Further reading and references

Armstrong, M. (2012) *A Handbook of Human Resource Management*, 12th edn, London: Kogan Page.

Beardwell, J. and Claydon, L. (2010) *Human Resource Management*, 6th edn, Harlow: Prentice Hall.

D'Annunzio-Green, N., Maxwell, G. and Watson, S. (2002) *Human Resource Management – International Perspectives in Hospitality and Tourism*, London: Continuum.

Goss-Turner, S. (2002) *Managing People in the Hospitality Industry*, 4th edn, Kingston-upon-Thames: Croner Publications.

People 1st (2011) *State of the Nation Report 2011, Analysis of labour market trends, skills, education and training within the UK hospitality, leisure, travel and tourism industries*, London: People 1st.

Pugh, D. S. and Hickson, D. J. (2007) *Writers on Organizations*, 6th edn, London: Penguin.

Sisson, K. (ed.) (1989) *Personnel Management in Britain*, Oxford: Blackwell.

Smethurst, S. (2004) 'The allure of online', *People Management*, 10(15): 38.

Storey, J. (ed.) (2001) *Human Resource Management – A Critical Text*, 2nd edn, London: Thomson Learning.

Storey, J. (ed.) (2007) *Human Resource Management – A Critical Text*, 3nd edn, London: Thomson Learning.

Torrington, D., Hall, L., Taylor, S. and Atkinson, C. (2011) *Human Resource Management*, 8th edn, Harlow: Pearson Education.

Members of the UK's Institute of Hospitality can access publications including Management Guides which summarize key information of relevance to hospitality operations (www.instituteofhospitality.org).

Members of the UK's Chartered Institute of Personnel and Development (CIPD) can access a range of materials including Fact Sheets and articles from over 300 online journal titles relevant to HR. CIPD members and *People Management* subscribers can see articles on the People Management website (www.peoplemanagement.co.uk).

Questions

1 Describe the objectives of selection, the alternative methods and the various steps you would normally expect to find in a systematic selection procedure.

2 Discuss which you consider to be the most effective selection method and explain why.

3 Compare and contrast interviews, psychological tests and group assessment procedures.

4 Discuss what changes are likely to be made in the future to improve selection procedures.

5 Visit several hospitality recruitment websites, using some principles outlined in this chapter compare and contrast them concluding which you consider to be the most effective.

6 Evaluate the approach to selection used by an employer you know well.

CASE STUDY QUESTION – see the Lux Hotels case study Appendix 5

In this chapter key approaches to selection have been described. Now discuss which main approach or approaches would be most suited to Lux Hotels. Consider the main different levels of employee giving reasons for your recommendation for each different level.

Would the countries in which the hotels are located have any influence on the methods used? (See also Chapter 21.)

Chapter 6

Appointment and induction

The process of inducting or introducing new staff to an organization goes under several different titles including induction and orientation. Induction was defined some years ago by the Department for Education and Employment in England as the 'Arrangements made by or on behalf of the management to familiarize new employees with the working organization, welfare and safety matters, general conditions of employment and the work of the departments in which he (*sic*) is to be employed. It is a continuous process starting from the first contact with the employer.'

As this definition shows, induction or orientation is the process by which an employer integrates the new worker or workers into the working organization. The process is concerned with general conditions of employment, welfare, health and safety matters, and the work of the departments in which the new employee is to be employed. It is a continuous process starting from the first contact with the employer. This process of correctly inducting an employee starts even before the formal offer of employment. When the employer has made a decision, the successful applicant should be told immediately that the employer wishes to make an offer. This should be done, if possible, at an interview, by telephone or by email so that agreement can be reached about details such as starting date and any outstanding arrangements such as holidays, to be confirmed later in writing.

Letter of appointment

A formal letter or email should then be sent off incorporating all significant conditions of employment and also the job description. An example of a typical letter of offer is shown in Figure 6.1. Figure 6.2 shows a North American example.

Such a letter of offer should incorporate several requirements:

1 It gives the new employee full details concerning the job and conditions.
2 It demonstrates an efficient, businesslike and, by its tone, sympathetic approach that should make the person feel he or she is joining a caring organization.
3 It obtains written acceptance of the offer and also written permission to write off for references.
4 It states exactly when and where the person is to come, and what to bring on the first day.

Also, note the approach of the American employer (Figure 6.2) who asks for a US$25 dollar commitment fee which will be returned once employment has started.

From a legal point of view such letters may be structured to fulfil the requirements of employment legislation such as the UK's Employment Rights Act 1996. This Act requires that a written statement of

PRIVATE AND CONFIDENTIAL

Dear

Following your recent interview, I am pleased to offer you the position of
Terms of employment are as follows –

Salary	**£ per hour**
Start Date	
Contracted Hours	hours per week, worked over days
Pension Scheme	After six months' service you are entitled to join either the Whitbread Group Pension Fund or the Personal Pension Plan. Please speak to Human Resources for further details.
Incentive Scheme	You will be entitled to participate in the Whitbread Hotel Company reward scheme called PRIDE. Full details will be given when you join.
Staying for Pleasure	You are entitled to two weekends at our UK hotels each year, after completion of one year's service. Full details will be given when you join.
Staff Discount Scheme	After three months' service you are able to participate in the staff discount scheme. Full details will be given when you join.
Uniform	We will order your uniform and name badge on your first day. However, we would be grateful if you would wear smart attire for your arrival at the hotel. You will need to supply black shoes and socks (Males), and either flesh coloured tights 15 denier or less (Female supervisors, managers and administration staff) or navy tights 15 denier or less (all other associates). **Navy** court shoes need to be worn by all female members of staff. A temporary name badge will be given to you on your first day.

Although you are employed as   , you may be required to work in other areas of the hotel
to meet the needs of the business.

You will be required to serve a 90 day probationary period, at the end of which time, provided that your progress in the
job is satisfactory, you will be appointed to the permanent staff.

This offer is subject to:

1 Our receipt of two satisfactory references. I would, therefore, be grateful if you would let me have the names and
   addresses of two referees whom we may approach on your behalf.
2 Medical clearance by our Occupational Health Department. I would, therefore, be grateful if you would complete the
   enclosed questionnaire and return it to me as soon as possible.

The Company reserves the right to vary the Terms and Conditions of your employment relating to your working hours
to give effect to the Working Time Regulations 1998. This may involve varying the numbers of hours you work and
when you work, even though you may or may not be directly affected by the details of the Regulations.

We have enclosed two copies of this letter and would be grateful if you would sign and return one copy as soon
as possible to the Human Resources Department at the Leeds Marriott Hotel. Also, I would be grateful if you
would complete the enclosed New Starter Form and return it to me as soon as possible. Please note that until
I receive this form, I cannot set you up on Payroll.

Please could I ask that on your first day you arrive at 9 am for your induction. Please ask for me at the reception desk.

Finally, I would like to take this opportunity of welcoming you to the Whitbread Hotel Company and the Leeds Marriott
Hotel and I hope that your career with the Company will be a long and happy one.

Yours sincerely,

Michelle Walton
Human Resources Officer

I have read and agree to the above terms and conditions of this offer of employment. I confirm that my start date is

Signed ....   Date ....

Figure 6.1 Example of a letter offering employment
Source: Reproduced by courtesy of Marriott Hotels.

FLAMINGO LODGE
Marina & Outpost Resort
IN EVERGLADES NATIONAL PARK
Flamingo, Florida 33034

Dear Katherine:

Congratulations! You have been selected from among several hundred applicants to fill an important position at Flamingo Lodge for the winter season. You were chosen because we felt you stood out as an individual who shares our commitment to quality guest services. Working together, I know we can be the best concession operation in the National Park system. I look forward to having you as part of our team.

Please review your employment agreement and dates. Contact me directly if you have any questions. Return one signed copy of your employment agreement, the Employment Fact Sheet, and a $25.00 check or money order by the date indicated in order to secure your position. Your $25.00 deposit is used only to establish your commitment to be with us this winter. It will be returned upon your arrival.

If, for any reason, you cannot accept our offer for employment we would appreciate your letting us know so that we can offer the position to another individual.

I look forward to meeting you soon.

Julie Fondriest

Julie Fondriest
General Manager

JF:ml
enc.

(305) 253-2241 • (813) 695-3101 • FAX: (813) 695-3921

TW RECREATIONAL
SERVICES, INC.
CANTEEN CORPORATION

Figure 6.2 An alternative letter offering employment

the main terms of employment are given to all employees within two months of starting employment. These include:

- name of employer and employee
- date employment began including continuous employment
- job title
- place of work
- scale or rate of pay

- pay intervals (e.g. weekly, monthly)
- working hours and patterns of work
- if not permanent, the date of termination
- holiday and public holiday entitlements
- any sick pay schemes, other than Statutory Sick Pay
- any pension scheme rights
- length of notice
- any collective agreements
- disciplinary and grievance procedures.

Note: some of these conditions may be contained in separate documents but should be referred to.

Documentation

The first step when the employee arrives is to arrange that all documentation proceeds smoothly. In the UK this includes obtaining the P45 (record of tax and national insurance paid to date) and, if the employee is to be paid through a bank, the bank details. A personal file or dossier will have to be opened, which will contain all relevant correspondence and documents including the application form and acceptance of offer, and in time a variety of other documents such as training records (needed for 'due diligence' purposes), maximum working hours opt-out agreements.

In larger companies an engagement form should be completed to ensure that no documentation procedures are missed out.

Introduction to workplace, colleagues, rules, etc.

The second part of inducting new employees is concerned with ensuring that they know and understand what is required of them in order to do their jobs satisfactorily. This includes telling them or preferably showing them the layout of the place of work, introducing them to colleagues and explaining to them the function of other relevant departments. It will also be necessary for them to know about house rules such as 'no drinking', 'no smoking' and relevant laws such as licensing hours and what the disciplinary procedures and consequences are.

Training needs

The third aspect is concerned with determining the employee's ability to do the job itself effectively and this will depend upon the person's training and experience. On the one hand no training may be needed, or merely working under close guidance and supervision for a few days may be adequate. On the other hand, detailed training may be required and this is often the case in larger organizations that are prepared to employ untrained people and have standard methods common to many branches.

Induction checklist

Whatever the level of competence, however, it is advisable to use a checklist to ensure that an induction procedure deals adequately with all necessary aspects of induction. In this context it is important to remember that what may not appear important to the employer may be very important to employees. Figure 6.3 shows the checklist used by a hotel.

NEWPORT
Marriott

Name of Employee	Department	Hire Date

Manager, please check each item as it is covered with the employee and return to personnel by_____

1. **INTRODUCTION**
   Department Head/Supervisor/Co-workers

2. **EXPLAIN WORK SCHEDULE**
   Work schedule (posted as soon as business for following week can be forecasted)
   Changes must be approved by manager

3. **EXPLAIN ATTENDANCE REQUIREMENTS**
   Attendance (Mandatory on scheduled days)
   Punctuality (Must be on time)
   Reporting absences (Phone supervisor/manager at least 2 hours in advance of scheduled time and if unable to reach, leave a message with Security)
   Punch own time card
   Punch in in uniform at shift starting time.
   All work must be on the time clock & a mgr. must approve any overtime before it is worked.

4. **EXPLAIN GENERAL RULES**
   Employee entrance/exit (by Security)
   There is no employee parking
   No return after work policy
   Red sticker policy (items subject to inspection by Security or Management)
   No personal phone calls & employee pay phone
   Hotel telephone number and department extension
   Groom standards (dress code & hygiene)

Professional conduct/behavior required
Smoking policy
No gum chewing
Uniforms (includes name tag)
Employee restrooms (uniformed employees use locker rooms)
Employee cafeteria (time card stamped/wear name tag)
NOTE: Proper behavior is required in the Cafeteria; including cleaning up after eating—emptying trash and ashtray. No food/beverage is to be taken out of the Cafeteria.
Use service elevators
No eating in areas outside cafeteria without management approval
Notify supervisor before leaving at the end of your shift
No wandering out of work area without management approval
Phone answering procedures (give name, do not screen calls)
Employee lockers (unauthorized substances or materials)

5. **EXPLAIN TRAINING PROGRAM**
   Who will train
   90-day probation period
   Encourage asking questions

6. **MEAL**
   30 minute meal period (punch in and out for meal)

7. **EXPLAIN RELATION OF WORK TO OTHERS**
   Chain of command
   Guarantee of Fair Treatment
   Relation of job to other jobs
   Relation of department to other

Figure 6.3 Orientation checklist for new employees at Newport Marriott Hotel (USA)
Source: Reproduced by courtesy of Marriott Hotels (USA).

departments and to hotel
Individual responsibility to guests
(Aggressive Hospitality/Customer
Concern)

8. **EXPLAIN IMPORTANCE OF JOB**
Employee's contribution to job
Rewards of enthusiasm, job
satisfaction, advancement
(Promotions based on qualifications)

9. **QUALITY/QUANTITY OF WORK**
Importance of accuracy/speed when
experienced
Importance of courtesy and smile

10. **SAFETY**
Fire/emergency procedures
Nearest fire extinguisher (location)
Report ALL accidents IMMEDIATELY
(no matter how minor) to your
supervisor/manager
Clean as you go policy
Job safety analysis

11. **EXPLAIN PAY POLICIES**
Starting pay rate/performance
reviews/increases (PAF)
Pay periods (Sat.–Fri.) payday/time
Thursday
Accurately report all tips on tip sheet
each week and sign name

12. **EXPLAIN BENEFITS**
NOTE: Full time is 30 hours or more
per week

Vacation policy (eligible if full-time
after 1 yr., part-time after 2 yrs.)
Sick leave (for full-time employees,
after 6 months)
Holidays (full/part-time)
Medical Insurance (full-time; if not
enrolled within 1st 30 days there is a
90 day waiting period before
insurance is effective! May also have
to take a physical exam)
Group Term Life Insurance (additional
life insurance; same enrollment
requirements as Medical Plan)
Dental Plan (full-time/after 6 mos. in
Medical Plan sign up at hire or at
change from PT-FT)
Credit Union (full-part-time
employees)
30% Gift Shop discount

13. **DISCIPLINARY PROCEDURES**
Verbal Warning
Coaching and Counseling
Written Warning
NOTE: Policies on this list with an (*)
are important. When not followed an
automatic written warning may result.
Suspension pending termination

14. **REVIEW POSITION DESCRIPTION**

Initial

I have received the Newport Marriott Hotel Handbook and understand that it is my
responsibility to study and use the handbook as a reference to the benefits and rules of
the company. If I have any questions I will ask my manager or the Human Resources
staff.

I understand that the Human Resource Director is my Equal Employment Opportunity
representative, and that he/she will insure my rights under the Marriott Guarantee of
Fair Treatment.

Regarding medical, dental, group term-life, and disability insurance coverages, I
understand that I must see the human resources representative and complete the
enrollment forms within 21 days of hire, or eligibility, to assure full coverage without
an additional waiting period.

FOR EMPLOYEES WHO HAVE BEEN ISSUED UNIFORMS AND/OR EQUIPMENT: The
uniforms and/or equipment issued to you are to be used only while performing services
for Marriott Corporation. In the event you leave the Corporation, you must return the
uniforms and/or equipment in good condition minus normal wear and tear. Also,
uniforms and/or equipment damaged due to normal wear and tear shall be returned for
replacement and, if lost, you will be personally responsible to accept the expense of the
uniforms and/or equipment. Marriott Corporation will be authorized to deduct (by your
signature below) from any of your earnings, present or future, the value of said
uniforms/equipment.

I have read, or have had read to me, the items listed above. The items on the other side
have been explained to me and I understand and agree to abide by these and all other
rules of this hotel.

Employee's Signature:_____   Date:_____

Explained by (Mgr/Supervisor):_____   Translator:_____

Figure 6.3 Orientation checklist for new employees at Newport Marriott Hotel
(USA) (contd.)

Each employee is an individual

Introducing staff into an organization inevitably involves some of the mechanistic processes just described, but it has to be remembered that each member of staff is an individual. Precisely how one introduces or inducts each new individual to an organization depends upon many factors, such as the newcomer's experience and knowledge and the type and level of job he or she is to undertake. It is vital, however, if induction is to be successful, to try to put oneself in the new employee's place. As Rafael Steinberg wrote in 1977, 'He arrives unknown. His face is not recognized. His interests and idiosyncrasies are ignored by people he meets. He has suddenly become a number, an anonymous replaceable cog. Quite naturally, without thinking about it, he resists this depersonalization and strives to introduce a measure of humanity to his strange new world.'

Probably the simplest and most common method of induction is a short discussion in a supervisor's office followed by informal chats. This may be quite practical where a person's superior is readily available. However, where this is not the case, unless a checklist is used, many points may remain unclear for a considerable time.

Another method is the 'sponsor' or 'mentor' method in which a newcomer, after an initial talk with their own supervisor, is introduced to an established employee who will 'show them the ropes'. This should not be confused with 'sitting next to Nellie', which is concerned primarily with training and not induction. If this sponsor technique is used, however, the sponsor should be carefully selected to ensure that he or she knows what the duties are and has the necessary knowledge to carry them out. These would include many of the items listed on the induction checklist. In addition, however, a well-chosen sponsor will introduce the new employee to the inner face of the organization, i.e. informal systems, unwritten rules, etc. Sponsors in larger companies receive appropriate training and sometimes financial benefits as well.

A copy of the induction checklist should be given to the sponsor, to be returned to the newcomer's supervisor once everything has been completed. The process might take as little as a few minutes, or could be spread over several days.

Finally, some induction programmes make use of formal training techniques in classroom situations. This is normally only used by larger employers that can afford the facilities, and these programmes, apart from the initial documentation, may include talks, discussions, films, DVDs, online material, etc. on the company's history, organization, rules and regulations. In addition, a large part of the programme may be devoted to job training.

The advantage of formal systems such as the sponsor and classroom methods is that because one person is clearly responsible for the induction of newcomers it is more likely to be organized and conducted properly resulting in consistency.

Induction can be considerably simplified by the preparation of clear handouts, manuals, DVDs, etc. elaborating aspects of employment that may need some explanation. Pension schemes and grievance procedures, for example, are ideally explained in written form owing to the amount of detail involved. Many other subjects, too, can be included in manuals such as leave and employee benefits, staff association agreements, suggestion schemes, holiday arrangements, sick benefits, etc.

What a job consists of

Induction is not always something that takes place on the first morning of a new job; it can be a relatively long process, with some people taking many weeks, even months to settle in. This is because every job has two elements. First, there is the work itself. Second, there is the overall organizational environment including work conditions and social contacts, which go to make up the work community in which the work is performed.

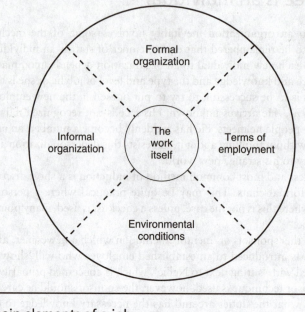

Figure 6.4 The main elements of a job

People will not be able to cope with the 'work' part of their job unless they understand and are familiar with the surrounding elements. These include

- location and physical layout
- management, supervision and formal relationships
- colleagues and informal relationships
- customers
- conditions of employment and contracts
- company, house and legal rules.

These may be further complicated by the need to understand the complexities and demands of franchise, consortium and management contracts.

The induction process is concerned with introducing an employee to all these elements as quickly as possible so that he or she can concentrate on the work, which is the main purpose of the job, rather than having to learn and worry about all the elements surrounding the work (Figure 6.4).

Benefits of induction

The employer benefits from effective induction by

1 reducing staff turnover and improving the retention rate
2 improving staff efficiency, work standards, revenue and profits
3 improving staff morale
4 meeting a number of legal obligations such as health and safety expectations.

The employees benefit by

1 fitting in and feeling part of the team
2 being accepted as part of the team
3 becoming competent and hence confident in the shortest possible time.

Measuring the effectiveness of induction programmes

The purpose of induction procedures is to introduce new employees into the workforce and, with most employers, to reduce the likelihood of the new employee leaving. The effectiveness of induction can be measured by measuring labour turnover in three specific ways. These are

1 the survival curve, which measures an employer's ability to retain its entrants; it shows employee wastage as a curve which can be divided into the induction crisis, differential transit and settled connection
2 the labour turnover and retention rates, which measure leavers as a proportion of the labour force, and the average length of service
3 the length of service distribution, which shows the employer's ability to build a stable team.

These are discussed in more detail in Chapter 14.

In meeting the individual's needs it is important to recognize features of the employer's organization and the industry. The hospitality industry has a number of features that distinguish it from many other sectors and these should be borne in mind when induction programmes are being prepared:

1 The industry employs a large number of people from the secondary labour market, i.e. people such as students who have not trained specifically for employment in the industry and who may not want a career.
2 The industry has its own traditions and jargon, much of it either based on a highly specialist use of normal words or, in the case of kitchen work, based on French.
3 Immediate customer contact, frequently with little, if any, supervision.
4 Complex interdependent operations which can be seriously interrupted by one person not performing his or her role properly.
5 Many units employ a high proportion of foreign workers, often from different cultures, with different values, expectations and behaviour.

Effective induction is important also because of the wide range of responsibilities imposed on employers by various national laws. At the least, effective induction can demonstrate that the employer has exercised 'due diligence', i.e. all reasonable precautions have been taken to prevent a breach of the law, such as health and safety or food safety law.

In the obviously difficult field of managing people, comparing human beings with machines should be avoided, but in the case of induction a very useful parallel can be drawn. Time spent in carefully installing and running in a new piece of machinery usually results in that machinery giving long reliable service.

Further reading and references

Armstrong, M. (2012) *A Handbook of Human Resource Management*, 12th edn, London: Kogan Page.
Beardwell, J. and Claydon, L. (2010) *Human Resource Management*, 6th edn, Harlow: Prentice Hall.
Department for Education and Employment (1991) *Glossary of Training Terms*, 3rd edn, London: DfEE.

Goss-Turner, S. (2002) *Managing People in the Hospitality Industry*, 4th edn, Kingston-upon-Thames: Croner Publications.

Lashley, C. and Best, W. (2002) 'Employee induction in licensed retail organisations', *International Journal of Contemporary Hospitality Management*, 14(1): 6–13.

Pugh, D. S. and Hickson, D. J. (2007) *Writers on Organizations*, 6th edn, London: Penguin.

Steinberg, R. (1977) *Man and the Organization*, London: Time Life International.

Storey, J. (ed.) (2007) *Human Resource Management – A Critical Text*, 3rd edn, London: Thomson Learning.

Torrington, D., Hall, L., Taylor, S. and Atkinson, C. (2011) *Human Resource Management*, 8th edn, Harlow: Pearson Education.

Members of the UK's Institute of Hospitality can access publications including Management Guides which summarize key information of relevance to hospitality operations (www.instituteofhospitality.org).

Members of the UK's Chartered Institute of Personnel and Development (CIPD) can access a range of materials including Fact Sheets and articles from over 300 online journal titles relevant to HR. CIPD members and *People Management* subscribers can see articles on the People Management website (www.peoplemanagement.co.uk).

Questions

1 Describe the objectives of induction and the various steps you would normally expect to find in a systematic induction procedure.

2 Discuss which you consider to be the most important issues in job induction and why.

3 Describe who should be involved in the induction procedure, what they should be responsible for and how they may be motivated.

4 Evaluate the approach to induction used by an employer you know well.

CASE STUDY QUESTION – see the Lux Hotels case study Appendix 5

In this chapter key approaches to appointment and induction have been described. Now discuss which main approach or approaches would be most suited to Lux Hotels. Consider the main different levels of employee. Who would be responsible for introducing each different level of employee to the company and the hotel in which they work? Estimate how long induction should take for the main different levels, giving reasons for your recommendation for each different level. Would your recommendations be the same for all the hotels in the Group?

Developing the human resource

Part 3

Developing the human resource

Chapter 7

Performance management

In exploring the defining characteristics of the contemporary concept of HRM, as discussed in Chapter 2, the contribution of people management practices towards improved performance at work is proposed as a critical aspiration and goal. Alongside the need to attain high commitment from the workforce has been the competition-driven aim to manage a high-performance work system (Appelbaum *et al.*, 2000). Whilst early considerations of performance management concentrated on performance appraisal of the individual, this basic HR function has been developed to be one part of a system of managing performance in an integrated fashion which links the performance objectives of the organization, the work groups and the individual. As such, the current interpretation and understanding of the term 'performance management' may be extended to an all-embracing activity which seeks to align the organization's goals and targets with those of the work team and individual employee (Torrington *et al.*, 2008).

A concern for performance improvement across the workforce in general has been evident at the highest levels of government in recent times, as exemplified by the report by MacLeod and Clarke (2010), commissioned by the then Department for Business, Innovation and Skills. Their comprehensive response emphasizes the importance of performance enhancement and its interrelated links to sound HRM policies and the critical factor of positive engagement of employees. In this way, performance and performance targets are interlinked with the HRM activities which consider training and development, performance appraisal, payment and reward systems, succession planning and organizational culture and change initiatives. The precise nature of these activities will depend on the organization and its external environment but may include fundamental changes to business policy, market positioning, objectives, structures, sourcing materials and work systems. Many different approaches to achieving these ends are used by organizations, with greater or lesser effect. These include particular management ideologies such as empowerment; reward strategies such as performance-related pay (PRP) systems; nationally recognized programmes such as Investors in People; and high-performance work systems approaches such as Total Quality Management (TQM) or Just in Time (JIT) logistics models.

Figure 7.1 summarizes what many would consider to be the essentials of effective performance management. How each of these is dealt with will vary from one employer to another. In some cases staff will be fully involved in decisions. In other cases senior management take all the decisions and communicate them to supervisors and staff. It can readily be seen that there are consistent linkages between the factors highlighted in Figure 7.1 and some of the key components of HRM in the modern workplace.

One aspect considered to be an essential element of HRM in contrast to earlier versions of the so-called personnel or people management is its concentration on individual and organizational performance. Holbeche (2001: 123) is unequivocal in supporting the notion, arguing that HR helps to implement high-performance work practices, 'by creating a culture which is supportive of high performance ... conducive to productivity and quality improvement'. She stresses the importance of issues such

Standards of performance for the manager and/or departments or functions are established (see Chapter 3).

Standards of performance for individuals and groups are established (see Chapter 3).

Policies, objectives, targets and plans are communicated to appropriate people (see Chapter 3).

Individuals and teams are involved in work organization and allocation, with clear targets, roles and responsibilities set.

Appropriate human resources, in numbers and skills, are made available (see Chapters 3, 18 and 19).

Resources and support are made available to support the achievement of the policies, objectives targets and plans (see Chapters 2–9).

Problems and opportunities are identified through proper communication and consultation (see this chapter and Chapters 19 and 20).

Individual and group training and development needs that match the employer's, individual's and group's objectives are established (this chapter and Chapters 8 and 9).

Monitoring and evaluation systems are set up and operated to provide accurate and timely information on performance (see Chapters 3 and 18).

Opportunities for individuals and groups to participate in their own performance reviews are provided (this chapter and Chapters 3 and 15).

Appropriate feedback is provided and development plans are reviewed (this chapter).

Causes of conflict and instances of actual conflict are identified and procedures are developed for their resolution (this chapter).

Legal requirements are met such as the need for health and safety consultation and grievance procedures (see Chapter 16).

Similar elements are to be found in the 'performance criteria' listed in NVQ/SVQ Key Role C, Manage People, Hospitality Training Foundation, 1998.

Figure 7.1 Managing performance – some key elements

as communication between management and staff, the trust factor, and productivity measurement. Beardwell *et al.* (2004) also point to performance management being a crucial aspect of the 'HRM Mantra', which consists of cohesive cultures, flatter structures, a customer focus, productivity through people and strong HR-aware leadership. With a planned and direct correlation to contingent pay and rewards systems, performance management can be seen as a bridge between HRM and the achievement of strategic goals of organizations.

Establishing the contribution of HR to performance

However, a continual challenge to HRM practitioners and academics has been to establish the true value of HRM practices in achieving improved performance. At one level it is a normative argument, a rhetoric easily replayed which declares without hard empirical evidence that HRM in service-dominated sectors, such as the hospitality industry, must be a critical business policy area of strategic and operational significance. But it is a more difficult case to make when challenged to provide quantified proof of the value of HR in improving the overall performance of the business and the individual. In the forefront of tackling this challenge were US researchers such as Huselid (1995), MacDuffie (1995) and Pfeffer (1998). Huselid (1995) applied a range of variables of business performance to evaluate the HR contribution, selecting labour turnover and retention as key indicators of organizational and HRM effectiveness. In the case of labour turnover he aimed to demonstrate that by adopting a range of HRM practices and procedures (referred to as 'bundles' of HR interventions after the work of MacDuffie), a statistically significant and actual decrease in labour turnover would result.

In a study of nearly 1,000 US firms, Huselid claimed substantial returns for the investment by firms in high-performance work systems, expressed in quantitative terms as a 7 per cent decrease in labour turnover, and increased sales per employee of $27,000 and increased profit per employee of $3,800.

Appelbaum *et al.* (2000: 201) conclude that high-performance work systems possess characteristics which generally enhance workers' levels of job satisfaction and organizational commitment, citing a 'bundle' of practices including: participation and involvement in decision making; incentives and reward systems; and skills development programmes. Their research found that staff in such organizations, including retail and hospitality businesses, are 'more willing to work hard on its behalf and more apt to want to continue their attachment to it'. Here we also see the close relationship between HRM, performance management and also employee commitment (see also Paauwe, 2008). The idea of employee commitment to an organization is of particular relevance to hospitality organizations, which can suffer from high labour turnover and fragmentation of work groups whilst attempting to improve service quality and business performance.

In line with the work of Meyer *et al.* (2002), the nature of the employee's commitment and therefore engagement with the organization may vary depending on the circumstances and nature of the business and job characteristics. Most positively, affective commitment is experienced by staff when they genuinely feel satisfied and positive about their work experiences and wish to stay in the employment (see also Kuvaas, 2007; Yang, 2008). Employees may also increasingly experience a continuance commitment, a realization that they also need to stay in the job because of the pay level, benefits and relative security that have been accumulated over time. Finally, employees may feel a level of commitment known as normative commitment, feeling that they ought to stay in a particular job because of a moral commitment connected to personal values and relationships with their colleagues.

In considering the overarching principles of performance management, it is probably most rational and appropriate to understand that the particular approach taken by an organization must be aligned with its position in the external environment, finding the best possible 'fit' between the HRM policies and procedures, and the overall business strategy and policy (Guest *et al.*, 2003). Integrated with the organization's strategy and culture, performance management seeks to introduce a rigorous system of improving performance via a number of linked stages. Torrington *et al.* (2008) propose a model at the employee level that flows from one level to another within the overall business context, summarized here as:

Stage 1: Definition of the role, its job description and objectives.
Stage 2: Planning the performance levels, the individual objectives and development plans.
Stage 3: Monitoring the delivery of targets and reviewing performance.
Stage 4: Annual formal assessment (appraisal) with link to pay and rewards.

The final stage in this approach leads us clearly into that aspect of performance management which has most often been the outward manifestation of the performance-oriented business, the individual's performance appraisal.

Performance appraisal

At the heart of performance management in practice lies the need to evaluate or appraise the performance of the people concerned. This systematic approach to performance management requires that performance targets are set and evaluated at every level of the organization, from main board directors to front-line employees. For example, the individual business targets of the international, multinational hotel company's chief executive must be linked to, and 'fed into' by, the objectives and targets of the regional directors of the company in Europe, North America or the Asia/Pacific, to their hotel managers in these regions, and then each hotel manager's targets must be linked to every assistant hotel manager, head of department and finally to every front-line employee. This cascade of performance objectives ultimately forms part of the daily work standards and practices of all employees. For example, by servicing a hotel bedroom in 37 minutes as outlined by the standards of performance training, a room attendant is contributing to the productivity of the housekeeping department, which in turn is contributing to the profitability of the hotel rooms division and to the financial targets of the entire hotel.

Individual performance appraisal should not always be seen as a once-a-year formality. Each time a supervisor reviews performance over a single shift, counsels, praises or gives corrective guidance to a subordinate, some form of informal appraisal is taking place. However, to give a systematic and reasoned feedback to an employee on their performance over an extended period of time, that supervisor will need to carry out a formal performance appraisal, normally annually but such a procedure might be more frequently undertaken depending on the circumstances or the issues involved. Also, the supervisor needs to get away from the hurly-burly of the workplace and to examine objectively the performance of his or her team. The supervisor needs to do this because the employer should know the strengths and weaknesses of the employees and because employees need to know whether or not they are considered to be working to the agreed standards and quality of performance. The supervisor should examine each employee's performance against previously agreed plans and expectations and at the same time consider the person's potential as well. He or she should then decide what steps should be taken in both the employer's and the individual's best interests.

The hospitality industry is a sector that structurally fits this systematic approach, consisting of many different departments, with line managers responsible for a number of employees. However, its record in carrying out such appraisals is patchy, and some cynics have pointed to the lack of appraisals being a result of the lack of time that employees stay in their jobs. The sector needs to employ people who genuinely feel engaged or attached to their work and workplace; who feel themselves to be part of a worthwhile organization and group of colleagues. Too many hospitality employees suffer from seeing the work as temporary, the work demeaning and the prospects minimal. The employee engagement or attachment issue is one that many in the industry are fully aware of and are trying various means to address the problem. In its *State of the Nation Report 2011*, the hospitality industry's skills training body, People 1st (2011), provides evidence from its survey of the hospitality industry which supports the view that organizations are not just paying lip-service to the HRM, performance management, and employee commitment agenda. The survey clearly points to the importance of involving employees in appraisals, with 61 per cent of the employers surveyed believing that regular and properly applied performance appraisal was a key factor in attaining engagement from employees. There are significant links also to more recently developing approaches to management development, which will be discussed in Chapter 9, and which place strong emphasis on the identification and development of 'talent' within an organization – the term 'talent management' fast entering the discourse of contemporary practitioners and academics connected with the development, engagement and retention of high-performing managers of the future.

The Chartered Institute of Personnel and Development (CIPD) reported that performance appraisals 'are a definite motivating factor . . . with over 60 per cent of workers feeling positive and only 11 per cent feeling demotivated' (*Employment News*, March 1996). The CIPD reviewed the value and reasons for undertaking performance appraisals. These are shown in Figure 7.2.

	%
To assess training and development needs	97
To help improve current performance	97
To review past performance	98
To assess future potential/promotability	71
To assist career planning decisions	75
To set performance objectives	81
To assess increases or new levels in salary	40
Others – e.g. updating personnel records	4

Figure 7.2 Reasons for reviewing performance (% of respondents)
Source: IPM Fact Sheet No. 3 (1988).

From this it is apparent that performance appraisal is aimed at improving performance both of the individual and of the employing organization. This is achieved by:

- identifying both the individual's and work group's weaknesses and strengths so that weaknesses can be corrected and strengths recognized, developed and built upon
- identifying each individual's hopes and aspirations so that, where these do not conflict with the organization's objectives, they can be addressed and potentially realized.

From a properly conducted appraisal programme an employer should obtain the following:

- commitment to a 'performance contract', a mutually agreed set of performance targets and desired outcomes
- an analysis of development needs which enables individual competencies to be extended and group or employment category training needs to be identified
- a succession plan and supervisory/management development programme that earmark individuals for promotion and identify their particular development needs
- a reasonably objective basis for allocating rewards
- improved communications.

The individual also benefits by knowing:

- how he or she stands and what help is to be given to improve performance and competencies
- what his or her career prospects are.

There are three main steps in conducting appraisals correctly:

1. having an up-to-date and objective job description, and performance targets or performance contracts
2. comparing the person's performance with the job description and targets or performance contracts
3. communicating and discussing the supervisor's and the person's views regarding his or her performance, and recording both the supervisor's and the subordinate's views (also see '360-degree' approaches outlined below).

Job descriptions have been discussed in Chapter 3; it now becomes apparent why they should contain as many objective, measurable items as possible: for example, if the word 'satisfactory' is used, superior and subordinate may interpret the word differently. On the other hand, if an objective term such as '60% gross profit' is used, neither person can so easily dispute or challenge the interpretation of this figure so long as each is clear about what is included in the calculation. In comparing a person's performance with their targets, therefore, it is necessary to bring together as much relevant information as possible, such as performance data, key statistics, budgets, forecasts and other records. These quantitative forms of evidence of performance may also be supplemented by more qualitative reflections on the person's performance, such as being a good team member or excelling in customer service. It has been a practice in many organizations to remember the mnemonic 'SMART' when setting targets, which should be:

Specific
Measurable
Achievable
Relevant
Timely.

The approach to performance appraisal

There are many different approaches to performance appraisal but it is possible to divide schemes into those concerned mainly with:

- outputs, i.e. results-oriented
- inputs, i.e. job behaviour or personality traits-oriented
- a combination of the two.

Roberts (in Beardwell and Holden, 1997) reports a number of different approaches, which include the following:

Absolute methods
In such methods individuals are assessed relative to an absolute standard, e.g. achieving a qualification, such as an NVQ Level 3 Catering Assistant, which is a requirement for the role.

Comparative methods
- Ranking whereby individuals are assessed and placed in a hierarchy using certain criteria as a benchmark.
- Paired comparisons whereby each individual is compared with each other individual until everyone has been compared with everyone else, from which a ranking scale may be produced.
- Forced distribution whereby individuals' performances are ranked and then allocated to some predetermined distribution point.

Critical incident techniques
Assessment is based upon positive and negative behaviour in the employee's performance, exemplified by their reaction to specific, 'critical' incidents, e.g. reaction by a hotel receptionist to an over-booking situation or a customer complaint. Often such incidents or examples of how the employee reacted in a specific situation are effective as qualitative and discussive feedback mechanisms.

Results-oriented methods
Assessment is based upon results and not upon behaviour, such as achieving the targeted average restaurant spend or maximum occupancy levels.

Pratt and Bennett (1990) describe three commonly used techniques for rating performance. The first is the 'linear rule', which requires the appraiser to place a tick along a numerical scale or in a box to represent ratings for the characteristics. They point out the distinction that needs to be made between measuring results, such as quantity of work, and traits, such as reliability. The second technique is known as BARS (behaviourally anchored rating scale). In this technique people familiar with a job select appropriate aspects of it and describe examples of behaviour ranging from ineffective to effective along a scale for each aspect. An appraiser can then identify individual performance on the scale. Third, Pratt and Bennett describe MbO (management by objectives), derivatives being also termed as key performance indicators (KPIs) or key result areas (KRAs).

Some schemes require the manager making the assessment to place ticks in graded boxes, or to award letters, grades or points, as judged appropriate. They are relatively easy to operate, but just how reliable or fair they are is very debatable. They are particularly difficult to use for the assessment of unquantifiable factors such as personality traits. The British Psychological Society was reported to have found that such schemes were less popular because of the difficulties associated with them. In written assessment schemes much greater importance is attached to a freely written report. These types of scheme have the

Performance review: Part 1   Confidential

Name of employee _____   Job _____   Branch _____
Completed by   _____   Name _____   Position _____

Overall assessment   Whichever grade you award please
Tick appropriate box   elaborate here on this person's
                                           performance:

Excellent   ☐   Satisfactory ☐
Good   ☐   Poor   ☐

Detailed assessment	Excellent	Good	Satisfactory	Poor	
For all staff					Remarks
Technical competence	☐	☐	☐	☐	
Application	☐	☐	☐	☐	
Initiative	☐	☐	☐	☐	
Relations with:					
Supervisor	☐	☐	☐	☐	
Colleagues	☐	☐	☐	☐	
Customers	☐	☐	☐	☐	
For supervisory staff					
Ability to direct others	☐	☐	☐	☐	
Planning and organizing ability	☐	☐	☐	☐	
Expression:					
Written	☐	☐	☐	☐	
Oral	☐	☐	☐	☐	

Performance review: Part 2   Confidential

Is this person promotable, and if so, what type of job would most suit his/her
abilities and aspirations?

List what training can be given, or other action taken, to assist in improving
performance or preparing for promotion

What salary increase would you recommend? Give reasons
High   ☐   Low   ☐
Standard   ☐   None   ☐

Have you discussed this appraisal with your subordinate? Yes/No

If yes, what were his/her comments?

Figure 7.3 Example of appraisal form

advantage of encouraging the manager making the assessment to think broadly rather than having to use preselected labels.

There are systems that find a compromise between these two extreme types and which ask the manager to fill in grades against a grid of boxes and also to write a broad statement as well. One such scheme is shown in simplified form in Figure 7.3.

Who appraises?

As organizations reduce the number of layers of management, perhaps adopting more flexible, flatter organizational structures and devolved management practices, the question of who should carry out the appraisal can become more complex. It is also the case that as more companies, including hospitality firms according to People 1st, are adopting the principle that every employee should be appraised, the number of appraisals to be undertaken has increased to a point where managers would find it difficult to undertake all the appraisals themselves. Traditionally the superior was responsible for assessing their subordinates' performance, usually moderated by the assessor's own superior and sometimes a personnel officer. This has been modified by the adoption by many organizations of self-assessment methods in which a subordinate has a role in assessing his or her own performance. Nowadays it is increasingly common for an employee's peers and even subordinates (upward appraisal) or clients (like students reporting on a teacher's performance) to be involved. In some cases, outside agencies such as client firms or suppliers are also being involved.

The 360-degree feedback method

According to a Towers Perrin survey, the use of a method known as '360-degree' feedback has been increasing over the past decade. The growing adoption and importance of this system is confirmed later by Redman and Wilkinson (2006). This system sets out to assess employees' performance based on feedback from a wide circle of work contacts including superiors, subordinates, peers, customers and, in some cases, suppliers. The survey found that 94 per cent of firms use it for training and management development, 31 per cent use it to assess potential, 27 per cent use it for succession planning and 13 per cent for promotion. One of the reported advantages is that 'it crosses the cultural divide – the tool will work in any country' (*Management Consultancy*, September 1998). This is important within international organizations, where transnational HR systems are required and performance appraisals feed into succession plans and management development programmes. International hospitality firms need to have knowledge of their managers and their potential across the globe so that they can appoint the most suitable employee in future vacancies, wherever they may be.

There is further evidence in recent commentaries that 360-degree appraisal techniques are being used more widely (see Armstrong, 2002), particularly regarding behavioural aspects such as communication skills and teamwork capabilities. Robbins (2005) reports that following a survey in the USA, 21 per cent of US organizations are utilizing 360-degree formats and that sophistication of technique is growing within consultancies. However, whilst it is clear that many HR managers and line managers value the method, Redman and Wilkinson (2006) also point to the possible downsides of the system. They question just how accurate are the data being generated from very different sources, how subjective they might be and therefore how valid and meaningful. It can also be a time-consuming and potentially rather bureaucratic system, and employers must be clear on the suitability and benefits of such an approach to appraisal.

More generally, a linkage has been established between such sophisticated appraisal systems and the increasing usage of a balanced scorecard approach to management, strategy and performance measurement (see Kuvaas, 2007). In this process, organizations set specific objectives or targets, directly related to overall strategy, for the business, and evaluate performance against these defined aims (Norton and Kaplan, 1992). These objectives normally fall within a matrix of four key imperatives for performance, such as: financial/shareholder value, employee-focused elements, e.g. labour turnover level, customer-perspective issues and, for example, innovations in products or service delivery concepts/systems. Individual performance targets would therefore need to be set and appraised with a direct linkage to these elements of the balanced scorecard. This approach has been found to be an important and successful part of the performance management system of Marriott Hotels, as reported in a study by Millett (2002).

The appraisal interview

A crucial aspect of successful performance appraisal is naturally the conduct and effectiveness of the interview itself. Some managers find that asking their subordinates to examine and complete an appraisal report for themselves makes the situation easier. This is sometimes known as 'self-appraisal' and enables a supervisor to study beforehand a person's own reflective views concerning his or her own performance. This means that the supervisor is better equipped to get the best results from the interview, as he or she knows where the person is likely to be most sensitive. At the same time, if the person has identified known weaknesses, the supervisor can concentrate on the means of improvement and future development without dwelling too much on shortcomings and the past. Some schemes are now going even further and allow the appraisee to actually design the basis of the performance review – selecting what he or she thinks is relevant to a review of their own performance.

The appraisal form

The type of form used to record the appraisal should be incidental but helpful to the interview itself; a well-designed form can assist in preparing for and conducting an interview, but must not be a bureaucratic distraction. In cases where the form itself is of more importance than the interview, the approach to the management of people is likely to be mechanistic. It enables employers to achieve some of their objectives without fully considering the individual's own needs and aspirations.

The contents of the form therefore should be dependent upon the purpose of the appraisal scheme and the nature of the approach. One concerned with 'inputs' would include the following type of information:

1 personal details, e.g. name, length of service, job
2 performance report covering:

- knowledge
- skill
- application
- initiative
- expression – written and spoken
- ability to plan and to organize
- ability to work with others
- ability to direct others
- specific job targets or objectives and the measure of achievements.

3 training needs in present job
4 individual potential
5 training or development needs for future development/promotion
6 general salary recommendation
7 employee's comments.

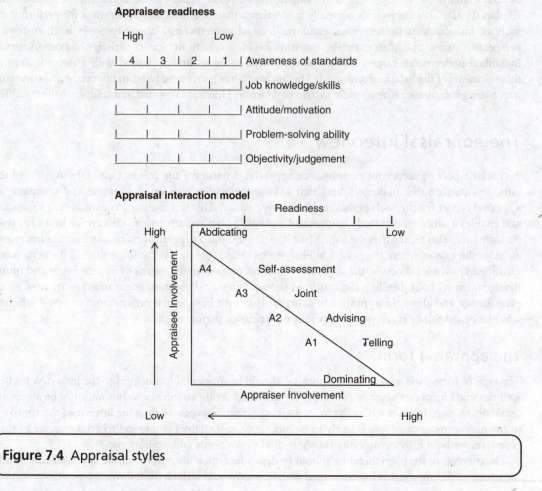

Figure 7.4 Appraisal styles

Appraisal styles

It is suggested that there are six styles on a continuum consisting of dominating, telling, advising, joint, self-assessment and abdicating. These relate to the interaction between the appraiser and the appraised and can be seen on the appraisal interaction model in Figure 7.4.

Effective appraisal interviews – some tips

As with selection interviewing, appraisal interviewing is a skilled technique and those responsible for conducting these interviews need training and practice, along with the ability to examine and criticize their own performance. Here are some useful rules to follow:

1 Plan the interview by obtaining all necessary information and by giving the person to be interviewed prior notice of the interview and its purpose.
2 Remember that interviews are a means of two-way communication and that the best interviewers do little talking themselves.
3 Suspend phone calls, turn off the desktop, avoid interruptions and allow plenty of time for the interview.

4 Put the interviewee at ease and try to make the occasion an informal one. For example, avoid having the desk between yourself and the interviewee.
5 Make the interviewee feel that the main purpose of the interview is to benefit him or her.
6 Start by praising strong points. Remember that the appraisee is in a vulnerable position and that unremitting criticism may be disheartening and possibly be rejected as unfair or even untrue, unless the balance is maintained by acknowledging good points as well (sometimes this balance of the good and the not-so-good feedback is known as the 'praise sandwich').
7 Ask the interviewee their reasons for any shortcomings against targets or performance below standard, and ask for suggestions for improvement.
8 Finish the interview firmly on a positive, developmental note by reiterating what performance has been agreed and what assistance the employee can expect in the form of training or other help.

Do NOT!

1 Rush the interview or omit good preparation. It is one of the most important occasions in a person's working year.
2 Prejudge the outcome of the interview; and therefore don't finalize the form until afterwards.
3 Read out the printed form as if it is the first time you have seen it. The discussion should come over in your own words in a natural manner.
4 Preach or be pompous. This is an occasion to discuss how a person's performance targets may be consolidated/achieved and their individual potential realized to the maximum.

In smaller organizations, which predominate within the hospitality industry, with no more than a few employees, a formal approach may be unnecessary and could even disrupt some healthily close superior–subordinate relationships. However, all employees should receive feedback on their performance and will value a meaningful discussion that makes it clear they are not taken for granted, and that the manager expects high levels of performance, however informal the working relationship.

Appraisal can be one of the most personal and potentially unsettling situations that occurs in a working person's life. It is, after all, an examination and judgement of a key aspect of their self-esteem and self-worth as an employee and consequently it can be very damaging to the ego and more general morale if handled badly. It must therefore be honest and truthful but also developmental and constructive. It should not be an occasion for apportioning blame or responsibility for past shortcomings or failures. If these are discussed, they should be used as examples to illustrate points from which both sides can learn in order to take steps to improve for the future. Appraisal should be creative and aim to enhance performance and should result in new objectives and in agreement on the means by which these objectives can be achieved. Whether or not the appraisal outcome should be linked to pay and rewards is often debated. Some would prefer a system that has development plans and personal improvement plans as the only outcomes. Others see the issue in more contemporary strategic HR terms, and believe that if staff are reaching their targets which are in turn contributing to the achievement of the company's targets, then there should be some link to compensation and benefits systems within the organization. Performance-related pay and performance-linked bonus schemes are examples of this approach, items that will be discussed later in this book.

Further reading and references

Appelbaum, E., Bailey, T., Berg, P. and Kalleberg, A. L. (2000) *Manufacturing Advantage*, Ithaca, NJ: Cornell University Press.
Armstrong, M. (2002) *Employee Reward*, London: CIPD Publications.

Beardwell, I. and Holden, L. (1997) *Human Resource Management*, 2nd edn, London: Pitman.

Beardwell, I., Holden, L. and Claydon, T. (2004) *Human Resources Management – A Contemporary Approach*, 4th edn, Harlow: Prentice Hall.

Guest, D. E., Michie, J., Conway, N. and Sheehan, M. (2003), 'Human resource management and corporate performance in the UK', *British Journal of Industrial Relations*, 41(2): 291–314.

Holbeche, L. (2001) *Aligning Human Resources and Business Strategy*, Oxford: Butterworth-Heinemann.

Huselid, M. A. (1995) 'The impact of human resource management practices on turnover, productivity, and corporate financial performance', *Academy of Management Journal*, 38(3): 635–672.

Institute of Personnel Management (1996) Employment News, London: IPM.

Institute of Personnel Management (1998) Fact Sheet no. 3, London: IPM.

Kuvaas, B. (2007) 'An exploration of how the employee–organization relationship affects the linkage between perception of developmental human resource practices and employee outcomes', *Journal of Management Studies*, 45(1): 1–25.

MacDuffie, J. P. (1995) 'Human resource bundles and manufacturing performance: organizational logic and flexible production systems in the world auto industry', *Industrial and Labor Relations Review*, 48(2): 197–221.

MacLeod, D. and Clarke, N. (2010) *Engaging for Success: Enhancing Performance through Employee Engagement*, London: Department for Business, Innovation and Skills.

Meyer, J. P., Stanley, D., Herscovitch, L. and Topolnytsky, L. (2002) 'Affective, continuance and normative commitment to the organization: a meta-analysis of antecedents, correlates and consequences', *Journal of Vocational Behaviour*, 61: 20–52.

Millett, B. (2002) 'Performance management in international hospitality and tourism', in D'Annunzio-Green, N., Maxwell, G. and Watson, S. (eds) *Human Resource Management – International Perspectives in Hospitality and Tourism*, London: Continuum.

Norton, D. and Kaplan, R. (1992) 'The balanced scorecard: Measures that drive performance', *Harvard Business Review*, January/February: 71–79.

Paauwe, J. (2008) 'HRM and performance: achievements, methodological issues and prospects', *Journal of Management Studies*, 46(1): 129–142.

People 1st (2011) *State of the Nation Report 2011, Analysis of labour market trends, skills, education and training within the UK hospitality, leisure, travel and tourism industries*, London: People 1st.

Pfeffer, J. (1998) *The Human Equation: Building Profits by Putting People First*, Boston, MA: Harvard Business School Press.

Pratt, K. J. and Bennett, S. C. (1990) *Elements of Personnel Management*, 4th edn, Wokingham: GEE.

Redman, T. and Wilkinson, A. (2006) *Contemporary Human Resource Management*, 2nd edn, Harlow: Pearson Education.

Robbins, S. (2005) *Organizational Behaviour*, 11th edn, Upper Saddle River, NJ: Pearson Education.

Torrington, D., Hall, L. and Taylor, S. (2008) *Human Resource Management*, 7th edn, Harlow: Financial Times Prentice-Hall.

Yang, J-T. (2008) 'Effect of newcomer socialisation on organisational commitment, job satisfaction, and turnover intention in the hotel industry', *The Service Industries Journal*, 28(4): 429–443.

Members of the UK's Institute of Hospitality (IoH) can access publications including Management Guides which summarize key information of relevance to hospitality operations (www.instituteofhospitality.org).

Members of the UK's Chartered Institute of Personnel and Development (CIPD) can access a range of materials including Fact Sheets and articles from over 300 online journal titles relevant to HRM. CIPD members and *People Management* subscribers can see articles on the People Management website (www.peoplemanagement.co.uk).

Questions

1 Describe the objectives of a performance appraisal scheme and the various steps or phases that you would normally expect to find.

2 Discuss which you consider to be the most important steps in a performance appraisal and why.

3 Discuss what changes are likely to be made in the future to improve performance appraisal procedures.

4 Discuss the relationship between performance appraisal and the characteristics of contemporary HRM practices.

5 Evaluate the approach to performance appraisal used by an employer you know well.

CASE STUDY QUESTION – see the Lux Hotels case study Appendix 5

What HRM performance measures would you recommend that Lux Hotels adopts in developing its performance management systems?

Chapter 8

Training

One of the features of working life today is that whatever education and training is received early in life, it will almost certainly become only partially relevant, perhaps even obsolete during one's working lifetime. Change in economic and social conditions is a constant within contemporary society as technological advances and globalization affect whole industries as well as the skills component of almost every job. The need to learn and to acquire new knowledge, new skills, new approaches and attitudes has become an everyday aspect of each individual's career. In some cases this may merely be an updating and reskilling process, but in others it will require a complete change from one occupation to another. The rapid alterations to everyday working lives brought about by digital technology, the Internet, email and social media are unlikely to grind to a halt.

Some jobs and traditional industries in the UK and throughout Western Europe have already disappeared or been relocated to other countries in a fast-changing and highly unpredictable age, whilst other, new roles and forms of organizations have and will emerge. Fortunately for the hospitality industry, there is no likelihood of the main customer services it provides becoming totally redundant in the immediate future. Some types of jobs may disappear through technological advancement or through outsourcing, but the industry itself is predicted to continue to flourish, not only at a national level but most certainly at an international level as emerging service industry markets in nations like Brazil, Russia, India and China (the so-called 'BRIC' nations) become globally influential. Their economic growth and strong manufacturing base will inevitably lead to demand for services, including tourism and hospitality.

The responsibility for ensuring that the working population is equipped to cope with these changes lies with a number of interested parties. The state carries part of the responsibility, particularly in providing the infrastructure of appropriate, vocational education and training frameworks (e.g. apprenticeship schemes) for school leavers and for those who need retraining due to the decline of specific industries. Colleges, universities and private training providers also contribute significantly to the overall training effort. Many such organizations are working together to provide coherent and meaningful training pathways for people to follow and qualifications to strive for, from the vocational qualifications at levels 1, 2 and 3 (in the UK national qualification framework), up to foundation degrees (levels 4 and 5), undergraduate degrees (levels 4, 5 and 6) and postgraduate degrees (level 7) in economically relevant subjects such as hospitality management.

The current high levels of unemployment in young people in the UK is a real challenge to both government and industry in terms of developing an effective workforce for the future and providing young people with the skills and the hope of a fulfilling career in work. A recent report for the Work Foundation by Sissons and Jones (2012) relates how the number of people under the age of 25 who are not in employment, education or training (termed 'NEETS'), has grown steadily over the past decade towards 300,000. Furthermore, and of significance to the hospitality industry, the report highlights the need for more training and development of people towards service sector employment, more awareness of the soft skills of interpersonal behaviour and customer service, rather than the traditional hard skills that might prepare for the manufacturing sectors. The following conclusion from within the Work Foundation report illustrates the challenge for the service sector as a whole and hospitality in particular:

> While apprenticeships are now more visible in sectors like retail and hospitality, and the numbers have grown, there is further work required to make these true vocational routes which offer rounded training, employment and career progression for young people.
>
> (Sissons and Jones, 2012: 42)

The hospitality industry itself, with many employers throughout the different sectors, has an enormous responsibility and challenge in ensuring that its vast workforce, much of which is young people, is trained to the correct level in order to deliver high quality products and high quality service standards. One recent report (People 1st, 2011) puts the challenge in sharp focus. Whilst employers in hospitality, tourism and leisure sectors are attributed as spending more than any other economic sector on training (over £4 billion per annum), one in ten of the hospitality workforce is lacking the basic skills necessary to carry out their job.

At one in ten, this figure may sound relatively small, but it equates to nearly 200,000 employees who are inadequately trained. The People 1st report points to the fact that skills gaps are perennial problems for the industry, especially in key functions such as customer service jobs and chef skills, with one in four establishments declaring skills gaps in these areas. More generic skill issues are also suggested as being customer handling, team working, problem solving, written communication and literacy skills. The industry, its professional bodies, the colleges and universities as well as employer organizations are seeking to address this great challenge, as the global hospitality industry becomes more competitive and such skills and competencies are key elements of contemporary society and events, as exemplified by the substantial training and development plans put in place for the London Olympics in 2012.

As discussed in other sections of this book, one of the factors that creates the need for so much costly training is the high labour turnover rates within the industry, the People 1st report (2011) estimating that labour turnover counts for over £33 million annually in terms of wasted recruitment and training efforts. Training is an investment, an investment in the future of the individual but also in organizations' prosperity, but an employee needs to be in the job long enough for that investment to see some return through consolidation of the learning and then long-term efficiency, productivity and effectiveness. Here we see the link between training and the successful engagement and commitment of employees, which in turn can enhance the probability of reducing labour turnover and having a motivated and efficient workforce. From induction onwards, employers have the chance to fully engage their staff in their work, creating an attachment between worker and company, and laying the foundation for a long and rewarding career.

However, the disparate and fragmented nature of the hospitality industry has an impact on the incidence of a lack of proper training and skills development. Too many of the industry's traditional employers, particularly the smaller, privately owned businesses, do not implement systematically planned training for a number of reasons:

1 Many proprietors and managers have had no formal training themselves and, therefore, are unaware of the standards that can be achieved and of the benefits of training.
2 Many employers are concerned constantly with immediate operational problems and do not plan ahead.

3   Many are undercapitalized and cannot afford the investment.
4   Many believe that it is the responsibility of others, such as government, schools and further education colleges, to provide them with 'work-ready', trained staff.

At the same time, however, there is a constant upgrading in the industry and a move towards both 'high tech' (modern technology and costly capital investment) and 'high touch' (high customer contact and high wage costs), each demanding more training, with the leading employers now putting more and more resources into training. Larger hospitality chains have introduced some highly professional strategies on training which guide managers and employees from the first day of their employment at induction, through to on-job training and beyond to career development, ensuring that the company culture is a coherent thread through that training. The following case study note (researched by the author as part of a research project) provides an example of this contemporary approach, in this instance by an international licensed retailer and restaurants operator (given here the pseudonym 'GastroPubs & Bars plc'):

Mini case study: 'GastroPubs & Bars plc'

'GastroPubs & Bars plc' has developed an induction and training programme known as Your First Steps, an HR initiative that has to be implemented in every outlet of the company, whatever the brand, in whatever country it operates. This initiative developed out of a corporate policy commitment to ensuring that every employee receives an appropriate induction into the company, and receives effective job training. Your First Steps is operated and monitored through the centralized, head office-based HRM department of the company. The basic principles of corporate marketing and branding have been applied to this project, the programme possessing its own logo, presentation and print style. The content and messages within the programme are strongly predicated on specific principles, particularly exceptional customer service as demanded by the customers of up-market pubs and eateries. It is implemented across all outlets and therefore should be experienced by all staff. Indeed, within the respondent interviewees for the research project, there was a high level of awareness of the Your First Steps programme and acknowledgement that they had experienced an effective induction programme when they had first commenced their employment.

   A review of company documentation, coupled with discussions with pub and restaurant managers, revealed a highly structured approach to induction and initial job training, beginning with the issuing of a Team Associates Handbook for each employee. Managers confirmed in interviews that they must keep a team member record system, tracking the induction plan, the training plan and the progress of each employee against an Induction Checklist. The employee's training handbook is attractively presented and printed on high quality paper. The first page is dominated by the sub-heading of Company Mission and Purpose, and the following sections are headed Terminology, Our Customers, Identifying Customers and Customer Service. The prominence of these topics indicates the agenda of the corporate and HR strategy in terms of the concentration on the customer and customer service and the corporate culture values of this hospitality firm.

The first page stresses the company's strategic aim: 'To be Europe's leading pub, bar and restaurant chain . . . we will be the No. 1 choice for gastronomy, beverages and hospitality.' Such rational and strategic objectives for the company move quickly into the 'softer', employee development aspirations: 'We are committed to the continuing training and development of the employees who make our business a success – in other words, YOU!' The rest of the handbook addresses a set of topics related to training and development and career possibilities, and then to the statutory aspects of health and safety legislation, ending with the formal terms and conditions of employment.

It must be noted that the content and tone of the Team Associates Handbook reflects earlier research findings concerning induction and training in the licensed retail sector by Pratten (2003) and by Lashley and Best (2002: 9), the latter authors concluding that induction programmes are 'focused on the companies' agenda, rather than meeting the social and psychological needs of the new employees'. The 'GastroPubs and Bars plc' handbook is undoubtedly a helpful guide for those first few days, but its detailed prescriptive approach to customer service gives little mention of the challenge and stress associated with customer service in a pressurized hospitality work environment. This challenge appears to be potentially overcome by recourse to a number of basic, straightforward instructions, and controlled by the Mystery Customer inspections. The following quotations, featuring important use of language and terminology, are taken from the Customer Service section:

'Be open, welcoming, delighted to see another customer'

'Give eye contact to each customer and remember you smile with your eyes'

'Don't wait until they speak, give recognition and initiate the conversation whenever possible'

'Go that all-important Extra Mile for every customer'

'We have a Mystery Customer Programme that measures our service standards and gives us lots of feedback'

'We need to constantly measure ourselves against the standards of performance guidelines'

'This is done by our Mystery Customer Programme'

'The Mystery Customer Report for your unit can be found on associates notice-board – go and check out the last report'.

Within such an influential document for new entrants into the organization and into the work groups within every outlet, these extracts reflect research output from the hospitality and retail sectors which juxtaposes the managerial emphasis on controlling employee behaviour and emotions (see Ogbonna and Harris, 2002), with the need to ensure compliance to a set of behavioural instructions through training and learning the emotional rules (Seymour and Sandiford, 2005).

The focus for such behaviour is the customer, imbued with a supreme authority and power by the organization ('the customer is King'). The customer's expectations need to be exceeded rather than satisfied. The customer needs to be 'delighted', not only in the language of the 'enchanting myth of customer sovereignty' (Korczynski, 2002), but also in the language of the corporate handbook itself. There is much instruction on providing the service standards and emotional behaviour required by the average customer, but there is also a noticeable lack of help and guidance on how to deal with the stress and pressure of dealing with difficult customers and difficult situations. Training programmes need to be aware that hospitality staff work under the dual-pressure of needing to delight the customer whatever the circumstances, as well as be efficient and effective for the organization.

The main components of training

At its most fundamental level, training is concerned with bridging the gap between individuals' and groups' existing competence or actual performance and the performance required to achieve the organization's objectives. These objectives may include such activities as company expansion (including overseas merger/acquisition), obtaining repeat business, increasing sales turnover, increasing productivity and therefore profitability, and improving standards. On other occasions training may be needed merely to maintain the employer's position in the market, or to ensure that new legislation is complied with; however, there are some useful signs, or symptoms, that may indicate to a manager/HR manager that there is a need for training and these include:

- failure to attain targets such as gross profit on food or liquor, sales turnover, average spends, revenue per available room (called 'revpar') and net profit levels
- customer complaints and general comments/feedback/suggestions
- inconsistent service delivery: standards and timeliness issues
- increased labour turnover rates, exit interview details, staff morale issues raised at staff meetings/consultative committees
- departmental problems/friction amongst staff/lack of collaboration between departments
- high accident, breakage and wastage levels
- inappropriate and costly misuse of equipment and IT systems, e.g. reservations system, and higher maintenance costs
- staff sickness/absenteeism/emotional stress evidence
- to ensure compliance with prevailing legislation and new legal obligations, e.g. health, hygiene, safety, COSHH (Control of Substances Hazardous to Health) training, service of alcohol/licensing acts.

There are three main components that an individual requires in order to do a job effectively: knowledge, skills and attitudes. Each of these can be developed or improved upon (from the organization's point of view) by effective training. Each component, however, needs a different training approach. Knowledge, for example, can be imparted by briefings, lectures and videos, but these techniques would prove almost valueless in imparting the second component, that of skills, such as knife drill or operating the reservations system. In this case, practice is necessary. The third component, individuals' inherent attitudes, towards customers and colleagues for example, is often the most difficult to shape or to change, even with soundly based training, and it requires understanding of human behaviour among those responsible for training. Training techniques in this field may include psychometric tests, online programmes, group discussions, case studies and role-playing. The high quality handbooks and guides on attitudes towards customers referred to in the case study example above is a common contemporary approach which emphasizes to all employees the service culture approach. Attitudes can be extremely difficult to modify, however, and it is better to begin by the planned, systematic and professional selection of people with inherently appropriate attitudes rather than attempt to train and change individuals who have in-built attitudes that conflict with the needs of the employer.

In order to design effective training programmes the following principles should be known and understood:

1 Training can only be successful if it is recognized that learning is a voluntary process, that individuals must be keen to learn and consequently they must be properly motivated; for example, if trainee food service assistants are losing earnings in the form of tips in order to attend a course, they may well begrudge the time and therefore may be unwilling to participate actively.
2 People learn at different rates and, particularly in the case of adults, often start from different levels of knowledge and skill and with different motives and attitudes.

3 Learning is hindered by feelings of nervousness, fear, inferiority and by lack of confidence.

4 Instruction must be given in short frequent sessions rather than isolated, long events; for example, if a trainee is being instructed in the use of kitchen equipment, ten lessons lasting 15 minutes are far better than one lesson lasting several hours, allowing consolidation of learning and the development of competencies.

5 Trainees must play active roles – they must participate; for example, lecturing puts the trainees into a passive role, whereas discussions or practical work/role-plays/online training exercises and 'games' give them active roles.

6 Training must make full use of appropriate and varied techniques and of all the senses, not just one, such as the sense of hearing.

7 Trainees need clear targets, and progress must be checked frequently.

8 Confidence has to be built up by praise and encouragement, not broken down by negativity and reprimand: learning ought to be motivating and emotionally rewarding.

9 Skills and knowledge are acquired in stages marked by periods of progress, standstill and even a degeneration of the skill or knowledge so far acquired: instructors must know about this phenomenon (the learning curve), as it can be a cause of disappointment and frustration for many trainees, and their trainers!

These principles of learning illustrate and emphasize that it is both difficult and inefficient to treat individuals as homogeneous groups. So far as possible, training needs to be tailored to suit individual needs. The techniques to be used depend on a variety of factors, including whether it is knowledge, skills or attitudes that are to be imparted and whether individuals or small groups/specific departmental teams are to be trained. The two main basic approaches are 'on-the-job' and 'off-the-job' training.

'On-the-job' training

In the hospitality industry much of the staff's work is performed in direct contact with customers. For this reason much of the training of new staff has to be performed 'on the job' so that experience of repeatedly dealing with customers and other employees can be obtained. 'On-the-job' training, therefore, plays a vital part in the industry's approach to training. In one large survey conducted in the USA, 'experiential learning' was ranked as the most effective form of training. If handled correctly, it can indeed be very effective for the teaching of manual and social skills, but it requires that training objectives are clearly defined and that those responsible for instruction are themselves proficient in applying appropriate training techniques.

Unfortunately, newcomers are too often attached to experienced workers who are not in any way equipped to train others, and may not even wish to be involved in developing another employee. This is often referred to as 'sitting next to Nellie'. Apart from having neither a suitable personality nor the necessary training skills, the trainer may not even have been told exactly what to instruct. Instead, if experienced workers are to be entrusted with the training of newcomers, they should be chosen because of their ability to deal sympathetically with trainees, not just because of their knowledge of the job itself. They should then be given appropriate instructor training before being asked to train newcomers. The progress of trainees must be checked regularly, preferably by a systematic procedure that is properly documented and carried out by the person responsible for training, who may be the line manager, departmental head or training and development manager within a larger HR department. Responsibility for managing the training should not be abdicated to the instructor. An example of an 'on-the-job' training programme for a cocktail bartender is shown in Figure 8.1. Please note that the training scheme in Figure 8.1 is organized into carefully planned and progressive stages. It requires each phase to be completely covered and successfully achieved before the next stage is started. In addition, this particular

First Stage

1 Bar preparation and cleanliness
- a) Washing down of bar counter, bottle shelves
- b) Polishing of mirrors, glass shelves
- c) 'Bottling up'
- d) Use of counter towels, drip mats and trays
- e) Preparation of accompaniments including lemon, olives, cherries
- f) Use of beer dispense equipment

2 'Cash'
- a) Price list
- b) Use of cash register
- c) Cheques and credit cards
- d) Charging to customer accounts
- e) Computation of costs of rounds and 'change giving'

3 Main points of law
- a) Licensing hours and drinking-up time
- b) Hotel residents and guests
- c) Adulteration
- d) Weights and measures

4 Service of simple orders
- a) Beers, wines by the glass
- b) Spirits and vermouth with mixers
- c) Use of accompaniments such as ice, lemon, cherries
- d) Customer service skills

Second Stage

1 Bar preparation and cleanliness
- a) Requisitioning of stock
- b) Cleaning of beer dispense equipment
- c) Preparing weekly liquor and provisions order

2 'Cash'
- a) Checking float
- b) Checking till roll/electronic read-out
- c) 'Off sales'

3 Further law
- a) Betting and gaming
- b) Young persons
- c) Credit sales of intoxicating liquor

4 Service of mixed drinks
- a) Shandies
- b) Gin and Italian, gin and French

Third Stage

1 Bar preparation and cleanliness
- a) Rectification of faults such as 'fobbing beer', jammed bottle disposal unit
- b) Preparation for stocktaking

2 'Cash'
- Cashing up

3 Service of all drinks contained in the house list
- a) Knowledge of recipes
- b) Use of shaker and mixing glass

Figure 8.1 Example of an 'on-the-job' training programme for a cocktail bartender – basically a list of duties and tasks

programme is only a checklist and therefore presupposes that the instructor already has the detailed knowledge. Because of this, in many cases it will be necessary to expand this type of list by specifying in a document such as a training manual exactly what has to be instructed under each new heading.

'Off-the-job' training

'Off-the-job' training takes place separated from the direct working environment. A variety of methods and techniques may be used but the particular choice will depend on what is to be imparted. The main methods are listed below:

1 Briefings are best used for imparting knowledge such as company history and policies, legal matters, regulations, recipes, and outlines of methods and procedures. In giving a briefing, progress must be checked frequently by the use of questions and answers, and briefings may be supported by short company videos and by printed material for the trainees to take away as a future reference.
2 Discussions are best used to elaborate on and to consolidate what has been imparted by other techniques and to share best practice.
3 'Lectures' often mean little more than talking at trainees and are therefore to be avoided, as there is usually little trainee participation.
4 Case studies, projects and business simulation games are best used to illustrate and to consolidate principles of management such as planning, analytical techniques, etc.
5 Role-playing is best used to develop social skills such as receiving guests, handling customer complaints, selling and interviewing, and can also be useful when the social skills have to be simultaneously applied with technical skills, such as hotel check-in or check-out situations.
6 Videos/DVDs, podcasts, PowerPoint presentations, flip charts and other visual aids should not normally be used as instructional techniques by themselves, but should support briefings, discussions, case studies and role-playing.
7 Programmed texts, interactive videos/DVDs, CDs and Internet-based online programmes satisfy many of the principles of learning. In addition, they can be used by individuals at any convenient time – not always requiring the presence of an instructor. They cannot, of course, be used to teach something such as manual skills, and they can be very expensive to design if customized.

An example of a fairly typical 'off-the-job' training programme for chefs is shown in Figure 8.2. Figure 8.3 ranks the effectiveness of different forms of training.

Time	Subject matter	Method of instruction
9.00–9.45	Company history Present organization and objectives Personnel policies	Talk, discussion and film
9.45–10.30	Kitchen equipment; cleanliness, safety, uses	Demonstration and discussion
10.30–11.00	Hygiene	Film and discussion
11.00–11.15	Coffee	
11.15–12.00	Principles of cooking; grilling	Demonstration and discussion
12.00–1.00	Portion, preparation and presentation	Demonstration and practical work
1.00–2.00	Lunch	
2.00–4.00	Practical cookery	Practical preparation of simple dishes
4.00–4.15	Tea	
4.15–5.00	Costing and portion control	Talk and discussion
5.00–6.00	Clearing up	

Figure 8.2 Example of first day of an 'off-the-job' training programme for cooks employed by a firm with many establishments offering standardized service

1   Personalized experiential learning; e.g. on-job training, 'mentor' supervision
2   Textual material; e.g. textbooks, manuals
3   Self-directed learning resources; e.g. resource area, programme learning
4   Observational learning; e.g. exhibits, working models
5   Interactive simulations; e.g. games, role play
6   Visual lecture aids; e.g. flip charts, overhead projectors (OHPs)
7   Expert formal presentations; e.g. lectures, panel presentations
8   Impersonal passive electronic media; instructional TV and radio.

Figure 8.3 Rank order of training effectiveness for non-supervisory jobs
Source: Dr R. Foucar-Szacki (1988) CHRIE conference paper, Syracuse University, USA.

Training and development needs analysis

Having considered what training and development attempts to do, the main principles of learning and the main techniques available, the next step is to consider the design of training programmes. Figure 8.4 gives a simple overview of the complete process. This starts with an identification of training needs, sometimes referred to as a 'training needs analysis', which is conducted by the person responsible for training in consultation with line management. It should attempt to identify those problems and opportunities that line management could solve and exploit with the assistance of appropriate training. It should be produced by studying the training needs of individuals as identified in appraisals and performance progress checks and by detailed discussions with the line managers. The individual's job description, actual performance and potential should be the basis for these discussions, together with organizational plans for the future. One useful approach is to adopt the 80/20 'Pareto' principle, e.g. what (20 per cent) activity is causing most (80 per cent) of the problems? In the commercial context it is always vital to concentrate limited resources on areas that will give the biggest rewards.

From the collation and amalgamation of individual training needs, HR or line managers will develop a composite plan for the wider organization's training needs. Some aspects of this plan will be categorized as 'essential' and some as 'desirable', dependent on the firm's overall objectives and priorities. These priorities should be informed by, and confirmed by, senior management and will consequently fit in with the undertaking's overall business strategy.

In the case of a catering contractor or a group of restaurants, for example, there may be plans to expand the number of units, and in order to do this a variety of key staff for the new units will be needed over a given period of time. It will be important, therefore, to identify those employees who can be transferred or promoted and the training that will be needed in order to prepare them for such a change. This may range from preparing some assistant managers for more senior management roles, to preparing junior kitchen operatives to take over more skilled responsibilities in food preparation and presentation. The question of having sufficient trained personnel to fit into expansion plans is critical to the successful growth of an organization and it is one HRM area where the training function together with effective recruitment and selection can prove to be of considerable value to a company. This is increasingly important where a hospitality firm embarks on international expansion and yet has to maintain the standards and reputation of the company and brand. Not all training needs emerge from the annual training needs analysis. They also arise from unexpected changes in trading conditions or business emphasis; a change of

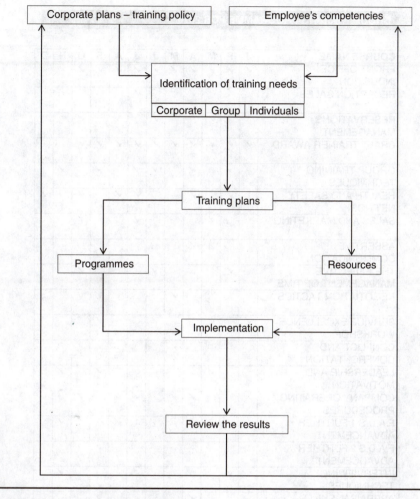

Figure 8.4 Meeting training needs

business strategy from a wholly owned restaurant business to a franchised operation across Europe would require training of area managers in order that they can collaborate with overseas franchisees, very different to managing and supervising home-grown, unit managers employed directly by the company.

Training needs may be sorted into three broad categories. The first is the organization's needs; for example, improved service and customer relations in order to tackle vibrant local competition. Such a need may affect all employees, and may be influenced by local events and festivals. The second need is a work group need; for example, a particular group of employees such as receptionists may need training in rooms division yield management techniques in order to increase revpar, the revenue from rooms in terms of maximizing room rates. The third is that of individual employees; for example, the proposal to computerize the payroll could result in the need for the payroll clerk to be trained in appropriate computer skills and HR information systems. Figure 8.5 illustrates one hotel company's off-job annual training plan.

GROUP TRAINING PROGRAMME FOR 2010

COURSE NAME	J	F	M	A	M	J	J	A	S	O	N	D
FRONT OFFICE INDUCTION	✓	✓	✓	✓	✓	✓	✓	✓	✓	✓	✓	✓
RECEPTION SALES				✓			✓			✓		
RESERVATIONS MANAGEMENT			✓			✓				✓		
CRAFT TRAINER AWARD	✓	✓	✓	✓	✓	✓	✓	✓	✓	✓		
GROUP TRAINING TECHNIQUES		✓		✓		✓	✓			✓		
HEALTH AND SAFETY NETWORK		✓		✓			✓	✓		✓		✓
SALES AND MARKETING			✓				✓			✓		
ASSERTIVE COMMUNICATION				✓								
THE EFFECTIVE MANAGEMENT OF TIME		✓				✓				✓		
NEGOTIATION TACTICS					✓				✓			
SERVICE EXCELLENCE WORKSHOP	✓		✓			✓			✓			
CONFLICT AND CONFRONTATION					✓				✓			
LEADERSHIP AND MOTIVATION			✓			✓			✓		✓	
COMPANY OPERATING PROCEDURES				✓	✓		✓		✓			
F.A.D.S 1 FURTHER ADVANCEMENT		✓				✓		✓			✓	
F.A.D.S 2 FURTHER ADVANCEMENT				✓					✓			
INTERVIEWING TECHNIQUES		✓				✓		✓			✓	
APPRAISAL SKILLS				✓					✓			
PERSONNEL OPERATING PROCEDURES				✓								

Figure 8.5 Example of a company's off-job annual training plan
Source: Reproduced by courtesy of Choice Hotels.

Line management support

It is vital that line management is seen to lead from the front in this HR aspect, supporting training by continuously emphasizing its importance, and by participating in training activities as much as possible; if all training and instruction is left to the HRM team and training instructors, an undesirable 'gap' can develop between the line management and the trainers. HR must not be seen as the expert training service to which responsibility may be abdicated, but regarded rather as a facilitator of a framework or system within which training and development of the workforce takes place, led by line managers and supervisors. One way to overcome this is to ensure that line management, such as unit and departmental managers, and the most skilled and suitable employees, are trained in on-the-job training skills so that they can personally undertake training sessions and be given specific responsibilities for training. Senior managers should consistently demonstrate their support and commitment towards training activities, by being there at the start of a programme whenever possible and introducing the event, outlining the importance of the training for the employees and for the business as a whole. Training is one of the tools of management that should be used to increase an employer's efficiency and productivity and customer service focus. It enables the organization's objectives to be achieved by properly equipping its personnel with the competencies, knowledge, skills and attitudes necessary to achieve those objectives and be a successful hospitality business. At the same time training should also enable individuals, through increased competence and confidence, to achieve whatever realistic aspirations they have in their work and ultimately in their careers.

In a modern conceptualization of HRM, training and development are also the activities that can reinforce the service culture of the organization (as illustrated in the case study earlier in this chapter) and place appropriate strategic emphasis on the 'soft' and 'hard' aspects of the hospitality business. HR has very much embraced the strategic training role within major hospitality companies, as a critical aspect of corporate policy, from the first days of a new employee's job induction and skills training to the management development activities required to ensure the retention and advancement of talented senior managers for the future. The next chapter specifically considers this area of management development and its fast-developing contemporary interpretation known as 'talent management'.

Further reading and references

Armstrong, M. (2012) *A Handbook of Human Resource Management Practice*, 12th edn, London: Kogan Page.

Beardwell, J. and Claydon, T. (2010) *Human Resources Management – A Contemporary Approach*, 6th edn, Harlow: FT Prentice-Hall.

Foot, M. and Hook, C. (2011) *Introducing Human Resource Management*, 6th edn, Harlow: FT Prentice Hall.

Foucar-Szacki, R. (1988) CHRIE conference paper, Syracuse University, USA.

Goss-Turner, S. (2002) *Managing People in the Hospitality Industry*, 4th edn, Kingston-upon-Thames: Croner Publications.

Kelliher, C. and Perrett, G. (2001) 'Business strategy and approaches to HRM: a case study of new developments in the UK restaurant industry', *Personnel Review*, 30(4): 421–437.

Korczynski, M. (2002) *Human Resource Management in Service Work*, Basingstoke: Palgrave Macmillan.

Lashley, C. and Best, W. (2002) 'Employee induction in licensed retail organisations', *International Journal of Contemporary Hospitality Management*, 14(1): 6–13.

Lucas, R. (2004) *Employment Relations in the Hospitality and Tourism Industries*, London: Routledge.

Nickson, D. (2007) *Human Resource Management for the Hospitality and Tourism Industries*, Oxford: Butterworth-Heinemann.

Ogbonna, E. and Harris, L. C. (2002) 'Managing organisational culture: insights from the hospitality industry', *Human Resource Management Journal*, 12(1): 33–53.

People 1st (2011) *State of the Nation Report 2011, Analysis of labour market trends, skills, education and training within the UK hospitality, leisure, travel and tourism industries*, London: People 1st.

Pratten, J. D. (2003) 'The importance of waiting staff in restaurant service', *British Food Journal*, 105(1): 826–834.

Seymour, D. and Sandiford, P. (2005) 'Learning emotion rules in service organizations: socialization and training in the UK public house sector', *Work, Employment & Society*, 19(3): 547–564.

Sissons, P. and Jones, K. (2012) *Lost in Transition? The Changing Labour Market and Young People Not in Employment, Education or Training*, Lancaster University: The Work Foundation.

Torrington, D., Hall, L. and Taylor, S. (2008) *Human Resource Management*, 7th edn, Harlow: FT Prentice Hall.

Members of the UK's Institute of Hospitality (IoH) can access publications including Management Guides which summarize key information of relevance to hospitality operations (www.instituteofhospitality.org).

Members of the UK's Chartered Institute of Personnel and Development (CIPD) can access a range of materials including Fact Sheets and articles from over 300 online journal titles relevant to HRM. CIPD members and *People Management* subscribers can see articles on the People Management website (www.peoplemanagement.co.uk).

Questions

1 Describe the objectives of systematic training and the various steps or phases that you would normally expect to find in its operation.

2 Discuss which you consider to be the most important elements in training and why.

3 Discuss what changes are likely to be made in the future to improve training and what areas employers are most likely to concentrate on.

4 Discuss the relationship between training and approaches to management, such as management by objectives (see Chapter 3).

5 Consider the 'GastroPubs & Bars plc' case study in this chapter and consider how you would feel as a new employee in the group in terms of being on the Your First Steps training programme.

CASE STUDY QUESTION – see the Lux Hotels case study Appendix 5

How can this organization learn from the approaches taken by 'GastroPubs & Bars plc', despite being in a very different market and sector of the hospitality industry?

Chapter 9

Management development

In the preceding chapter it was seen that much of the training effort within the hospitality industry focuses on developing the competencies needed to perform particular tasks and roles. It is concerned, in the main, with the present training needs and the immediate future, with meeting customers' immediate needs, as well as emphasizing key elements of longer-term business policy and HRM strategy. However, organizations also need managers who are able to interpret external environmental influences, plan ahead, organize and deploy resources, develop and interpret business information, and motivate a committed workforce. Management and leadership within the contemporary organization is a significant challenge in any sector. To ensure that such people are available in the right place and at the right time, organizations need to adopt some form of management development programme.

It has been estimated that managers make up 29 per cent of the hospitality workforce (Wilson *et al.*, 2006), and this vital segment of employees is increasingly required to be effective and efficient within an ever more competitive and changing international environment. In the specific area of HRM, it has been made clear in other sections of this book (e.g. Chapter 2) that it is essential to have managers throughout the hospitality organization who have the capability to address key questions of employee performance and commitment, of retention of capable staff, and with the drive and confidence to promote the critical aspects of organizational and service culture such as customer-oriented approaches. The move towards flatter management structures has also created the need for more rounded and competent management at all levels within the firm, as noted by Philippe Rossiter, Chief Executive of the Institute of Hospitality, the professional management body of the hospitality industry (People 1st, 2011). However, the industry continually seems to have difficulty in recruiting, developing and, most importantly, retaining management of the most competent kind (Watson, 2008). Hence the importance of having management development programmes which fulfil this vital aim and which prepare managers of the future for the specific company and for the industry as a whole, both nationally and where appropriate within an international environment.

What is meant by management development?

The term 'management development' has developed over the years to be an all-embracing function that encompasses the development of the management personnel of an organization, often from graduate management trainee to chief executive. It may be interpreted as giving a focus to recruitment and selection of managers most suitable for the company's activities, their subsequent training and development as future senior managers and their ongoing updating and development towards executive and senior specialist roles, such as hospitality sector area managers, HR and marketing managers. Watson (2008: 758) reviews recent literature in this area of hospitality management development, and considers management development to encompass, 'training, education and learning practices that are intended to assist managers realise their potential, either for personal or organisational benefit'. Gosling and Mintzberg (2003) discuss the twin concepts of management development and of leadership in terms of five mindsets: the reflective mindset concerned with managing oneself; the analytic mindset in terms of managing the organization; the worldly mindset concerned with the wider context and environment of the business; the collaborative mindset regarding working relationships; and finally the action mindset for making change happen and getting tasks completed. It can be seen just how many varied competencies may be required by managers, how much support the developing manager needs, and that is before we add in the industrial context of a complex and multidisciplinary sector such as hospitality.

The recent increased effort in devising more sophisticated management development strategies to meet these needs has been energized by a range of factors connected to the external and internal environment of the industry, such as:

- increased global competition from hospitality employers seeking the best managers of the present and future
- increased development and competency needs
- expectations of managers in flatter organization structures with fewer promotion opportunities
- internationalization of markets, brands and operators
- demographic changes in many countries, creating shortages of young people who make up such a large portion of the hospitality workforce around the world
- linkages to longer-term succession planning for the senior managers of the future
- the diversity of the industry and the workforce and the graduates entering the industry from university and college courses
- the need to continually address the image of the sector and its skills gaps in terms of management competencies
- part of a drive towards more effective leadership in terms of developing contemporary HRM practices, higher performance and worker commitment within the industry.

Within the hospitality industry research literature, there has also been criticism of the offering of management training and development, much of it being reactive and unplanned responses to immediate difficulties, rather than linked closely to the achievement of business objectives (see McGunnigle and Jameson, 2000). It is also true, however, that major hospitality chains are amongst those service businesses to have developed 'management academies' or management training centres, in an attempt to inculcate management training and learning into a clearly articulated developmental culture. The importance given to corporate culture within multi-site companies has also been a boost to the significance of strategic-level management development plans and activities, exemplified by the recent programme of training and development within the Compass Group, impacting on all its 400,000 worldwide workforce.

The culture argument has strong resonance with the need for tailored management learning approaches, as it is a key role of managers to reinforce the precepts of the prevailing organizational culture, so crucial to the achievement of business plans. Again we see strong threads to business strategy and performance management (see Chapters 2 and 7), where planned training and development, such as executive courses, events and mentoring, attempt to satisfy the strategic aim of merging the career development aspects of HR with the priorities of the business. In a rapidly developing contemporary hospitality business environment, management development forms a major component of the wider change management processes (Mabey and Salaman, 1995).

The components of a national or, as required in many multi-unit hospitality firms, an international management development strategy requires significant financial investment, whether the training courses are carried out by specially appointed internal HR department training personnel or whether outsourced to specialist training consultancies and business schools. The need to retain well-trained and high-performing managers is often a major challenge for the industry, and this retention factor needs to be tightly bound into the aims of the management development plans, so that the return on investment may be harvested by the firm that has put in the investment, rather than some other organization that might just come along and 'poach' a near-finished article! Thus a stable management workforce is vitally important in many ways in ensuring that an organization has an effective management team in the future (Deery, 2008).

Succession planning

To achieve this, an organization also needs to plan for natural replacement caused by reasons such as retirements, transfers and resignations and it needs to ensure that sufficient competent management is available for expansion plans. However, in a healthy organization these plans must also extend to satisfying each individual's reasonable aspirations; for example, if an employer stands in the way of an employee's attempt to obtain a recognized qualification, by not allowing adequate time off and support, the employee may place the qualification before the job and seek an employer who will assist. Plans that accommodate only the employer's needs may result in dissatisfaction, frustration, low morale and high labour turnover.

The senior management of an organization must therefore ensure that adequate plans and resources exist to recruit, motivate, train, develop and obtain commitment from a stable management team. This leads us to consider contemporary developments within the field of management development; in particular, it is important to note the value of systematic succession planning, but also the recent drive towards specific plans for the most capable of employees, often termed 'talent management'.

In larger organizations, management development and succession plans will be interdependent. The approach to succession planning itself will vary according to an organization's own needs. In an organization that operates within one large homogeneous market (McDonald's, Burger King, Premier Lodge, for example) it may be possible to develop the entire organization's management along similar lines and principles. In another organization, operating in very different markets with very different products and brands (Whitbread, Mitchells & Butlers or Accor, for example), it may be necessary to develop managers specifically for particular market segments.

Succession planning has two main elements. First, there have to be decisions regarding the sources of future management. These may be all home-grown or developed internally, or they may be recruited from other organizations or there may be a mixture of both these sources. Second, there is the process needed to identify management needs and the individuals to fill these needs. In small businesses, such as owner-run restaurants or ten-bedroom hotels, this will be a simple informal system because the management is likely to work with and be fully aware of those employees with potential. In large organizations, complex and often formal IT-based systems may be needed because of the large number of job opportunities, managers and potential managers involved. There will also be a need to manage the entire process so that an appropriate management team results. This is particularly the case in multinational companies such as Accor or Starwood, whose management potential may be currently working within any one of 100 countries.

A succession plan is produced by comparing future management requirements with currently available management. In order to do this, organization charts may be drawn up, which show the structure of the undertaking at the present time and at various future dates, such as in three months, one year, three years or five years. Each job shown may have two boxes immediately next to it or under it in which the names of suitable successors can be inserted. A replacement form is shown in Figure 9.1, and a succession chart in Figure 9.2.

Position	Present job holder	Most suitable replacement Put present job in brackets	Second recommendation Put present job in brackets
Hotel Manager (Splendide)	J. Jones	A. Smith (Food and Beverage Manager, Splendide)	R. Barker (Front Office Manager, Grand)
Promotion potential		Ready for promotion	Promotable with training
Training and/or development needed		None	Food and beverage experience needed
Signed by Approved by	J. Jones J. Walker	Date (Area Manager)	20/1/06

Figure 9.1 A management succession or replacement form

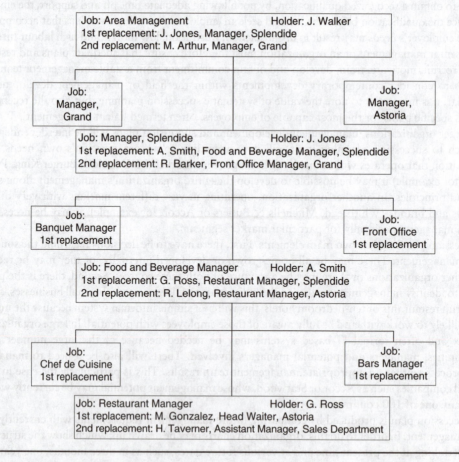

Figure 9.2 A succession chart

The managers' names inserted into Figures 9.1 and 9.2 would result from discussions between the most appropriate levels of management, using performance appraisal reports as a basis (see Chapter 7). This emphasizes the need for a section on promotion potential to be included in the appraisal report. Increasingly, promotion potential is being assessed through the use of assessment centres, with often the assistance of business schools, consultants, psychometric tests and occupational psychologists (see Chapter 5).

So long as the basis for discussion is that replacement will be due to normal retirement, accident or the voluntary departure of the incumbent, the most appropriate levels of management to be involved in discussions will be:

1 the present holder of the job for which a replacement is being discussed
2 the present job holder's superior
3 the superiors of those proposed as replacements
4 a member of senior management who is fully aware of future plans
5 a human resources specialist.

In some organizations, dependent on size and scope, one person will frequently fulfil more than one of these roles. The final plan, particularly for the more senior levels, must carry the approval of senior management. In order to identify likely successors in the first place it is common practice to ask each member of management to nominate those he or she considers to be the most suitable as successors. However, where this is done it must be recognized that there may arise a danger of rigid departmental career paths, whereas in some cases interdepartmental transfers and promotions will be more desirable in order to broaden the experience of individual managers.

In the largest organizations, which are structurally subdivided into global, regional or functional operating divisions, the danger of 'sitting on' talent, consciously or subconsciously, has to be avoided. In multinational, multi-divisional organizations, the executive responsible for a particular division may well wish to retain within their own division the most capable management colleagues, rather than seeing the resource as one available to the whole company. This can lead to frustration in some managers who really want to move onward and upwards within the wider organization. To assist multinationals in 'tracking' the ability and potential of their managers around the world, some HR departments have invested in succession planning software systems as part of their overall HR information system package, which provide considerable rafts of information about the company's management personnel.

As part of this more holistic approach to management development and succession planning, it is important for us to consider the well-documented recent management practice towards recognizing that some people have more potential than others in terms of being the senior executives of the future. 'Talent management' is being much discussed in the HR professional and academic journals as a means of fast-tracking individuals from graduate schemes onwards, and focusing elements of the management development investment budget specifically on such individuals.

Talent management

In the search for innovative approaches to the training of managers, a strand of research and practice has recently developed around this concept of 'talent management', a concept that sits alongside management development and embraces the challenge of recruiting, developing and retaining high-potential employees. This concept is open to a variety of interpretations within the hospitality environment (Christensen Hughes and Rog, 2008) and might be trivialized as a fad or merely a contemporary 'spin' on management development. However, it can also be considered as a further step in the integration of HRM policies and practices into the overall strategy of the business. It highlights the importance of high quality selection and well-planned training and development programmes that are aligned with the organization's goals. There are major influences on talent management from both internal factors (e.g. culture and values) and external factors (e.g. image of the industry), and the concept is also connected to further issues such as skills and competencies, career paths, and learning and development approaches within the organization.

Christensen Hughes and Rog (2008) also conceptualize talent management within the domain of employee engagement and retention in the hospitality industry, and strongly advocate the importance of organization-wide commitment to the talent management project from the chief executive to the front-line employee, a perpetual thread through the company's culture and mindset. They conclude that within hospitality organizations, 'talent management presents a particularly intriguing opportunity' (2008: 757). However, the opportunity will only be realized if there is clarity about the nature and objectives of the programme itself and commitment from the top of the organization.

There is also a need for an analysis of internal HR and development systems, and the structure and availability of training and learning schemes, in order for individual potential to be maximized. Baum (2008: 729) also rightly points to the diffuse nature of talent within the hospitality industry – so many different skills and competencies across so many different jobs – and recommends that 'most hospitality and tourism organizations need to focus on inclusiveness and an open-minded approach to training and development which provides opportunities for all staff to participate and enhance their skills and knowledge sets'. Deery (2008) also takes us back to the discussion about emotional labour and stress within hospitality work, by making a clear linkage between employee retention and work–life balance, and how talent management must not be immune from seeking to address these matters through its developmental activities.

The hospitality industry, whether in its small-scale SME version or the multinational large-scale entity, needs to consider seriously the meaning and implications of the principles underpinning talent management. The People 1st survey of employers in 2011 indicated that the difficulty in recruiting and keeping managers with the right skills and competencies is getting worse, not better. In particular, employers reported that the causes of the management skills gaps experienced by them included lack of experience (partly no doubt due to the vicious circle of high labour turnover); inability to motivate staff; failure to train and develop staff; inability to keep up with change.

Education of managers

In accordance with the succession plan, individual training and development programmes have to be designed. It is here that an understanding of how a manager acquires his or her knowledge, skills and attitudes is vital. The hospitality industry has a good record of providing a platform for an individual to start in a purely operative role, perhaps from leaving school, and still achieving a management role of seniority in the course of time. Climbing the career ladder up the organization's structure is earned by the individual's hard work and commitment, and often a seemingly natural talent for the industry, as in looking after customers or managing a successful team of hospitality employees. However, the educational system has increasingly provided a range of possibilities for potential hospitality employees first to gain some learning and qualifications at college or as a part college/part work-based learning programme. The Institute of Hospitality and colleges of further education (FE) offer a range of vocational qualifications from Levels 2 to 4 in the national framework, under the general nomenclature of a Diploma in Hospitality and Tourism Operations. These qualifications may be undertaken in a variety

Year	Approximate age	Position
1	21	Trainee management programme, various departments and establishments
2–3	22–24	Junior supervisory position, e.g. assistant manager of a hotel restaurant
4	24	Specialized function, e.g. new projects department, sales office, training department
5	25	Line management, e.g. unit management, food and beverage management
6	27	Specialist function, e.g. sales management, training officer
7	28	Assistant to area manager
8	30	Line management, e.g. manager of a medium to large unit, area manager

Figure 9.3 Example of a career path for a young executive

of flexible learning programmes as part of continuing professional development (CPD). Beyond Levels 2 and 3 are also Level 4/5 foundation degrees in hospitality management.

Foundation degrees are two-year, non-honours degree programmes validated by universities but usually delivered at FE colleges, and are designed for those with strong work-oriented approaches. They are available to those with considerable prior work experience and/or those with prior qualification levels that may not be accepted by a university for honours degree admission. An example would be the offering of City College Brighton and Hove, which delivers foundation degrees (FDs) in hospitality and event management, travel and tourism management, and food and culinary arts. Students may, subject to their performance levels, then transfer to the University of Brighton to 'top-up' their FD by taking the final year of the BA (Honours) degree in the same subject areas.

There are a wide range of universities throughout the UK that offer hospitality management degrees at both undergraduate and postgraduate levels, and students with these higher qualifications are much in demand by larger, chain organizations, often the international hotel and tourism companies such as Starwood, Hilton, Marriott Hotels, Disney and Virgin Atlantic.

However, becoming a graduate is only part of the management development journey towards senior executive roles. Many companies in hospitality design their own management development programmes which are tailored to their particular organization's needs and nature. In this way, trainee managers from whatever educational background experience a mixture of learning, both on-job and off-job, and are exposed to the operational challenges that might seem very different in practice in contrast to the more theoretical perspective gained at college or university. The hospitality industry's great diversity of roles, tasks and activities, and its dependence on the successful human interaction of so many employees and customers, requires that the training is both intellectually and practically focused.

A management development programme must therefore contain a balance of formal training and planned experience. It is not something that operates for one period only of a manager's life. It should be updated constantly to continue throughout a manager's career. Over a period of years, therefore, a programme may include spells in line management and in various specialist departments; for example, a young executive's first eight to ten years with a company could be as shown in Figure 9.3.

During this period the trainee executive may also attend a number of 'off-the-job' development courses on such subjects as:

- supervisory skills
- budgetary control and forecasting
- techniques of instruction/on-job training

- managing people/teams
- interviewing and selection techniques
- project planning
- finance for non-financial executives
- selling and skills of negotiation
- marketing and merchandizing techniques.

Whether these are internal or external courses depends on the needs and resources of the organization and the individual. Generally, internal courses are more precisely designed to satisfy the needs of the organization and cost much less, whereas external courses have to be broadly based to appeal to a wider market and are often more expensive.

The value of external courses also lies to some extent in the opportunity to exchange views with managers from other organizations, but this only has value if those attending can bring about necessary organizational changes and effect improvements on return to the business. This prerogative normally lies only with more senior managers and therefore the value of external courses probably increases with the seniority of those attending (so long as the courses are geared to their needs).

An example of internal management development activity implemented by a restaurant chain is given below:

Mini case study: management development in practice

The national quick service restaurant company known here for reasons of confidentiality as 'Sprinters', conducted a nationwide, multi-site questionnaire survey of all its unit managers (over 300), seeking their priorities in terms of how the company could improve its effective team working practices. This was seen as a priority by the senior management team and the main board HR Director, part of a need to develop an appropriate management culture, fostering effective leadership approaches required for a highly competitive market. Most of the restaurant outlets of the company were located on the brand-dominated high streets of the UK towns and cities such as Reading, Oxford and Manchester. Following statistical analysis of the results, a set of eight key result areas were identified and communicated to the survey participants by the head office HR department. These were:

- the need for clear objectives and agreed company and brand goals
- openness and strategies to avoid confrontation
- need for more support and trust
- more cooperation and reduced conflict
- strong, sound company procedures, well communicated
- leadership of consistency and appropriate to the type of business
- regular review in a supportive manner
- more emphasis on individual development.

Following publication of these results, which were of statistical significance, the HR team organized a series of one-day workshops (15 in all) across the country, inviting every manager to attend. There were company presentations of the detailed findings, group discussions and participatory training methods – adopted to ensure the active involvement of normally hands-on operational managers, not comfortable as recipients of a talk-and-chalk session for more than 30 minutes. These sessions were considered hugely successful in building a company-wide management spirit and teamwork culture which resulted in many collaborative initiatives across the brands and outlets. In this case, a very tailored and systematic approach to management development paid great dividends, and the investment in time and money was seen by senior executives as well spent. Follow-up sessions with area managers were arranged so that the value was not lost within the hectic everyday life of the business.

Trainee management programmes

There is a long history of trainee manager development within the hospitality industry, from graduate management schemes to the 'training up from within' style of mentoring and development of talented young employees who display the potential for a future supervisory or managerial career. The approach to trainee management courses varies considerably. In some cases they will consist of job rotation through a variety of jobs for a sometimes indeterminate period, the length of time in each department being more dependent upon business needs than upon those of the trainee. In other cases programmes will be individually designed, taking into account previous experience such as industrial release or work placements, and the trainees' progress will be carefully monitored by the managers responsible for them.

As the first step in a person's career, the design of trainee management courses is critical. It is in the first months that the basis of knowledge and skills and, in particular, an understanding of the employer's policies, attitudes and cultural values will be formed.

There are many critics and opponents of the traditional 'Cook's tour' training and development plan, involving spells of 'training' in the most important departments. In some cases this criticism is well deserved because no objectives are laid down and the trainees are merely used as cheap labour, or not used at all. However, in order to be a successful hospitality manager, knowledge and experience of certain departments are vital and the well-designed 'Cook's tour' serves this purpose; at the same time objectives must be agreed with departmental supervisors, and trainees should be given their training objectives preferably in written form. They should not move from one department to the next until departmental training objectives have been attained. Trainees should maintain training logs or diaries and, in addition, they may be given specific and challenging, meaningful projects. Regular progress interviews and performance appraisal meetings should be held to ensure that the trainees' objectives are being achieved. This approach should also be applied to those many students who undergo supervised work experience (often called internship or 'stage' within international companies) within industry as part of their hospitality management degree course.

In considering an individual's development programme, which is updated and modified year by year, it is vital to examine both strengths and weaknesses, remembering that they may well be strengths and weaknesses only so far as the employer is concerned. In another type of organization the same characteristics may be seen in a completely different light. Ideally the weaknesses should be corrected and the strengths built upon. However, this will not always be possible, because some weaknesses may not be merely lack of knowledge or skill but rather may be of a personality or attitudinal nature and these are often very difficult to correct even if it were in the individual's interest to do so. For example, a highly creative person may prefer to work as an individual, perhaps in a non-standardized type of operation. He or she may not enjoy or wish to work with others, nor to control them. The weakness, so far as the employer is concerned, is that he or she cannot direct or lead others, so the employer decides to give the individual a spell managing others to develop them into more of an all-rounder. In some cases this may work out, but in others it could have detrimental results, with the person concerned eventually leaving.

A major research report into hospitality management development conducted by the Council for Hospitality Management Education (CHME), *Getting Ahead: Graduate Careers in Hospitality Management* (2001), revealed interesting features regarding the growing demand for hospitality qualifications within the sample of leading firms across all sectors of the hospitality industry. Key findings included a confirmation of the importance of qualifications for career development to senior managerial roles; the developing need for management qualifications and competencies at unit manager level; the linking of in-house development to externally awarded qualifications; and the preference of the major companies for hospitality graduates because of their industry understanding and enthusiastic commitment to the sector. The ultimate success of those graduates will in part be due to the effectiveness of the organization's management development programme.

Further reading and references

Armstrong, M. (2012) *A Handbook of Human Resource Management Practice*, 12th edn, London: Kogan Page.

Baum, T. (2008) 'Implications of hospitality and tourism labour markets for talent management strategies', *International Journal of Contemporary Hospitality Management*, 20(7): 720–729.

Christensen Hughes, J. and Rog, E. (2008) 'A strategy for improving employee recruitment, retention and engagement within hospitality organizations', *International Journal of Contemporary Hospitality Management*, 20(7): 743–757.

Council for Hospitality Management Education (2001) *Getting Ahead: Graduate Careers in Hospitality Management*, London: CHME/HEFCE Publications.

Deery, M. A. (2008) 'Talent management, work–life balance and retention strategies', *International Journal of Contemporary Hospitality Management*, 20(7): 792–806.

Gosling, J. and Mintzberg, H. (2003) 'The five minds of a manager', *Harvard Business Review*, November: 1–9.

Mabey, C. and Salaman, G. (1995) *Strategic Human Resource Management*, Oxford: Blackwell.

McGunnigle, P. and Jameson, S. (2000) 'HRM in UK hotels: a focus on commitment', *Employee Relations*, 22(4): 403–422.

People 1st (2011) *State of the Nation Report 2011, Analysis of labour market trends, skills, education and training within the UK hospitality, leisure, travel and tourism industries*, London: People 1st.

Torrington, D., Hall, L. and Taylor, S. (2008) *Human Resource Management*, 7th edn, Harlow: FT Prentice Hall.

Watson, S. (2008) 'Where are we now? A review of management development issues in the hospitality and tourism sector: implications for talent management', *International Journal of Contemporary Hospitality Management*, 20(7): 758–780.

Wilson, R., Homenidou, K. and Dickerson, A. (2006) *Working Futures 2004–2014*, University of Warwick, Coventry: Institute for Employment Research.

Members of the UK's Institute of Hospitality (IoH) can access publications including Management Guides which summarize key information of relevance to hospitality operations (www.instituteofhospitality.org).

Members of the UK's Chartered Institute of Personnel and Development (CIPD) can access a range of materials including Fact Sheets and articles from over 300 online journal titles relevant to HRM. CIPD members and *People Management* subscribers can see articles on the People Management website (www.peoplemanagement.co.uk).

Questions

1 Describe the objectives of management development and the various steps or phases that you would normally expect to find in the operation of an effective management development programme.

2 Discuss which you consider to be the most important steps in management development and why.

3 How do you think that the concept of 'talent management' could be effectively introduced within a hospitality firm?

4 Discuss the relationship between management development and the concept of contemporary human resource management as outlined in Chapter 2.

CASE STUDY QUESTION – see the Lux Hotels case study Appendix 5

How could Lux Hotels integrate the concept of talent management into its development plans for the organization and its future management team?

Part 4

Rewards and remuneration

Chapter 10

Reward systems

Reward or remuneration systems, are central to the employee–employer relationship. In essence they should be the free exchange of work for money and other benefits of value. In modern society, however, this relationship can be extremely complex. At its simplest a reward system can consist of an hourly rate being paid for each hour worked. At the other extreme a remuneration system might consist of a career-long package of benefits including salary, paid holidays, pensions, company car, health insurances, training and development, regular promotion, clubs, special purchasing arrangements, family benefits and a range of other benefits.

Within the hospitality industry, reward systems can be very simple such as a rate per hour or per session for casual or part-time workers. Or the remuneration package can be complex consisting, as described above, of annual salary, free or cheap meals and accommodation, tips and service charges, performance bonuses, paid holidays, pensions, company car, health insurances and a range of other benefits.

Since the recent economic crisis, which started around 2008, much has been written about its causes, with many observers laying the blame for the crisis on incentive systems that encouraged and rewarded short-term risk-taking on unprecedented scales with the consequent failure of a number of banks. Nobel Prize-winning economist, Joseph Stiglitz, said that the banking system 'encouraged excessive risk-taking. In fact it paid them to gamble' (reported in *People Management,* July 2011). Whilst hospitality businesses are very different from the world of banking, the reasons behind the failure of banks illustrate the need to align business policy with reward systems, recognizing that some hospitality businesses are large multinational even global companies. Following the 2008 financial and economic crisis serious concern began to emerge concerning the divisive effects of excessive pay awards to many top executives, not just in the UK but in other countries as well.

In the UK the High Pay Commission addressed the issue. To summarize, it found that excessive high pay damages companies, is bad for the economy and has negative impacts on society as a whole. At its worst, excessive high pay bears little relation to company success and is rewarding failure. There was an impression that business leaders are 'in it for themselves' – especially at a time when most workers are seeing little or no increase in their pay (High Pay Commission, 2011).

Its findings demonstrated that some company senior management reward systems totally contradicted principles of sound company-wide reward systems. The earnings of many top managers have grown at rates which many observers consider to be excessive. Many CEOs now earn well over 100 times the average pay of their workforce. Such comparisons can be difficult to make, particularly in multinational companies where operative staff wages in many countries may be much lower than those paid in the parent company's host country. Even so, such differentials can cause serious resentment within a company. Peter Drucker (1909–2005), one of the most respected and influential management gurus wrote that CEOs' earnings should not exceed 20 to 25 times their average employees' earnings, believing that larger differentials generated resentment, writing 'I'm not talking about the bitter feelings of the people on the plant floor ... It's the mid-level management that is incredibly disillusioned' by king-sized CEO compensation (reported at the Davos G20 Conference 2010). What he was writing about then, we might now refer to as 'staff engagement', an issue dealt with in the report *Engaging for Success* (MacLeod and Clarke, 2009).

There is little evidence that such differentials are common within the hospitality industry, although hospitality workers feature amongst the lower paid in many economies. However, other issues related to pay also exist which can cause serious dissatisfaction. Many of these issues including relatively low pay are to be looked at in the next three chapters.

One of the problems for the hospitality industry and its pay levels is that, relatively speaking, each employee does not generate large sums of revenue for the employer. In hotels, for example, hotel workers generated £67.81 per hour worked, from which the cost of earnings, overheads, loans, taxes, etc. have to be deducted. The figures for restaurants and food services are even lower (People 1st, 2011).

Such levels of sales per employee do not leave much room for significant rates of pay, particularly when compared to other industries where each employee may generate hundreds of thousands of pounds each year. This is illustrated in Figure 10.1 by the employee contribution to gambling, the highest in the sector and where there are few 'consumable' costs.

Many organizations have wage and salary systems that have evolved over time and which in many cases have not really addressed the crucial task of matching an organization's goals closely to its reward systems. This is particularly so in the hospitality industry, where the majority of enterprises tend to be small and where there is a lack of professional management expertise.

In order to be effective, a reward policy and its dependent package needs to be aimed at achieving the owner's overall business objectives. For example, if an owner's business policy focuses on quality and repeat business, the rewards system must not conflict with that policy by focusing staff effort mostly on other objectives such as maximizing sales volumes. From the human resource policy perspective, if an employer's policy is to encourage long service and career development among most of its employees, the employer may offer an incremental payment system that rewards long service in itself. If the employer chooses to recruit from a volatile, young and relatively cheap labour market, it will probably offer low rates of pay with little room for significant increases. Some employers will mix their policies, encouraging managers to make careers with them whilst not encouraging long-serving operative staff.

Hourly revenue generated per employee	
Gambling	£121.44
Travel services	£102.74
Pubs, bars and nightclubs	£80.89
Hotels	£67.81
Visitor attractions	£67.28
Tourist services	£51.80
Restaurants	£47.53
Food and service management	£41.61
Events	£39.72
Self-catering accommodation, holiday parks and hostels	£30.93

Figure 10.1 Economic contribution per employee by industry
Source: People 1st (2011).

Apart from the lack of method in setting basic rates in some sectors other factors such as tipping, service charges and the provision of meals and living accommodation all have to be taken into consideration, all within the context of minimum wage and other employment legislation. Within a single establishment it is quite possible to find a complex range of permutations of all the various benefits received by employees and workers. Some live in and earn tips, some live out and do not earn tips, some are provided with meals and some are not. In addition, in the largest organizations, some subsidiaries encourage tipping, whereas others do everything to eliminate it and also levy service charges. This may be even further complicated by some managers and executives being provided with company cars and other benefits. On closer examination, however, it may well be found that these same executives are worse off (in cash and kind) than their own residential managers.

In the contract catering field the problems can be exacerbated by other factors. The client's employees, for example, may enjoy extremely high rewards (e.g. in the City of London) which make the catering staffs' rewards look very insignificant.

'Fiddles and knock-offs'

Over thirty years ago Mars *et al*. (1979) claimed the payment system in hotels had particular problems because it provided opportunities for 'fiddles and knock-offs'(i.e. pilferage/theft).

Since then regular surveys among returning work experience students indicate that little has changed in this respect. Mars *et al*. attached particular importance to the fiddles element because of the power it provided to management. They suggested that management laid down parameters within which fiddles are acceptable, but at the same time if someone displeased them for other reasons they could dismiss the person for fiddling. Undoubtedly, whether fiddling is institutionalized or not, it is a major source of income to employees, and causes headaches to the industry's employers.

Types of employee

Within the hospitality industry, irrespective of any legal definitions (see Chapter 16), there are several types of employee. From a payment or earnings point of view these are:

- *Salaried employees*: usually paid monthly and usually consisting of managers and senior supervisors, often receiving performance-related bonuses.
- *Full-time employees*: usually working around 30–45 hours a week and who know from week to week that they have guaranteed work; paid usually weekly or monthly.
- *Part-timers*: usually working fewer hours than a full-timer and who generally know from week to week that they have work, usually paid by the hour. As a result of the EU decisions most part-timers qualify, pro rata, for the same fringe benefits, such as holidays, as the full-time members of staff.
- *Casuals*: normally working on a session-by-session basis (e.g. one evening) with no guarantees about future work. Usually paid by the session in cash.
- *Zero hours*: a form of agreement whereby an employee may be available for work as and when required but with no guarantees. Sometimes a guaranteed minimum or retainer may be paid.
- *Subcontract (including outsourced)*: such workers are not employees of the organization but they work within or for the organization. These may include, for example, security staff, musicians and contract cleaners attending to the servicing of public areas and in the case of hotels, guest rooms. The advantage of employing such workers is that they can be called in or laid off with little or

no notice and they may involve no or little 'payroll burden', i.e. national insurance, pension contributions, etc.

- *Offshored*: similar to subcontract but employed in another country where rates of pay may be lower and/or where recruitment is easy. Examples include call-centre services.

Most pay systems are based on two principles: to reward for time or for performance. In the first case, obviously, there is also an element of performance – one is not paid indefinitely for 'time' if the performance is not satisfactory. In the second case, however, payment for performance, there are a number of questions that have to be addressed, e.g. is it the individual's, the group's or the enterprise's performance that is rewarded, or is it the 'inputs' or the 'outputs' that are rewarded?

Formal administration of wages

A major issue for owners and their managers is to decide how to distribute fairly among all employees the money set aside for payment of staff. This may range from as little as 10 per cent of revenue in some efficient public houses to over 40 per cent in top-class hotels. This money may derive from normal revenue or may also come from retained service charges. In determining what to pay, owners and managers may decide by looking at what competitors are paying, what has been historically the employer's practice and, in many cases, what is necessary to overcome a current staffing crisis. The result is that considerable anomalies exist in many hospitality establishments and, indeed, whole companies. As mentioned in the last chapter, newcomers may be paid more than similar staff with long service and more senior staff may earn less than some juniors.

Market pricing

Larger companies will tend to adopt a practice called market pricing which is a system of collecting data on pay for comparable jobs in other organizations in order to establish their market rate or 'price'. The process aims to determine the organization's own pay rates in order to recruit and retain the staff it needs.

The exact policy to be adopted by an employer with regard to wage and salary systems will depend to a great extent upon the business objectives, human resource policies and style of management; for example, in organizations where labour turnover is not considered to be important, there may be little method or formality in setting rates of pay. In other organizations, however, where it is recognized that a stable labour force is a valuable asset, much more method will be applied to wage and salary matters. This is typically so in the public sector, where for many years employers set out to be exemplary.

Job evaluation

Where there are many employees with differing levels of skills, fair salary administration may depend upon job evaluation, which measures the relative importance to the organization of different jobs. But after jobs have been evaluated, pay rates will have to be set for each grade to ensure that there are realistic differentials between grades so that more senior jobs and promotions are rewarded by worthwhile differences in earnings; promotion then becomes something to aim for (Figure 10.2).

Determining the rate for each job or for key jobs depends on many factors, including the make-up of the workforce, statutory requirements, competitors' rates of pay, other industries' rates of pay, cost of living and the location of the employer.

Grade	Basic wage (£ week)
1	200
2	220
3	240
4	265

Figure 10.2 Example of a grade and wage table

Because of this, in order to establish or to maintain competitive rates of pay, it will be necessary to study advertisements in the press and to keep in touch with staff agencies, local Job Centres and the local associations of hoteliers and caterers (see market pricing in the previous section).

In making decisions as a result of this research, it is vital to ensure that all factors affecting rates of pay are taken into account, such as tips and service charges, actual hours worked, anti-social hours worked and the provision or otherwise of meals, taxis, accommodation, etc. Some employers may, in addition, require different rates or even entirely different structures for each branch, brand or region.

Increments – merit and service

In some situations, in order to encourage good performance and long service, it may be appropriate to provide merit and service increments. Where this is done there will normally be overlaps between grades, enabling someone in a low grade, but with long service or high merit, to earn more than someone in a higher grade with short service. This recognizes that a person's competence and value to an organization may increase with service, and because of this the increment is granted both as an increased share of the employees' overall contribution and to encourage them to stay. Figure 10.3 shows a scale for such a scheme.

In the example shown in Figure 10.3 an employee could anticipate, with satisfactory service, to move from the minimum to the maximum in a period of about four years, giving an average annual increase of about 6–7 per cent. The exact rate might be determined by performance appraisals and by the employer's financial policy and performance. The advantage of this system, when publicized, is that

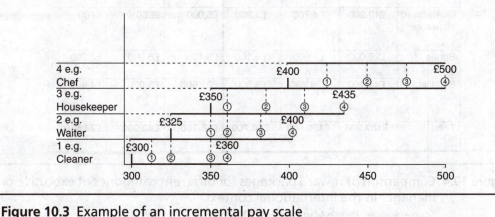

Figure 10.3 Example of an incremental pay scale

employees know what they can expect to earn by gaining promotion or by staying with an employer. In addition, some employers have age-related scales or rates of pay, usually for employees up to about 21 years of age. Increases in these cases would normally be granted on each employee's birthday. There may be percentage links to statutory minimum wages.

In some cases starting wages or salaries offered to newcomers may not normally be more than 20 per cent above the minimum and this would only be permitted where appropriate experience in the type of job justifies it.

Reviews should take place regularly and should fit into the employer's budgetary and financial cycle. In seasonal establishments reviews may take place towards or at the end of the season in order to retain those employees management want to keep.

Apart from increases for merit, service and promotion, some systems also allow for cost-of-living increases to be made. These will probably be related to government data such as a cost-of-living index, but where such increases are granted it is important to bear in mind that they have little positive motivational effect – unlike a promotion or merit award. That is because they are usually granted to all employees without discriminating between good performance and poorer performance.

On the other hand it is important to keep in mind that the absence of cost-of-living increases may have a negative effect – i.e. the employees' relative level of earnings may fall and force them to seek employment elsewhere. It can be said that although cost-of-living awards have little positive motivational effect, their absence may have a negative effect such as a higher labour turnover (see Herzberg's 'hygiene' factors, Chapter 2).

So far as multinationals are concerned, remuneration policy becomes even more complex. A range of factors has to be taken into account, in particular comparability within the company itself and also within the host country. Such issues are discussed in more detail in Chapter 21 but Figure 10.4 illustrates how remuneration varies within a country dependent upon the origins of the employee concerned.

	Executive board			Management position		
	Expat from Western country	Locally hired foreigner	Local resident	Expat from Western country	Locally hired foreigner	Local resident
Base pay	£91,600	£94,700	£41,100	£50,000	£31,200	£17,250
Guaranteed allowance	£19,200	£4,700	£1,200	£5,000	£800	£700
Bonus	£25,000	£7,000	£6,100	£9,400	£5,900	£2,200
Benefits	£44,400	£24,200	£6,300	£21,900	£5,000	£4,400
Total	£182,200	£130,600	£54,700	£86,300	£42,900	£24,550

Figure 10.4 Comparison of reward packages for different categories of executive or manager in the international context

Source: Mercer, *People Management* (2010).

Remuneration committees and recruitment consultants

In most larger organizations an employer's reward policies and practices may be overseen by a remuneration committee. Their role should be to ensure that sound systems for job evaluation and market pricing are in place.

However, some remuneration committees, particularly those concerned with senior management, have recently come under serious criticism because of the role they have played in encouraging what some observers consider to be excessive earnings and earnings inflation amongst senior management. This is because remuneration committees tend to have external members from other comparable employers, with the result that they realize if they support, even encourage, large increases in earnings, they themselves will benefit when 'market pricing' comparisons are made. Similar criticisms are aimed at recruitment consultants 'who have a vested interest in driving up pay levels, and placing too much importance on assumed comparative rates' (Brian Bailey, *People Management*, February 2012).

Further reading and references

ACAS (2010) *Job Evaluation: Considerations and Risks*, Advisory booklet, London: ACAS.

Armstrong, M. (2007) *A Handbook of Employee Reward Management and Practice*, London: Kogan Page.

Armstrong, M. (2012) *A Handbook of Human Resource Management*, 12th edn, London: Kogan Page.

Armstrong, M. and Brown, D. (2009) *Strategic Reward: Implementing More Effective Reward Management*, London: Kogan Page.

Armstrong, M., Brown, D. and Reilly, P. (2010) *Evidence Based Reward Management*, London: Kogan Page.

Bailey, B. (2012) *People Management*, London: Chartered Institute of Personnel and Development.

Beardwell, I., Holden, L. and Claydon, T. (2004) *Human Resource Management – A Contemporary Approach*, 4th edn, Harlow: Prentice Hall.

High Pay Commission (2011) *Cheques with Balances: Why Tackling High Pay Is in the National Interest*, London: High Pay Commission.

Income Data Services (2011) *A New Era for Job Evaluation?* Executive Compensation Review No. 365, London: IDS Executive.

Income Data Services (2011) *Total Reward*, HR Studies, London: IDS.

Kessler, I. (2001) 'Reward system choices', in Storey, J. (ed.) *Human Resource Management – A Critical Text*, 2nd edn, London: Thomson Learning.

Langley, A. (2008) *Employee Reward Structures*, 3rd edn, London: Spiramus Press.

MacLeod, D. and Clarke, N. (2009) *Engaging for Success: Enhancing Performance through Employee Engagement*, London: Department for Business, Innovation and Skills.

Mars, G., Mitchell, P. and Bryant, D. (1979) *Manpower Problems in the Hotel and Catering Industry*, Farnborough: Saxon House.

Mercer Human Resources (2010) *People Management*, London: Chartered Institute of Personnel and Development.

Office of Manpower Economics and Chartered Institute of Personnel and Development (2008) *Public/Private Approaches to Pay and Progression*.

People 1st (2011) *State of the Nation Report 2011, Analysis of labour market trends, skills, education and training within the UK hospitality, leisure, travel and tourism industries*, London: People 1st.

Perkins, S. J. and White, G. (2011) *Reward Management: Alternatives, Consequences and Contexts*, 2nd edn, London: Chartered Institute of Personnel and Development.

Thompson, P. (2002) *Total Reward*, Executive briefing, London: Chartered Institute of Personnel and Development.

Torrington, D., Hall, L., Taylor, S. and Atkinson, C. (2011) *Human Resource Management*, 8th edn, Harlow: Pearson Education.

Members of the UK's Institute of Hospitality can access publications including Management Guides which summarize key information of relevance to hospitality operations (www.instituteofhospitality.org).

Members of the UK's Chartered Institute of Personnel and Development (CIPD) can access a range of materials including Fact Sheets and articles from over 300 online journal titles relevant to HR. CIPD members and *People Management* subscribers can see articles on the People Management website (www.peoplemanagement.co.uk).

Questions

1 Describe the objectives of a systematic rewards administration system.

2 Discuss in which sectors of the hospitality industry systematic wage and salary administration is least likely and most likely to be found and why.

3 Discuss what you consider to be the most likely consequences of a lack of systematic wage and salary administration and why.

4 Discuss the relationship between rewards administration and performance appraisal (see Chapter 7).

5 Evaluate the approach to wage and salary administration used by an employer you know well.

CASE STUDY QUESTION – see the Lux Hotels case study Appendix 5

In this chapter key approaches to remuneration have been described. Now discuss which main approach or approaches would be most suited to Lux Hotels bearing in mind that they are seeking to encourage mobility between levels of employee, their different brands and the countries where their hotels are located. Consider the main different levels of employee, giving reasons for your recommendation for each different level.

Chapter 11

Job evaluation

Job evaluation contributes to two absolute essentials in reward systems: external competitiveness and internal equity or fairness.

One of the major causes of friction between employers and their employees, between individual employees and between groups of employees is a real or perceived lack of fairness in the distribution of wages. For many years in the past, British industry was bedevilled with industrial strife caused by 'pay differentials' between ordinary workers, each group constantly protecting its pay advantage over other groups. Today dissatisfaction is caused frequently by the differentials between top management and other employees in a company. The UK's High Pay Commission was set up to look into pay at the top of UK companies. As a result of the inquiry the Commission was highly critical of many senior management payment systems.

The Commission found evidence that excessively high pay damages companies, that high pay is bad for the economy and has negative impacts on society. Sadly, it found that excessive high pay bears little relation to company success. Failure also was rewarded. Some figures show that pay at the top of some of our biggest companies spiralled. For example, at BP in 2011, the lead executive earned 63 times more than the average employee. In 1979 the multiple was 16.5. In Barclays, top pay is now 75 times more than the average worker's. In 1979 it was 14.5 times (High Pay Commission, 2011).

Peter Drucker wrote (see also Chapter 10) that CEOs' earnings should not exceed 20 to 25 times their average employees' earnings, believing that larger differentials generated resentment, writing 'I'm not talking about the bitter feelings of the people on the plant floor … It's the mid-level management that is incredibly disillusioned' by king-sized CEO compensation (reported at the Davos G20 Conference 2010).

Today we have two extreme approaches to the determination of wages. At one extreme we have total transparency in which every employee can know what everyone else earns, e.g. in most public sector organizations. At the other extreme are employers who not only keep secret what they pay each employee but also make it a condition of employment that salaries are not to be discussed between staff. In some countries, Germany for example, this can be written into employment contracts. In the case of the UK the High Pay Commission found 'remuneration reports to be complex … opaque and unclear' (High Pay Commission, 2011).

If dissatisfaction is to be avoided, and if other issues such as equal pay for work of equal value disputes are to be avoided, a methodical, fair and transparent approach to the award of wages and salaries is essential for harmonious relationships to exist at all levels within an enterprise. In organizations of any reasonable size, this can probably be achieved only if the relative value of each job is recognized. To do this, a system of ranking jobs in order of importance needs to be used. It is important that a person, such as a chef, who has completed a relatively long and formal training and has acquired knowledge and skill should be paid more highly than a person whose job needs little knowledge or skill. It is simple to distinguish between jobs with skill and those without, but the problem arises when comparing jobs that are less easily differentiated; for example, when comparing those of a cook and a waiter. Both demand particular skills and knowledge but management may have to decide whether to award more, and how much, to one rather than to the other. A system of comparison that embraces all jobs within an enterprise needs to be adopted to ensure that wages are distributed fairly. Such a system, usually called 'job evaluation', provides a sound basis for comparisons to be made. Some systems attempt to be objective and analytical, whereas others are somewhat subjective, but if managed properly they can be equally successful. Job evaluation may, therefore, be defined as the process that establishes the relative value of jobs in a job hierarchy.

In essence job evaluation is concerned with internal fairness but it also has to take into account external competitiveness through 'market pricing' (see Chapter 10).

Not all employers are in favour of job evaluation. One criticism is that it evaluates a job rather than the person's contribution to the employer. This criticism can be met, however, through a well-designed combination of job evaluation and merit awards in a well-designed salary structure.

The following symptoms can indicate a need for methodical job evaluation:

1 Employees leaving because earnings are not awarded fairly and, in particular, because some newcomers earn more than long-serving employees.
2 A need to pay unexpected increases in order to retain existing employees.
3 Difficulties, due to earnings levels, in transferring and promoting employees. (This can be a common problem in promoting a single unit manager to a multi-unit management role.)
4 A need to pay extras or bonuses to get people to do what is, or should be, part of their normal job.

In order to carry out effective job evaluation, precise job descriptions and even job specifications are required because without these the comparison of jobs becomes difficult, if not meaningless. Also, because comparisons of jobs are to be made, the preparation of job descriptions must be standardized throughout the undertaking, and the actual evaluation should be conducted by one specialist or the smallest possible number of people to ensure a consistent result.

As Figure 11.1 shows, there are many different job evaluation techniques. The first type – the non-analytical – considers the whole job when jobs are being compared.

For ranking, jobs are placed in order of importance. They may then be placed in clusters of closely ranked jobs.

For grading or classification, a number of grades will have been decided upon. A typical job illustrating the grade will be chosen, known as a 'benchmark' job. All other jobs are then placed into the most appropriate grades using the benchmark job for guidance. Figure 11.2 shows a typical approach – the system devised by the Institute of Administrative Management – and demonstrates its application to jobs in the hotel and catering industry.

The other approach consists of analytical methods. Most of these involve some form of point scoring of job elements or factors such as level of responsibility (e.g. sales volumes or number of staff managed) or competencies such as technical skills needed.

Points assessment

This method allocates points for each factor of a job. The points for all factors are added up and the total indicates the job's relative position in the job hierarchy. In some cases some factors may be considered to

Title	Broad description	Advantages	Disadvantages
Non-analytical methods			
Ranking	A simple method whereby the relative importance of the total job is assessed. Jobs are put in order of importance and may then be divided into groups.	Very simple to use.	Assessors need to know all jobs in some depth.
Grading or classification	A simple method in which a grading structure indicating relative job values is designed. Each job is then placed within the most appropriate grade.	Very simple to use.	Assessors need to know all jobs in some depth. Marginal jobs may be placed in higher or lower grade because system may not be sufficiently discriminating.
Analytical methods			
Points assessment	A commonly used and very acceptable method. Factors common to most jobs in the organization are identified such as knowledge and responsibility. Maximum points are allocated to each factor weighted according to importance. Each job examined is broken into the various factors. Each factor is then awarded points between zero and the maximum. The total of points awarded will give the score for the job and thereby its standing relative to other jobs. Benchmark jobs will be used to assist in allocating points.	Simple to understand and operate.	Takes longer to implement than ranking or grading. It can lead to considerable discussion on weighting of factors.
Factor comparison	Similar in some respects to points assessment but in some cases monetary values are used instead of points. Fewer factors, also, will normally be used than in points assessment. Benchmark jobs will normally be used.	Simple to operate once it has been designed.	Difficult to arrive at monetary values.
Direct consensus method or paired comparisons	A complex technique where evaluators representing all interested parties are asked to indicate which job of a pair or which factors within pairs of jobs they consider more important. The evaluators will probably deal with several or even many jobs. The paired comparisons of all evaluators may then be fed into a computer which will produce the ranking of all jobs considered.	Reduces individual subjectivity to a minimum.	Complex, usually needs a computer.
Time span of discretion	This technique measures one factor only: the length of time in which an individual's work or decisions remain unchecked, e.g. a typist four hours, a managing director four years.	Simple, once the concept has been fully understood.	Sometimes difficult to determine true discretion span.

Figure 11.1 Job evaluation

be more important than others, so they either have a wider points range or they may be given more weighting by a multiplier. The type of factors evaluated in each job may include the following:

- *Knowledge* – This may be simple knowledge acquired in a few days or, at the other extreme, may be knowledge acquired by several years of study and application.
- *Skills* – This refers mainly to manual skills. These may be acquired within a very short period, such as the skills needed to operate a limited range of equipment, or they may take many weeks,

even months, of practice, as in the case of keyboard skills or the varied skills needed by a competent cook.

- *Responsibility* – This may be of the type in which a person makes important decisions that are not checked for a long period; alternatively they may be simple decisions that are checked immediately. This factor may include responsibility for investment, people, equipment or cash.
- *Physical demands* – Some jobs, such as cooking, are physically demanding, or they may make little physical demand, as in book-keeping or word-processing.
- *Mental demands* – All jobs, to a greater or lesser extent, make demands on a person's mental abilities including the abilities to concentrate and to apply oneself; for example, a senior receptionist's job will be much more demanding mentally than a kitchen porter's.
- *Social skills* – Some jobs require more social skills than others. A restaurant manager, for example, will require a high degree of tact and patience, whereas a chef may require fewer social skills.
- *Working conditions* – This includes physical and social inconveniences such as heat, long hours and whether one sits or stands while working. This may also take into account hazards such as risk of burns, cuts or even physical violence.

Grade	Definition	Example
A	Simple tasks requiring little training; closely supervised or controlled through self-checking	Cleaner
B	Simple jobs that consist of standard routines and require a short period of training	Room attendant
C	Some experience or aptitude needed; standardized duties; little room for initiative	Assistant waiter, Clerk
D	Considerable experience; limited degree of initiative but mostly within predetermined procedures	Receptionist
E	Technical or specialist knowledge or both; supervision of up to five other workers	Head waiter, Head hall porter
F	Technical or professional operations at intermediate membership level of a professional institute; performance or control of complex work; supervision requiring leadership skills and training of others	F & B manager, Bars manager
M1	Professional or specialized knowledge up to professional institute membership level; performance or control of work of wide complexity; management of sufficient staff to need grade F subordinates as supervisors	Hotel manager
M2	Jobs requiring the final qualification of a professional institute or university degree; regular non-routine decision making; use of judgement and initiative; assistance in policy making; management of specialist functions involving more than one level of supervision	Group human resource manager
M3	Jobs requiring the final qualification of a professional institute or university degree plus several years' experience of wide-ranging authority; performance or control of work over several functions, demanding general as well as specialist expertise and policy making at the highest level; management of a series of specialist functions where management level jobs report in for guidance, control and monitoring	Group chief executive

Acknowledgement to Institute of Administrative Management.

Figure 11.2 A job grading or classification system

Source: Based on the Institute of Administrative Management grading scheme.

In the case of a large public sector organization such as a university, excluding academic staff but including catering and other support staff, a wide range of factors may be considered including:

- communication
- liaison and networking
- managing people
- planning and managing resources
- teamwork
- initiative, problem solving and decision making
- sensory, physical and emotional demands
- work environment
- expertise.

Evaluation of these factors may then allocate jobs into around 50 different points values on a scale, in turn allocated into ten different job grades.

These examples give a broad indication of the types of factors to be considered. Others may be used and, in addition, a breakdown into sub-factors may also be desirable. The normal method of awarding points for each factor is to have a scale with benchmark jobs on it. When evaluating a particular factor of a job it will be placed at or between what appears to be the most appropriate benchmark job or jobs; i.e. in evaluating one factor, such as knowledge, the list of benchmark jobs is examined and the job being evaluated is then placed in the most appropriate position on the scale (Figure 11.3).

The knowledge required of a head waiter, for example, would fall between the station waiter and the restaurant manager in Figure 11.3, consequently being awarded about 15 points. The same procedure would then be adopted for all other factors to be evaluated. The benchmark jobs will not necessarily be the same for each factor. After this has been done for all factors, the points are totalled and the job grade should be determined by reference to a grade table such as that shown in Figure 11.4.

Points	Benchmark jobs for knowledge: maximum points – 30; minimum points – 0
30	Hotel manager
24	Front office manager
18	Restaurant manager
12	Station waiter
6	Hall porter

Figure 11.3 Example of benchmark jobs (for one factor only)

Grade	Points (Total of all factors)	Example of job
7	121–140	Chef de cuisine
6	101–120	Restaurant manager
5	81–100	Senior receptionist
4	61–80	Waiter
3	41–60	Clerk
2	21–40	Hall porter
1	0–20	Kitchen porter

Figure 11.4. Example of a grade table

Factor	Maximum points	Example evaluation of two jobs	
		Commis waiter	Restaurant manager
Knowledge	30	5	18
Skill	20	10	20
Responsibility	30	3	24
Physical demands	10	5	4
Mental demands	20	8	15
Social skills	20	12	18
Working conditions	10	5	3
Total	140	48	102

Figure 11.5 Example of a points assessment system showing the evaluation of two jobs

Figure 11.5 shows the technique applied to two jobs: a restaurant manager's and a commis waiter's. In this example the factors outlined above are used, but in designing a scheme other factors may be considered. After the points have been totalled, a look at a grade table will indicate the grades of the two jobs – refer back to Figure 11.4. The commis waiter's job, therefore, is Grade 3 and the restaurant manager's is Grade 6.

This is a very simplified example of a points assessment system. Some systems, for example in large organizations and in the public sector, may be much more complex than this, but no matter which technique is used, the principles of job evaluation are as follows:

1 Job descriptions must be precise and up to date.
2 Because wages and salaries depend on the results, evaluation must be scrupulously fair and consistent.
3 It is the job, not the job holder, that is being evaluated.

People at work tend to measure the value their employer places upon them by reference, among other things, to how much they are paid, relative both to their own colleagues and to the outside market. If they perceive their level of pay (and other conditions) as inferior to that of their colleagues and of similar workers elsewhere, the relationship with the employer may well be affected adversely. This could take a number of forms, including absenteeism, pilferage, theft and even vandalism.

Arriving at a fair system for awarding wages and salaries is not easy and too often is a matter of expediency. Too often in the hospitality industry, due largely to the large number of small businesses, wages, salaries, bonuses and other earnings are the result of expediency rather than methodical planning and application. If potential causes of dissatisfaction are to be removed it is vital to recognize the relative importance of each job and to adopt a methodical system of evaluating jobs so that wages, salaries and other earnings are fairly distributed to all.

Job evaluation in the hospitality industry

Job evaluation is commonplace in the public sector of the hospitality industry. Many jobs are evaluated using one or other of the job evaluation methods. It is also used by a number of larger operators, including some major hospitality companies, that use companies such as Hay-MSL (a specialist consultancy) to determine pay rates and scales for their managers. Otherwise job evaluation is not very common in the private sector, owing to the large number of small employers. Instead wage levels are frequently determined by expediency rather than by a methodical approach.

Further reading and references

ACAS (2010) *Job Evaluation: Considerations and Risks*, Advisory booklet, London: ACAS.

Armstrong, M. (2010) *Armstrong's Handbook of Reward Management Practice: Improving Performance through Reward*, 3rd edn, London: Kogan Page.

Armstrong, M. (2012) *A Handbook of Human Resource Management*, 12th edn, London: Kogan Page.

Armstrong, M., Brown, D. and Reilly, P. (2010) *Evidence Based Reward Management*, London: Kogan Page.

Beardwell, J. and Claydon, L. (2010) *Human Resource Management*, 6th edn, Harlow: Prentice Hall.

High Pay Commission (2011) *Cheques with Balances: Why Tackling High Pay is in the National Interest*, London: High Pay Commission.

Incomes Data Services (2010) *Job Evaluation*, HR Studies, London: Incomes Data Services.

Incomes Data Services (2010) *Pay Progression*, London: Incomes Data Services.

Lucas, R. (2004) *Employment Relations in the Hospitality and Tourism Industries*, London: Routledge.

Office of Manpower Economics and Chartered Institute of Personnel and Development (2008) *Public/ Private Approaches to Pay and Progression*. Available at: www.cipd.co.uk/surveys.

Perkins, S. J. and White, G. (2011) *Reward Management: Alternatives, Consequences and Contexts*, 2nd edn, London: Chartered Institute of Personnel and Development.

Stiglitz, J. (2011) *People Management*, London: Chartered Institute of Personnel and Development.

Torrington, D., Hall, L., Taylor, S. and Atkinso, C. (2011) *Human Resource Management*, 8th edn, Harlow: Pearson Education.

Members of the UK's Institute of Hospitality can access publications including Management Guides which summarize key information of relevance to hospitality operations (www.instituteofhospitality.org).

Members of the UK's Chartered Institute of Personnel and Development (CIPD) can access a range of materials including Fact Sheets and articles from over 300 online journal titles relevant to HR. CIPD members and *People Management* subscribers can see articles on the People Management website (www.peoplemanagement.co.uk).

Questions

1 Describe the objectives of job evaluation.

2 Describe the alternative approaches and their suitability to different types of organizations.

3 Discuss what you consider to be the most important issues in job evaluation and why.

4 Discuss in which sectors of the hospitality industry job evaluation is most likely to be found and why.

5 Evaluate the approach to setting rates of pay and other conditions used by an employer you know well.

6 Read the High Pay Commission report and discuss the principles it contains relative to hospitality companies.

CASE STUDY QUESTION – see the Lux Hotels case study Appendix 5

In this chapter key approaches to job evaluation have been described. First, discuss the reasons for adopting job evaluation and then discuss the benefits, if any, of job evaluation to Lux hotels.

Which main approach or approaches would be most suited to Lux Hotels bearing in mind that they are seeking to encourage mobility between levels of employee, their different brands and the countries where their hotels are located.

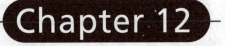

Chapter 12

Incentives

Since the economic crisis of 2008 much attention has been paid to incentive schemes, particularly those offered to top managers, and to CEOs (chief executive officers) in particular. It has been argued that many incentive schemes were the cause of the economic crisis. The incentive schemes offered reward for very short-term results, in many cases rewarding for 'non-achievement', even failure (High Pay Commission, 2011).

Some of these issues are discussed in Chapter 10. This chapter concentrates, in the main, on incentive schemes designed and operated for more junior employees.

Competition among employers to attract and motivate effective employees, and other factors, such as the nature of the taxation system, have obliged employers over the years to seek ways and means of making the total remuneration package more attractive to employees. In some cases benefits such as free health care insurance are offered, often because other competing employers do so. At the most senior levels (CEOs) a major driver of incentive schemes has been comparison with the total reward packages of other CEOs.

In other cases, incentives are offered in order to focus employees' attention on the business objectives of the employer, e.g. to support a yield management system or to increase the profitability of contracts run by a contract caterer. The CEO of Compass, the world's largest contract caterer, serving ten million meals a day, was reported to have a multi-million pound rewards package, spread over several years. For this he had to:

- tackle cost base (each 1 per cent waste of materials equals £40 million pounds)
- reduce workforce
- eliminate poor contracts
- introduce MAP (management and performance).

What motivates?

In Chapter 2 the contributions of a number of different theorists were considered. Most of these are crucially concerned with what motivates people to work. In spite of the vast body of concepts coming from people like Taylor, Mayo, McGregor, Maslow, Herzberg and Drucker, there is still no absolute consensus. Many managers still hold to the belief that money, because of what it can buy (including security and status), is a major motivator. Others tend to the more complex views of Maslow, Herzberg and others, arguing that people work for a composite package, including money, security, self-esteem, esteem of others, job satisfaction, etc. At a practical level this discussion obviously concerns the merits or otherwise of reward systems and incentive schemes.

Some people argue that employees should be given an adequate wage or salary and so long as other conditions and prospects are adequate, such as regular review of earnings and the likelihood of promotion, people will give what they consider to be a fair day's work. The prospect of incentives will not spur them to continued greater efforts. This is reflected in a statement by Jeroen van der Veer, former CEO of Royal Dutch Shell: 'You have to realise: if I had been paid 50% more, I would not have done it better. If I had been paid 50% less, then I would not have done it worse' (High Pay Commission, 2011).

Of course this is the statement of a very highly paid executive. On the other hand it is argued that incentive payments are most effective when people are dependent upon them, i.e. the nearer the basic pay is to subsistence levels, the more effective an incentive scheme. A good example is that of waiting staff who are almost totally dependent upon tips earnings.

In works of a highly creative nature the prospect of incentive payments is considered unlikely to stimulate greater creativity. There are others, however, who argue that incentives will certainly influence productivity, saying, for example, that in a selling situation the prospects of earning commission will definitely stimulate greater selling effort. It is also argued that because of the growing interdependence of working people they can no longer increase their own earnings without the involvement of their colleagues. In many cases nowadays this is true, and this is recognized in various schemes that reward teams as opposed to individuals.

In the hospitality industry, because of its nature, there are many opportunities for individuals to increase their earnings considerably – particularly in the selling areas, such as waiting, bar work, hotel reception and function catering. Within the scope of this book it is not possible to consider further the arguments for and against incentive schemes. There are innumerable examples supporting both view-points. It is intended here to look at the main forms of incentives operated in the hospitality industry, including tips, service charges, 'tronc' (a system for distributing tips, gratuities and service charges), bonuses and commissions. Other financial incentives such as profit sharing are considered in the next chapter.

In other industries other forms of incentive payments are used. These include methods such as payment by results (PBR), piece rates or measured day work, which are usually based on work measurement techniques, whereas those commonly used in the hospitality industry are more normally related to financial targets such as sales targets, occupancy rates, gross profits, turnover and control of variable costs (e.g. gas, electricity). In some cases they may be entirely discretionary.

Although tipping and the tronc were mentioned along with other forms of financial incentive, it is probably better to think of them as part of normal earnings. Financial incentives should normally stimulate and promote extra effort and/or results, whereas tips, the tronc and service charges are considered by many employees as part of normal earnings, a matter of right and something without which they could not have a reasonable living standard.

Tipping is a form of payment that originated when many workers in the old inns were not employed by the innkeeper but were retained by guests to do particular jobs such as carrying bags, cleaning garments, etc. Many consider it an anachronism in this day and age, and a view that has been expressed by many people for many years is that it needs to be eliminated as rapidly as possible. Professor Nailon of Surrey University, however, wrote in 1978 that it is not necessarily a bad practice but that it may have profound effects on interdepartmental relationships. Also it removes from management an important area of personal control by making the customer, rather than the employer, the paymaster (Nailon, 1978). Many countries, including most European countries, have tried to eliminate it by encouraging all-inclusive pricing on menus, room tariffs and other price lists. In spite of this tipping continues and will continue.

Service charges, many argue, on the other hand, are quite acceptable methods for an undertaking to use to raise revenue. In many tourism-based economies it is common to find that tariffs are inclusive of taxes and service charges, and attempts are made to eliminate tipping, although in many countries, such as France, where service charges are included, staff still expect some tip, if not the traditional 10–15 per cent. Sometimes where a service charge is included in the bill, tipping may be discouraged, and notices on bills, menus, brochures and in guest rooms discourage guests from giving tips in addition to paying the service charge.

Principles of incentive schemes

In designing an incentive scheme, whether for the hospitality industry or any other, there are several principles that should be adhered to for it to be effective in the long term:

1 The undertaking's major business objectives should be promoted and their achievement assisted by incentive payments. These payments should enable individuals to identify with the success of the undertaking; for example, if food gross profit is vital, the chef and maybe his staff as well should be rewarded for achieving gross profit targets. But only elements over which a person exerts control should be included. A chef, for example, has no control over the rent and the rates, so there is no point in including these in a scheme for the chef.
2 When an incentive scheme is to be introduced, all workers should be considered because of the effect the scheme may have on existing earnings differentials and the possibility of creating friction between staff.
3 Payments should be related to results by comparing actual performance with forecasts, targets, standards or budgets. This may be done individually or on a group basis.
4 Targets should be realistic, i.e. achievable with reasonable effort and agreed with the person or group concerned.
5 Targets should be reviewed regularly, and at least annually, so that payments are something to be earned with effort rather than something that becomes a matter of right. They should also be reviewed if circumstances change considerably; for example, if a large new office block opens next door to a snack bar, trade will probably increase greatly, through no effort of the manager. The turnover and other targets should, therefore, be reviewed at the same time, bearing in mind that extra work will be created and that wages and salaries may have to be increased.
6 An incentive scheme should be simple and clearly understood by those within the scheme.
7 Payment of the incentive should be made as near as possible to the period in which it was earned. Long delays in payment cause irritation and reduce the incentive element.
8 All elements of a scheme and any rules should be objective. Management should not incorporate discretionary rules such as 'management reserves the right to withhold payment without giving a reason'. Incentives, if earned, should be a matter of right, not for management to dispense on a discretionary basis, and the terms of the incentive scheme should become part of the contract of employment.
9 An employer's objectives, short, medium and long term, should be considered and allocated to the levels of employee who have responsibility and control, e.g.:

   • short term: junior staff and supervisors
   • medium term: departmental managers
   • long term: senior managers, e.g unit managers, area managers.

10 Finally, and importantly, account for cultural differences – some forms of incentives just do not work in some cultures.

Rewards and remuneration

Incentives are normally used to stimulate performance and particularly to increase sales and to control costs. Figures 12.1–12.3 are included as examples. Having looked at these examples, which are intended to illustrate principles only and which demonstrate that incentive schemes can be designed for many departments in an organization, it is vital to bear in mind that their introduction may have undesirable consequences which could exclude their being used; for example, the chef may well place commission above customer satisfaction and buy cheap materials or keep labour costs too low for efficient service; the receptionists may overbook (more than is desirable) and consequently lose customers for the future.

1 *Job*	Chef			
2 *Commission*	1 per cent of all 'gross profit' (for this purpose revenue less purchases and labour costs) in excess of £2,000 per week, after achieving the following targets			
3 *Targets*	1 Purchases not to exceed 45 per cent of revenue 2 Kitchen labour not to exceed 15 per cent of revenue			

4 *Example of calculation*
Period 7

Food cost	£6,000	(37.5%)	Revenue	£16,000
Labour cost	£2,200	(13.75%)		
	£8,200			
'Gross profit'	£7,800	(48.75%)		

Gross profit £7,800 – £2,000 = £5,800 x 1/100 = £58.00

Commission to be £58.00

Figure 12.1 Example of an individual incentive scheme (chef)

1 *Department*	Front Office
2 *Commission*	£120 for every 1 per cent in excess of occupancy targets, distributed to all front office staff pro rata to salaries
3 *Target*	85 per cent occupancy

4 *Examples of calculation*
Period 7
Actual occupancy 90.0% therefore 5.0 x £120 = £600 to be distributed

Salaries: Head receptionist	£14,000
2 Senior receptionists @	£13,000
2 Cashier/receptionists @	£10,000
Total salaries	£60,000
£600 commission	
£30,000 salaries =	£0.01 per £ salary

Therefore the following commissions will be paid

Head receptionist*	£14,000 x £0.01 = £140
Senior receptionists*	£13,000 x £0.01 = £130
Cashier/receptionists (part time)	£10,000 x £0.01 = £100

* live-in staff

Figure 12.2 Example of a group incentive scheme

1 Job	Restaurant manager
2 Commission	5 per cent of net profit up to budget, 10 per cent of net profit between 101 and 130 per cent of target budget, 20 per cent of net profit in excess of 130 per cent of target budget
3 Target budget	£40,000 net profit

4 Example of calculation
Year ended 31 December 2015 Actual net profit = £56,000

Commission rate	Qualifying net profit	Commission
5%	£40,000	£2,000
10%	£12,000	£1,200
20%	£4,000	£800
Total	£56,000	£4,000

Note: In this example it is interesting to note that although the top rate of commission is 20 per cent and consequently well worth striving for, the actual rate of total commission is only just over 7 per cent.

Figure 12.3 Example of an individual incentive scheme (manager)

On the other hand, from the restaurant manager's scheme it can be seen that, because the commission is related to net profit, the manager has an interest in successfully controlling all aspects of the business, including revenue, purchases, wages, variables and, of course, customer satisfaction.

In designing an incentive scheme, therefore, one has to ensure that the benefits to the individual do not stimulate the manager to take measures that may not be in the employer's interests. Incentives can cover such things as sales, gross and net profits, occupancy, average room rates, suggestion schemes, new staff introduction bonuses and new business introduction bonuses.

Financial incentives can reward individual employees or groups of employees through increased payment for their increased contribution to the enterprise. More than anything else they have to be designed with the employer's long-term objectives in mind. It was this lack of foresight that contributed, to a major extent, to the financial and economic crises of 2008 and onwards. Incentives themselves may achieve little on their own. They should be part of a comprehensive, well-balanced human resource policy that is based upon achieving the employer's main objectives, short, medium and long term.

Further reading and references

Armstrong, M. (2010) *Armstrong's Handbook of Reward Management Practice: Improving Performance through Reward*, 3rd edn, London: Kogan Page.

Armstrong, M. (2012) *A Handbook of Human Resource Management*, 12th edn, London: Kogan Page.

Armstrong, M., Brown, D. and Reilly, P. (2010) *Evidence Based Reward Management*, London: Kogan Page.

Goss-Turner, S. (2002) *Managing People in the Hospitality Industry*, 4th edn, Kingston-upon-Thames: Croner Publications.

High Pay Commission (2011) *Cheques with Balances: Why Tackling High Pay is in the National Interest*, London: High Pay Commission.

Kessler, I. (2001) 'Reward system choices', in Storey, J. (ed.) *Human Resource Management – A Critical Text*, 2nd edn, London: Thomson Learning.

Langley, A. (2008) *Employee Reward Structures*, 3rd edn, London: Spiramus Press.

Nailon, P. (1978) *HCIMA Review*, 2(4), London.

Perkins, S. J. and White, G. (2011) *Reward Management: Alternatives, Consequences and Contexts*, 2nd edn, London: Chartered Institute of Personnel and Development.

Storey, J. (ed.) (2007) *Human Resource Management – A Critical Text*, 3rd edn, London: Thomson Learning.

Torrington, D., Hall, L., Taylor, S. and Atkinson, C. (2011) *Human Resource Management*, 8th edn, Harlow: Pearson Education.

Members of the UK's Institute of Hospitality can access publications including Management Guides which summarize key information of relevance to hospitality operations (www.instituteofhospitality.org).

Members of the UK's Chartered Institute of Personnel and Development (CIPD) can access a range of materials including Fact Sheets and articles from over 300 online journal titles relevant to HR. CIPD members and *People Management* subscribers can see articles on the People Management website (www.peoplemanagement.co.uk).

Questions

1 Describe the objectives of incentive schemes and the various alternatives in regular use.

2 Discuss which you consider to be the most important principles if incentive schemes are to be effective. What do you understand by 'effective'?

3 Identify an operative job, a supervisory job, a departmental job and a unit manager's job. Design incentive schemes for each.

4 Discuss what external factors influence the nature of incentive schemes.

5 Discuss the relationship between incentive schemes and other elements of reward packages.

6 Discuss the role played by wages, salaries and incentives in implementing an employer's human resource policy.

7 Evaluate the approach to incentive schemes used by an employer you know well.

CASE STUDY QUESTION – see the Lux Hotels case study Appendix 5

In this chapter key approaches to incentives have been described. What are Lux Hotels' key objectives and how can the company focus employees' attention on these company's key objectives. Consider the main different levels of employee including hotel managers, supervisors and key operative staff such as receptionists, giving reasons for your recommendation for each different level.

Chapter 13

Employee benefits

Employee benefits, sometimes also known as fringe benefits, benefits in kind, perquisites, 'perqs' or 'perks', are various non-wage compensations provided in addition to normal earnings. These have to be seen in conjunction with other rewards such as salaries and incentive payments.

The range, variety and importance of such benefits in employment policies include benefits that may attract little or no tax, such as meals, and deferred earnings such as pensions. Employee benefits have considerable value to many employers in that they represent a form of reward that does not necessarily have progressive or long-term effects in the way that a salary increase does. A salary increase is usually for all time. It affects all future settlements because most settlements are usually percentage based. Also a salary is the basis for settlements such as redundancy and separation payments which have grown in recent years.

The total list of benefits offered today is considerable and is continually growing as employers look for new ways to woo employees. For the purposes of this chapter employee benefits have been divided simply into three main types: financial, part-financial and non-financial. There is, of course, overlap between these three main types

- Financial benefits include commissions, bonuses, profit sharing, share options.
- Part-financial benefits include pensions, meals, cars, subscriptions.
- Non-financial benefits include holidays, sick pay, medical insurance.

See Figure 13.1 for a list of employee benefits selected from various companies' information.

In considering employee benefits it is vital to recognize that what may be considered an 'incentive' or 'motivator' today may lose its motivating effect with time. This may be because what is offered by only one or two employers to start with will be offered by many employers as they follow suit. Alternatively, what may have been offered as a reward for exceptional services one year becomes expected and a 'matter of right' within the next two or three years.

Having made this point, it is necessary to bear in mind also that, although the presence of many employee benefits in a rewards package may not be a positive incentive to work harder or to perform better, the absence of employee benefits, on the other hand, may be a disincentive and will put an employer at a disadvantage in recruiting or retaining staff.

Staff restaurant, free meals	Social and sports clubs, cinema and
Luncheon vouchers	theatre passes
Accommodation	Company newspaper, staff newspaper
Staff hostel	Discount buying
Assistance with finding	Discounted holidays
accommodation	Familiarization weekends
Training and	Discounted accommodation, meals in
educational fees	company hotels or restaurants
Use of customers' facilities	Savings schemes
Free uniform, laundry	House purchase assistance
services	Relocation grants
Paid holidays in excess of	Long service awards
statutory minima	Christmas bonus, birthday gift/cards
Pension scheme, sickness	Suggestion bonus
leave	Language proficiency
Company car – personal use,	Employee introduction bonus
fuel for private use	Jury service pay
Mobile phone, personal use	Share option scheme
Maternity leave, paternity	Volunteer reserve paid time off
leave	Time off for charitable works
Medical services, private	
medical insurance	

Figure 13.1 Some employee benefits offered in the industry

Source: Company induction materials.

In some cases, offering high salaries, commissions or bonuses may compensate for lack of other employee benefits, but owing to the fact that non-cash benefits may be taxed lightly or not at all, these have been playing a bigger part in employee compensation in recent years. They can add another 25 per cent to the total payroll costs but a similar increase to salaries, due to personal tax, would almost certainly not enable employees to purchase the same type of benefits or to enjoy the same standard of living.

Employee benefit programmes should be designed to further the employer's objectives and should, in particular, be designed to assist in human resource planning and management. Where, for example, it is desirable to have a stable, mature management team providing plenty of continuity, an incremental salary scheme, generous pension and life assurance scheme, along with loan facilities (e.g. for house purchase, among other things) will assist in retaining the management team. On the other hand a dynamic young organization may want a fairly steady flow of 'high flyers', the majority of whom will not want to stay for long because there will not be room for all of them. In this case high salaries and good incentives payments will be preferable, as this type of person may not be interested in benefits such as pensions. The differing needs of employers along with pressures exerted by competing organizations and by statutory requirements will all help to dictate what type of employee benefits programme needs to be offered. There are many different components and the permutations can be numerous. Increasingly, employee benefits may be elements of a 'flexible' benefits scheme, which may consist of core benefits, plus some choice of benefits (a la carte!).

Choice, in turn, can be limited or very open. In some cases, for example, employees may be able to choose the type of car they would like, up to a limit (a user-chooser scheme). In a more open scheme an employee may be able to exchange the car benefit for an equivalent cash addition to salary. Such schemes recognize that each employee may have particular needs, which may vary at different points in their career.

Financial benefits

Financial benefits were covered in more detail in Chapter 12; as was said there, they should be directly related, as far as possible, to measurable performance. Discretionary handouts have little positive motivational value long term.

Profit sharing

Profit-sharing schemes, as the name implies, distribute some share of profit to all or selected employees. Some profit-sharing schemes may not be justified directly on individual motivational grounds. This is because individuals do not receive a share of profit related to their own efforts, and sometimes because these awards may come to be expected as a matter of right. On the other hand such schemes may contribute to developing a team spirit.

Share option schemes

These enable employees to buy options, usually at favourable prices, on company shares with loans provided by the employer. The better the company performs, the more the value of the shares increases. These schemes are strictly controlled by law; for example, they do not allow an employee to sell the shares until a certain number of years have elapsed. Once reserved for executives only, many organizations in the service sector are now offering such schemes to all staff with a certain length of service, full and part time. The supermarket chain Asda has had considerable success with its scheme and attributes a lowering of labour turnover to the scheme and the way it ties staff in to remaining with the company for a specified number of years, at least three years in the case of Asda. Of course such schemes are only of real motivational value if the company is successful and its share price improves.

Part-financial benefits

There are many benefits which may be awarded which can be described as partly financial. These are benefits that the employee cannot normally dispose of in cash or kind, but which enable him or her either to avoid spending personal resources on these benefits or to enjoy a higher standard of living. These benefits include such things as pensions (sometimes described as deferred earnings) and life assurance schemes, company cars, mobile phones, expense accounts. The major part-financial benefits are as follows.

Pensions

Pension arrangements throughout advanced nations are undergoing significant changes, due mainly to demographic changes such as increased longevity.

In the UK the best schemes, known as 'final salary' schemes, grant a percentage of final salary (sometimes the average of the last few years) for each year's service, thereby enabling a person with forty or more years' service to retire on forty-sixtieths (or two-thirds of final salary), the maximum pension currently permissible. Provision is also normally made for a person's dependents, whether he or she dies in service or in retirement. Some schemes are index linked; some are not.

Such schemes, as stated above, are being revised largely because of increased longevity and the consequent costs. They are being replaced by 'average earnings schemes', in which the pension is based on the employee's work lifetime average annual earnings, and not on final salary. In some other countries, France for example, state pension schemes largely replace private company pension schemes.

One of the benefits to employers of comprehensive pension schemes is that they enable employers to retire their older employees, particularly for health reasons, replacing them by younger people, knowing that the older ones will be provided for in retirement. This is assisted by some countries, again France as an example, obliging most working people to retire at a specific age such as 65.

Life insurances

In itself this is hardly a benefit that will persuade a person to join one employer rather than another. From the employer's point of view, however, the major value is that it provides for the dependents of employees who die in service. Without this provision the employer may feel that there is a moral, if not a legal, responsibility to look after an employee's dependents, particularly if that person dies in the course of work. If no insurance is provided, some other provision may have to be made on a discretionary basis and, where large numbers of people are employed, cases may be treated inconsistently. Also, the burden may fall more heavily in one year rather than another and, worst of all, if the employer goes out of business the dependents of ex-employees may be completely un-provided for.

Company cars

Generally speaking, these are provided for one of two reasons. First, because an employee needs a car in order to do the job. This would include people such as regional or area managers, marketing and training staff, and audit staff. Second, cars are provided to improve a person's standard of living without incurring the full tax liability that paying an equivalent cash amount would impose.

The provision of company cars is a highly contentious benefit, however, for reasons such as these:

1 Cars are very nearly cash equivalent and therefore if a car is provided to one employee in a particular job grade because it is needed, another employee of similar grade but who does not need or receive a car may well expect a cash equivalent.
2 Cars are status symbols both within the organization and within the community at large and wherever status is concerned people are very sensitive and often irrational.

House purchasing

Purchasing a house is usually the biggest investment that a person ever makes and often moving house is one of the biggest obstacles to employee mobility. (The fact that labour mobility in the hospitality industry is high while home ownership by many of the industry's employees is relatively low is probably not unrelated.) By helping employees to buy a house, employers can increase the stability of their labour force. At the top of the scale this assistance can take the form of soft (cheap) loans, but, more practically, it can be confined to the employer acting as guarantor or negotiating favourable rates for employees with one of their banks or insurance providers.

Relocation expenses

These payments are intended to indemnify an employee for the cost incurred in moving home when being appointed, transferred or promoted by the employer. The amount allowed should be such that the employee is no worse off financially as a direct result of moving house. The expenses included in this, however, can be extensive, including estate agent costs, legal fees, furniture removal, new school uniforms, temporary accommodation, etc. In multinational companies such expenses may be considerable.

These are the major part-financial employee benefits offered by many employers. There are many others as well which enable employees to enjoy a better standard of living and these include advantageous purchasing of food and beverages, insurance, furniture, etc. These can all be arranged through the employer's own suppliers or agents.

Non-financial benefits

Although the main benefits in this category can cost the employer considerable sums of money, they do not normally provide employees with any direct financial advantages. Instead they afford employees other benefits such as a degree of security or more time for leisure.

Paid holidays

Paid holidays can be used as a stimulus to labour stability; for example, extra days over the statutory minimum can be granted after a certain number of years' service.

Sick pay schemes

As with several other conditions of employment, details of pay during sickness have to be entered into the statement of conditions of employment. This is required by employment legislation (see Chapter 16) and, in the absence of such details, an employer may have to pay a sick employee the full wage or salary until dismissal of the employee after giving full notice of termination.

It is for this reason, as well as for normal employee relations considerations, that employers should formulate a sick pay policy that is consistent with their human resource management practices and which is affordable. It is important to recognize that in some employment situations sickness leave, with pay, can increase considerably the incidence of absence. This appears to be particularly so in the public sector, where sick leave ('sickies') may be seen as another form of holiday entitlement.

Statutory rights

In most developed nations governments create certain rights to time off and pay in the case of holidays, sickness, maternity and paternity. In the UK such rights may be determined by European Union regulations and directives. Many employers offer conditions additional to the minima laid down by legislation.

Private medical treatment

Private medical treatment is one particular employee benefit that is being granted to many employees these days. The direct advantage to the company is that employees can be treated at a time convenient to the company and not when it is convenient to health services. This is particularly appropriate for key members of staff. Sometimes the cover provided by the company includes employees' family as well.

Some employers may feel it is too expensive or even inappropriate to pay for this service, but even so employers can arrange 'group rates' and monthly deductions of premiums from salaries, enabling their employees to benefit from preferential rates at no cost to the employer. A combination of these two methods can be adopted in which senior employees are paid for by the company and the remainder of the employees have the option of participating in the group scheme. The Institute of Hospitality has negotiated a group rate with health insurance providers for members who may not have the benefit of a company scheme.

Tax pitfalls

It should be noted that although some employee benefits may offer tax advantages this is not always the case. The provision of company cars and fuel for private use creates tax liabilities. Various incentives such as Christmas parties and foreign trips can catch the unwary. It is for the employer to account for any tax due on any employee benefits that are taxable.

This chapter has dealt with the major benefits that can be offered to employees. Many companies will offer some of these, some will offer none. Employees will not qualify for all such benefits automatically. Some benefits should be offered as incentives to stay with the organization and to seek promotion; therefore they may be granted only for service and seniority. On the other hand certain benefits may be offered to all employees upon joining or shortly after joining, for example, discounted purchasing facilities.

Employee benefits play a vital part in an employer's human resource policy, since the nature of all the benefits offered influences considerably the type of employees who will be attracted to the employer and who will stay. And since the cost of employee benefits can add significantly to the payroll cost, it is essential that the range of benefits offered and their likely effects are planned within the overall business strategy.

Further reading and references

Armstrong, M. (2012) *A Handbook of Human Resource Management*, 12th edn, London: Kogan Page.

Armstrong, M., Brown, D. and Reilly, P. (2010) *Evidence Based Reward Management*, London: Kogan Page.

Beardwell, I., Holden, L. and Claydon, T. (2004) *Human Resource Management – A Contemporary Approach*, 4th edn, Harlow: Prentice Hall.

High Pay Commission (2011) *Cheques with Balances: Why Tackling High Pay Is in the National Interest*, London: High Pay Commission.

Kessler, I. (2001) 'Reward system choices', in Storey, J. (ed.) *Human Resource Management – A Critical Text*, 2nd edn, London: Thomson Learning.

Torrington, D., Hall, L., Taylor, S. and Atkinson, C. (2011) *Human Resource Management*, 8th edn, Harlow: Pearson Education.

Members of the UK's Institute of Hospitality can access publications including Management Guides which summarize key information of relevance to hospitality operations (www.instituteofhospitality.org).

Members of the UK's Chartered Institute of Personnel and Development (CIPD) can access a range of materials including Fact Sheets and articles from over 300 online journal titles relevant to HR. CIPD members and *People Management* subscribers can see articles on the People Management website (www.peoplemanagement.co.uk).

Questions

1   Describe the objectives of employee benefits schemes and the various alternatives in regular use.

2   Discuss which you consider to be the most important principles for employee benefits to be effective. What do you understand by 'effective' in this context?

3   Discuss what external factors influence the nature of employee benefits.

4   Discuss the relationship between employee benefits, incentive schemes and alternative methods of wage and salary administration.

5   Discuss the role played by employee benefits, wages and/or salaries and incentives in implementing an employer's human resource policy.

6   Evaluate the approach to employee benefits used by an employer you know well.

CASE STUDY QUESTION – see the Lux Hotels case study Appendix 5

In this chapter key approaches to employee benefits have been described. What are Lux Hotels key HR objectives? Discuss the role of employee benefits in helping to achieve these HR objectives. Now, consider the main different levels of employee including hotel managers, supervisors and key operative staff such as receptionists and make recommendations concerning key employment benefits, giving reasons for your recommendation for each different level. Would these be the same for all the countries where Lux Hotels operates?

Part 5

The employment relationship

Chapter 14

Labour turnover and workforce stability

The issue of unacceptably high rates of labour turnover within the hospitality industry has been a recurring theme in this book in terms of the detriment to successful human resource management caused by the lack of workforce stability created by frequent incidence of labour turnover. Indeed, the challenge to retain more skilled employees within the industry has been a much-researched topic within every report or study conducted into the hospitality workforce characteristics, not just in the UK, but world-wide (see Lucas, 2004: 32–34). Too often, the hospitality and tourism sectors have topped the 'league table' of labour turnover rates. However, there are reasons to be more cheerful than in the last edition of this book, when it was reported that the industry norm in 2000 was 48 per cent per annum (according to government statistics) and this was compared to a 2003 report by the CIPD that the UK's national, all-sector average was 16 per cent per annum. More recently, however, the hospitality industry labour turnover rate for the UK industry has been reported as declining to 31 per cent in 2009 and down again to 23 per cent in 2011 (People 1st, 2011: 62).

It is wise to note that the recent lower levels of turnover have been recorded during a time of deep economic recession and it would be foolish to conclude that the challenge is on its way to being resolved, as the figure is still well above those of other economic sectors. Also, the bare statistics do not demonstrate the real difficulty that employers are still reporting in terms of retaining the most skilled staff and the further difficulty in finding their replacements when they do move on to pastures new. There are also sectoral statistical differences, as highlighted in Figure 14.1.

Furthermore, the survey of hospitality employers revealed a strong belief that the industry was still relying too heavily on transient employees, workers such as students and international 'tourist-workers', who fund their travels by getting short-term jobs in hotels, pubs and restaurants. This practice appears necessary because the employers just cannot recruit and retain sufficient local staff. It also contributes to the systemic high levels of employee turnover, and, more insidiously, may lead to a lack of effort to train such staff with a resultant impact on the quality of customer service. The responses of hospitality employers are summarized by sectors in Figure 14.2, illustrating the strength of feeling about the over-reliance on transient workers.

The extent of the challenge has inevitably led to a significant amount of research into the causes and impacts of high levels of labour turnover, much of the discussion debating the disadvantages and dysfunctionality of such levels. There are also pertinent research notes about the potential advantages of turnover at a healthy level, such as skills development, labour market regeneration and the 'fresh blood' argument. This chapter will consider the wider perspectives regarding workforce stability by

Industry	Turnover (%)
Pubs, bars and nightclubs	31
Events	31
Visitor attractions	29
Restaurants	26
Hotels	25
Travel and tourist services	16
Self-catering accommodation, holiday parks and hostels	12
Gambling	11
Food and service management	9

Figure 14.1 Labour turnover rates by industry sector
Source: People 1st, 2011.

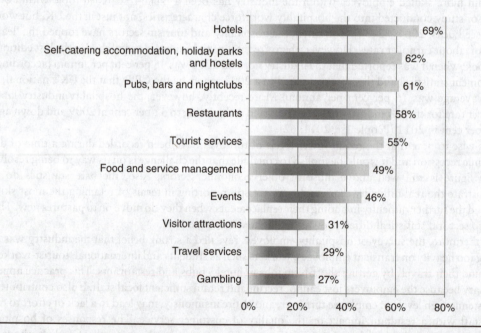

Figure 14.2 Proportion of businesses who believe the reliance on transient workers is too high
Source: People 1st, 2011.

reference to labour turnover theory and also more recent innovative research connected with organizational culture and emotional labour concepts.

Labour turnover theory

Consideration of labour turnover within the employment context of service work in the hospitality industry needs to be informed by an understanding of the phenomenon of labour turnover. Given the potential impact of labour turnover on organizational effectiveness, it is not surprising that there has been a long and abundant history of research concerning this phenomenon (e.g. Hom and Griffeth, 1995; Morrell *et al.*, 2001, 2004; Davidson *et al.*, 2010). The incidence and nature of labour turnover needs to be analysed, so that action may be taken to influence the turnover and its potential impacts on key result areas such as recruitment and training costs, on overall profitability and service quality levels. Labour turnover is a key measure or index for the success of an organization's human resource management practices but also of the organization as a whole and its image as an employer of choice.

From a review of research output on labour turnover for this chapter, four distinct approaches have been identified. First, as indicated above, there is some consideration of whether or not labour turnover is avoidable in such a diverse industry and workforce, whether or not it is detrimental, considering the positive as well as the negative effects of turnover (Deery and Shaw, 1997). Whilst the negativity of high turnover dominates research findings and consultancy reports, there is also recognition that some positive effects can be gained by a degree of mobility in the labour force, by a surge of fresh energy, enthusiasm and ideas.

A second approach is to consider employee turnover as a matter connected to the prevailing labour market, an essentially economic analysis, concerned with assessing the relevant supply of labour, the current demand for labour and skills, local employment and unemployment trends and wage levels (Hom and Griffeth, 1995). This approach is concerned with modelling the labour market and assessing the predictability of labour turnover. Much of the hospitality industry is particularly susceptible to local economic trends as exemplified by pubs and restaurants where local people will spend much more of the disposable income on eating out and other hospitality events in times of job security and prosperity. The industry needs to be aware of local trends in employment and be ready to compete with the terms and conditions of other, perhaps new, businesses in the area.

A third framework for understanding labour turnover is more concerned with the variables within the firm itself, and with the employee's intentions and decisions over staying or leaving their job. It is about how an employee feels about their job and whether or not they want to stay or leave. It is more concerned with psychological matters and individual intention rather than the harder, economic and labour market issues. These variables include the level of satisfaction experienced within the hospitality job (Yang, 2008); the 'fit' between the organization and its values, with the behaviour and the individual's personal values, and the employee's reaction to the firm's treatment of them (Bellou, 2009); and the employee's personal commitment and strength of belonging to the company (Kuvaas, 2007). This approach stresses the fact that people stay in their jobs not just because of wage or salary, but because of factors such as loyalty to colleagues, work group affiliations and positive worker relationships.

A fourth approach links labour turnover to workplace or organizational culture (Deery and Shaw, 1999), concerned with the development of shared understandings and shared values and beliefs amongst the employees, supported appropriately by the culture of the organization itself. Deery and Shaw (1997: 378), from research within the hotel sector, develop the concept of a labour turnover culture as being 'a set of shared understandings about the legitimacy of leaving an organization'. This reinforces a degree of compatibility between the labour turnover culture idea and the wider psychological school of labour turnover theory outlined above.

This psychological school places emphasis on the organization in terms of its characteristics such as goals, values and expectations, and also on the individual in terms of the personal factors that have resulted in their own values and thus their expectations of work and the organization. The favourable meeting of these characteristics leads to job satisfaction, employee decision making over whether to stay or leave the employment, and therefore to the level of commitment. The level of affective commitment has been found to be especially significant in its potential for predicting labour turnover (Meyer *et al.*, 2002; Shore *et al.*, 2006; Kuvaas, 2007).

Turnover culture

The turnover culture construct proposed by Deery and Shaw (1997, 1999) is based on their research in the Australian hotel industry, and on an amalgamation of two sets of research output and concepts, namely organizational culture and labour turnover. They isolated variables that gave credence to their initial notion that, 'an organizational turnover culture would encourage employee intentions to leave the organization' (1997: 380). They discovered hotel managers and employees who coexisted within an organization culture that basically 'expected' employees to be in their job for a short period of time, a situation where it was the norm to be dissatisfied and therefore leave. After a time, managers may come to accept this situation as inevitable, and (even subconsciously) reduce their commitment to induction and training programmes and other associated activities, and related to the costs of taking on new employees. The performance and commitment of these employees is likely to be inadequate, they achieve little satisfaction and therefore soon begin to intend to find a better, more satisfying role somewhere else. A vicious cycle has become firmly established.

Deery and Shaw (1997, 1999) stress the importance of small work group dynamics and how such groups influence the values and assumptions of employees, particularly new employees. They suggest that the precursors to an employee determining to find a new job are connected with the culture of the organization and the work group. They develop connections with the concept of absenteeism and absence culture, and its inference that it is 'legitimate' to be absent from time to time, just as it might be 'legitimate' to seek another job. Their research also notes the importance of the compatibility between the individual and the organization, declaring that 'employees who do not fit the organization's task or cultural requirements will have reduced satisfaction and commitment and be more likely to leave the organization' (1997: 379).

The important conclusions to this hotels-based study by Deery and Shaw are that a turnover culture does indeed exist, but also that it has two versions, as a positive turnover culture and a negative turnover culture. The positive version emphasizes an enthusiastic work-orientation (a 'work culture' in their term), the employee satisfied and committed to stay. Ironically this might also lead to a 'high-flying' employee leaving, but for positive reasons, to pursue career development elsewhere. A hotel or restaurant chain may well still retain that talented employee by internally promoting to another unit in the group, and developing their career within the wider organization. The negative turnover culture is directly connected with an employee's dissatisfaction with the current job, where the employee is leaving to get away from the current role, organization and possibly the sector. This decision to leave is not born out of a positive perspective and outlook (that a better job is in prospect) but rather out of a negative determination that the employee needs to leave because of factors such as a lack of 'fit' between personal and organizational values, or the stress of the current job, the perceived lack of organizational support and perhaps because the supervisory management is considered to be ineffective.

Acknowledging the turnover culture concept, Rowley and Purcell (2001) prefer to consider the 'push' and 'pull' factors in terms of the causes of high labour turnover rates revealed in their study of the hospitality industry. Rowley and Purcell consider that positive turnover culture or 'pull' factors might be the availability of mobility and career progression within the sector, whereas negative turnover culture factors, the 'push' factors, include stress, burnout, false expectations and poor management practices (2001: 166). Critical findings from their research included the significance of management's understanding of 'emotional labour' issues, which will be considered later in this chapter, linked to stress and pressure on the emotions of a hospitality worker. Rowley and Purcell suggested that labour turnover was minimized within a supportive culture, where staff training and development were given high priority, where managers 'inculcated a sense of value and organisational membership among their staff' (2001: 183).

Labour turnover and the hospitality industry

The preoccupation with labour turnover of many HR managers and researchers within the hospitality field is testament to its continual significance within the sector as compared with other industrial sectors. Such turnover also mitigates against a cohesive culture, as a plentiful supply of employees 'come and go' in a negative turnover culture; as work groups regularly change membership; and as managers come to see training as a waste of time and money for staff with limited expected length of service, a factor particularly noted within the pubs and bars of the licensed retail sector (Pratten and Curtis, 2002).

The causes of labour turnover within the hospitality industry have been extensively reviewed in sector-specific HRM literature (Rowley and Purcell, 2001; Nickson, 2007) and the real cost (direct and indirect) of such turnover frequently estimated (Lashley, 1999). Such persistent high rates of labour turnover are deeply concerning for a sector where service efficiency, effectiveness and service quality are deemed to be such critical, competitive factors. It has been argued, as noted above, that there may be some benefits to high labour turnover, an almost natural way of adjusting hospitality employment levels or benefiting from an influx of new ideas, that such labour market mobility assists skills development. Such possible benefits to hospitality businesses are generally considered of marginal significance compared to the instability created by high turnover levels (Lashley, 1999). One is left with the notion of an industry seeking 'acceptable' levels of turnover, due to its fragmented and transient workforce demographics and characteristics, levels that do not affect detrimentally the necessary standards of product and customer service.

The causes of high labour turnover within the hospitality industry and the service sector in general have been analysed from a variety of disciplines and perspectives. Earlier studies tended to highlight 'traditional' causal factors such as poor pay and conditions, long hours, ineffective training, a lack of in-company development in terms of promotional opportunities, and also the general stressfulness and pressures of service encounter work. These factors may impact negatively upon employee satisfaction in the job, as well as the employee's commitment to the organization (see Riley et al., 1998).

There is also an additional complexity in terms of different patterns of labour turnover within different hospitality sectors and within different job categories and occupations, as exemplified by the statistics in Figure 14.1. For example, in a study of the luxury restaurant sector, Kelliher and Perrett (2001) found that there was lower labour turnover within the core, committed employees and much higher turnover in the staff that were part-timers and casuals; they also assessed lower turnover in the kitchen than in food service, particularly noting that chefs tended to leave their current job in a more planned and strategic manner, aiming for personal and professional skills development with the possibility of learning from other renowned chefs. Turnover patterns may also vary with the nature, size and market segment of the business, as noted in Lynn's (2002) study of US restaurants, where high sales/ high volume restaurants with high labour turnover rates were particularly at risk of declining service standards and low customer satisfaction. This was much less prevalent in low volume and smaller, less complex businesses, where existing staff and supervisors were able to deal more effectively with short-term staffing shortages.

Similarly, high volume licensed retail outlets operated by the large national pub chains in the UK, those often most bound to corporate strategies and branding, experience high turnover rates. Lashley and Rowson (2000) emphasize the stress associated with this type of bar work, hurried recruitment and training leading to early uncertainty for the new recruit in terms of their skills and confidence with colleagues and customers. Lashley and Best (2002) highlight the influence of poor staff induction programmes, often rushed and ineffective, sometimes non-existent due to the high staff turnover that has itself caused the hurried and less discerning recruitment process. The significance of staff induction (sometimes referred to as 'socialization') and initial training has also been noted within the sector by Seymour and Sandiford (2005) and Yang (2008).

Emotional labour and labour turnover

The emotional challenge of service work in general, and the hospitality industry specifically, has been increasingly seen as a reason for serious worker dissatisfaction, high absenteeism and high labour turnover within service sectors where so-called 'emotional labour' is paramount (Mann, 1997, 2007). The concept of emotional labour came to prominence with the work of Arlie Russell Hochschild and her 1983 publication, *The Managed Heart*. Hochschild professed that service workers, notably airline cabin crew in her own primary research, were required to conform to very prescribed displays and behaviours as laid down by the organizational or occupational cultures and norms, but that often such conformity clashes with the worker's own inner emotions and feelings. Hochschild's thesis is that such a 'clash' leads to inner conflict and emotional difficulties. The hotel receptionist may have personal difficulties, ill-health, perhaps fatigue, but when they go on duty they are expected to smile, be welcoming to every guest, display all the emotions of being caring and happy, and to hide their true, inner emotions and feelings.

Such acting out of emotions within the workplace might be skilfully contrived ('surface') or a more deeply felt response, induced by empathy and the deliberate marshalling of appropriate inner feelings. Some hospitality employees may find satisfaction in successfully facing the challenge of emotional labour, placating the difficult and complaining customer for example, by skilful behavioural application. The benefit of 'being yourself' and gaining satisfaction within emotionally demanding service jobs is attracting considerable recent scholastic attention, as in Seymour and Sandiford (2005) and later in a special edition of the journal *Employee Relations* (e.g. Bolton and Houlihan, 2009). It is critical that managers fully understand this area and adopt training and supervisory approaches that support the employees in this very real challenge. Other positive aspects in learning to cope with emotional labour consequences have also been cited as an increased solidarity of the work group (Korczynski, 2003), the need to promote mutual support and empathy between colleagues, as well as managerial approaches to ensuring staff take sufficient breaks, have access to proper relaxation areas, even have specific places to let off steam and vent frustrations (see also Noon and Blyton, 2007: 201).

The ability of hospitality organizations to cope effectively with emotional labour tensions and stress and the other challenges to service workers are frequently seen as an HRM responsibility, while Seymour and Sandiford (2005: 554) confirmed that the multi-site, branded chains, such as national pub companies, were most likely to give formal training to staff in such matters as interpersonal skills, behavioural skills and customer care. These possible remedies are all focused on the ultimate aim of retaining the most skilled and competent workers within the industry, workers who will delight the customers and make a fundamental contribution to the overall commercial success of the business.

Managing and monitoring labour turnover

From the overview of issues and thinking about the phenomenon of labour turnover, it is now necessary to consider the practical management and analysis of specific labour turnover trends at unit level. In order to understand and control labour turnover and employee retention levels, it is important to have an in-depth

Sampled departments	Two large London hotels		Medium-sized county town hotel
	A	B	
Kitchens	140%	80%	47%
Wash-up, porters	550%	135%	
Coffee shop	125%	100%	17%
Hall porters	68%	105%	0%
Housekeeping	150%	146%	28%
Weighted average *all* departments	110%	105%	40%

Figure 14.3: Labour turnover in three hotels

analysis of the turnover rates not only at unit level, but also by department (as illustrated in Figure 14.3). This enables managers to explore any particular reasons for disparity in labour turnover rates across different departments, and whether there are management interventions that can be introduced by departmental heads and managers to tackle a specific problem area. The organizational structure of many hospitality businesses, especially larger hotels for example, mean that the overall figure for labour turnover may mask specific 'hotspots' of very high turnover when these departments are compared with others that perhaps have much less of a problem. Reasons for leaving are also an important element of this analysis and HR systems such as exit interviews for leavers must be considered so that some accurate data are available, and that actions are not just taken on hunches and departmental anecdotes.

There is also a means of analysis based on the 'survival curve', a means of identifying when labour turnover is most critical, mapping the leavers against a time continuum. This may help to answer questions such as: Is labour turnover occurring during the early induction period, or in the subsequent settling-in period of on-the-job training, or at some critical point after job training when staff lose motivation and satisfaction with their work? Such an analysis (see Figure 14.4) can indicate causes such

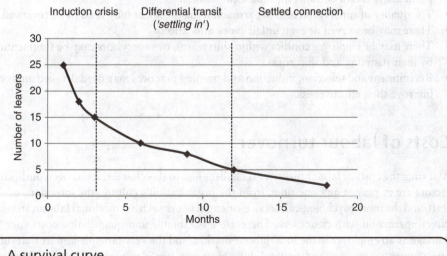

Figure 14.4 A survival curve

169

```
Codes

 1 Another job                      11 Retirement
 2 Returned to college or school    12 Failure to return after leave of absence*
 3 Medical reasons                  13 Conclusion of temporary employment*
 4 Marriage                         14 Reduction of labour force*
 5 Relocation                       15 Unsatisfactory performance*
 6 Dissatisfaction with wages       16 Misconduct*
 7 Undisclosed personal reasons     17 Gross misconduct*
 8 Resigned without notice          18 Absenteeism*
 9 Dissatisfaction with work        19 Permanent disability*
10 Dissatisfaction with conditions  20 Death*

* Involuntary leavers
```

Figure 14.5 An analysis by code of reasons for leaving

as poor induction, ineffective skills training, poor supervision or incompetent management. Whilst labour turnover is analysed both by department and by length of service, the actual reasons for employees leaving needs full understanding and recording. Some employers, perhaps those within a long-standing negative turnover culture as outlined earlier, do little or nothing about such an analysis, whereas others obtain very detailed information. Figure 14.5 shows how one fast food company analyses employee reasons for leaving.

In possession of such data, management may then be in a better position to consider changes and improvements to management and supervisory practices and procedures in order to reduce labour turnover, with the larger organizations involving the HRM team in advising on such changes. Action may be required within the following categories:

- Wages and salaries may have fallen behind the rates offered by competitors in the local labour market.
- Better terms and conditions may be prevalent within the employment contracts of competitors, particularly recent entrants into the local market.
- The quality of supervision and departmental management may need to be reviewed.
- There may be uneven or even unfair work allocation.
- There may be employee conflict within shift teams, or supervisors may be fragmenting settled teams by their rostering and shift rotas.
- Recruitment and selection, induction and training practices may need detailed analysis and review to improve their effectiveness.

Costs of labour turnover

Assessing the costs of labour turnover is challenging. In this chapter, it has been outlined just how many factors are in play at any one time, from the organization's culture, the intentions and perceptions of staff, and the more psychological, service-oriented issues such as emotional labour, stress and pressure of direct interaction with customers. There are less tangible and quantifiable costs such as reputational damage as an employer in the local labour market, and the very tangible impact that turnover can have on commercial success and profitability. However, the day-to-day financial data and commercial implications of high labour turnover and workforce instability can be useful tools in the manager's toolbox for illustrating to departmental managers that this is not something just to accept and at which to shrug their supervisory shoulders (the negative turnover culture reaction). Major costs can be assessed and analysed as some examples below indicate:

- the costs associated with termination of employment such as HR administration, payroll administration, exit interviewing
- costs associated with replacement, including direct costs such as advertising, recruitment, selection processes which involve application assessment, shortlisting of candidates, selection interviews and possibly psychometric testing costs, online applications and assessment costs, agency commission perhaps, possibly travel expenses
- costs associated with transition, direct and indirect costs such as relief cover and overtime payments, training costs, low productivity during training, possible wastage, more time invested in induction and orientation activities
- costs of an indirect nature, such as HR, line management and supervisory time dedicated to recruitment, selection and induction/training activities
- and the potential loss in customer satisfaction and repeat business and therefore loss of sales and profitability.

Cultural alignment and labour turnover

The author's research within the UK's licensed retail sector, particularly the large multi-brand pub chains, provides a new framework for gaining insight into the relationship between organizational culture and labour turnover intentions within the hospitality industry (Goss-Turner, 2010). In particular it identified three key components of the service sector workplace culture that influence the nature of the turnover culture and the resulting likelihood of an employee staying in the job or leaving. First, there is what the anthropologist Mary Douglas (1978) termed the *grid* or constraints that are imposed on the workplace culture; these constraints were exemplified by the corporate culture values and tightly branded specifications from which employees must not deviate. Second, there is the *group* dimension of the workplace culture (Douglas, 1978), derived from individual employee and work group commitment, the degree of belonging between group members and the mutual support members feel for each other. Third, there is the degree of *service encounter complexity*, derived from the level of pressure felt from the customer in terms of their dual-need for substantive consumption (a meal for food, a drink to quench thirst) and symbolic consumption (recognition by name and feeling of power). This latter dimension is linked to the work of Korczynski (2002), referred to earlier in Chapter 8.

From the research into highly specified pub brands, it was evident from the qualitative research with employees that these key factors affected the workplace culture and that the more alignment between the three factors, the more a positive turnover culture prevailed, and a reduced intention to quit the job resulted (see Figure 14.6). As an example, a brand with very low labour turnover was revealed to be a concept for young people and students where the values of the company, the values of the employees and the values of the customer base (also mostly people of a similar age) were perceived to be in alignment. As a result, there was more harmony in the workplace *group*, less of a feeling of being dominated by the *grid* of company standards and a desire to retain membership of specific shifts and work teams. The alignment and relative harmony with the customers led to a feeling that the employees were able to deal more effectively with the stress and emotional challenge of the work. This cultural alignment helps to understand the positive turnover culture and its potential for finding solutions to the labour turnover challenge.

Labour turnover is clearly a measure or barometer of the success or otherwise of HRM practices and line management competence within the labour-intensive hospitality industry. It is a measure of the

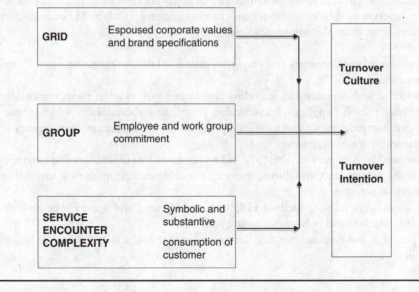

Figure 14.6 Service workplace: cultural alignment and labour turnover

overall well-being of the organization with special reference to the underlying state of employee relations within the business, a topic which will be considered in the following chapter. However, labour turnover is a hugely complex phenomenon, and its full understanding remains a constant preoccupation of hospitality practitioners and researchers alike. To aid this challenge, it is increasingly seen as important to analyse the issue in terms of the specifics of a particular job and individual, but also at the far broader scale of the overall organizational culture and its reliance on a stable workforce.

Further reading and references

Bellou, V. (2009) 'Matching individuals and organizations: evidence from Greece', *Employee Relations*, 31(5): 455–470.

Bolton, S. C. and Houlihan, M. (2009) 'Are we having fun yet? A consideration of workplace fun and employment', *Employee Relations*, 31(6): 556–568.

Davidson, M., Timo, N. and Wang, Y. (2010) 'How much does labour turnover cost?', *International Journal of Contemporary Hospitality Management*, 22(4): 451–466.

Deery, M. A. and Shaw, R. N. (1997) 'An exploratory analysis of turnover culture in the hotel industry in Australia', *International Journal of Hospitality Management*, 16(4): 375–392.

Deery, M. A. and Shaw, R. N. (1999) 'An investigation of the relationship between employee turnover and organizational culture', *Journal of Hospitality and Tourism Research*, 23(4): 387–400.

Douglas, M. (1978) *Cultural Bias*, Occasional Paper No. 34, Royal Anthropological Institute of Great Britain and Ireland.

Goss-Turner, S. (2010) 'The relationship between organisational culture and labour turnover', unpublished PhD thesis, University of Brighton.

Hochschild, A. R. (1983) *The Managed Heart: The Commercialization of Human Feeling*, Berkeley: University of California Press.

Hom, P. W. and Griffeth, R. W. (1995) *Employee Turnover*, Cincinnati, OH: South Western Publishing.

Kelliher, C. and Perrett, G. (2001) 'Business strategy and approaches to HRM – a case study of new developments in the United Kingdom restaurant industry', *Personnel Review*, 30(4): 421–437.

Korczynski, M. (2002) *Human Resource Management in Service Work*, Basingstoke: Palgrave Macmillan.

Korczynski, M. (2003) 'Communities of coping: collective emotional labour in service work', *Organization*, 10(1): 55–79.

Kuvaas, B. (2007) 'An exploration of how the employee–organization relationship affects the linkage between perception of developmental human resource practices and employee outcomes', *Journal of Management Studies*, 45(1): 1–25.

Lashley, C. (1999) 'Up against the wall: the cost of staff turnover in licensed retailing', *The Hospitality Review*, October: 53–56.

Lashley, C. and Best, W. (2002) 'Employee induction in licensed retail organisations', *International Journal of Contemporary Hospitality Management*, 14(1): 6–13.

Lashley, C. and Rowson, B. (2000) 'Wasted millions: staff turnover in licensed retailing', *Proceedings of 9th Annual Research Conference of the Council for Hospitality Management Educators*, University of Huddersfield.

Lucas, R. (2004) *Employment Relations in the Hospitality and Tourism Industries*, London: Routledge.

Lynn, M. (2002) 'Turnover's relationships with sales, tips and service across restaurants in a chain', *International Journal of Hospitality Management*, 21(4): 443–447.

Mann, S. (1997) 'Emotional labour in organisations', *Leadership and Organisation Development Journal*, 18(1): 4–12.

Mann, S. (2007) 'Expectations of emotional display in the workplace', *Leadership and Organisation Development Journal*, 28(6): 552–570.

Meyer, J. P., Stanley, D., Herscovitch, L. and Topolnytsky, L. (2002) 'Affective, continuance and normative commitment to the organization: a meta-analysis of antecedents, correlates and consequences', *Journal of Vocational Behaviour*, 61: 20–52.

Morrell, K., Loan-Clarke, J. and Wilkinson, A. (2001) 'Unweaving leaving: the use of models in the management of employee turnover', *International Journal of Management Reviews*, 3(1): 219–244.

Morrell, K., Loan-Clarke, J. and Wilkinson, A. (2004) 'The role of shocks in employee turnover', *British Journal of Management*, 15: 335–349.

Nickson, D. (2007) *Human Resource Management for the Hospitality and Tourism Industries*, Oxford: Butterworth-Heinemann.

Noon, M. and Blyton, P. (2007) *The Realities of Work*, 3rd edn, Basingstoke: Palgrave Macmillan.

People 1st (2011) *State of the Nation Report 2011, Analysis of labour market trends, skills, education and training within the UK hospitality, leisure, travel and tourism industries*, London: People 1st.

Pratten, J. D. and Curtis, S. (2002) 'Attitudes towards training in UK licensed retail: an exploratory case study', *International Journal of Hospitality Management*, 21(4): 393–403.

Riley, M., Lockwood, A., Powell-Perry, J. and Baker, M. (1998) 'Job satisfaction, organisation commitment and occupational culture: a case from the UK pub industry', *Progress in Tourism and Hospitality Research*, 4: 159–168.

Rowley, G. and Purcell, K. (2001) 'As cooks go, she went: is labour churn inevitable?', *International Journal of Hospitality Management*, 20: 163–185.

Seymour, D. and Sandiford, P. (2005) 'Learning emotion rules in service organizations: socialization and training in the UK public house sector', *Work, Employment & Society*, 19(3): 547–564.

Shore, L. M., Tetrick, L. E., Lynch, P. and Barksdale, K. (2006) 'Social and economic exchange: construct development and validation', *Journal of Applied Social Psychology*, 36: 837–867.

The employment relationship

Yang, J-T. (2008) 'Effect of newcomer socialisation on organisational commitment, job satisfaction, and turnover intention in the hotel industry', *The Service Industries Journal*, 28(4): 429–443.

Members of the UK's Institute of Hospitality (IoH) can access publications including Management Guides which summarize key information of relevance to hospitality operations (www.instituteofhospitality.org).

Members of the UK's Chartered Institute of Personnel and Development (CIPD) can access a range of materials including Fact Sheets and articles from over 300 online journal titles relevant to HRM. CIPD members and *People Management* subscribers can see articles on the People Management website (www.peoplemanagement.co.uk).

Questions

1   What are some of the connections between labour turnover and organizational culture?

2   What do you understand by positive and negative labour turnover cultures?

3   What external factors affect labour turnover and how may they be limited?

4   What means are available to managers to analyse the issues and address the problem of unacceptably high labour turnover levels?

CASE STUDY QUESTION – see the Lux Hotels case study Appendix 5

What particular emotional labour issues might be prevalent in a company such as Lux Hotels and how might such issues affect employee retention levels?

Chapter 15

Employee relations

In many respects this whole book is concerned with the relationship between employers and their employees. Whether one is considering recruitment, induction, grievance and disciplinary procedures or reward systems, all have important inputs into the employment relationship. However, all of these can be concerned with the relationship of an individual employee and the employer, a situation of a manager directly managing an individual employee.

This chapter, instead, is to focus on the collective relationship traditionally referred to as 'industrial relations' but which, with the changed nature of trade union roles and power, is increasingly referred to as 'employee relations' (Bacon, 2006). At one extreme, such relationships are seen as being concerned with purely economic issues, i.e. the 'pay for effort' bargain or relationship. At another extreme are those who see industrial relations as being concerned with politics and as an extension of party politics. The term 'employee relations' is generally used to describe the relationship that exists between the management of an undertaking and its work people predominantly through their representatives, in the collective sense. An important contributor to the subject of employment relations as it pertains to the hospitality industry is Rosemary Lucas, whose definition of the employment relationship also introduced the consumer within its scope:

> Employee relations in hotels and catering is about the management of employment and work relationships between managers and workers and, sometimes, customers, it also covers contemporary employment and work practices.
>
> (Lucas, 1995: 81)

In a later work, Lucas (2004) develops this important theme for service industries, where the role and behaviours of hospitality employees are impacted upon crucially by the organization, its culture, its management and the customer they are serving. The challenge for many hospitality employees is to satisfy the needs and demands of all these stakeholders, and this complexity of relationship can create significant problems for individual workers through the role conflict and potential stress that can result. The hotel receptionist dealing with a stressed guest, disappointed and angry about the poor decorative order of a hotel bedroom, is in a parlous position, faced with the 'power' of the customer, and the 'power' of the organization and management that demands maximum occupancy and revenue from all rooms, including the substandard accommodation not yet featuring on the carefully budgeted and phased refurbishment schedule.

Bacon (2006: 188) points to the frames of reference, the underlying assumptions of managers towards their workforce as a critical element within employee relations, impacting on the managers' behaviour and management style. A unitarist approach seeks harmony and collaboration, believing the workforce to be all members of the same team; a pluralist perspective sees an organization as composed of different subgroups and subcultures, all needing a clearly defined structure and framework to work within; the radical frame of reference sees a power struggle between groups of unequal power as exemplified by the power of the owners and managers of the enterprise and their less powerful employees.

The traditional and collective term of industrial relations is sometimes still applied in employment situations where employees are organized and represented within a strong trade union. In the hospitality industry the degree of organization of employees within trade unions varies considerably. At one end of the scale, in sectors such as public sector and contract catering, it is possible for all employees' conditions of employment to be determined by negotiation (collective bargaining) and national agreements resulting in a high degree of union membership; yet at the other end of the scale, in most private enterprise hotels and restaurants, trade union membership is comparatively low, and often non-existent. Upon close examination it appears that there are certain factors that either contribute towards or militate against strong union involvement. Bain and Price (1983) identified a number of determinants of union growth or decline, factors still relevant today. These include:

- industrial structure
- government action
- business cycle
- composition of potential membership
- employer policies
- personal and job-related characteristics
- union leadership.

Using some of these determinants identified by Bain and Price (1983), supported by the later work of Noon and Blyton (2007), it is possible to conclude that union membership is extremely low and sporadic in the hospitality industry, and service sector work in general, for the following reasons:

- The very large number of small establishments, often managed by the proprietor of the business, which makes it difficult for trade union officials to approach individuals and canvass potential members and to organize meetings.
- The highly dispersed and departmentalized labour force, even in the largest establishments, resulting in the absence of cohesive groups of workers with common interests and common issues.
- The large number of part-time employees, predominantly female and also many young employees, all people who are rarely interested in belonging to a trade union and paying any membership fees.
- The large number of transient employees and 'tourist workers', employees who are in hospitality industry employment for relatively short periods of time and cannot envisage their conditions being affected.
- Shift working, which again makes it difficult to contact potential members directly and organize employees.
- Tipping, which introduces an entrepreneurial (perhaps selfish) element into hospitality work; many employees fear a trade union would try to eliminate, or try to distribute in a more collective manner, rather than a tip being an extra reward for giving good customer service as an individual.
- Individual and unwritten cash payments/contracts made between the employer and the employee.
- No history and tradition of trade union membership within some sectors of the industry, unlike manufacturing industry; indeed, many hospitality employees appear to 'side' with their employers in a scenario of paternal benevolence rather than be seen to be at the behest of left-wing unionists.
- Employers' resistance, because employers fear that they have more to lose than to gain from the trade union movement, and feel that the involvement of unions will only cause friction and potentially damage their perceived close relationships with their employees.
- High labour turnover in some hospitality sectors mitigates against membership, association and the ability of trade unions to organize effectively.

Low union membership	High union membership
Small units – small workforce	Large units – large workforce
Many part-timers and casuals	Few part-timers and casuals
'Entrepreneurial' opportunities, e.g. tipping	No 'entrepreneurial' opportunities
Ownership and management combined or closely related	Management distinct from ownership
'Secret' contracts	No 'secret' contracts
Hostile ownership	
No other union involvement	Other unions involved in the enterprise
No tradition of union involvement	Traditions of union involvement
Some examples	*Some examples*
Restaurants, fast food outlets, hotels, public house staff	Hospitality catering, university and college catering, school meals, Civil Service catering, public house manager

Figure 15.1 Factors contributing to low or high levels of union involvement

Figure 15.1 illustrates how these factors can be applied to the hospitality industry and lead to low or high union membership.

Development of unions and worker representation

In order to see the hospitality industry's employee relations in perspective it is important to look at the historical development of industrial relations generally and, in particular, to examine the development of organizations of work people and of employers. The organization of employers and workers came about from the eighteenth century onwards with the emergence of the modern industrial society. Before this time most conditions of employment had been regulated by the state, often through the local magistrate, and it was an offence in common law to do anything (even with the intention of improving one's own conditions of work) that might have been in restraint of trade. A combination of workers, therefore, to strike or to do anything else to improve conditions that adversely affected the employer's business was a criminal act of conspiracy. But at the same time it was illegal for employers to form such combinations. As industry became more complex, the state regulations of wages fell into disuse and employers themselves were able to fix conditions of employment. Legislation followed, banning combinations in one trade after another until the situation was made quite clear when the Combination Acts 1799–1800 provided for a general prohibition in all trades of combinations of employees or employers.

However, following the Napoleonic Wars there was an economic depression together with a movement to improve conditions, which resulted in the repeal, in 1824, of the Combination Laws. The effect of this was to allow workers to enter into combinations for the purpose of regulating wages and other conditions without committing the crime of conspiracy. This Act (the Combination Laws Repeal Act 1824) was followed shortly by another that somewhat circumscribed workers' rights, but still preserved the right to withhold labour by collective action and this right has never been withdrawn, although current legislation makes it more difficult to instigate certain types of industrial action without risk of penalties.

Subsequent acts, including the Trade Union Act 1871 and the Conspiracy and Protection of Property Act 1875, gave trade unions legal status and also permitted peaceful picketing. Then the Trade Disputes Act 1906 protected a trade union from being sued for alleged wrongful acts committed by it or on its behalf. Thus trade unions were freed of any risk of a civil liability arising from their actions. A variety of other legislation followed which repealed certain preceding legislation, covered the amalgamation of trade unions and tied up some other aspects that were not satisfactory.

However, the most notable legislation to date was the Industrial Relations Act of 1971, which replaced most preceding legislation regarding trade unions and followed both the main political parties' examination of the increasingly complex and potentially disruptive industrial relations scene. This Act granted to an individual the right to belong or not to belong to a trade union. This was subsequently repealed with many other provisions by the Trade Unions and Labour Relations Act 1974. Certain provisions particularly relating to 'unfair dismissal' remained to protect the individual, but have since been altered by subsequent employment legislation. Principal statutes enacted concerning employment rights and trade unions rights in the intervening period have been the Trade Union and Labour Relations (Consolidation) Act 1992, the Trade Union Reform and Employment Rights Act 1993 and the Employment Relations Act 1999.

The trade union movement, along with other elements of our society, has undergone a period of consolidation, merger and rationalization. At the end of 1972 there were about 480 trade unions, whose members totalled about 11 million; in 1987 there were only 373 unions with 10.7 million members; in 1989 there were about 8.6 million members in unions affiliated to the Trades Union Congress (TUC). The number of union members was the same in 1993 (8.6 million) but the number of certificated unions had fallen to 267, of which 67 were affiliated to the TUC. Brown (2000) reports that the number of UK workers with trade union membership decreased from 53 per cent of the total workforce in 1979 to just 28 per cent in 1999. Brownlie (2012) reports that in 2011, trade union membership stood at 6.4 million or just under 25 per cent of the working population of the UK. Recent trends seem to suggest that membership has begun to rise slightly in the public sector, as people worry more about their terms and conditions, especially pension rights, in a period of economic austerity imposed by the Coalition Government since 2010.

Other statistics in the Department for Business, Innovation and Skills (BIS) report on trade union membership in 2011 (Brownlie, 2012) reveal further reasons why membership density within the hospitality industry remains low. Of the 6.4 million members of trade unions in 2011, 80 per cent were full-time workers, whereas only 20 per cent were part-time workers, a dominant group in hospitality. It also notes that 43 per cent of members are aged between 35 and 49 years, whereas only 4.6 per cent of members are aged between 16 and 24, an age group of significance within hospitality. The hospitality sector, as analysed by the Workplace Employee Relations Survey in 1998, had no members at all in 92 per cent of establishments. Recent estimates of the percentage of the hospitality labour force who are members put the figure at as low as 4 per cent (Brook, 2002, cited in Lucas, 2004). The BIS report puts the accommodation and food service sector as the lowest density of trade union membership in the UK of all industry classifications, at just under 4 per cent (Brownlie, 2012).

HRM and employee relations

The development of the contemporary practices of HRM, as indicated in Chapter 2, owed much of its developmental roots to practitioners and academics in the United States. However, HRM's development through the late twentieth century developed within a very different context in the UK, characterized by industrial unrest, especially in the 1970s and 1980s. During this damaging period of industrial conflict, the traditional economic and employment sectors of manufacturing and heavy industry fought for survival in a changing, globalized market, alongside a national UK economy increasingly focused on the service sector (Sisson and Storey, 1993). The 1970s experienced turbulent industrial relations against a background of oil and energy crises, increased competition and technological advances. Those involved in HRM or, as it was often termed in those days, personnel management, mainly fulfilled 'go-between' roles in mediating the relations between managers, unions and workers (Mabey and Salaman, 1995).

The 1980s experienced further industrial unrest but also a UK government committed to deregulation of the labour market and the gradual dismantling of the voluntary collective bargaining processes and institutions (Lucas, 2004). The impact of these changes on the development of people management practices was significant. Personnel Managers, now often retitled Human Resources Managers, had to reappraise their role in a new-style workplace and service-dominated economy. They were more concerned with the corporate strategy of the business and with employee relations (rather than industrial relations) in a post-industrialization society (Millward, 1994). Bacon (2006) suggests that the main aim of HRM in this new era of employee relations was to steer a complementary course, aligning both individual and collective approaches, but, it is argued here, within a context of HR being firmly placed within the management of the business and not a somewhat parlous go-between.

Employee relations and employee involvement

The HRM approach in the late twentieth and early twenty-first century has moved some way from the large-scale conflict between managers and employees, especially in the service sector and hospitality, where the low trade union membership has resulted in few high-profile disputes. As noted above, there is some resurgence of unrest amongst public sector workers as the Coalition Government elected in 2010 seeks to reduce the national debt in part by reviewing pension arrangements and other terms and conditions that can be affected by the government itself. More generally, contemporary employee relations can be seen as part of the wider aim of HRM that seeks to involve the employees in the organization, encouraging participation and consultation. All this activity is predicated on the unitarist principles of everyone pulling together but also that employees who are involved in the future of the enterprise will be more engaged and committed, more readily achieving high performance levels. As has been discussed earlier, especially in Chapter 2, employee commitment and performance are key central tenets of the contemporary interpretation of HRM.

Within the hospitality industry, there are probably three main types of consultative procedure. The first and probably the least formal is found in the many small and medium-sized enterprises (SMEs) in hospitality, the individually owned hotel or restaurant, managed by a proprietor who works in the establishment with a staff (full-time and part-time/casuals) numbering no more than about 20. In this case any formal joint consultation or negotiation may be unnecessary, since the employer is close to the employees and has more opportunity to be aware of their issues and views. It is in the employer's interest to be well informed of the employees' opinions and feelings, and for this purpose the employer may well hold informal meetings at regular intervals with all staff or small representative groups. Meetings or briefings may also be held to discuss menus, special functions and other priority issues and from time to time these meetings could be enlarged and extended to cover methods of work and conditions of employment.

The next level may be found in larger hotels or restaurants with groups of employees in several different, discrete departments. Typically this would be a hotel or restaurant complex with from 20 to over a 100 employees. There needs to be some more formal system of involving and engaging staff in such establishments, ensuring that they feel they are being listened to, consulted with and considered. Departmental feuds are not uncommon in the hospitality industry, and meetings of cross-department staff are a good means of contributing to solving problems or just gathering issues and concerns from the employees. In this case it might be that each department nominates a representative to meet management's representatives on a regular basis – probably between four and eight times a year. Some formality and structure to the meetings is needed, and items for the agenda for each meeting should be requested from the representatives well before the event, so that they can discuss issues with their colleagues in a meaningful way, and also that management may be better prepared on the issues and not caught 'on the hop'.

The third level of consultation process is the multi-site, perhaps multinational, company or multi-unit organization. Each establishment may have its own joint consultative committee, and in addition it may find it worth organizing a company-based joint consultative committee where representatives from each establishment meet head office management. This system is most appropriate where a company is heavily represented in an area – London, for example – and where management might wish to discourage unnecessary movements between units caused by varying supervisory or personnel practices within the company's establishments. On the other hand it may not be necessary where an employer's establishments are located far apart in areas where conditions are very different.

Large organizations, with no collective agreement with trade unions, also try to utilize staff handbooks and other information materials to convey to staff the key issues in the relations between employees and employer. Such handbooks can serve two purposes: to give information to the employee and also to encourage discussion and involvement with the management of the outlet to ensure good employee relations. Frequently such handbooks will cover the practical implications of terms and conditions of employment such as pension schemes, in-company discounts, bank holiday work and possibly share-save schemes. Other employee relations aspects covered might be the firm's equal opportunities policy, a statement about bullying and harassment, and smoking at work regulations.

Benefits of employee consultation

Managers may ask what benefits can result from their taking the initiative in establishing joint consultation and even bargaining or negotiating procedures with their employees. First, and most important, it must be recognized that although employees may have no formal, union-backed negotiating machinery, they may still push up rates of pay and win other concessions by voting with their feet. They could move from employer to employer continuously looking for higher earnings and employers in turn have continually to increase their rates to attract replacement staff.

Because of continuous, collective pressure from the employees, through consultation, their conditions could be seen to steadily improve, and job security would become greater, with the result that the staff turnover rate would almost certainly drop to reasonable proportions. There are cases in certain sections of the hospitality industry where trade unions are relatively strong and where the annual staff turnover is not above 10 per cent per annum, the contract food service sector being one such example. As a result the economies to be made through not having to recruit and train a steady flow of replacement staff are considerable, apart from the benefits of being able to maintain consistent standards, and engage employees in a positive and motivational manner.

A further benefit of consultation is to encourage a workforce to be more willing to accept change. By nature most people resist or even oppose change, but if they have been involved in discussing changes that affect them and they understand the underlying reasons, they are more likely to be more prepared to make the changes work. A further benefit is that many employees, at all levels within the organization, have ideas that can improve working methods, and, by consultation, management can provide the opportunities for these to be expressed and implemented where appropriate.

Establishing consultation

Once the decision has been taken to establish a consultation protocol within an organization, the scope of the ensuing discussions may cover all matters of interest to both sides, including the overall reward system, hours of work, working methods and company plans. It should be clear, however, that the purpose of such consultative committees is consultation and not ongoing, endless negotiation. Setting up a staff consultative committee sometimes presents problems, because it is essential that the employees' representatives are chosen, perhaps even elected, by their colleagues and not by management. The outline of a constitution and rules for a staff consultative committee, taken from a multi-unit hotel company, is illustrated in Figure 15.2.

1 Objectives

The object of the Staff Consultative Committee is to provide a means of communication and consultation between the management and staff of the hotel on all matters of mutual interest, including:

(a) Explanation on general information concerning company activities, policies and procedures.
(b) Business plans for the hotel and current results, expressed in broad terms as percentages, etc.
(c) Ideas for improving sales, standards of performance, efficiency and productivity.
(d) Discussion on staff rules and regulations, and discussion on security matters.
(e) Terms and conditions of employment, staff amenities and welfare facilities. Wage rates/wage reviews may be discussed in general terms only. The wages or status of an individual member of staff may not be discussed.
(f) Training activities.
(g) Health and safety at work, including hygiene and welfare. (The hotel Safety and Hygiene Officer should be in attendance during discussion on these items.)
(h) Organizing of social, sporting and recreational activities.

2 Membership

The Committee shall consist of:

(a) **A Chairman** who shall be the General Manager.
(b) **Another Management Representative** preferably the Human Resources Manager or Assistant Manager responsible for Human Resources.
(c) **A Head of Department or Supervisor**: normally a different Head of Department or Supervisor attending the meeting in rotation.
(d) **Elected Staff Representatives** for each Department of the Hotel (normally there should be between 6 and 12 staff representatives on the Committee depending on the size of the hotel). They will also act as Safety Representatives for their Departments – see *Guidelines for the Duties of Staff Safety Representative*.
(e) **A Secretary** to record the Minutes of meetings of the Committee. Staff Representatives will be chosen annually by election, other members of the Committee being nominated by management. Should members of the Committee cease to be employed by the hotel, then membership shall immediately terminate.

3 Attendance

Any member who is absent without adequate reason for two or more consecutive meetings may, at the discretion of the Committee, be disqualified from membership.

4 Co-option

The Chairman may invite additional members of management and/or staff to attend meetings to provide special information.

5 Election of Staff Representative

All staff over the age of 18 years who have been employed for over three months by the hotel shall be entitled to stand for election which shall be conducted annually by Departments. Elections, which shall normally be by secret ballot, shall be organized by the Head of Department in consultation with the Hotel Manager, and shall be held normally in January or as required as a vacancy arises during a term of office. All staff on the payroll at the time of the election shall be entitled to one vote. Staff Representatives are entitled to wear a special Company badge whilst they hold office. These badges will be issued by the Hotel Managers and must be returned if the person concerned is no longer the Staff Representative.

6 Officers

The officers shall consist of the Chairman, a Management Representative and Head of Human Resources Representative as referred to in Paragraph 2 (a), (b) & (c).

7 Retirement

Staff Representatives shall be elected for one year and may be eligible for re-election every year.
Management members shall hold office at the discretion of their superiors.

Figure 15.2 Example of a formal staff consultative committee constitution

---

8 Meetings

(a) Ordinary meetings shall be held at least every two months during normal working hours if possible, and 14 days' notice of the meeting should be given. Items for the agenda may be submitted to any member of the Committee and the agenda should be distributed to members with a copy placed on the staff noticeboard at least 7 days before the meeting. Fixed items on the agenda should be:

> Minutes of last meeting
> Matters arising
> Training
> Health and safety
> Business results and objectives
> Security
> Energy conservation
> Date of next meeting.

(b) Special meetings may be convened at the request of any four members or the Chairman.
(c) The meetings shall conform to committee procedure, members addressing the Chair.
(d) Discussion shall be opened by the members in whose name the item on the agenda stands.

9 Minutes

The Chairman shall ensure that accurate Minutes of all meetings are kept which summarize the discussion and define clearly the action being taken and who is responsible for that action. (Minutes must always have an Action column.) The Minutes must be prepared and circulated within 7 days of the meeting with copies distributed to all Committee members, all Management and Heads of Department and all Staff Noticeboards. Copies of the Minutes are also to be sent to the Area Operations Director, the Hotels Human Resources Department and the Group Human Resources Director.

10 Alterations of Rules

Additions or amendment to these rules may only be made by the Committee, with the approval of the Company.

Figure 15.2 Example of a formal staff consultative committee constitution (contd.)

In concluding this chapter, it must be stressed that the approach of managers towards the subject of positive employee relations will vary greatly across the enormous diversity of business within hospitality. However, it is noteworthy that the lack of formal trade union representation and evidence of 'traditional' collective industrial relations is not an excuse for ignoring this critical aspect of managing people and promoting a contemporary approach to HRM. The hospitality workforce is itself diverse and composed of so many different skills and experience levels, and these very facts demand that management teams talk and listen to staff in a meaningful way, confident that if staff feel involved and engaged, they are more likely to achieve the levels of commitment and performance that will supply the business with its commercial prosperity.

Further reading and references

Armstrong, M. (2012) *A Handbook of Human Resource Management Practice*, 12th edn, London: Kogan Page.

Bacon, N. (2006) 'Industrial relations', in Redman, T. and Wilkinson, A. (eds) *Contemporary Human Resource Management*, 2nd edn, London: Prentice Hall.

Bain, G. and Price, R. (1983) *Industrial Relations in Britain*, London: Blackwell.

Brook, K. (2002) 'Trade union membership: an analysis of data from the autumn 2001 LFS', *Labour Market Trends*, July: 343–356.

Brown, W. (2000) 'Putting partnership into practice in Britain', *British Journal of Industrial Relations*, 38(2): 299–316.

Brownlie, N. (2012) *Trade Union Membership 2011*, report for the Department of Business, Innovation and Skills, London: National Statistics Publication.

Farnham, D. and Pimlott, J. (1995) *Understanding Industrial Relations*, 5th edn, London: Cassell.

Knights, D. and Kerfoot, H. (2012) (eds) *Introducing Organizational Behaviour and Management*, 2nd edn, Andover: Cengage Learning EMEA.

Lucas, R. (1995) *Managing Employee Relations in the Hotel and Catering Industry*, London: Cassell.

Lucas, R. (2004) *Employment Relations in the Hospitality and Tourism Industries*, London: Routledge.

Mabey, C. and Salaman, G. (1995) *Strategic Human Resource Management*, Oxford: Blackwell.

Millward, N. (1994) *The New Industrial Relations*, London: Policy Studies Institute.

Noon, M. and Blyton, P. (2007) *The Realities of Work*, 3rd edn, Basingstoke: Palgrave Macmillan.

Sisson, K. and Storey, J. (1993) *Managing Human Resources and Industrial Relations*, Milton Keynes: Open University Press.

Storey, J. (2007) *Human Resource Management – A Critical Text*, 3rd edn, London: Thomson.

Torrington, D., Hall, L. and Taylor, S. (2008) *Human Resource Management*, 7th edn, Harlow: Pearson Education.

Members of the UK's Institute of Hospitality (IoH) can access publications including Management Guides which summarize key information of relevance to hospitality operations (www.instituteofhospitality.org).

Members of the UK's Chartered Institute of Personnel and Development (CIPD) can access a range of materials including Fact Sheets and articles from over 300 online journal titles relevant to HRM. CIPD members and *People Management* subscribers can see articles on the People Management website (www.peoplemanagement.co.uk).

Questions

1 Describe the structure of industrial/employee relations in the private (commercial) sector of the hospitality industry and also in the public sector of the same industry.

2 Discuss the factors contributing to high or low levels of union participation in different sectors or employers of the hospitality industry.

3 Discuss the external factors that influence the nature of employee relations.

4 Why should larger organizations set up staff consultative committees?

5 Evaluate the approach to employee relations used by an employer you know well.

CASE STUDY QUESTION – see the Lux Hotels case study Appendix 5

What international differences regarding employee relations might influence the policies and procedures of Lux Hotels in development plans and actions?

Chapter 16

Employment law

Employment legislation is one of the more complex areas of law affecting employers so this chapter needs to be viewed as a very brief overview intended to illustrate its scope rather than its detail, particularly as such legislation is subject to constant change. Major areas of employment law have been selected and summarized below. Before looking at these, however, it is important to define an 'employee'.

Under section 230 of the Employment Rights Act 1996, the word 'employee' is defined to mean somebody with a 'contract of employment'. This means someone who has a 'contract *of* service' and not a 'contract *for* services', which distinguishes between someone who is working for another, under their control, and someone who is working *on their own* account, controlling their own work. In other words, it is meant to be the difference between the truly 'employed' and the 'self-employed'. This has implications for issues such as tax and national insurance. Similar definitions will exist in many other jurisdictions. There are advantages to employers to employ 'contractors' or subcontractors because these have no employment rights such as sickness and pension rights and no additional charges.

The aim of this chapter is not to describe in detail legislation relating to employment. Instead the chapter sets out to identify the general scope of employment law which is subject to national political, economic, social and technological development. As a consequence employment law changes very regularly over time. The evolution and development of modern, complex societies have been accompanied by the need to regulate many of the activities of various groups of people. In the case of employment in England and Wales, the activities of employers were long regulated by various legal institutions such as magistrates, who had, among a number of powers, the power to set rates of pay. Craft guilds also played a significant role throughout much of Europe. The guilds set duties and conditions for apprentices and their masters. A master craftsman was entitled to employ young people in exchange for providing food, lodging and formal training in the craft.

From the nineteenth century onwards, the activities of employers became subject to increasing regulation in order to provide employees with greater protection in economic, social and physical terms. In England early legislation was the Factories Act 1833. The basic Act legislated:

- no child workers under 9 years of age
- employers must have an age certificate for their child workers
- children of 9–13 years to work no more than nine hours a day
- children of 13–18 years to work no more than 12 hours a day
- children are not to work at night.

At the geo-political level various international conventions set out to protect employees from exploitation such as the International Labour Organization's (ILO) Convention on Human Rights. The ILO was created in 1919 in order to protect against injustice, hardship and privation. The ILO now has 174 member states which are committed to:

- freedom of association, i.e. to join a union
- recognition of right to organize collective bargaining
- elimination of forced and compulsory labour
- elimination of child labour
- elimination of discrimination.

In some jurisdictions regulation of work conditions rests largely on governments and local officials. In other jurisdictions a laissez-faire approach prevails, with employers and employees negotiating working conditions.

The role of the European Union (EU) has become increasingly important also – not just to improve employment conditions but also to ensure that all member states are competing on equal terms.

Before employment

Sex, race, age discrimination – e.g. advertising and interviewing
Rehabilitation of offenders – certain offenders do not have to reveal spent convictions
Employing overseas workers – work permits needed in certain cases
Employing children – local authority approval needed
Employing young persons – e.g. licensing law restrictions
Employment agencies – who is the employer? who pays the agency?
Disabled workers – physical impediments or obstacles to their employment to be removed
Trade union membership – free to belong or not to belong

On starting employment

Contract of employment – certain terms and conditions to be given in writing
Health and safety – e.g. induction, fire training, safety precautions
Employer's liability insurance – needed to indemnify employees in case of accidents at work

During employment

Maximum hours
Statutory paid holidays
Health and safety at work – range of health and safety measures
Disciplinary procedures – need to be communicated and fair
Time off – for sickness, maternity, jury service, etc.
Trade union membership – free to belong or not to belong
Harassment – employer to take reasonable measures to prevent harassment
Discrimination – e.g. in promotion
Discipline and grievance procedures

Pay and other benefits

Minimum wages
Equal pay – pay to be equal for men and women doing work of equal value
Statutory pay for sickness and maternity
Taxation and national insurance – who is responsible for collecting tax and deductions
Deductions – lawful and unlawful deductions

Termination

Termination procedures – resignations and dismissals
Written reasons for dismissal
Transfer of undertakings – protection of employment.

Figure 16.1 An illustration of the areas of employment regulated to a greater or lesser extent by the law in most developed nations (this is illustrative only)

Examples of such legislation include the introduction or extension of legislation into the United Kingdom covering minimum wages, maximum working hours and statutory paid holidays.

Common law rights and obligations

In the UK, and many other 'common law' countries, many aspects of the relationship between employer and employee are regulated by the contract of employment, much of it with origins in the common law. The employer's duties are to pay the agreed wages, to provide work, to select and to train competent workers, to provide adequate materials and to provide safe systems of work. Any breach of these common law obligations means that an employee could sue for damages, when an injury is sustained; or even to resign without notice and to sue for constructive dismissal, i.e. when an employer creates such circumstances that an employee feels justified in resigning.

In turn, common law lays obligations upon employees as well. These include the duty to serve the employer according to the terms of the contract, to be obedient (i.e. to follow reasonable instructions), to work competently, to work for the employer in good faith – which includes not taking secret profits or commissions, to keep confidential information and not to set up in competition.

In addition to the common law the employment relationship is regulated by statute (i.e. Act of Parliament), much of it driven by EU regulations and directives.

In 'civil law' countries such obligations will be written into codes (legislation) such as the *Code du Travail* in France.

Important legal responsibilities of employers

Vicarious liability

An employer may be 'vicariously' liable, for negligent acts or omissions of their employees in the course of employment. This is an important legal concept which makes an employer responsible for the civil or criminal acts of his employees, where the acts are committed in the normal course of their work, such as overcharging, short-measuring, hygiene offences. Vicarious liability does not extend to acts which are outside the normal duties, so an assault upon a customer may not be the responsibility of the employer, excepting where force might be required, such as nightclub door supervisors. This legal concept exists in very many jurisdictions.

Due diligence

Employers are expected to take reasonable precautions to ensure the safety of the customers, staff and others coming onto their premises. The owner or the manager or responsible employee should take all reasonable precautions and exercise all due diligence to avoid committing an offence. One example of exercising 'due diligence' would be the use of Hazard Analysis and Critical Control Points (HACCP) to ensure food safety. Another would be the proper training of bar staff to ensure that under-age people are not served alcohol. Again, this legal concept exists in very many jurisdictions.

Contracts of employment

A contract of employment is the basis of the working relationship between employer and employee and is subject to the general principles covered by the law of contract. In common law countries there are a number of essentials for a contract to be valid. These are as follows:

1 *Offer and acceptance* – there must be an offer and an acceptance
2 *Intention to create legal relations* – each party must intend to create a legally binding contract
3 *Capacity* – each party to the contract must be legally able to make the contract
4 *Consent* – must be genuine and freely given
5 *Consideration* – something of value must be exchanged, e.g. money for work
6 *Legality* – the purpose of the contract must be legal
7 *Possibility* – it must be possible to perform the contract.

In most common law countries a contract of employment may be oral, written, or the terms may be merely implied. It consists of an offer by one of the parties and an acceptance by the other. The consideration must have an economic value. The offer is usually (but not necessarily) made by the employer and should contain details of remuneration, hours, location and holidays. The offer may refer to other documents such as pension scheme booklets. Not all conditions have to be included, as some may be implied by custom and practice. The contract comes into existence when the offeror receives acceptance from the offeree.

Although, in common law, many contracts need not be in writing, it is advisable, in the case of employment contracts that all offers and acceptances are in writing in order to avoid misunderstanding and possible problems. Furthermore, because employers are obliged to issue a written statement of the main conditions of employment (see below), there is no real reason today for not preparing a proper, written contract of employment.

In civil law countries, as noted above, employment contracts may be largely regulated by codes leaving less room for negotiation.

Zero hours contract

A zero hours contract is effectively an 'on-call' arrangement between employer and employee. Such contracts, not uncommon in the hospitality industry, are used to cope with varying customer demand so that an employer may have staff available on demand. The employer is under no obligation to offer an employee work but, when the employer does, the employee is expected to accept the offer. In many cases the employer may send staff home early (e.g. in a bar) where demand drops off, paying only for the actual hours worked.

Black or shadow economy

The black or shadow economy has many definitions. For the purpose of this book it may be defined as 'business activities or revenues which evade a country's rules on taxation, in order to reduce or evade paying tax'. This occurs in the main where transactions are conducted in cash, a proportion of which is not recorded or reported, and amongst smaller businesses. Larger businesses tend to be strictly audited. It was estimated that at the European level in 2005, the shadow economy of the hospitality industry was in the region of 15 per cent of the industry's total revenue (Schneider, 2005).

Because of the nature of the hospitality industry (i.e. many small businesses taking cash) the industry is host to a significant 'black or shadow' economy. One consequence is that workers may have no legally enforceable contract of employment and no rights such as protection from unfair dismissal and no rights to sickness benefits, pensions or industrial injuries benefits.

In the UK the tax authorities (HMRC) suggest that the UK's black economy is of the order of 6 to 8 per cent of GDP and probably higher in the hospitality industry. In 2011 it was reported that tax inspectors were to investigate restaurants in London and other parts of the UK to hunt down tax dodgers in the food trade.

In countries such as Spain, Italy and Greece the black economy ranges between 21 and 26 per cent of their GDP. In Germany the level is said to be 15 per cent of GDP (Schneider, 2005).

The Equality Act 2010 (UK)

This legislation requires equal treatment in conditions of employment such as pay, and access to employment regardless of age, disability, gender reassignment, marriage and civil partnership, race, religion or belief, sex, and sexual orientation. In the case of gender, there are special protections for pregnant women. In the case of disability, employers and service providers are under a duty to make reasonable adjustments to their workplaces to overcome barriers experienced by disabled people.

Discrimination in employment

Discrimination against applicants for jobs and those in employment can be directed at a range of different groups of people including women, men, people of some ethnic groups, people with certain beliefs or with disability, people of gay, lesbian or bisexual orientation, people with criminal convictions and older people. The UK legislation, largely repeated in European Union legislation and many other jurisdictions (e.g. USA, Canada, Australia) is directed at eliminating discrimination in the workplace which is aimed at women, ethnic minorities, people with disability and those who may be discriminated against because of their religion or beliefs.

Under UK legislation, the Equality Act 2010 identifies a range of discriminations:

1 Direct discrimination, which includes:

- associative discrimination
- perceptive discrimination.

2 Indirect discrimination, which includes:

- harassment
- third-party harassment
- victimization.

Direct discrimination

This consists of acts that discriminate against another on grounds such as gender, racial origin or disability. To refuse to employ someone on the grounds that they may be too old would be an example of direct discrimination. This legislation presents problems for employers in some situations. For example, a bar operator might prefer to employ attractive young women. *Associative discrimination* arises when someone is treated less favourably because he or she might be connected to someone who might present problems, such as having a disabled partner. *Perceptive discrimination* occurs when someone is discriminated against because they might be perceived to present problems such as a woman who might be about to start a family, or someone whose religious beliefs could interfere with their ability to do certain tasks (e.g. a strict Muslim cannot consume or serve alcohol).

Indirect discrimination

This consists of applying conditions that make it more difficult for certain people, for example, of one sex or of a particular racial group, to fulfil them. An example would be specifying a condition such as to be able to lift heavy weights, without this being a necessary task; the result would be to exclude most women.

Harassment is defined as 'unwanted conduct … which has the purpose or effect of violating an individual's dignity or creating an intimidating, hostile, degrading, humiliating or offensive environment for that individual'. Sexual and racial harassment are examples.

Third-party harassment consists of harassment by people such as customers. An employer has to protect employees from such harassment.

Victimization occurs for example when a member of staff is the subject of a disciplinary measure, or some other detrimental action, as a result of having complained to an employment tribunal.

Rehabilitation of Offenders Act 1974

This Act permits people convicted of certain crimes to treat their sentences as 'spent' after a specified period of time has elapsed. Applicants for jobs do not have to reveal the conviction and sentence and the employer cannot dismiss the employee on the grounds of that conviction if they subsequently learn of the sentence. For example a sentence of up to 30 months in prison becomes spent after ten years.

The Employment Rights Act 1996

This Act provides the rights of employees, who work over a certain number of hours, to minimum periods of notice dependent on their length of service, and the Act also requires that employees are given written details of certain conditions of employment, known as the 'written statement of particulars'. It confirms the main express terms of the employment contract. Whilst not definitive of the entire contract, the written statement is intended to be a guide for employees of their rights.

Where a contract provides for longer periods of notice the terms of the contract will apply, whereas contracts containing shorter periods are overridden by the periods laid down by the 1996 Act. Payment in lieu of notice may be made by the employer or the employee.

Written particulars

These must be given to people within two months of employment commencing. This does not apply to casual workers whose contract is for one session of work at a time.

Written statements need not take any particular form but the contents are prescribed and they can refer employees to other documents such as manuals and booklets, which must be reasonably available to them. There is no requirement in law for the employee or the employer to sign the statement. But it is advisable to issue all employees with a statement and to retain signed copies in the personal dossiers. The ideal procedure is to design letters of offer so that they satisfy the Employment Rights Act 1996 requirements.

Restraint on employees

In the case of some employees, such as chefs, sales staff or managers, employers feel it necessary to include a clause in a contract which restrains an employee from divulging trade secrets, entering into direct competition by operating his or her own business, working for another person in the same line of business or using lists of customers prepared in the course of employment in order to entice customers away.

To obtain protection against such eventualities any terms in a contract need to be clearly stated and not implied. It is important, however, to make such a term reasonable in the circumstances, otherwise the right to any protection could be forfeited. At the same time such restraint clauses must be shown to be in the public interest and it is unlikely that such a restraint clause will be upheld.

Searching employees

It is always advisable to obtain an employee's permission before attempting to search his or her person or property. To search a person without permission, and without finding evidence of theft, can result in the employer being sued for assault and battery. In those cases where the employer's right to search is considered to be vital, a clause to this effect should be written into every person's contract of employment. Even so, an employee cannot be forcibly searched if he or she refuses. Such a refusal instead becomes the subject of disciplinary or dismissal proceedings for breach of a condition of employment.

Dismissals

Under the Employment Rights Act 1996 there is protection for employees against unfair dismissal. Similar rights exist in many other jurisdictions where dismissal can be much more difficult and expensive than in the UK. Valid reasons for dismissal may include:

- lack of capability or qualification for the job for which an employee was employed
- misconduct (e.g. theft, rudeness)
- redundancy, within the definition of redundancy legislation (e.g. no further need for a job to be performed)
- unsuitability due to legal restrictions (e.g. loss of alcohol licence, driving licence where driving is part of the duties)
- some other substantial reasons (e.g. chronic sickness).

In most states of the United States similar concepts apply under their 'just cause' principles. However certain US states have the 'at will' concept under which employment can be terminated, by either party, at any time, irrespective of length of service.

Instant or summary dismissal

In certain instances an employer may be justified in dismissing an employee without giving the required period of notice or money in lieu. Although this may be permitted in such cases as an employee's permanent incapacity to perform his or her duties, in most cases it occurs where employees are guilty of serious misconduct such as theft. To dismiss a person instantly can have serious consequences for the employer if a dismissed employee sues the employer successfully for damages, so it is not a step to be taken lightly. Examples of reasons for instant dismissal include:

- serious or repeated disobedience or other misconduct
- serious or repeated negligence
- drunkenness or drug offences while on duty
- theft
- accepting bribes or commissions.

The argument underlying instant dismissal is that the employee, through serious misconduct, has repudiated the contract, and the employer chooses not to renew it.

An employer can normally only dismiss an employee for misconduct committed outside working hours and away from the place of work if other employees were involved, or which could have an effect on the employer's business, or if the employee is in domestic service.

Where an employer dismisses a person instantly it should be done at the time of the misdemeanour or when it first comes to the attention of the employer. To delay may imply that the employer has waived his or her right to dismiss, but see the discussion of suspensions below. The reason for dismissal should be given at the time of the dismissal.

An employer may, in some cases, withhold money earned by an employee who has been instantly dismissed for good reasons, unless a contract states otherwise. However, legal advice should always be sought before taking such action.

Suspensions

In some circumstances, particularly involving alleged misconduct, an employer may wish to suspend an employee until the circumstances have been looked into and a decision has been taken regarding the employee's future. It is quite in order to do this so long as pay is not withheld – unless a contract specifically permitting the withholding of pay is in existence.

Maternity and paternity rights

Many legal jurisdictions provide for maternity rights and parental leave. At the time of writing (2012) in the UK there are three levels of maternity leave. Certain paternity rights also exist.

Transfer of Undertakings Regulations

These regulations implemented the EU Business Transfers Directive, under which employees of an undertaking who are transferred from one owner to another, usually as a result of the sale of the business, have their employment rights protected. Effectively this means that a new employer is required to treat all of an employee's previous service with the undertaking as uninterrupted. This is of crucial importance on matters such as pension, redundancy, protection from unfair dismissal, etc.

Payment of wages

As wages or salaries are central to the employment contract there is extensive legislation concerned with this subject. One of the key issues is minimum wage legislation. This is common in many but not all countries. Where there are powerful trade unions and where collective bargaining works effectively, such as in Germany, minimum wage legislation does not exist. In many other countries minimum wage legislation does exist, ranging through much of Europe including the UK and France. Minimum wages also exist in the USA, Australia and Canada. In many cases minimum wages are modified for catering workers because of their tips or service charge earnings, as well as meals and accommodation.

Generally speaking, arrangements for the payment of wages are regulated by the contract of employment. In the UK the Employment Rights Act 1996 provides specific rules on deductions. These specify that an employer must not make deductions or receive payment (e.g. as a fine) unless

- the deduction is authorized by statute, e.g. national insurance, income tax, court order
- the deduction is authorized in the contract of employment
- the worker has agreed in writing to the deduction.

Certain deductions are exempted from the above conditions, such as the recovery of an overpayment of wages.

In the case of the retail trade, including hospitality, cash and stock shortages are relatively common. During a busy work session mistakes can be made and some employers hold the staff responsible. In such cases employees can be required, as a condition of the contract, to make good stock or cash shortages. However, such a deduction or payment must not exceed 10 per cent of the gross pay due for the period. On termination of employment, however, such deductions may exceed 10 per cent. They cannot be made retrospective for more than 12 months. Notice of intention to make such deductions has to be made in advance, and a written demand also has to be issued.

Pay As You Earn (PAYE)

In the UK employers are obliged to deduct tax due on earnings falling under Schedule E (i.e. emoluments from any office or employment). In some other countries it is the employee's responsibility to make the necessary tax declarations.

This responsibility to deduct tax covers service charge earnings and 'tronc' (pooled tips) earnings where the employer or one of the employees is involved on behalf of the employer in the distribution of the 'tronc'. It is the duty of staff to declare tips where the manager or employer is not involved in their distribution.

Social security

Social security schemes vary considerably from country to country. Most people over school-leaving age and under pensionable age are obliged to contribute. Much of Europe has very supportive schemes, part of the 'social model', providing a wide variety of benefits and welfare services such as benefits for unemployment, sickness, industrial injuries and retirement. Some jurisdictions, in contrast, such as some states of the USA and less developed nations, offer relatively little support.

Employer's liability

In common law countries there are two separate categories of liability that employers bear in relation to injuries suffered by their employees while in their employment. These are common law and statutory liabilities.

In common law, employers are expected to provide protection that is reasonable in the circumstances. An employee will be compensated for injury if the employer was at fault in exposing the employee to unnecessary risk in the circumstances. The common law responsibilities extend also to employees of other employers, such as contractors, while working on the employer's premises, and also to the employer's employees carrying out work for him or her on another person's premises, for example an outdoor caterer's staff.

Common law, however, is not able to provide for all developments in industry and therefore statutes exist to specify the nature of protection to be provided and to lay down certain other regulations covering the working environment, the major one in the UK being the Health and Safety at Work Act 1974. This is largely replicated through much of the EU.

Health and Safety at Work Act 1974

The hospitality industry is not as dangerous as some other industries such as construction. However, there can be significant levels of risk to employees, managers and customers. These may include risks that are simple to recognize – such as slips and trips, cuts and burns and food poisoning – through to less obvious risks such as damage to hearing due to very high noise levels, e.g. in discos, or violence from customers and other staff.

The Health and Safety at Work Act 1974, reflecting EU legislation, is largely implemented through a number of different sets of regulations including:

- Management of Health and Safety at Work Regulations 1999
- Provision and Use of Work Equipment Regulations 1998
- Manual Handling Operations Regulations 1992
- Workplace (Health, Safety and Welfare) Regulations 1992
- Personal Protective Equipment at Work Regulations 1992
- Control of Substances Hazardous to Health (COSHH) Regulations 1994.

The 1974 Act, in principle, obliges employers to ensure the safety of their employees and other people at their premises, by maintaining safe plant, safe systems of work and safe premises, and also by ensuring adequate instruction, training and supervision. This Act also covers such aspects as cleanliness, over-crowding, lighting, temperature, ventilation and sanitary arrangements for work people. Other people, too, such as designers, manufacturers, installers, importers and suppliers of goods for use at work, are to ensure, in so far as they are responsible, that any health and safety risks are eliminated. Employees also are responsible for the safety of others.

Health and safety policy statement

All employers, other than those with fewer than five employees, must have a health and safety policy statement. Typically such a policy will include an overall policy statement regarding the company's and the employees' responsibilities for health and safety. It will then be specific about certain key issues such as: risk assessment, uniforms and protective clothing, first aid, accidents and reporting accidents, manual handling, dangerous machinery, use of dangerous utensils such as knives, electrical equipment, visual display units, hazard spotting, hygiene, fire precautions, bomb alerts, COSHH (Control of Substances Hazardous to Health).

Risk assessment

From a management point of view probably the most important issue is that of risk assessment. 'Risk assessment' is the term used to describe the process an employer uses to identify risks associated with a business's day-to-day operations. If risk assessment is carried out effectively it will almost certainly reduce the risk of injury, but should an incident occur which leads to litigation it can be used to demonstrate 'due diligence' (see above), a legal term used to demonstrate that an employer has taken all reasonable steps to minimize risk.

Risks and the likelihood of occurrence may be classified as follows:

Hazard severity	Likelihood of occurrence
1 Minor injury	1 Low – seldom occurs
2 Off work for three days or more	2 Medium – frequently occurs
3 Death or major injury	3 High – near certain

Multiplication of the two factors (severity and likelihood, resulting in a score of, for example, 2, 4, 9) indicates the overall degree of risk.

Employment of children

The legal definition of a child varies from country to country, the determining criterion being age which ranges from around 14 to 18. The International Labour Organization has within its charter the Elimination of Child Labour, as one of its major aims.

In the UK 'children' are defined as being under the minimum school-leaving age. The principal Acts are concerned primarily with protecting the physical well-being of children and with specifying the hours that they are permitted to work. Children, for example, are not permitted to work during school hours and where a child is under 13 years of age the legal restrictions are particularly strict, for example, limiting their hours of work to no more than one hour per day outside of school hours. Restrictions on the working hours of young persons who have left school but are under the age of 18 are also included in the Working Time Regulations 1998.

Employment of children and young persons in the hospitality industry, where alcohol is sold, is covered by the Licensing Act 2003.

Employment of non-European Union (EU) subjects

Most countries have strict rules and quotas concerning the employment of foreign workers. In the case of the UK the employment of EU subjects is permitted. Non-EU subjects needs Home Office approval, through the granting of a work permit. Under the Asylum and Immigration Act 1996 it is a criminal offence to employ a person who does not have authorization to work in the UK. The penalty (in 2012) is £10,000 for each offence.

Trade union legislation

Membership of trade unions in Europe has been in decline over the last 20 years. In the UK in 2012 around 6.5 million workers were members of trade unions, 25 per cent of the workforce (and see Chapter 15). Trade union membership in the hospitality industry generally is very low, even non-existent, in the private sector of the industry. Membership, however, can be significant in some public sectors.

Legislation covering trade unions varies considerably from country to country. In many countries union membership and activities are protected in a country's constitution. The convention of the International Labour Organization, to which many countries are signatories, states that 'the right of workers and employers to form and join organizations of their own choosing is an integral part of a free and open society'. In some other countries, however, usually autocracies of one type or another, worker organizations are not condoned, because they are seen as a challenge to the ruling power.

In the UK the main legislation currently covering trade unions is contained in a number of Acts, including the Trade Union and Labour Relations (Consolidation) Act 1992, the Trade Union Reform and Employment Rights Act 1993 and the Employment Relations Act 1999. These Acts contain legislation concerned with 'collective' employment issues and the rights of individuals to belong or not to belong to a trade union.

To qualify for most rights under trade union legislation, trade unions have to be certified as independent by the Certification Officer.

Trade disputes and immunities

Trade disputes only attract immunity from actions for damages if they are disputes between employees and their employer and are concerned with matters central to their employment relationship. In addition, any action must have been approved in a ballot by a majority of those voting.

Picketing

Picketing is only lawful if carried out as part of a trade dispute and should be at or near the place of work.

Concluding statement

As stated at the start of this chapter, employment is an extremely complex area of law so this chapter must be viewed as a simple introduction to some of the key issues.

Further reading and references

Boella, M. J. (ed.) *Catering: Reference Book for Caterers*, London: Croner Publications, (updated every four months).

Daniels, K. (2012) *Employment Law*, 3rd edn, London: Chartered Institute of Personnel and Development.

Institute of Hospitality (2009) *Employing Ex-Offenders*, London: Institute of Hospitality.

Lewis, D., Sargeant, M. and Scwab, D. (2011) *Employment Law: The Essentials*, London: Chartered Institute of Personnel and Development.

Schneider, Friedrich (2005) 'A. T. Kearney analysis', Johannes Kepler University of Linz, Austria.

Members of the UK's Institute of Hospitality can access publications including Management Guides which summarize key information of relevance to hospitality operations (www.instituteofhospitality.org).

Members of the UK's Chartered Institute of Personnel and Development (CIPD) can access a range of materials including Fact Sheets and articles from over 300 online journal titles relevant to HR. CIPD members and *People Management* subscribers can see articles on the People Management website (www.peoplemanagement.co.uk).

Questions

1 Describe the main distinct areas of law affecting employment.
2 Describe the 'fair reasons' for terminating employment.
3 Describe a 'fair disciplinary' procedure (see also Chapter 14).
4 Discuss the proposition that a contract of employment is much more than the 'written statement' required by the Employment Rights Act 1996.
5 Evaluate the approach adopted by an employer you know well to managing their labour force as the law requires.
6 Discuss the proposition that government intervention through statute law has no place in the employment relationship which according to contract law is an agreement between two willing parties.

Chapter 17

Human resource planning and information systems

Hospitality management is characterized by an immediacy and an endless cycle of everyday activities and events. It requires a keen sense of the priorities and challenges of the immediate future in order for production and service to come together in a simultaneous offering to the customer. It is about managing resources in the short term, but also demands managers and staff to ensure resources will be properly planned for the future. It is all too easy to pay full attention and energy to today's events and to allow tomorrow's and longer-term business to come as a nasty surprise.

The employment relationship can also be dominated by the 'here and now', ensuring that there is effective workforce and management action and cooperation, that the underpinning HR systems of recruitment and payroll are fulfilling the need of the operation and that employment is administered and enacted within the prevailing legislation. However, the development of contemporary HRM has also placed more strategic, long-term emphasis on the need for organizations to plan and prepare for the future of the business. Indeed, one of the frequently espoused differences between traditional 'personnel management' and HRM is that the former tended to be a reactive, subservient implication of the corporate plan of the organization, whereas the latter is seen as critically central to the business planning process (Kerfoot and Knights, 2012). The alignment of HRM and future business planning requires that the HR decisions are based on appropriate and relevant data, just as any strategic plan, rather than be left to happenstance and external pressures alone. This chapter considers the planning elements and contexts for HRM and employment and the way that modern technology can assist this vital planning process through computerized personnel information systems (CPIS) and the provision of data that give direction to plans and justification for actions.

The importance, value and future impact of an organization's human resources have become much more apparent in recent times as employers seek competitive advantage through improved performance, service and product. In the hospitality industry, the workforce is of substantive and quantifiable importance as well, because of the considerable costs of labour in service work and the growing staff and skill shortages in some sectors of hospitality. The 'demographic time bomb', i.e. the reduction in the number of young people available for work, may contribute to the scale of the problem for many hospitality employers who are reliant on certain employee profiles, such as the fast food sector. With the volatility of the hospitality industry, the arrival of new employers in the local labour market may frequently create new demands on an ever more competitive labour market. Larger firms might also develop plans to expand, both nationally and internationally, through merger and acquisition. Such growth necessitates the companies concerned to plan carefully the impact on the human resource policies and practices in different locations, different countries with very different local factors, traditions and employment environments. Hotel companies such as Intercontinental have recently announced major international expansion plans in countries like China and Russia, two of the so-called 'BRIC' nations (supplemented by Brazil and India), where rapid economic growth is providing enormous future opportunities for international hospitality businesses.

Such developments lead to a need for more accurate planning so that an employer has the appropriate quantity and quality of human resources available when required, from managers to front-line service workers. HR plans are essential to ensure that labour costs associated with growth and development are soundly considered, not unnecessarily overly burdensome on an expanding business. Because of this, well-conceived human resource policies and plans are now playing an increasingly important part in furthering many companies' wider business objectives. HR plans need to be an integrated element of the overall business or corporate plan, not an adjunct or afterthought, and need to be recognized by all senior management as a critical part of ensuring future competitiveness and profitability. The strategic HR plans will then be cascaded into more detailed, operational HR plans that give meaning and guidance to all managers and employees in their everyday work. This means the strategic plans related to all-embracing issues such as organizational culture and service quality are ultimately enacted within the commitment and performance of the workforce in its dealings with the customer.

Strategic HR planning

Successful human resource policies can only be achieved through a thorough understanding of the organization, its objectives, its management, its operating style and its social, technical and political environment. HR planning can therefore be described as the process of interpreting the employment environment, predicting its effects on the organization, evaluating these effects and planning and controlling appropriate measures in order that the company possesses an effective and efficient human resource; basically the right people in the right place at the right time. In effect, HR strategists need to compare the organization's existing workforce with the forecast demand created by the corporate plan, and hence the planning and implementation of HR activities in order that the organization can recruit, train and develop appropriate human resources. This process will often be placed within a scenario of commercial success and development, planning the recruitment of more staff for a healthy, growing organization. However, it may require there to be consideration of the less positive and comfortable aspects of HRM, such as the restructuring of organizations, possibly the redeployment of reluctant employees to other parts of the company or into alternative jobs, and, most regrettably, it may also reveal the need for some redundancies.

In the main, however, human resource policies must be crafted in order to play a positive and creative role in the plans, developments and future activities of an organization. They must be designed to provide appropriately competent human resources as and when required. The need to plan on a sound basis of reliable and pertinent information needs to be emphasized, and much of a manager's work revolves around certain basic and fundamental information; for example, precise job or role descriptions have been shown to be vital not only to recruitment but also to training, performance appraisal, job evaluation and salary administration.

Human resource planning may be divided into two separate and distinct parts: strategic and operational. The strategic part of planning is concerned with ensuring that the right people will be available in the longer term, for example for hotels and resorts that are not yet even purchased or built. Strategic human resource planning for larger organizations requires a thorough understanding of the operation, the sector and the wider economic and social environment. Figure 17.1 shows a 'systems thinking' diagram – how an organization's plan and planning can be significantly affected by its environment.

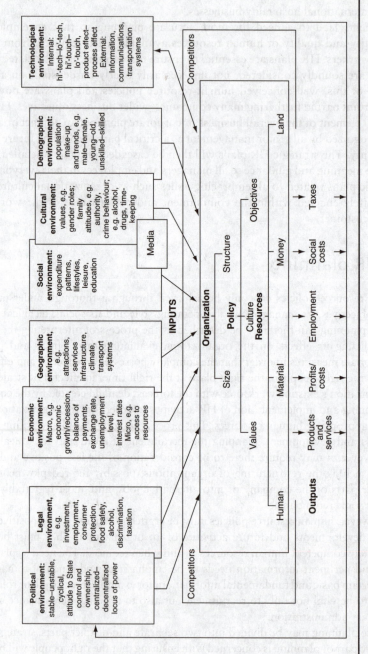

Figure 17.1 A 'systems thinking' diagram

Strategic human resource planning seeks to align the corporate business plan and the HR plan, ensuring as far as possible that the organization has an ability to respond to the HR needs of the corporate plan, and hence the ability to adapt to market trends and customer needs, and maintain a competitive advantage (Holbeche, 2001).

This is a particularly relevant approach for hospitality companies in an international expansion setting as exemplified by the following (anonymized) case study:

Mini case study: Oakwood International Hotels

This company owned and operated 120 hotels in the United Kingdom, predominantly aimed at the corporate business market, often located near to main road transport routes and hubs. As a result of a full strategic review the company had determined that within its specific business travel accommodation markets of the UK, a degree of market saturation had been achieved by its principal brand concepts. However, it operated only a handful of properties on mainland Europe and an expansion strategy was developed in order to benefit from more corporate referral of its core business travel clients and to benefit from EU expansion and, at the time, relative economic strengths. The new strategy was given the title of 'FIGS', the acronym standing for France, Italy, Germany and Spain. A strategic planning team was given the task of seeking suitable sites for new hotel builds or existing properties that may be potential purchases. The nearness to major road networks was continued as a strategic driver. The ambitious business plan stated an expansion of 30 hotels within five years.

However, the company also realized that its existing workforce was demographically home-based, locally resident to the hotels, and that its approach was somewhat parochial and that the management team as a whole was short on international experience as well as weak in intercultural exposure and linguistic abilities. It determined to put together an HR expansion and development team as well as the strategic planning team, but with one senior manager common to both teams to ensure coordination. The HR plan of this team eventually crystallized into an aim to recruit and develop a European management workforce for the future organization.

The more detailed plan that emerged began with an objective of recruiting 20 high quality hotel management graduates from the leading hotel schools and colleges within the 'FIGS' countries and also Switzerland, due to its provision of renowned international hotel management colleges. In this way, the company would be employing graduate-level talent with appropriate cultural and linguistic capabilities and with a desire to train within a highly respected UK business before taking up management positions within the expanded organization, perhaps back in their home country. The HR plan did not finish at recruitment though, as there was a need for a comprehensive training and development plan to be put in place within the UK hotels, so that the new recruits could gain invaluable knowledge and experience within the existing organization, from its culture and service standards to its operating systems and procedures. These talented young people could then provide a coherent bridge of HR into the hotels of the future of the company.

With agreement on a substantial budget to underpin all this HR activity, the company clearly signposted its strategic determination to bring the HR plan to full realization. Once recruited, an HR executive was given the job of managing the progress of the new recruits within the UK head office and specific hotel units. This entailed the development of a special induction and orientation week, with a welcome from the chief executive and sessions with senior managers from across the company's central departments and regional operations. Each recruit was allocated a mentor from within the senior management team as well as a more local mentor within their specific hotel. Further off-job training courses were planned over an 18-month period, covering a range of management development activities and topics. These courses were generally carried out in the Oakwood Hotels Management College, an education and learning facility within the company, forming a wing of its Hemel Hempstead hotel operation. There were also half-yearly formal appraisals of the graduates and eventually they were interviewed and placed within hotels for their first management position. The entire strategic plan and HR plan was eventually deemed to have been a success in the main, although it was apparent that the acquisition of new properties did not fully match the number of graduates prepared, leading to some of the graduates leaving the company after training as they were dissatisfied with the positions available within the UK.

Strategic HR planning can be seen from this example to be a link to strategy implementation and action, to change and transformation, but also to financial planning and budgeting formulation – as this HR plan shows, from recruitment across Europe to systematic and customized training incorporates significant investment on behalf of the organization. This level of HR planning requires HR strategists to consider the existing organizational culture, worker behaviours, skills and the management competencies of the organization, and plan for those key aspects to change and adapt for the future business model.

HR planning also needs to be aware of the demographic profile of its labour market. This requires the gathering of relevant data and statistics, from the locality of a single business to the impact of population trends across a continent. In the case of European expansion as in the case study above, contemporary plans for EU developments would not only need to consider the current economic issues within Europe, but also the age profile of the labour market. Recent reports such as from the Office for National Statistics (ONS), put the ageing population issue into a striking reality, predicting that by 2032, 23 per cent of the UK population will be aged 65 or over, and that there will be 30 per cent more pensioners than the proportion in 2011. In Europe (the 27 countries of the EU making a total population of about 500 million), it is forecast that 39 per cent of the population will be aged 65 or more by 2032. Life expectancy rates continue to rise in the EU, the average age for men in 2011 in the EU was 76 and the average age for women was over 82 years. These fundamental trends are significant for the hospitality industry both in terms of implications for its customer base, but also its future workforce. HR planners should also not be complacent about more contemporary issues, such as high youth unemployment in Europe at the time of writing, as highlighted recently by a report from the Chartered Institute of Personnel and Development (CIPD):

> despite the continuing economic downturn, it is predicted that UK employers will need to fill an estimated 13.5 million job vacancies in the next 10 years, but only 7 million young people will leave school or college over this period.

> (CIPD, 2012)

Operational HR planning

From the broadest of issues at a strategic HR level, hospitality managers also need to translate and interpret the wider HR policies and plans for the shorter term within an operational HR plan (see Figure 17.2) that seeks to match the labour supply with the labour demand. Such a plan needs to consider the more immediate issues of a plan for recruitment and selection (based on staffing ratios and forecast business), for training and development, for performance monitoring and appraisal, for succession planning and for associated plans for future compensation and benefits for employees.

Operational plans frequently require the planning and actioning of specific and customized initiatives. Recruitment plans may lead to plans for advertising or agency consultation, or may be better served by local open days, a well-publicized invitation for local people to come along for a chat about potential jobs and training within the organization. This is often used for new hotel and restaurant openings, and may be preceded by specific advertisements and articles sponsored within the local press and on local radio stations to raise awareness of the company's plans for local development and jobs. Plans for selection methods may lead to the practical outcomes of the introduction of assessment centres and psychometric testing of potential recruits, all designed to employ people most suited to the job and the

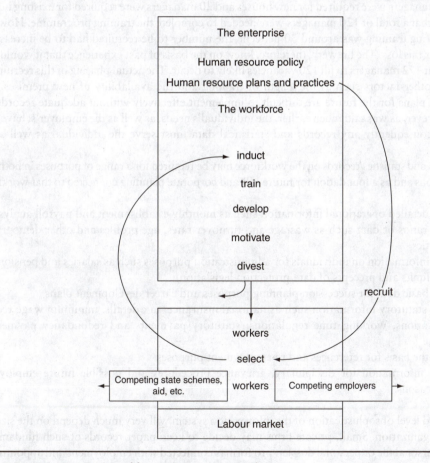

Figure 17.2 Operational human resources plan

organization and its culture, not just in the technical skills but also in attitudes and behaviours needed to ensure customer service standards are achieved and competitiveness attained.

The need for information

At the strategic and operational HR planning levels, management needs accurate data, information and statistics in order to develop the long-term strategies and in due course to implement shorter-term plans. This can be illustrated by a real example with which one of the authors of this book was associated. A brewery and pub company reviewed its business strategy and this resulted in a strategic driver or imperative to expand its number of managed licensed retail houses by 100. It needed to recruit at least 100 new management teams (often husband-and-wife teams or partner couples) to run these public houses. In addition, as it had 100 managed houses already, it would have to anticipate finding replacements for some of these existing 100 managers. If wastage (labour turnover) rates of pub managers had been unavailable, it would not have been possible to calculate accurately the numbers to recruit and train. On the other hand the company had kept records and these showed that wastage among established managers was 20 per cent per annum and among trainees 30 per cent. It was then simple to determine how many to recruit in a year.

Since 100 managers were required for new houses and 20 managers were required for existing houses, this indicated that a total of 120 managers were needed to complete the training programme. However, as wastage during training was around 30 per cent, the number to be recruited had to be increased to compensate for this loss. The brewery, therefore, knew on the basis of past experience that it would need to recruit about 172 managers to fill 120 vacancies likely to occur. The actual phasing of this recruitment depended on other factors such as the length of training and the availability of new premises. This illustrates that plans for the future are difficult to implement effectively without adequate records and statistics. However, as was said much earlier, the individual's needs, as well as the employer's, have to be recognized – consequently any records and statistical data must serve the individual as well as the employer.

Information and statistics/records on the workforce may be required for a range of purposes in both day-to-day operations and as a foundation for future HR and corporate planning connected to that workforce:

- to provide detailed operational information such as monthly establishment and payroll analyses
- to provide ratios or data such as wastage and turnover rates, age profiles and other demographic characteristics
- to provide information on individuals for administration purposes such as salaries and pensions (all within the limits and precepts of data protection legislation)
- to provide basic data for succession planning purposes and career development plans
- to provide statutory information such as national insurance, tax details, minimum wage records and implications, working time regulations, statutory payments and redundancy payments if appropriate
- to provide the basis for references and re-employment purposes
- to provide information for disciplinary, grievance procedures and possible future employment litigation reasons.

The format and level of sophistication of the information system will very much depend on the size and scale of the organization. Small, private firms may decide to keep paper records of such fundamental aspects as: a personal file or personal dossier; pro formas connected with employment and appointment; disciplinary, grievance and termination forms; establishment and labour turnover analyses; payroll data; accident and medical reports; absentee records. However, with the benefit of modern computerized personnel information systems (CPIS), even small businesses can be reassured that for a relatively small cost for a very basic system, they have an information base that both protects them from legal processes and provides a basis for operational planning.

Computerized personnel information systems (CPIS)

For hospitality organizations such as multi-site and multinational chains, with large and disparate workforces, there is now a wide range of software systems that can be acquired. Some systems are basic IT versions of the personnel record systems of the past, and can be purchased from as little as £300, but for multinationals, much more sophisticated designs need to be considered, and the cost–benefit factor assessed. Advanced CPIS provide stores of data, providing the necessary and essential information required for both short-term, everyday management needs and also the basis for longer-term strategic HR planning. Human resources software packages aim to provide the employer with all the necessary data in one, secure location. A basic system can store:

- personal details
- holiday records
- absences/sick leave
- payroll records
- disciplinary records
- working patterns/shifts/rosters
- performance and training data
- legislative/statutory and required data.

With regard to this last point, these packages have the inherent advantage of giving the employer some peace of mind over compliance with employment law and regulations. Regardless of size, an employer is required by law to retain and maintain accurate basic details of employees of all levels and status, from full-time to part-time and casuals, as well as details of other subcontractors and volunteers. Systems will normally ensure there is adequate provision for systematic keeping of records connected with legislation such as work permits, right-to-work forms and CRB (Criminal Records Bureau) and ISA (Independent Safeguarding Authority) checks where relevant. They might have the facility to generate written statements of employment for new employees within two months of their start dates and also flag up renewal dates for important legal issues such as CRB checks where supervision of children is involved.

Other, more sophisticated systems might include the following features:

- full HR software for personnel database management for comprehensive, safely stored employee records
- payroll software with full integration of payroll with the HR information above, reporting needs and statutory forms
- online recruitment facility with full vacancy management features from applicant management to uploading of CVs by the candidate (sometimes referred to as career portals, allowing firms to access the same tools as used by commercial recruitment agencies)
- training solutions for managing courses: scheduling, budget and course documentation
- work patterns and effective performance analyses, for most efficient approaches to work shifts and ergonomics/design of work patterns and rotas
- analysis features which can be customized to the needs of the employer, perhaps producing charts and graphs required for presentations as well as management interpretation and action

- links to social media platforms and guidance on how to use them for collaboration and connections across different parts of the company, to improve communication and engagement of personnel across a multi-site organization
- 'HR Dashboards' can be part of some systems, providing analysis and metrics on-screen, segmenting the workforce data into different formats as required by management, e.g. payroll summaries, salary costs, overtime trends, sector benchmarks against which to judge HR performance trends and achievements.

Auditing HR

As with the contemporaneous HR Dashboard concept, some of the largest employers also conduct detailed studies periodically which provide a complete breakdown of their workforce, from job grades and salary bands to age profile and lengths of service. There may be a requirement to review staff training activities, qualifications levels, performance assessments and appraisal data. Put together, such information may provide a dossier of data to underpin and inform an HR planning function. It may also be useful to try to determine the economic value of the human organization by placing values on all activities, such as recruitment and training, and in effect preparing a human resource account. This approach, sometimes referred to as human asset accounting, can be relevant if the HR team wish to find correlation between business success and profitability and the input from HR activities.

However, it is a difficult task to discover and calculate absolute correlations between HR inputs and business success outputs. Contemporary management strategists, especially in the hospitality and related service sectors, do not always need the hard evidence of values to convince them that their human resources are key to commercial viability; or that planning, both strategically and operationally, is an integral and essential part of managing a hospitality enterprise in the twenty-first century.

Further reading and references

Armstrong, M. (2012) *A Handbook of Human Resource Management Practice*, 12th edn, London: Kogan Page.

Chartered Institute of Personnel and Development (CIPD) (2012) *Managing a Healthy Ageing Workforce: A National Business Imperative*, London: CIPD Publications.

Holbeche, L. (2001) *Aligning Human Resources and Business Strategy*, Oxford: Butterworth-Heinemann.

Kerfoot, D. and Knights, D. (2012) 'Managing people: contexts of HRM', in Knights, D. and Willmott, H., *Introducing Organisational Behaviour and Management*, 2nd edn, Andover: Cengage Learning EMEA.

Pratt, K. J. and Bennett, S. C. (1990) *Elements of Personnel Management*, 4th edn, Wokingham: GEE.

Storey, J. (2007) *Human Resource Management – A Critical Text*, 3rd edn, London: Thomson.

Torrington, D., Hall, L. and Taylor, S. (2008) *Human Resource Management*, 7th edn, Harlow: FT Prentice Hall.

Members of the UK's Institute of Hospitality (IoH) can access publications including Management Guides which summarize key information of relevance to hospitality operations (www.instituteofhospitality.org).

Members of the UK's Chartered Institute of Personnel and Development (CIPD) can access a range of materials including Fact Sheets and articles from over 300 online journal titles relevant to HRM. CIPD members and *People Management* subscribers can see articles on the People Management website (www.peoplemanagement.co.uk).

Questions

1 What are the objectives of human resource planning?

2 What are the critical differences between strategic HR planning and operational HR planning?

3 What purposes can be served by information systems in connection to HR planning?

4 If deciding to purchase a CPIS software package for HR data, what criteria would you assess in order to make a worthwhile purchase?

5 What aspects and HR performance measures would you want as part of the data analysis on an 'HR Dashboard'? Consider an organization with which you are familiar as a context for answering this question.

CASE STUDY QUESTION – see the Lux Hotels case study Appendix 5

Apply the principles considered in this chapter to the Lux Hotels case and its development plans for the business.

Chapter 18

Productivity and labour costs

In any industry in which labour is a significant cost, its monitoring and control is vital in ensuring profitability. This is certainly the case in the hospitality industry, especially in high labour costs regions such as the UK, European Union as a whole and North America. It is also the case that the hospitality industry must also consider the workforce as a key element in the provision of a quality product and standard of service. Hence any consideration of controlling labour costs must be simultaneously assessed alongside the need for maintaining the desired levels of quality and of service to the standards required to meet the expectations of customers. This is the challenge of understanding and monitoring productivity of the labour force.

The hospitality industry has frequently been criticized for its low productivity levels and apparent lack of concern and knowledge about its performance outside of the raw data of profit and loss accounts (Jones, 2007). In many ways it can be reasoned why this should be the case. Productivity measurement in terms of ratios of inputs and outputs has its history embedded within the manufacturing sectors, with mass production assembly lines being the epitome of a quantifiable situation where inputs of labour could be evaluated by the numbers of finished products and articles coming off the line and out of the factory. Motor car production under the precepts of scientific management and Taylorism (see Chapter 2), heralded an age of accurate and meaningful productivity measurement. The inputs and outputs of the service sector, including hospitality, are less easily evaluated. Outputs are particularly challenging in terms of accurate evaluation, often connected with intangible factors such as customer satisfaction, customer perceptions of value for money and the equally intangible combination of substantive consumption and emotion (the symbolic consumption) that determines the success of hospitality experiences.

The hospitality industry also has peaks and troughs of business, has many different departments and specific technical skills, and has inputs of the employees' interpersonal behaviour which are so difficult to put a value on with any certainty. A licensed retail chain may be able, through its sophisticated EPOS (electronic point of sale) technology, to gain an hourly assessment of transactions per employee, but how can that information be used to effect in the light of the periods within a day of sharply fluctuating sales volumes? However, this use of information technology does provide a basis for comparison and analysis and is only meaningful when compared with the inputs of labour costs. These costs form the comparator measurement for most productivity systems, such as a hotel using the basic measure of total revenue per hour worked, or rooms sold per hour worked or food revenue per hour worked in the food and beverage operation. It can be seen that at the heart of the issue of productivity is a need to have accurate but relevant labour cost and payroll information (the monetary inputs) in order to be able to take managerial decisions about the effectiveness and efficiency of the outputs such as revenue, average spend, rooms serviced in housekeeping and customer satisfaction.

Factors influencing labour costs

The factors that influence labour costs are numerous but a fundamental starting place for consideration is the precise nature of the enterprise, and the employer's particular policy; for example, if the business provides a subsidized staff meals service, with low selling prices to employees, then labour costs as a percentage of revenue will be high. Premium service levels, as in five-star hotels, require more skilled and plentiful employees and the wage percentage to sales will again be high. If, at the other extreme, the business model seeks to maximize profit on high volumes at low selling prices, by providing a product involving minimum service from capital-intensive plant, using low-skill staff, as in many fast food operations, then the labour costs will be low. Figure 18.1 illustrates some factors influencing labour costs and productivity.

Another major factor is efficiency of design. Modern, formulaic designed hotels (e.g. branded budget hotels) can expect room attendants to service around 17 bedrooms per section, in contrast to older, traditional properties (e.g. exclusive country house hotels), where sections often have to be much smaller due to room size and variety of configuration. Equally important of course is the level of service provided.

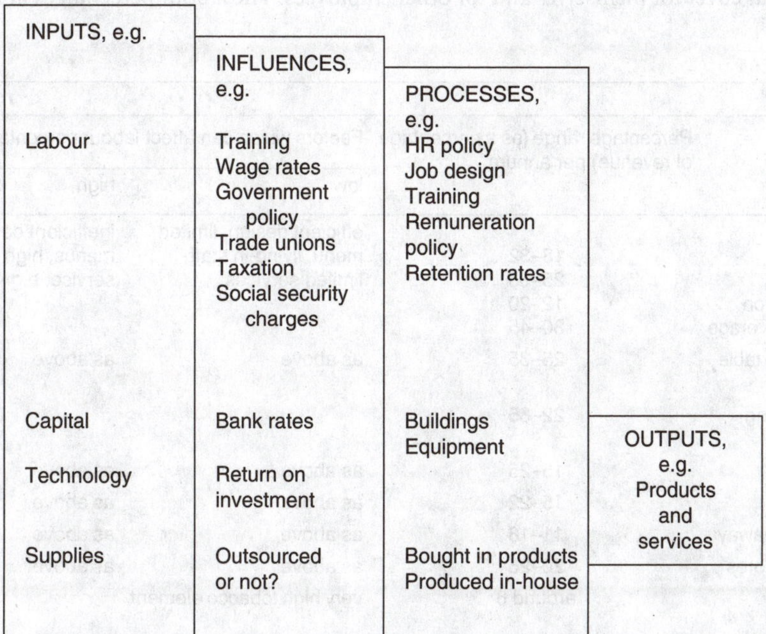

Figure 18.1 A simple 'input–output' productivity model

A fast food takeaway operation or a high street wine bar may operate with a labour percentage of around 15 per cent (alongside low selling prices), whereas a high-class restaurant offering skilled personal attention may need to operate at around 35 per cent labour cost (alongside high selling prices). Likewise a modern three-star hotel with minimal personal service can operate at around 18–20 per cent labour cost while some five-star hotels may need to spend up to 37 per cent on labour. Such percentages also vary from country to country, dependent on local workforce legislation, social and statutory costs and the level of trade union activity or national agreements. Of interest to HRM practitioners is also the influence of the level of multi-skilling across the workforce. Clearly there are potential productivity implications of a flexible workforce, employees able and willing to help out in a range of tasks across the business, thus giving management an invaluable tool in covering particular peaks in business activity (Jones, 2007).

In establishments at the smaller end of the scale, which make up such a large percentage of the hospitality industry, a factor influencing labour costs is whether an establishment is run by the owner or by an employed manager. Proprietors who are also managing the business can influence labour costs in a number of ways. First, some owners pay themselves unrealistic wages for a variety of reasons, not least to minimize tax liability. Second, owners are generally motivated to be much stronger in controlling costs (doing more hands-on work than their managerial counterparts). Third, they avoid employing excess labour as cover for themselves and for other employees. The labour percentages in Figure 18.2 are

Type of outlet	Percentage range (as a percentage of revenue) per annum	Factors which can affect labour percentage	
		low	high

Hotels
  2–3 star
  4–5 star
  rooms division
  food and beverage
	
	18–32
	25–35
	12–20
	30–45
		efficient design, limited menu, living-in staff, limited services	inefficient design, extensive menus, high level of service, e.g. room service

Restaurants – table service	25–35	as above	as above
Popular catering – table service	22–35		
Self-service	15–25	as above	as above
Wine bars	15–22	as above	as above
Fast food takeaway	11–18	as above	as above
Department stores	20–25	as above	as above
Kiosks, mainly confectionery and tobacco	around 6	very high tobacco element	
Public houses	10–20	efficient design, e.g. one bar, mainly liquor sales	high catering ratio, several bars/restaurants

Figure 18.2 Labour costs as a percentage of revenue

This table is intended to be a guide only, and it must be recognized that businesses may still operate successfully outside of these. These should be viewed as the range within which most viable businesses operate on a long-term (e.g. annual) basis. There can be considerable fluctuation on a short-term basis as labour costs are not a completely variable cost.
Note: Contract catering is not included as results are totally dependent upon client policy.

intended to indicate the approximate level of labour cost (as a percentage of revenue, net of value added tax) likely to be encountered in viable establishments. This does not mean that there are not successful establishments operating outside these ranges. Likewise, it must be recognized that labour costs are partly fixed and partly variable, so if trade drops dramatically there is a point beyond which labour costs can no longer be reduced to maintain them within the normally accepted percentages – a problem all too familiar to the management of seasonal establishments.

In some cases the wage percentage may well be reviewed on an annual basis. Most organizations, however, monitor labour costs on a shorter-term basis, monthly or maybe even weekly, with many of the fast food outlets now planning labour on an hourly basis.

Figure 18.3 illustrates a format used by some fast food operators. The consequence of this precise hour-by-hour planning is that labour costs are planned and controlled accurately to precise percentages. Such systems can also be linked to the 'HR Dashboard' information system reviewed in Chapter 17. One of the international fast food chains operates branches at around an 11.5 per cent labour cost, with management costs ranging from 2 per cent for the most efficient and busy branches up to 6 per cent for others. All employers must also consider the on-costs of labour costs, the national insurance payments that have to be made and other issues such as social security/sick pay schemes and pension schemes with contributions from the employer. As indicated above, the level of on-costs can vary markedly between countries, with much higher rates in countries like France and Sweden, much lower in the UK and USA.

Productivity measurement

As already mentioned, one of the problems of using labour percentage as the main means of labour cost control is that it does not indicate whether the cost is the result of employing a large number of low-paid people or of employing fewer people but paying them a higher wage. In addition, in many food service contracting sectors of the industry, such as school meals provision, hospital catering and employee meal services, labour costs cannot be expressed as a proportion of revenue because there may be little or no revenue, or because subsidies distort the picture. Other measures, therefore, become necessary. Basically these are concerned with relating labour input to the various forms of output. Such measures include physical and part-physical, part-financial measures and they vary among the different sectors and also within departments. These may be based on some constant (i.e. a factor unaffected by inflation) such as time. Some examples are shown in Figure 18.4. It should be borne in mind, however, that direct comparisons can be dangerous; for example, in one contract-catering situation a 'main meal' may offer each customer a wide choice, whereas in another situation there may be little or no choice. Other factors such as shift work and night work also play an important part, as do national and international work patterns; for example, an Industrial Society survey (*Catering, Prices, Costs and Subsidies*) showed that for every individual catering worker employed, about 22 main meals were served. The author's own consultancy work shows that in some other European countries the number of meals served is frequently between 50 and 60 for each food service contract-catering worker employed. The list in Figure 18.5 is taken from one North American hotel. Not all items listed are direct measures of labour cost or productivity but they all inform management decisions, most of which will affect staffing and HR planning (see also Sigla *et al.*, 2004).

In order to develop a more meaningful and comparative productivity measurement system or scheme, a hospitality manager must not only determine what the inputs are exactly, but also must set benchmarks for all activities and operational departments covered by the scheme. Agreeing benchmarks with other managers and departmental heads also provides a means of setting realistic targets and performance goals. Benchmarking is a very useful approach to the monitoring of productivity levels and of comparing

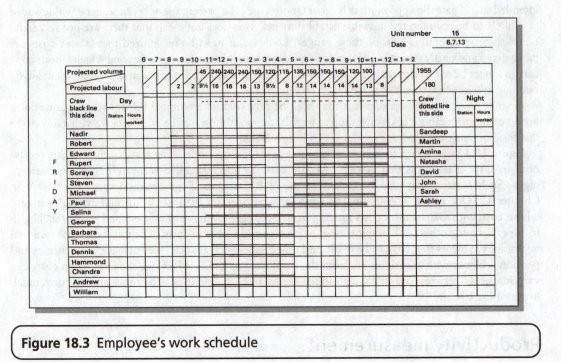

Figure 18.3 Employee's work schedule

'like with like' over time in order to identify trends and take management action as appropriate. Again, as noted by Harnisch (2012: 2), benchmarking must take into account the special characteristics of a particular business:

> For example the overall average rate of a hotel (revenue per worked hour) and its business mix (individual check-ins versus group/airline crew check-ins) impact scores. In terms of F&B [food and beverage] productivity, results are highly affected by the restaurant concept (buffet versus a la carte), and the physical structure of the restaurant.

For larger businesses, it is also noteworthy that the onward march of technology and IT/CPIS systems (see Chapter 17) to support hospitality managers has also reached the important subject of productivity and workforce costs. In addition to the generic computerized personnel information systems (CPIS) discussed in the previous chapter, there are now a range of software applications available to hospitality managers which address the specific challenge of productivity, labour costs and the efficient scheduling and rostering of employees. One leading provider proposes that its system enabled productivity levels to be enhanced, customer service improved and quality undiminished by use of its software. One such system offers and claims the following features:

- creates complex staff rotas/schedules across multiple units and locations
- aligns employee skills with tasks
- assists management in controlling labour costs
- eliminates unnecessary and costly manual procedures and processes
- increases productivity
- reduces labour turnover levels
- increases employee morale.

Department	Description of productivity measure	Some examples
Catering		
Employee meal service	1 Number of meals served by each member of staff (full-time equivalent)	30 meals a day
	2 Covers served per paid hour	4.5 covers
	3 Paid minutes for each meal served	
	plate wash	7 minutes
	food service staff	24 minutes
	cooks	15 minutes
	Coffee Shop	15 minutes
Hospitals	4 Labour as a percentage of direct costs $\dfrac{\text{Labour} + \text{Materials}}{\text{Labour}} \times 100$	e.g. 52%
School meals	5 Labour to materials ratio	£2 labour to £2 materials
Hotels	1 Employees per room	e.g. 0.9 per room
	2 Number of guest nights for each member of staff (full-time equivalent)	21 sleeper nights for each member of staff
	3 Number of rooms served for each member of staff on duty	17 rooms to 1 member of staff
	4 Number of paid minutes for each sleeper night	
	room-attendants	27 minutes per room (attendants on duty only)
	reception	33 minutes per guest night
Public houses/bars	1 Barrels and barrels equivalent per full-time equivalent	3–7 barrels per week

Figure 18.4 Some examples of productivity measures

Total food outlet sales

Breakfast, lunch, dinner 'capture': number of hotel residents taking breakfast, lunch and dinner

Breakfast, lunch and dinner average checks, i.e. spend per head

REVPAR (Revenue per available room)

House profit PAR (per average room)

Rooms division hours per occupied room: total of rooms division hours paid divided by total of occupied rooms

Laundry hours per occupied room: similar to the above

Kitchen hours per cover: total of kitchen hours paid divided by total of covers served

Stewarding hours per cover: similar to the above

Beverage sales per hour paid: total of beverage sales divided by paid hours

Banqueting hours per cover: total of banqueting revenue divided by total of banqueting hours paid

Total of administration and general expenses per available room: total administration and general costs divided by total relevant labour costs Including senior management.

Figure 18.5 A North American example of some key ratios

It may be considered somewhat ambitious that a system of technology can achieve such lofty goals, but it may be appropriate in multi-site and multinational organizations to assess the value of such a system and to test its claims against its own outputs. The most important point is that hospitality managers, whatever the size, type and location of the business, should undoubtedly consider those productivity measures that are significant for their particular business, and ensure that they have the most relevant data on labour costs available for the measurements to be meaningful. A summary of some examples follows.

Number of units sold per employee
A commonly used crude measure of productivity is that of the number of units produced/sold for each employee. This measure is frequently used, for example, to compare car-manufacturing productivity between nations. In order to make use of such a measure it is necessary to have additional information, e.g. how many components are outsourced. In hotels and restaurants one very simple measure is to relate the number of employees to the number of units of service, e.g. rooms, guests or meals served. These are usually extremely crude measures, since comparisons are rarely like with like. Some rooms may be larger than others, some meals may be more complex than others, some elements may be outsourced and some guests may stay for longer periods than others, reducing the variable costs of such items as replacement bed linen and towels.

Number of employees per X number of rooms
This is a simple measure which can (but not always) indicate the level of service provided.

Sales to payroll index
This is another way of expressing the labour cost as a proportion of revenue. It indicates the amount of revenue in pounds generated by each pound spent on labour.

Sales and payroll cost per employee
Another method is to look at the sales per employee and, after deducting the employee cost, the net sales per employee.

Added value
This method assesses the value added by each pound spent on labour. It is calculated by representing the gross profit (sales less material costs) as a proportion of the labour cost.

Materials-to-labour ratio
In many contract-catering operations where there may be little or no revenue, or where there is a subsidy element (e.g. hospitals, schools, employee meal services, clubs), expressing labour costs as a proportion of sales is either not possible or can be meaningless for comparative purposes. Other measures are therefore necessary – these can include the materials-to-labour ratio, i.e. how much labour is needed to process the materials required. In hospitals this can be around a 1:1 ratio, whereas in some school meals operations it can range from around 0.4:1.0 in centralized production operations to as high as 2.6:1.0 in some labour-intensive, localized production systems.

Effective use of available labour is obviously one of the key measures to controlling labour costs. Other factors to take into account include considering alternative ways of getting work done which can reduce the payroll burden. For example, some hospitality companies use contract cleaners to service their hotel bedrooms, even contract caterers to provide staff meals. Whilst this may appear an expensive method in the short term, in the long term their labour cost is reduced and management can concentrate their efforts on the core business.

Bahrain	1.42	London (upper tier)	1.62
Berlin	0.68	London (lower tier)	0.62
Brussels	0.51	London (all)	0.87
Cape Town	0.94	Moscow	1.20
Copenhagen	0.29	Paris (upper tier)	2.17
Helsinki	0.24	Paris (lower tier)	0.62
Jerusalem	0.57	Paris (all)	0.95

Figure 18.6 International staff-to-room ratios

The international context

Costs of labour and productivity of the workforce vary considerably from one country to another for a whole range of reasons – to do with skills, training, national government social and economic policy, management expertise and attitudes to work. Several of the leading specialist management consultancies produce regular reports on the worldwide hospitality industry and these show considerable differences in labour costs. Examples of these statistics are shown in Figure 18.6.

Soundly based and effective, realistic productivity measurement enables comparisons to be made between units or groups of workers employed on the same operations, or the same unit or groups of workers at different times. In spite of the many problems encountered in attempting to make comparisons, productivity measurement is a vital control tool for management, helping with budgeting, forecasting, human resource planning, incentive schemes and diagnosis of poor performance. Productivity measurement and internal benchmarking has the advantage over straight labour percentages of providing a constant measurement that is unaffected by inflation and changes in wage rates. Benchmarking productivity values may be internally derived from past records and current practice or standards, or might be informed by external benchmarking guidelines from other parts of the same organization or, indeed, other similar establishments within the sector.

Further reading and references

British Hospitality Association (1999) *British Hospitality Trends and Statistics*, London: BHA.

British Hospitality Association (2004) *British Hospitality Association: Trends and Statistics 2004*, London: BHA.

Catering Prices, Costs and Subsidies, London: Industrial Society, published annually.

Foot, M. and Hook, C. (2011) *Introducing Human Resource Management*, 6th edn, Harlow: FT Prentice Hall.

Harnisch, O. (2012) *Productivity Management in the Hospitality Industry*, Hospitality.net.

Ingold, T. and Yeoman, I. (2000) *Yield Management in the Hospitality Industry*, 2nd edn, London: Continuum.

Jones, P. (2007) 'Drivers of productivity improvement in the tourism and hospitality industries: practice, research evidence and implications for teaching', conference paper at Eurhodip, London.

MacLeod, D. and Clarke, N. (2010) *Engaging for Success: Enhancing Performance through Employee Engagement*, London: Department for Business, Innovation and Skills.

PKF (2003) *City Survey*, London: PKF.

Sigla, M., Jones, P., Lockwood, A. and Airey, D. (2004) 'Productivity in hotels: a stepwise data envelopment analysis of hotels' rooms division processes', *Service Industries Journal*, 25(1): 63–68.

Members of the UK's Institute of Hospitality (IoH) can access publications including Management Guides which summarize key information of relevance to hospitality operations (www.instituteofhospitality.org).

Members of the UK's Chartered Institute of Personnel and Development (CIPD) can access a range of materials including Fact Sheets and articles from over 300 online journal titles relevant to HRM. CIPD members and *People Management* subscribers can see articles on the People Management website (www.peoplemanagement.co.uk).

Questions

1 Describe the objectives of and alternative approaches to labour cost and productivity measurement.

2 Discuss the differences between labour cost measurement and productivity measurement.

3 Discuss what external factors influence (a) labour costs and (b) productivity.

4 Evaluate the approach to managing labour costs and productivity used by an employer you know well.

5 What is meant by productivity benchmarking?

CASE STUDY QUESTION – see the Lux Hotels case study Appendix 5

In regard to Lux Hotels, what productivity measures and benchmarks would you prioritize for the company in order for overall performance to be enhanced?

HRM and hospitality: contemporary issues

Chapter 19

Organizing human resources

The preceding chapters have concentrated largely on the various management techniques that are concerned with obtaining, training, motivating and administering staff. In addition to these various processes, however, managers also have to organize staff, that is to create groups of people who will meet the organization's objectives. This is normally one of the major responsibilities of line management, who organize their work people into groups in the manner they think best, basing their organization usually on what they have observed or experienced elsewhere. Nowadays, however, there is a growing recognition that organizing people into the most appropriate work groups is a highly skilled and complex task, often referred to as 'organization development', which is concerned with 'improving an organization's ability to achieve its goals by using people more effectively' (French and Saward, 1977). A great deal has been written about organizing people at work. Major ideas on the subject range from the Scientific School of Management through the Human Relations School to current ideas on systems and contingency. Some of the relevant key writers' ideas are summarized in Figure 2.5.

The object of this chapter is not to give a history of the evolution of thinking on organization structures but to highlight some key issues and the factors that influence choice about the nature of an organization. Organizations exist principally to achieve certain goals. In the modern commercial world, put very simply, this is usually to achieve some form of competitive advantage. This usually means market share and sometimes even market domination. In the public sector the goal is to provide service. These aims might be termed the organization's strategies which consist of long-term goals and objectives, courses of action and allocation of resources. These should determine the way the organization is put together with all the hierarchies and lines of authority. Such structures should follow strategy (see Chandler in Pugh and Hickson, 2007).

In order to achieve these goals an organization will manage its work according to certain principles, including planning, organizing, commanding, coordinating and controlling (after Fayol, see Figure 2.5). In addition, work will be specialized (after Taylor, see Figure 2.5) in a number of different ways, for example at the technical level, but also at a hierarchical level, i.e. there are both horizontal and vertical divisions of work.

Lynda Gratton, of the London Business School, writing in 'Mastering Management' (*Financial Times*, 1995), stated that an 'important issue for companies is to identify HR activities which link business strategy to performance. Key processes … include: reflecting business goals in individual and team objectives, and in performance measures; rewards and training; visualising the future; and identifying and encouraging individual talent'. Traditionally this required that a structure exists in which lines of authority, responsibility and communication exist. Ideas about how these principles are achieved have evolved over time, but are summarized simply by Mullins (1996):

- *The Scientific School*: strict division of labour, formal hierarchy.
- *Human Relations School*: recognition of workers' social needs and the informal organization.
- *Systems*: recognition of the socio-technical system, i.e. the need to integrate both the benefits of the Scientific School and the Human Relations School.
- *Contingency*: recognition that there is no one 'best' system for all management situations, e.g. managing the delivery of a fast food operation is very different from managing the planning of a new fast food restaurant.

Burns and Stalker (1966) identified two extreme types of organization – the 'mechanistic' and the 'organic'. The 'mechanistic' reflects the 'scientific school of management' in that it is very bureaucratic and has a hierarchical structure. The 'organic' organization, on the other hand, reflects the 'contingency' approach in that it is flexible and able to adopt new structures easily. Most organizations come somewhere between the two extremes.

Handy (1989) writes of the 'shamrock' organization, which consists of the professional core, the flexible labour force and the contractual fringe. This closely reflects the reality of the modern labour force, which in many cases consists of managers, core workers and peripheral workers – in the hospitality industry examples would include the management team, full-time employed key workers such as chefs and receptionists, casual workers such as casual waiters, and a range of subcontracted functions such as cleaners, security personnel, musicians and drivers.

Organization development as a process can have a number of different goals. The most common are:

- improvement in organizational performance, e.g. profits or service levels
- improvement in decision-making processes
- improvement in group or team work
- responding to change
- changing value systems and attitudes
- reducing costs.

A whole range of factors influence organization structures, each factor having some effect on the final type of structure, which may be either the result of careful design, the result of evolutionary development or merely expedient.

The main options open to organizations are as follows:

- *Functional*: where different individuals attend to the main management functions, i.e. finance, marketing, personnel, operations, research.
- *Product*: where different managers manage different products, e.g. hotels or public houses or popular catering.
- *Geographical*: where managers attend to everything within a geographic region, e.g. Europe, Scotland, Manchester, a motorway route such as the M1.
- *Project*: where groups are set up for specific projects and disperse upon completion, usually relying upon existing hierarchical roles.
- *Matrix*: a loose form of the above where individuals may be members of a number of different groups, with leadership roles depending more on expertise than on hierarchical roles.

In the larger organizations it is possible to find a combination of the above. For example, hotel and public house operating companies may be organized on both product and geographical bases.

Power and the decision-making process

Probably the most important influence on organization structure will be ownership. Is the organization owned by an individual, by a family, by a private company, a public company with shareholders, a private equity company or a hedge fund? Related to this will be whether the business is owner-operated, run by a management company, a franchise or member of a voluntary chain (a consortium).

Many of the largest hospitality companies have started out as small privately owned companies, progressing through various stages of the business life cycle to major multi-unit, national, international, even global companies operating in a variety of different formats. Serious human resource challenges arise at each stage of the evolution of such companies, for example, at what stage does the family relinquish or start to relinquish direct management control (see Chapter 22)?

Driving the process of organization should be an overall philosophy of the senior management towards their markets and their workforce (see Chapter 2). Unitarist (or autocratic) managers will tend towards concentrating decision making upon themselves, whereas a pluralist (or democratic) manager will be prepared to share decision making and to empower the workforce. Public sector organizations tend to require committee decisions, made within a legislative or bureaucratic framework, whereas private sector organizations tend to have far fewer legislative or bureaucratic restraints and decision making can be a simpler process, requiring fewer participants. Such differences in types of organization can influence quite considerably the formal and informal approaches to organization.

Organizational objectives

Each type of organization has particular objectives. In some cases the objective is to make a profit, in others to maximize profit, to increase shareholder value, to increase market share. In the public sector it is to provide a service such as caring for people, providing education. These objectives obviously influence staffing levels because where profit is the main motive, staffing levels will normally be kept close to the most economic level, with attendant risks of occasional understaffing. These considerations are present also in the public sector nowadays because of strict government spending restrictions.

The market

The single most important factor affecting structure is probably the type of market being catered for. Obviously consumer demands determine the type of staff required but the degree of seasonal fluctuation also influences organization structure. A hospital with predictable and stable levels of demand, where the catering service is ancillary to other services, will have staffing needs very different from those required by a highly seasonal resort hotel or holiday camp where the accommodation and catering services themselves are the end product. The hospital will need a relatively stable and permanent labour force, whereas the seasonal hotel will probably need a small nucleus of permanent, key staff which is boosted by seasonal and casual labour as demand increases (see the Shamrock organization, Handy, 1989, chapter 2).

Technology

The technology of a particular sector is also important. One simple example is airline catering. In this sector of the industry, space is at a premium, weight carries penalties, and constant supervision is not possible. These factors obviously influence the product offered, the equipment used and the staff selected.

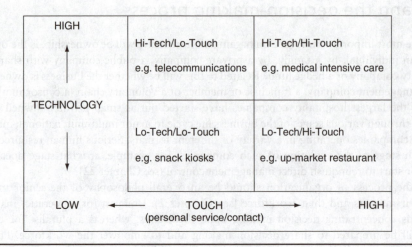

Figure 19.1 The tec–touch matrix

Product and process effects

The role of technology in shaping organizations is vital. One way to look at technology in the organization is to look at the 'tec–touch' matrix (see Figure 19.1). This diagram sets out to illustrate major approaches to the use of technology in industry. In some industries heavy investment in advanced technology is essential, such as in the information technology industries. Such technologies influence the hospitality industry mainly in an indirect way, for example through improved advance reservation systems and various social media such as TripAdvisor. Such influences may be known as the 'process' effect, i.e. the effect is mainly concerned with the process by which the customer receives or acquires the 'service' offering. New technologies may also enable a hospitality operator to offer new or enhanced 'service' products. This is known as the 'product' effect.

Hi-tech and hi-touch

In other cases most reliance is based on the human touch elements of service. Where the human element is high this may be known as a 'hi-touch' offering. In some cases there is a combination of hi-tech and hi-touch – an example is intensive-care hospital treatment. In many instances of hospitality offerings the technology used is relatively or very lo-tech and the human element of service is very low also – snack kiosks are examples of such lo-tech, lo-touch offerings.

Much fine-dining might be described as lo-tech and hi-touch.

Centralization and decentralization

The question of centralization and decentralization is at the heart of many organizational issues. In the hospitality industry this may focus on whether or not to centralize functions such as marketing and sales, reservations, financial management, purchasing, personnel, payroll and property management. In some cases, such as marketing or reservations, it is generally accepted that centralization can make good sense. In other cases, however, such as sales or personnel, unit managers often argue that they are better able to manage the activity.

Centralization of certain activities or functions has to address a number of different questions. Does centralization create opportunities to employ specialist skills, such as purchasing or marketing, which can bring significant benefits to the enterprise? Does it, on the other hand, create opportunities to reduce line management? A number of leading retail companies and hospitality companies have been developing 'cluster' management systems, by which one general manager is required to manage a number of outlets which were previously managed by their own managers. Arguably the increased expertise and skills of functional managers, supported by improved information technology systems, make this possible. It has to be seen, however, whether such approaches can work in those situations where the customer still expects to be received by a member of the senior management team, i.e. someone performing the role of 'mine host'.

The effect on employees also has to be considered. Centralization, whilst increasing some people's responsibility, may reduce another person's responsibility and hence job satisfaction. Decentralization, on the other hand, may well empower someone and hence give greater job satisfaction.

Size and diversity

Two other major influences on structure are the size of the organization and its diversity. However, there does seem to be some agreement among the largest organizations that they need to devolve responsibility to smaller, readily accountable units. This may be done on a geographic basis. An example is the way in which pubcos (public house operators) organize their public house districts. Their management may be responsible for all activities in an area, such as managed houses, tenanted houses, catering and entertainment. Alternatively, an organization may prefer to make its management responsible for particular types of products or services. An example is how some companies may concentrate their steak houses into one division, their music houses into another and leisure into yet another. For the largest companies both 'regional' and 'product' organization structures will be necessary.

At the individual unit level the degree of specialization is an important question, and of particular importance is the degree to which certain specialists such as sales executives and financial controllers may be responsible to the unit manager and to the head office specialist manager. Revenue control (yield management) managers in hotels, for example, may be responsible for developing (and even imposing) capacity management systems. This is a constant problem in hotels in particular, where revenue control managers and sales executives may see themselves as part of a head office team rather than part of the unit management. A consequence is that the sales staff often sell products the unit has difficulty providing.

Span of control

Something else discussed in the organizational context is the question of 'span of control', i.e. how many subordinates can each supervisor successfully supervise? While most will agree that 'one over one' is rarely, if ever, justified, beyond this all the factors listed above play their part in resolving the question of how many subordinates one person can control. There are situations where one supervisor can quite successfully control a hundred or more subordinates each of whom is performing similar and strictly controlled tasks. Likewise, however, there are many other situations where one person can successfully supervise, at most, a handful of subordinates. One very successful hotel executive who created at least three large, public hotel companies was reported to have over 20 executives reporting directly to him.

Levels of management – scalar chain

The number of levels of management (sometimes referred to as the 'scalar' chain) is another crucial element in any organization. Usually, this is a function of the size and diversity of the organization.

Recent trends, however, have been to delayer, i.e. to reduce the number of levels of management, giving more authority to those who remain. Improved information technology makes such measures more practicable. One such example is Harvester Restaurants, who went through this process in the mid-1990s. The process was described as 'an approach to employee empowerment which is based on a flat organization and autonomous work groups at unit level' (Ashness and Lashley, 1995). Such flatter organization structures are common at the time of writing (2012).

Outsourcing

'Outsourcing' is another influence on structure. Outsourcing is the process by which an enterprise acquires products and services from outside suppliers rather than providing them internally using its own employees. Up to the 1950s many of the larger hotels were like small towns, employing many different trades, including carpenters, upholsterers and silversmiths. Such practices have largely disappeared, it being thought more economic to buy in such expertise. Such outsourcing is now being extended into what may be described as pure management areas such as HR. One argument for outsourcing is that an enterprise should concentrate its management expertise on the core business. Outsourcing is also a very effective way of controlling labour costs, although it is also argued that management may lose control of the quality of some of the services which are outsourced.

Offshoring is another development. In this case companies arrange for work to be performed 'offshore', i.e. in another country where labour costs are significantly lower. Call centres are typical examples but other services, such as many administrative functions too, can be 'offshored'. At the time of writing (2012) there appears to be a reversal of some offshoring, largely as a response to customer dissatisfaction, but also because the cost benefits are declining.

The products and services

Obviously shaping all these factors is the product being provided. At one extreme there is the fine-dining meal experience involving an extensive range of technical, social and organizational skills which have taken many years of experience and training to acquire. At the other extreme nowadays we have fast foods and airline meals which involve very little craft skill at the point of sale but call upon management organization skills of a high order. In between these two extremes are numerous types and styles of product and service which make differing demands on capital, craft skill, social skill, training and organizational ability. Each combination creates a particular set of organizational needs and constraints which should be reflected in the consequent organization structure.

Age, size and culture

As successful organizations get older, so they have tended to become larger both through the natural growth of their business and often also through acquisition. Acquisition will bring problems both of managing the larger business but also of integrating the differing cultures. On the one hand, size creates opportunities for economies of scale; on the other hand, size increases problems of coordination and control adding to the administrative burden – the law of diminishing returns? Rosabeth Moss Kanter (1984) addresses a related issue, describing some organizations as 'segmentalist' or 'innovative'. In segmentalist organizations departments may be 'walled' from one another whereas in 'innovative' firms departments share issues.

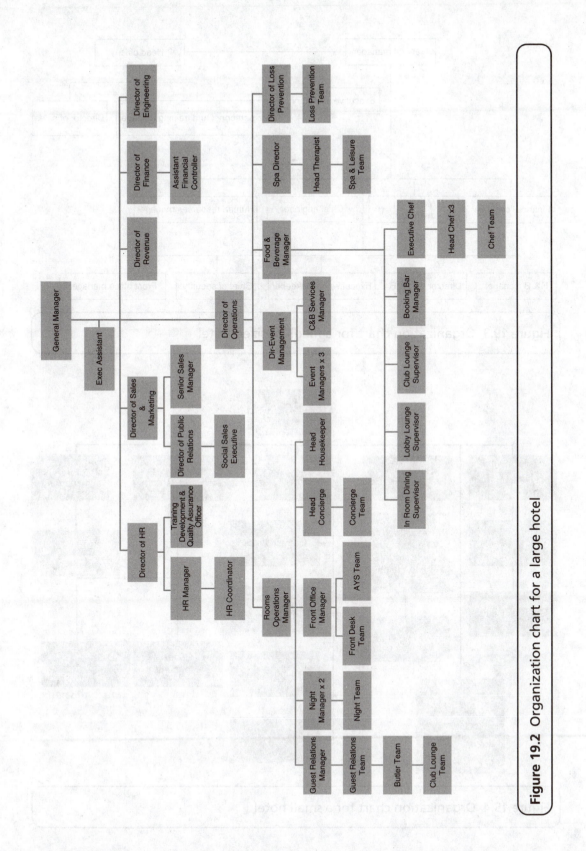

Figure 19.2 Organization chart for a large hotel

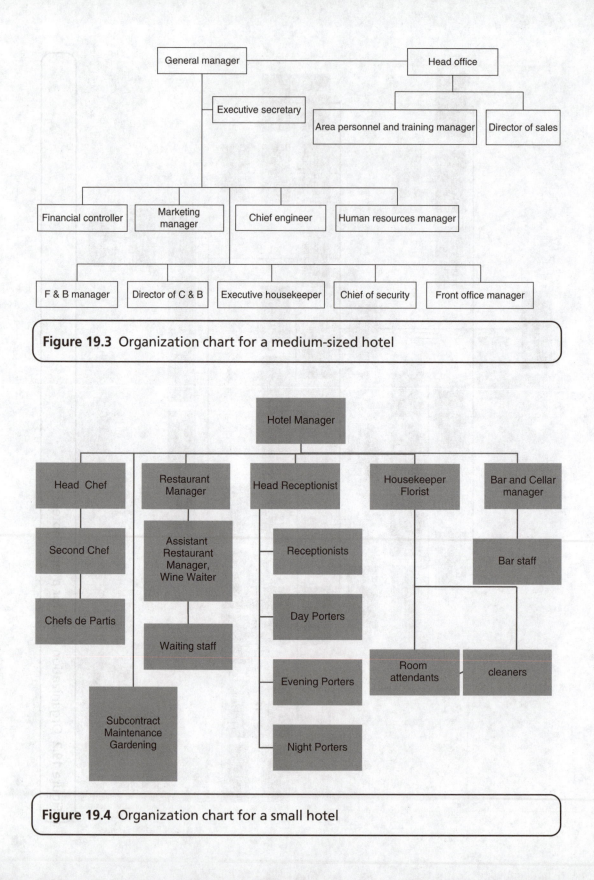

Figure 19.3 Organization chart for a medium-sized hotel

Figure 19.4 Organization chart for a small hotel

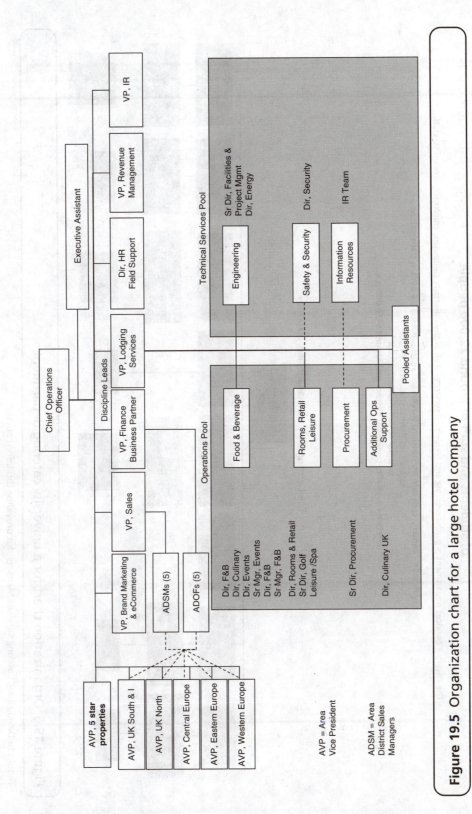

Figure 19.5 Organization chart for a large hotel company

The U.K.'s University of Brighton operates on five main campuses, and has a total population of students and staff of around 22,000 people.

The Catering Services department provides catering and residential services on all of the university campuses, employing around 90 staff.

Key figures – annual; cash sale transactions (beverages, snacks, meals) 1.6 million transactions
catered residential students: 134,000
summer school students 50,000
internal hospitality (meetings, visitors etc.) around £450,000 p.a.

The Catering Services Management Structure

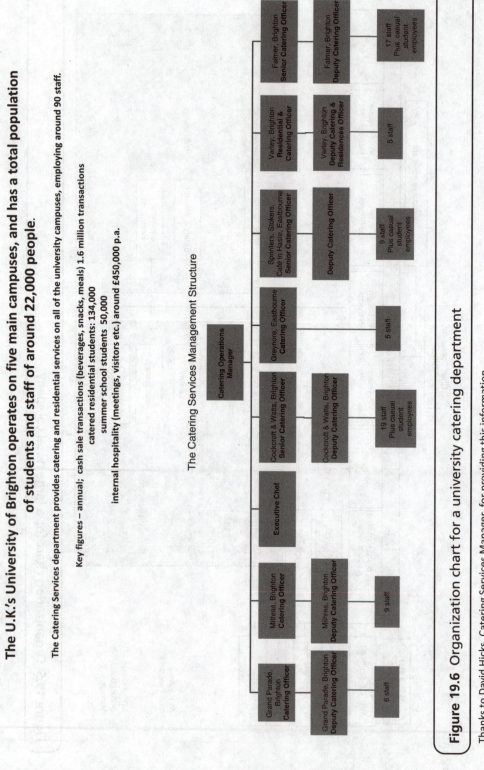

Figure 19.6 Organization chart for a university catering department

Thanks to David Hicks, Catering Services Manager for providing this information

Line managers and specialist managers

Once an enterprise reaches a certain size there will be a tendency for it to need to have specialist advice readily available. In the smallest organizations many specialist tasks will be performed by the owners or their managers. As the enterprise grows, the need for specialist advice grows and this can either be bought in from time to time – e.g. accountants or architects – or specialists may be engaged full-time. Human resource or personnel specialists are typical examples. Others include marketing, information technology and purchasing specialists.

The role of such specialists, usually referred to as 'staff' or 'functional' managers, varies considerably from one organization to the next. In some it will be, as the Human Resources Director of British Airways said, 'more strategic and less operational' (quoted from Goss-Turner, 1995). In any event, most believe that the role should be to advise and guide the line or operational managers, not to remove authority or responsibilities from them. In larger organizations, distinguishing the roles and relationships of line and functional managers becomes quite difficult in some situations. This is particularly so where a hotel, for example, has a revenue management team that is responsible (or perceives itself to be) to the head office marketing department as much as to the hotel general management. Figures 19.2–19.6 show organization charts of various different sizes and types of hospitality organization.

Further reading and references

Armstrong, M. (2012) *A Handbook of Human Resource Management*, 12th edn, London: Kogan Page.

Ashness, D. and Lashley, C. (1995) *Employee Empowerment in Harvester Restaurants*, Human Resource Management in the Hospitality Industry Conference Document, University of Brighton.

Beardwell, I., Holden, L. and Claydon, T. (2004) *Human Resource Management – A Contemporary Approach*, 4th edn, Harlow: Prentice Hall.

Burns, T. and Stalker, G. M. (1966) *The Management of Innovation*, London: Tavistock.

French, D. and Saward, H. (1977) *Dictionary of Management*, London: Pan.

Goss-Turner, S. (1995) *Human Resources and Line Management*, Human Resource Management in the Hospitality Industry Conference Document, University of Brighton.

Goss-Turner, S. (2002) *Managing People in the Hospitality Industry*, 4th edn, Kingston-upon-Thames: Croner Publications.

Handy, C. (1989) *The Age of Unreason*, London: Business Books.

Kanter, R. M. (1984) *The Change Masters: Corporate Entrepreneurs at Work*, London: Allen & Unwin.

Kanter, R. M. (1989) *When Giants Learn to Dance*, London: Simon and Schuster.

Kennedy, C. (2007) *Guide to the Management Gurus*, 5th edn, London: Random House.

Mars, G., Mitchell, P. and Bryant, D. (1979) *Manpower Problems in the Hotel and Catering Industry*, Farnborough: Saxon House.

Mullins, L. (1996) *Hospitality Management*, London: Longman.

Pugh, S. and Hickson, D. (2007) *Writers on Organizations*, 6th edn, London: Penguin Books.

Members of the UK's Institute of Hospitality can access publications including Management Guides which summarize key information of relevance to hospitality operations (www.instituteofhospitality.org).

Members of the UK's Chartered Institute of Personnel and Development (CIPD) can access a range of materials including Fact Sheets and articles from over 300 online journal titles relevant to HR. CIPD members and *People Management* subscribers can see articles on the People Management website (www.peoplemanagement.co.uk).

Questions

1 Discuss the factors that influence organization structure.

2 Discuss the various factors which can influence span of control and scalar chain in an organization.

3 Discuss the statement that structure follows strategy.

4 How does Handy's Shamrock concept apply to different sectors of the hospitality industry?

5 Evaluate the approach to organization structure and development used by an employer you know well.

CASE STUDY QUESTION – see the Lux Hotels case study Appendix 5

In this chapter key approaches to organization have been described.

What are Lux Hotels key strategies and how can organization structure contribute to the achievement of the principal strategic aims? Should the organization be based on issues such as brands, geography or property ownership? Prepare an organization chart for Lux Hotels as you perceive it now. Recommend a suitable organization structure for the future, giving reasons for your recommendation.

Chapter 20

Managing people

Within the hospitality industry virtually everybody works in groups of interdependent individuals. A key feature of much of the industry is the fact that most work people are very dependent, in an immediate sense, upon the work of colleagues. It is this working of interdependent individuals, brought together as groups, which determines the success or failure of many enterprises. The success of the group in turn is dependent upon the ability of some individuals, the managers or leaders, to lead such groups to achieve desired results.

What makes a person a successful manager or leader of others has, no doubt, been a subject of discussion since the time people began to live in organized societies. At one extreme are leaders who are in positions of power and leadership as a direct result of their personalities. This is referred to by some as 'charismatic' leadership. At the other extreme are managers who rely on strict procedures and peer support in their approach to management. This is often referred to as 'bureaucratic' management. As mentioned in Chapter 2, there are other approaches too. Figure 20.1 identifies some of the more common approaches.

With such a variety of different approaches it is not surprising that people are constantly asking which of these is the most likely to be successful, and it is not surprising either that there is no clear-cut answer. What may be successful in one situation may well prove a failure in another set of circumstances. For example, the type of leadership or management needed on the flight deck of an aircraft coming in to land will be very different from that needed in leading a team of architects designing a new building. Likewise the management skills needed to manage a fast food outlet will be very different from those needed to manage a small directors' dining room. Figure 20.2 illustrates some of the many factors that interact in any group/leadership situation.

Individuals and leadership

Considerable research has been carried out to identify which traits contribute to an individual being a leader or a follower. Many organizations invest considerable time and effort into identifying their future leaders. One example is the work of the armed services, which subjects applicants for officer rank to a series of tests lasting several days, plus months of officer/cadet training. Many other organizations adopt similar processes, now often referred to as 'assessment centres'.

Charismatic, Paternalistic, Bureaucratic	(Weber)
Theory X——Theory Y	(Douglas McGregor)
Exploitive authoritative, benevolent authoritative, consultative, participative group	(Rensis Likert)
Autocratic processes, consultative processes, group processes	(Vroom)
Relationship motivated – task motivated	(Fiedler)
Concern for people – concern for production	(Mouton and Blake)
Socio-technical system	(Trist et al.)

Figure 20.1 Some of the more commonly described approaches to management

Note: All of these are described in more detail in *Writers on Organizations*, Pugh and Hickson (2007).

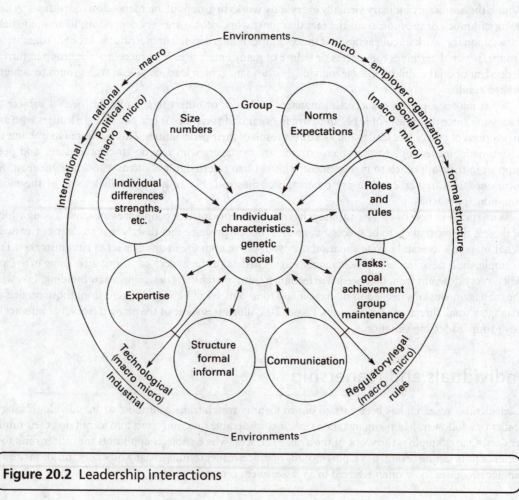

Figure 20.2 Leadership interactions

In the last century a number of researchers set out to identify and evaluate genetic and social or cultural factors which may contribute to leadership abilities. The works of J. Munro Fraser (five-point plan) and the National Institute of Industrial Psychology (seven-point plan), discussed in Chapter 5, were very significant. Many current selection methods, either assessment centres or individual interviews, still use similar categories. Other authorities developed psychometric tests, such as Raymond Cattell of the USA and his 16PF (Sixteen Personality Factor Questionnaire), which were designed to measure a range of psychological characteristics.

In looking at these different approaches it is apparent that a range of different characteristics are evaluated when individual potential is being considered. But in spite of there being a range of different methods of assessing leadership skills, many employers continue to devise their own methods of identifying and measuring management potential and performance, now often referred to as 'talent' (see Chapters 7 and 9). If, in fact, a single set of personality traits did make for successful management or leadership it is probable that, by now, some agreement would have been reached, as is more the case with single and maybe simpler personality traits such as 'intelligence'. It would appear therefore that successful management or leadership is not the result of a simple set of characteristics but is more likely to be dependent upon a whole range of interacting elements including the organizational environment.

Some of the key elements in Figure 20.2 are discussed more fully here. The division between genetic and cultural personality traits is illustrative only. There are conflicting opinions about many of the above traits and influences, e.g. introversion and extroversion may be as much culturally influenced as genetically determined.

The individual

At the individual level there are two main aspects that have to be considered – each consisting of many different elements. First, there are innate characteristics such as intelligence, height and gender. Second, there are culturally acquired characteristics such as beliefs, attitudes and values. These are illustrated in more detail in Figure 20.3.

Genetic characteristics

What is inherited genetically may contribute to leadership in a number of different ways. Relevant characteristics include intelligence, gender, height, physical build and even the ability to be persuaded. For example, some research has shown that successful managers generally tend to have above average intelligence and to be above average height. Also males generally are more likely to hold senior management positions than females even when females make up the majority of the workforce. In the case of the

Genetically determined characteristics	Culturally determined characteristics
Physical characteristics Gender, race, size, build, motor skills	Values, beliefs, attitudes, expectations, language, accent, behaviour, manners, perception of role, self-image, attitudes to work

Psychological characteristics
  Intelligence Introvert–extrovert
  Stable–unstable Creative	

Figure 20.3 Some individual characteristics

hospitality industry 44 per cent of senior managers are female, whilst 58 per cent of the workforce is female (People 1st, 2011). Whilst the reason for this may be more cultural than genetic, a person's gender (which is genetically determined) plays a significant part in determining whether a person will be more or less acceptable as a leader or manager.

It may also be that male assertiveness contributes to male 'success' in leadership in cultures where competitiveness is a key element in organization culture. Cattell (1957) identifies one factor, factor E, which is concerned with assertiveness, which, to some extent, may also be genetically influenced.

Cultural characteristics

Apart from the inherited characteristics, a society through socialization equips people with a whole range of beliefs, values, attitudes, prejudices and related behaviour patterns. For example, an individual's attitudes towards conformity, punctuality, honesty, work, the opposite sex, minorities, superiors and subordinates are all part of the individual's make-up and stem from the social context in which the individual has developed. For example, certain schools and types of schools build specific career expectations into their pupils, as do most higher education courses.

Groups

In any discussion on management or leadership it is essential to consider the nature of who or what is being managed. In most cases managers manage a range of resources including finance, equipment, buildings, land and a number of individuals, usually organized in a group or groups. Groups are the basic building blocks of society. Groups come in all shapes and sizes and have many different purposes and there are many different definitions of groups. For the purpose of this book, however, a group is defined as two or more people interacting together in order to achieve a common goal or goals.

Such a definition can include as few as two people working together and it can include an organization of many thousands of employees. For the purpose of this book the definition includes both the small group and the larger group, sometimes referred to as an organization, although some differences between groups and organizations will be looked at later. The reason for this definition is that management, even that of large organizations, functions through groups. Most chief executives of large organizations do not manage the organization, they manage a group of senior managers who in turn manage other groups.

Types of groups

The two most commonly distinguished groups are primary groups and secondary groups (Figure 20.4) plus another group called the reference group.

	Socio-economic	Affiliative
Primary groups	A family	A group of friends
Secondary groups		
Formal	A trading company	A sports club
	A district council	A professional body
	A trade union	A charity
Informal	A neighbourhood protest group	A group of fellow workers

Figure 20.4 Some examples of groups

Primary groups

Primary groups, of which the family is the best example, have few, if any, clearly written rules. The individual members are kept together through feelings for one another. Friendship groups are another example of a primary group. Objectives of primary groups generally are concerned with relationships between the members.

Secondary groups

Most other groups are formed for social and economic reasons, e.g. profit, fundraising, education, sharing resources and employment. In general they are more formal than primary groups. As a consequence they have clearly articulated rules and procedures. Typical examples may include schools, employers, sports clubs and professional associations.

Primary groups, such as friendship groups, may form as a result of membership of secondary groups, such as attending the same school or college or working under the same employer. In some cases primary groups will devolve into secondary groups.

Reference groups

A reference group (rather like a role model) is a real or imagined group that has attributes attractive to an individual who may aspire to become a member of such a group. Supervisors, for example, may aspire to becoming a member of the management group. The concept of the reference group can be used in a very manipulative fashion. Advertisers, for example, will suggest that the use of certain products will admit users to their reference group. Individuals may have several reference groups.

Apart from the many different definitions, there are also many different features of groups which can be isolated for discussion, such as: Why do groups form? How do they form? What effect does group membership have on the individuals making up the group? In order that a number of individuals may be described as a 'group' a number of elements have to be present to a greater or lesser extent. For the purpose of this book, only certain key issues will be discussed.

Features of groups

Shared goals

Ideally all members of a group share common goals. In work organizations the primary goals are likely to be task-oriented, with the making of profits and/or the provision of services as fundamental. The group is created or develops because it is likely to be more efficient than the individuals working independently. In non-work organizations, such as clubs, the goals are likely to be of a personal affiliation/fulfilment nature. In some situations, however, shared goals may hardly be present. In the work situation, for example, the sharing of goals can sometimes be minimal. Some trade unionists certainly do not share the same goals as their employers, whilst members of a trade union may share goals with one another. A major aim of many employers is to create a sharing of goals between the employers and the employees.

Etzioni (1980: see Chapter 2) writes that some managers have a coercive attitude to their workforce and that the work people in such a situation are likely to have an alienative attitude to the management. In such a situation the only shared goal is likely to be to exploit one another to the full. At the other extreme, Etzioni identifies managers with a 'normative' attitude to their workforce, who in turn have a 'moral' attitude to their work. In such cases there is a sharing of common values: all want the enterprise to succeed. Some countries' work cultures are better at this than others. It is suggested that Germany and Japan have successful economies because there is a sharing of corporate goals at the workplace.

Common values or norms

Ideally, members of a group should hold similar values. The readers of a national newspaper or users of a social medium, whilst possibly sharing many interests and values, can hardly be described as a group. Cooks working thousands of miles apart for the same fast food chain can hardly be described as members of the same group. For a group to exist, there needs to be a common purpose, activity and a relational interdependence.

Staff engagement

Human resource policies and procedures are largely concerned with identifying and developing individuals who share or will share the same values as the employer, i.e. to 'engage' with the employer. The word 'engagement' has recently entered the management vocabulary, as highlighted by the MacLeod report (2010), referred to elsewhere in this book. This report contains a number of definitions and for the purpose of this book 'engagement' as defined by the Institute of Development Studies in the MacLeod report has been chosen:

> A positive attitude held by the employee towards the organisation and its values. An engaged employee is aware of the business context, and works with colleagues to improve performance within the job for the benefit of the organisation. The organisation must work to develop and nurture engagement, which requires a two-way relationship between employee and employer.
>
> (MacLeod and Clarke, 2010)

To what extent, however, work people share values with their employers may be very questionable, particularly as a considerable proportion of the total workforce may be peripheral, i.e. drawn from the secondary labour market (see Chapters 1 and 2).

This question of the members of an organization needing to share common goals or values, and all that follows from this, constantly recurs as a major preoccupation of organizations. The MacLeod report discusses in detail both the barriers to 'engagement' but also initiatives being adopted by many companies, including hospitality companies, to develop staff engagement.

Communication between members

In order that individuals can work together to achieve their common goals, there will be a need for communication between some of, if not all, the members.

Group size – larger or smaller

Group size is a key feature affecting management. The smaller the group, the easier it is generally to coordinate its activities, and as membership increases so do the problems of coordination and control. Larger groups potentially, of course, can perform more work and have more skills available.

In employing organizations, because each member incurs costs, there is strong pressure to keep groups to a minimum size whilst aiming to have the number of individuals and skills necessary for the tasks to be performed. In other cases, such as trade unions, the pressure will be the reverse, to increase membership size because this increases economic and political power.

Group structure – formal versus informal

Because some individuals in a group will need to communicate – the leaders to exercise control – and because the individuals are interdependent, a structure will be developed. This may be very apparent and formal or it may be very loose, informal and changing.

Whilst larger organizations will set up formal structures that they believe will be most efficient from a task achievement, group maintenance and control point of view, other forces, informal ones, will be at work within the organization.

So, in any consideration of groups the two faces – the 'formal', as laid down by senior managers, and the 'informal', as determined by the emotional needs and the practical working circumstances – have to be considered. Rosabeth Moss Kanter (1984) addresses this issue describing some organizations as 'segmentalist' or 'innovative'. In segmentalist organizations departments may be 'walled' from one another whereas in 'innovative' firms departments share issues.

Group development

A newly formed group of individuals is also subject to a process of development, as the members become acquainted, begin to formulate agreed approaches and develop norms and other shared values across the group. This process can be difficult and can lead to conflict and argument between members. One of the most cited works concerning group behaviour was by Bruce Tuckman who reviewed around fifty studies of group development models and synthesized their common features (Tuckman, 1965). He described the process as a linear series of stages: 'forming' (finding out about each other and the task faced by the group), 'storming' (internal conflict and resistance), 'norming' (developing relationships and norms agreed across the members), 'performing' (effective teamwork phase). A fifth stage (adjourning) was added in 1977 when new sets of studies were reviewed (Tuckman and Jensen, 1977).

The power of a strong and effective group is considerable, and in HRM terms is a key factor in influencing reaction to change in the workplace. Many managers, when managing a group of people from similar ethnic backgrounds, often have to decide whether to split them or to leave them to work together. Another example of management recognition of the importance of groups is where some companies, including hospitality firms, are now involving the work group in the confirmation of appointment of a new colleague.

Group orientations

Groups, in the main, consist of both leaders and those being led, and each develop their own orientations or attitudes to work as well as towards those who work or organize their work. Etzioni (1980: see Chapter 2 and Figure 20.5 below) describes both managers' attitudes to their workforce and the workers' corresponding involvement or attitudes to work.

McGregor (1960: see also Chapter 2) described Theory-X managers who tend to expect the worst from their workers and Theory-Y managers who expect the best. Schein (1965: see Pugh and Hickson, 2007) goes further than McGregor and suggests four main assumptions that managers make of their work people:

- *rational–economic* – workers motivated by money
- *social* – workers motivated by work-group relationships
- *self-actualization* – workers motivated by a need to fulfil their potential
- *complex* – other models are too simple; workers are motivated differently at different stages of life.

From these models of attitudes to workers and to work it is apparent that attitudes may be dynamic in the sense that managers can create policies, working environments and styles of supervision that shape

Managers' power	Worker involvement
Coercive	Alienative
Utilitarian	Calculative
Normative	Moral

Figure 20.5 Etzioni: managers' power, workers' involvement

the nature of the workers' own attitudes to work and the employer. Furthermore, one of the problems of attitudes (not just to work) is that they may persist long after the reasons that created them have ceased to exist, a phenomenon at the basis of much prejudice.

Communications

Groups exist because communication is possible between individuals. The communication process has important effects on group behaviour and leadership because if information itself is seen as a valuable asset, it is possible to use that asset as a means of exercising control. If, for example, groups are structured A, B or C, as illustrated in Figure 20.6, one person can easily monopolize information (whereas in D all have access to everyone in the group). The person can choose to pass it on or not. There are two consequences of such a situation. First, the person with the information can automatically acquire the role of leader or second, a person with certain personality traits, recognizing the power of the position, will move into the focal position.

Communication is a complex subject and much has been written on it (see Figure 20.7). In essence, however, the process consists of information to be transmitted, a transmitter of the information, a means of transmission and a receiver of the information, followed sometimes by feedback that demonstrates whether the process has worked or not. Obstacles to transmission arise, however, including language or cultural differences and attitudinal or emotional states. Such problems are common in the hospitality industry where managers, employees and customers often come from many different cultural backgrounds and may have very different life experiences, perceptions and expectations. For the customer an undercooked steak may be a disappointment whilst the member of staff might be thinking that the customer is lucky to be able to afford a steak in the first place.

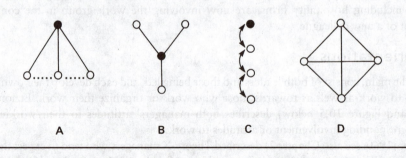

Figure 20.6 Some different channels of communication

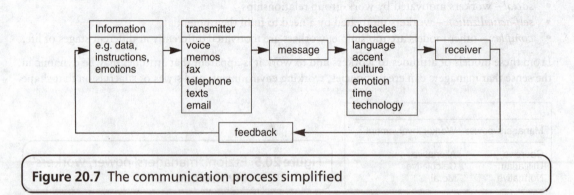

Figure 20.7 The communication process simplified

Group management

Where large groups of people have to be managed, as is the case with large enterprises, it is most likely that management will be, to a greater or lesser extent, of a bureaucratic nature. The word 'bureaucratic' is not meant in a pejorative sense but describes a particular approach to management, first described by Max Weber (see Chapter 2). Procedures will be formalized. Decision making is more likely to be a shared responsibility. Treatment of individuals will be based on clearly defined rules (as has been described in many chapters of this book). The key features of a bureaucratic approach to management, according to Weber, include:

- vertical authority structure
- maximum specialization
- close definition of duties, privileges and boundaries
- decisions based on expert judgement, technical competence and disciplined compliance with directives of superiors
- impersonal administration of staff
- employment consisting of a lifelong career.

The problem with Weber's view of bureaucracy is that it tends to imply that organizations are rational entities or systems, independent of the people who make up the organization. Another view, that of Silverman (1970), is that to understand organizations, it is necessary to view them from an 'action frame of reference', that is, as the product of the actions of the people who are the organization, pursuing their own objectives. This perspective, when contrasted with Weber's, indicates that organizations are not the rational system that many would like to believe they are, but are the results of the decisions of the leaders of the organization, pursuing their own ends. Many business failures are the result of owners and senior managers pursuing personal, often irrational goals as evidenced by some of the banking failures in the first ten years of this century.

Technology

Within an economy many different technologies are used to create goods and services. Different technologies create different organization structures and situations for managers. Joan Woodward (1965), in examining manufacturing industries, identified nine technologies grouped into three broad categories: unit and small batch, large batch and mass production, and process production. Each of these creates different management needs and structures.

Though not all hospitality operations fit into these categories, the industry does have many different market sectors with different technologies, ranging from the small, low volume (unit or small batch), fine-dining restaurant through to high volume (large batch), low price fast food outlets and flight catering (mass production). Each of these creates different situations for management.

The nature of the task

In addition to the individuals and groups being managed, the nature of the task also has to be considered. In some situations, e.g. the reception/cash desk of a hotel at 8.30 a.m. or a busy kitchen at 1.00 p.m., there is little room for debate about how things may be done differently and therefore a strict hierarchical structure may be vital to success. Some of the variables concerned with the task itself include:

- skilled – unskilled
- supervised – unsupervised

- pressured – unpressured
- self-paced – externally paced
- hi-touch – lo-touch (e.g. level of customer contact)
- hi-tech – lo-tech (e.g. level of reliance on technology/capital investment)
- creative – non-creative
- difficult – simple
- group work – individual work
- perishable – non-perishable (e.g. if not sold today can it be sold tomorrow?)
- low risk – high risk.

Different combinations of the above variables should lead to different forms of management. Skilled tasks will need more investment in training. Group tasks will need more coordination. Perishable tasks (e.g. bedrooms unsold tonight can never be sold again) may need more complex communications and control. High-risk tasks (e.g. preparation of large numbers of in-flight meals) will need very strict systems of supervision and control.

Environment

As the leadership function can only function within groups of people, so too groups can only function within a wider environment. Groups are not closed, isolated systems. They draw from the environment. Some examples of environmental factors influencing management of the workforce are listed below (see also Chapters 17 and 19):

- politico-legal
- economic
- social
- cultural
- demographic
- technological
- geographical
- environmental
- demand for products
- employment legislation
- capital investment
- educational attainments of employees
- employee expectations
- labour supply/demand.

What is successful management or leadership?

Successful leadership should consist of the ability to achieve specified goals through the proper use of the resources available. For most managers this comprises at least two key elements: goal achievement and group maintenance.

First, there is the achievement of the specified goals, e.g. of a financial profit or service nature. To some extent the specification of goals and their achievement occurs through job design, performance appraisal and approaches to management such as management by objectives (MbO) (see Chapters 3 and 7) and budgetary control.

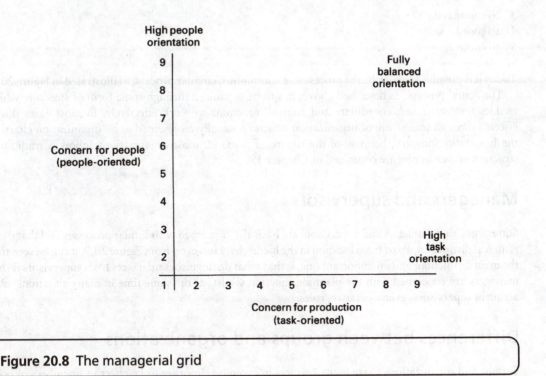

Figure 20.8 The managerial grid

Second, the other key responsibility is the group maintenance and development role which has been the subject of most of the chapters of this book. Again the achievement of this dimension of management can be measured, but usually with more difficulty, through approaches to management such as staff retention rates, performance appraisal and MbO.

Within the hospitality industry it could be argued that there appears to be more effort directed at the former goal than the latter – if the industry's high labour turnover is used as an indicator of the managers' concern with group maintenance and development goals.

Managers' orientations – production or people

Many believe that successful management consists of achieving a balance between task achievement and concern for the group. This has been expressed by Blake and Mouton (1985), who developed the concept of the managerial grid, illustrated in Figure 20.8. The report, *Engaging for Success* (MacLeod and Clarke, 2010), commissioned by the British government, highlighted the importance of engaging staff, and included examples from the hospitality industry.

The process of managing groups

The process of managing groups at work has been analysed by many management writers in the past. One of the earlier writers, Henri Fayol (Chapter 2), identified five key steps:

1 to forecast
2 to organize

3 to command
4 to coordinate
5 to control.

Today it is possible to describe the process as a continuous, circular process, as illustrated in Figure 20.9.

The actual process, as described above, has to be organized through some form of structure which enables the 'command, coordinate and control' functions to work effectively. In most cases this is effected through some form of organization structure, usually represented as an organization chart. In the hospitality industry, because of the nature of demand, most organizations follow a traditional structure and examples are contained in Chapter 19.

Managers and supervisors

Some argue that managers and supervisors are basically concerned with similar processes and that there is no real distinction, apart from location in the hierarchy. However, from Figure 20.9, it can be seen that the main distinction, and an important one, is that what distinguishes managers from supervisors is that managers are concerned with the planning function whilst, at the same time in many situations, also acting in supervisory, even operative, roles.

Differences between groups and organizations

Groups and organizations share many features in common. In order to be effective, members of both should have common goals and values. In many ways organizations are extensions of groups. Whereas

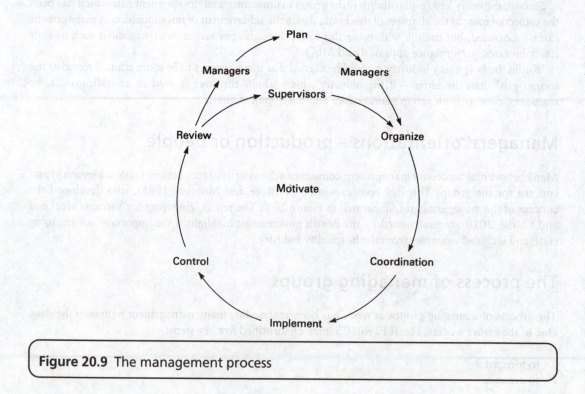

Figure 20.9 The management process

groups consist of interdependent individuals, organizations consist of interdependent groups with overlapping memberships. Whilst all the individuals are members of the organization, they are also members of smaller groups. The board of directors of a company, for example, makes up the group concerned with the overall direction of the company. Each director, apart perhaps from non-executive directors, in turn is a member, maybe the leader or manager, of specialist departments or groups. Figure 20.10 illustrates this.

From this it is apparent that, although the most junior members may be members of their own work group and of the organization overall, they are not members of 'similar interest' groups; most work people who have much in common from a work point of view, are not members of a wider work people's group. One of the reasons for the emergence and development of trade unions was a response to the need for work people to form a group or organization with common interests. Some enlightened employers also set out to develop ways and means of making every employee, including even their part-time and casual employees, feel an integral part of the wider group or organization.

Such techniques include induction, internal transfers and promotions, joint consultation, staff exchanges, company newspapers, staff parties and dances, and inter-unit competitions of a work or social nature. Some differences and similarities between groups and organizations are summarized in Figure 20.11.

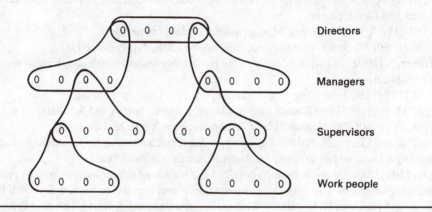

Figure 20.10 Organization and group membership

	Groups	Organizations
SIMILARITIES	Members may share common goals and values	
DIFFERENCES	Small	Large
	Simple structures	Complex structures
	Informal	Formal
	Emotional bonds	Economic/social bonds
	Simple decision making	Complex decision making
	Short-lived	Long-lived?
	All members know one another	All members do not know one another

Figure 20.11 Groups and organizations compared

Conclusion

Most of this book has been devoted to the various processes used by employers to attract, retain, develop, reward and motivate their workforces. This chapter has focused on considering what is involved in actually managing the workforce and what influences that process. It has suggested that managing work people successfully depends upon a complex interaction consisting of the make-up of the individuals involved, the nature of groups (which is different from the sum of their members), the nature of the work performed by the work people, and the environment in which the performance of the work takes place.

Further reading and references

Armstrong, M. (2012) *A Handbook of Human Resource Management*, 12th edn, London: Kogan Page.

Beardwell, I., Holden, L. and Claydon, T. (2004) *Human Resource Management – A Contemporary Approach*, 4th edn, Harlow: Prentice Hall.

Blake, R. and Mouton, J. (1985) *The Managerial Grid III: The Key to Leadership Excellence*, Houston: Gulf Publishing Company.

Cattell, R. (1957) *Personality and Motivation Structure and Measurement*, New York: World Books.

Daniels, K. (2006) *Employee Relations in an Organisational Context*, London: Chartered Institute of Personnel and Development.

Drucker, P. (1969) *The Practice of Management*, London: Heinemann.

Etzioni, A. (1980) *Modern Organizations*, Englewood Cliffs, NJ: Prentice Hall.

Goss-Turner, S. (2002) *Managing People in the Hospitality Industry*, 4th edn, Kingston-upon-Thames: Croner Publications.

Handy, C. (1993) *Understanding Organizations*, 4th edn, London: Penguin.

Kanter, R. M. (1989) *When Giants Learn to Dance*, London: Simon and Schuster.

McGregor, D. (1960) *The Human Side of Enterprise*, New York: McGraw-Hill.

MacLeod, D. and Clarke, N. (2010) *Engaging for Success: Enhancing Performance through Employee Engagement*, London: Department for Business, Innovation and Skills.

People 1st (2011) *State of the Nation Report 2011, Analysis of labour market trends, skills, education and training within the UK hospitality, leisure, travel and tourism industries*, London: People 1st.

Pugh, D. S. and Hickson, D. D. (2007) *Writers on Organizations*, 6th edn, London: Penguin.

Robbins, S. (2005) *Organizational Behaviour*, 11th edn, Englewood Cliffs, NJ: Pearson Education.

Silverman, D. (1970) *Theory of Organizations: A Sociological Framework*, London: Heinemann.

Sisson, K. (ed.) (1989) *Personnel Management in Britain*, Oxford: Blackwell.

Torrington, D., Hall, L., Taylor, S. and Atkinson, C. (2011) *Human Resource Management*, 8th edn, Harlow: Pearson Education.

Truss C., Soane, E. and Edwards, C. (2006) *Working Life: Employee Attitudes and Engagement 2006*, Research report, London: Chartered Institute of Personnel and Development.

Tuckman, B. (1965) 'Developmental sequence in small groups', *Psychological Bulletin*, 63: 384–399.

Tuckman, B. W. and Jensen, M. A. C. (1977) 'Stages of small group development revisited', *Group and Organizational Studies*, 2: 419–427.

Weber, M. (1947) *The Theory of Social and Economic Organization*, New York: Free Press.

Woodward, J. (1965) *Industrial Organisation: Theory and Practice*, Oxford: Oxford University Press.

Members of the UK's Institute of Hospitality can access publications including Management Guides which summarize key information of relevance to hospitality operations (www.instituteofhospitality.org).

Members of the UK's Chartered Institute of Personnel and Development (CIPD) can access a range of materials including Fact Sheets and articles from over 300 online journal titles relevant to HR. CIPD members and *People Management* subscribers can see articles on the People Management website (www.peoplemanagement.co.uk).

Questions

1 Describe what you consider to be the key features that contribute to effective management of people at work.

2 Discuss the proposition that leadership is an 'innate' characteristic.

3 What relevance does the 'informal' group have to the manager?

4 What effects does the 'nature of the task' have on the management of groups and organizations?

5 What does 'staff engagement', mean to you? Thinking of an employer you know discuss what measures, if any, they adopt in order to 'engage' their staff.

CASE STUDY QUESTION – see the Lux Hotels case study Appendix 5

In this chapter key approaches to managing people have been described. What are Lux Hotels key HR objectives? What are the key issues with the present organization and the management of the persons involved, particularly at senior level? Identify the strengths and weaknesses and make recommendations. What, if anything, does Lux Hotels need to do to ensure that its key corporate aims and its HR aims are achieved?

Chapter 21

Managing in the international context

The globalization of the hospitality industry and the development of worldwide groups, whether hotel groups or franchised fast food outlets, presents real challenges for the quality and effectiveness of HRM within the international context. At one level there is just the challenge of the numbers needed to open large numbers of new outlets often with strict quotas on the employment of 'expat' workers. At another level, cultural issues, national characteristics and regulations need to be considered. Employers need to be aware of the salary and benefit packages expected by truly mobile international personnel, and they may need to plan issues not normally part of the host-country operations such as language and culture training, schooling for management's families, taxation and legal aspects.

In addition there are different types of employees such as expatriates and local workers with different terms and conditions, family situations and expectations. The comparison in Figure 21.1 illustrates how pay and hence costs to the employer for a manager may vary between different categories of employee. Such costs can include: base pay, guaranteed allowances, bonus and benefits.

Much of the world's economy is now transnational (across one or two frontiers), international (across several frontiers), or global (across many frontiers), by nature. Several of the hospitality industry's major companies have long been large-scale international, even global, players. As examples, Hilton International, the InterContinental Hotel Group, Marriott, Accor of France, McDonald's, Burger King run outlets throughout the world. Most such companies expect that a significant proportion of their visitors will be foreign. Furthermore, many of the managers and staff in certain sectors of the industry are of foreign nationality or origin. In the UK around 35 per cent of restaurant workers are 'migrant workers'. In hotels migrant workers represent around 20 per cent of the workforce (People 1st, 2011).

One crucial point about the industry which has made this possible is that the knowledge and skills necessary to work in the industry are readily exportable or importable. These may be described as 'life skills'. As a result, most people joining the industry can anticipate working, whether in their own countries or abroad, with people of nationalities and cultures very different from their own – be they customers, staff, managers or, increasingly, owners.

The range of issues that differ from one country to another is vast, and it is beyond the scope of this book to go into detail. However, the major differences can be identified and evaluated using a systems thinking approach (see Figure 17.1). Figure 21.2 illustrates some of these points with a few simple examples, intended to highlight some dimensions on which countries differ in ways significant for HR

'Expat.'	foreigner	resident
£182.000 p.a.	£130,600 p.a.	£41,000 p.a.

Figure 21.1 Overseas pay differentials

Source: Mercer, www.peoplemanagement.co.uk, 7 August 2008.

Political	Stable/unstable? Business friendly/unfriendly?
	The UK attracts substantial inward investment because the UK has a reputation for being a stable economy and business friendly, which results in job creation. Some countries deter investment because of government policies, particularly on taxation, sometimes encouraging their own domestic companies to consider moving abroad (e.g. Sweden).
Legal	Business friendly/unfriendly?
	Compared with countries such as France it is easier to set up and to run a business in the UK. From the human resource viewpoint some countries are extremely protective of working people (e.g. France), which tends to slow down job creation, whereas other countries will adhere to free-market principles (e.g. the UK), believing that a healthy market economy will result in job creation.
Social	The social environment, generally speaking, shapes the attitudes and behaviour of the workforce. Attitudes to work, to religion and to authority derive from the social environment, as Hofstede has shown. Western companies entering Central European markets have encountered serious staffing problems because of the lack of a service culture.
Technological	The level of development of technology and attitudes to its adoption and use vary widely between countries. Some countries have a well-educated and developed workforce, so the adoption of new technology is relatively simple, whereas some other countries have attitudes towards machines and technology which will slow down their adoption. For example, when McDonald's entered the Russian market a major challenge to be overcome was the lack of suitable suppliers plus a lack of staff adapted to a service culture.

Figure 21.2 Some dimensions for evaluating differences between countries

management. It is intended to illustrate that when people go abroad to manage businesses the challenges they face are not just cultural. There are likely to be many very obvious differences, such as those of a legal nature. There are also likely to be some very subtle ones as well, many of a clearly cultural nature, such as attitudes to time and authority or towards the opposite sex. This chapter therefore concentrates on cultural differences likely to be encountered by hospitality managers. An understanding of such cultural differences may well provide the competitive advantage that many companies seek.

As a leading authority on intercultural management, Geert Hofstede (1989) states, 'cultural awareness is one of the subtle features of competition in world markets and firms which are better at it have a distinct advantage over their competitors'. Cultural awareness is much more than the ability to speak a foreign language or two, although this in itself may be vital. In Europe now, efforts are being made to improve the overall cultural awareness and foreign language ability of students through programmes such as Erasmus university student exchanges and multi-centre degrees.

Cultural awareness is the ability to anticipate, to recognize and to respond to cultural differences. This may include not only the ability to communicate correctly with staff, customers or potential customers in both written and spoken form but also to anticipate and to meet their particular cultural expectations. Besides language there are many other differences that exist between cultures. These may include differences in values, attitudes, behaviour, communication, personal space, technical differences, dress, religion, etc.

Hofstede's dimensions

Hofstede, in a study of over 1,000 IBM employees employed in over 70 countries, identified four key dimensions that help to distinguish one culture from another. These are shown in Figure 21.3. (Although IBM is not a hospitality company it has many features that are similar to those of multinationals operating in the hospitality sector, including companies such as Accor, Sheraton, Holiday Inn, Marriott and Hilton.) Hofstede has since added 'long-term orientation' and a sixth dimension, 'indulgence versus restraint'.

The power-distance dimension refers to the degree of inequality that exists within a society. In the organizational context it sets out to differentiate to what extent a country's organizational culture encourages supervisors to exercise power. High power distance means that a society accepts unequal distribution of power. France, for example, was found to have a high power-distance culture. Low power distance means that power is shared and that workers and managers may see themselves as equals. Nordic countries and the USA and the UK are examples. This explains to some extent why many British workers and students, accustomed to relatively relaxed relationships with British managers or lecturers, have difficulties with French managers. Likewise, French and German students sometimes have difficulty adjusting to the relatively relaxed, first-name style of lecturers in English colleges and universities.

The individualism dimension is concerned with the degree to which people in a culture learn to act as individuals as opposed to members of a group. Britain, Australia, Canada, New Zealand, Ireland and the USA are described as being high on individualism. This encourages personal initiative and achievement and a right to a private life. Countries low on the individualism dimension tend to value harmony, have collectivist cultures where age and wisdom are respected and where the extended family and the clan are more significant than the individual.

The masculinity dimension is concerned with values such as assertiveness, performance and success as opposed to feminine values such as warm personal relationships, quality of life and caring for others. Countries high on the masculinity dimension include Italy and Australia, whereas those at the other extreme include the Scandinavian countries and the Netherlands.

The uncertainty-avoidance dimension is concerned with the degree to which people in a country prefer structured or unstructured situations. Where the uncertainty-avoidance dimension is strong (e.g. Japan, Greece), people need clear guidelines and support. Business will be conducted very formally. In weak uncertainty-avoidance cultures, structures and rules are less important. Business will be conducted less formally. Change and risk will be accepted.

Dimension	High	Low
Power distance	Supervisors are distant from their staff	Supervisors are close to their staff
Uncertainty avoidance	Risk taking is encouraged	Risk taking is discouraged
Individualism	Individual initiative/and private life valued	Individual initiative discouraged, collectivist culture significant
Masculinity	Assertiveness valued	Warm, caring values significant

Figure 21.3 Dimensions for comparing cultures
Source: Hofstede (1991)

The long-term orientation refers to how society values traditions and values. In the business context managers in Western countries such as the USA and the UK are more concerned with achieving their aims than with following traditional ways of doing things.

Hofstede analysed each country using these dimensions and then grouped countries with similar sets of dimensions into eight clusters which tend to have historical developmental similarities rather than simple geographical connections.

Cultural dimensions versus individual personalities

Hofstede's cultural dimensions describe national averages which apply to a whole population but are not about differences between individual members of societies. These dimensions should be used as guidelines, not as absolutes.

Organizational level

Hofstede concluded that dimensions of national cultures are not relevant for comparing organizations within the same country. This is because national cultures reflect values whereas organizational cultures are evidenced by practices. In a limited study of 20 organizations in two countries, Hofstede identified six different dimensions of practices, or communities of practice:

- Process-oriented versus results-oriented
- Employee-oriented versus job-oriented
- Parochial versus professional
- Open system versus closed system
- Loose control versus tight control
- Pragmatic versus normative.

These may be compared to a large number of other authorities including Trompenaars, Mole (see below, p249) and others who are summarized in Chapter 2.

Project GLOBE

The GLOBE project took Hofstede's (1980) original findings into researching the differences of cultures. The research identified nine cultural competencies and grouped 62 countries into ten convenient clusters (Javidan and Dastmalchian, 2009).

The nine GLOBE cultural competencies are:

1 *Performance orientation* – refers to the extent to which an organization or society encourages and rewards group members for performance improvement and excellence.
2 *Assertiveness orientation* – is the degree to which individuals in organizations or societies are assertive, confrontational and aggressive in social relationships.
3 *Future orientation* – is the degree to which individuals in organizations or societies engage in future-oriented behaviours such as planning, investing in the future and delaying gratification.

4 *Human orientation* – is the degree to which individuals in organizations or societies encourage and reward individuals for being fair, altruistic, friendly, generous, caring and kind to others.

5 *Collectivism I: Institutional collectivism* – reflects the degree to which organizational and societal institutional practices encourage and reward collective distribution of resources and collective action.

6 *Collectivism II: In-group collectivism* – reflects the degree to which individuals express pride, loyalty and cohesiveness in their organizations or families.

7 *Gender egalitarianism* – is the extent to which an organization or a society minimizes gender role differences and gender discrimination.

8 *Power distance* – is defined as the degree to which members of an organization or society expect and agree that power should be unequally shared.

9 *Uncertainty avoidance* – is defined as the extent to which members of an organization or society strive to avoid uncertainty by reliance on social norms, rituals and bureaucratic practices to alleviate the unpredictability of future events.

The research then grouped over 21 primary leadership dimensions into six encompassing dimensions of global leadership.

The six GLOBE dimensions of culturally endorsed implicit leadership (CLT):

1 *Charismatic/value based* – characterized by demonstrating integrity, decisiveness and performance-oriented by appearing visionary, inspirational and self-sacrificing, but can also be toxic and allow for autocratic commanding.

2 *Team oriented* – characterized by diplomatic, administratively competent, team collaboration and integration. A toxic leader would be malevolent, alienating the team but driving cohesion.

3 *Self-protective* – characterized by self-centred, face saving, procedural behaviour capable of inducing conflict when necessary while being conscious of status.

4 *Participative* – characterized by (non-autocratic) participative behaviour that is supportive of those who are being led.

5 *Human orientation* – characterized by modesty and compassion for others in an altruistic fashion.

6 *Autonomous* – being able to function without constant consultation.

Fons Trompenaars

Trompenaars, another Dutchman who has contributed considerably to the literature of international business culture, writes that 'culture' comes in layers like an onion (Trompenaars, 1998). He suggests that the outer skin is the observable, such as buildings, language, dress and food. The middle layer consists of norms (what is right and wrong?) and values (what is good and bad?): when norms reflect values, a society can be described as stable. The innermost core contains the assumptions about existence, which he describes as the 'unquestioned reality'.

Trompenaars writes that cultures distinguish themselves by the way they solve particular problems. He groups the problems under three main headings:

- relationships with others
- treatment of time
- relationship with the environment.

He then divides these three into a total of seven dimensions, as follows.

Under relationships with people:

- *Universalism versus particularism.* This dimension contrasts those cultures in which there is an abstract notion of what is good and right to those cultures where relationships and unique circumstances may come before abstract societal codes. In many Latin countries, for example, obligations to the family will override any obligations to adhere to strict legal or societal codes.
- *Individualism versus collectivism.* This dimension is concerned with how people perceive themselves; as individuals or as members of a wider social group.
- *Neutral versus emotional.* This dimension is concerned with how people behave in their interactions. Is it permissible to express emotions? In northern European cultures the whole purpose of business is about achieving objectives whereas in many other cultures business is about relationships – expression of emotions in such cultures is quite in order.
- *Diffuse versus specific.* This dimension is concerned with the extent to which the business relationship is concerned only with achieving the narrow business objective or is concerned with a wider-ranging relationship.
- *Achievement versus ascription.* This dimension is concerned with the way society ascribes status. Does status derive from what you have achieved or gained from class, birth, gender and age?

And then under the next headings:

Attitudes to time
Trompenaars writes that the way societies perceive time varies considerably. For some societies what was achieved in the past may be more important than what is achieved now or will be achieved in the future. Links between the past, the present and the future are also perceived differently, so such things as forward planning and strategy may present serious problems for managers in cultures with which they are unfamiliar.

The environment
Trompenaars also identifies very different approaches to the environment. He writes that in some cultures individuals are very concerned about their impact on others and the environment and will take measures to reduce their impact. For example, the Japanese wear face masks in winter, not to protect themselves from infection but to protect others from being infected. In other cultures, in contrast, individuals take measures to protect themselves from the effects of the environment.

Using these seven main dimensions Trompenaars shows how societies differ and that preconceptions about a universal science of management ignore one major element – the culture within which management functions or attempts to function.

John Mole

Another writer, John Mole, identifies two main dimensions, organization and leadership, as cultural differentiators.

The organization dimension is based on the degree to which rational order is imposed. At one end of the dimension, the systematic end, is the belief that organizations 'are coordinated by well-defined, logical relationships' whilst at the other end of the same dimension, the organic end, 'is the belief that organizations are like living organisms growing out of the needs of their members, their environment and the circumstances of the moment' (Mole, 1995).

	Organic	Systematic
The organization dimension		
Forecasting	Plans based on hunches	Plans based on analysis
Decision making	Decisions evolve	Decisions are made
Supervision	Who you know?	What you know?
Control	Criticism is personal	Criticism is objective
Communication	Informal	Goes through the formal hierarchy
Reward	Success depends on luck	Success depends on skill
Motivation	Pride in status	Pride in achievement
Style	Rules are to be circumvented	Rules are to be obeyed
The leadership dimension		
Forecasting	Plans made by those involved	Plans made at the top
Decision making	Made by groups	Made by individuals
Supervision	Leaders are one of us	Leaders are different
Control	Groups are accountable	Individuals are accountable
Communication	Meetings are for sharing	Meetings are for briefing
Reward	Teams strive	Individuals strive
Motivation	Individuals work for the collective	Individuals work for themselves
Style	Hierarchy, status, titles are a convenience	Hierarchy, status, titles are essential

Figure 21.4 Mole's dimensions

The leadership dimension has at one end the individualistic (even absolutist) approach and at the other end the group (even collectivist) approach to leading others. At the 'individual end of the dimension is the belief that individuals are intrinsically unequal' (Mole, 1995). The group end of the same dimension is based on the belief that 'everyone has a right to be heard and to contribute to all decisions that affect them'. The two dimensions are then divided into sub-dimensions. Some examples from Mole are shown in Figure 21.4.

The main conclusion from research is that even if business practices within one type of business or company are similar across international boundaries there may be significant differences in culture. It follows that if countries have different values, then similar management styles used across different cultures will not necessarily work. For example, MbO (management by objectives), which involves managers negotiating targets and taking personal risks, may well succeed in Britain or the USA but not in France, Spain or Portugal.

Perlmutter

How multinational and transnational firms manage their human resources of course varies as much possibly as does their approach to marketing. A major contributor in this field is Howard Perlmutter, who describes a number of different management approaches adopted by multinationals. These include: ethnocentric, polycentric, geocentric and regiocentric.

- *An ethnocentric policy* implies the same HRM strategies in all countries, a strong head office role and home country's managers occupying all key roles.
- *A polycentric policy* implies that HRM is decentralized country by country, decision making is devolved to local managers and local managers trained and developed.

- *A geocentric policy* implies that HRM is managed on a global basis, harmonizes from the centre and allows for the best people to emerge irrespective of origin.
- *A regiocentric policy* implies that HRM is managed on a regional basis.

Each of these approaches may be adopted in the hospitality industry.

Cultural differences, however, should not be seen as being confined to differences between nationalities. Obviously each country, each company has its own cultural inheritance, which differs to a greater or lesser extent from other cultures. Cultural differences also exist within national cultures at geographical and sociocultural levels. Some socio-economic groups from different countries have more in common, in many respects, than with different demographic or socio-economic groups from their own country. For example, 20-year-olds from Britain are more likely to share tastes in music, clothes and leisure with 20-year-olds from other countries than with 50-year-olds from their own country.

How individual hospitality companies demonstrate or develop cultural awareness varies considerably. In many cases nothing whatever is done to accommodate the needs of other cultures. For example, no staff may be able to speak another language and menus may not be translated even where significant numbers of foreign customers are served. At the most basic, it may be that brochures, tariff displays, menus, etc., are translated. At the next level, employers may translate important signs or at least use internationally recognized symbols. Other employers may maintain a list of all languages spoken by their staff so that if a customer needs language help, an appropriate member of staff may be called.

Some employers will actively promote acquisition of language by paying 'language bonuses' and paying for or providing language tuition. Good language education not only equips people with basic communication skills but also introduces key cultural issues such as forms of addressing others. Some employers may go further by researching key cultural issues concerning potential and actual customers and setting out to meet these needs, such as the provision of a copy of the Koran in the bedroom rather than a Gideons Bible. Finally some employers train staff through role-play, etc., in how to meet the needs of people from many different cultures.

The purpose of this chapter was not to produce a list of cultural differences. Instead it is intended to create the awareness that cultural differences do exist, that they are important, and that they are ignored at the risk of high labour turnover, giving offence at the very least, of losing business and, maybe, at worst facing claims for discrimination.

When working with people of other cultures, whether as managers, employees, customers or owners, the relationship is likely to be more successful if cultural differences are anticipated and accounted for.

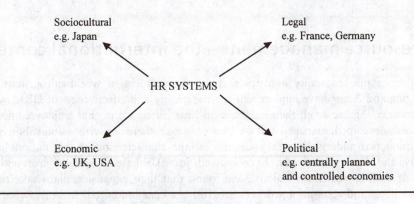

Figure 21.5 An example of the focus of HR systems

Aspects of culture	Some dimensions
Values, e.g.	
individual's place in society	autonomy valued .... collective effort valued
social status	material wealth .... social contribution
	ascribed at birth .... acquired through personal effort
religion	restrictive .... relaxed
	intolerant .... flexible
concern for others	caring .... unconcerned
Attitudes, e.g.	
towards work	economic necessity .... personal identity
towards authority	formal, respectful .... informal, unconcerned
towards those in subordinate social roles	demanding, superior .... relaxed, egalitarian
towards the other sex	strong gender role differentiation .... weak gender role differentiation
towards alcohol	consumed as adjunct to a meal....... consumed in order to get drunk
towards food & meals	important, symbolic .... unimportant, functional
towards time	punctuality very important .... punctuality unimportant
	one thing at a time .... several things at a time
Behaviour, e.g.	
relationship at work	formal .... informal
manner of dressing	formal .... informal
for work	important .... unimportant
personal space	close .... distant
forms of address	very formal .... informal
	important .... unimportant
non-verbal communication (e.g. gestures)	important .... unimportant
meals, eating habits	very formal .... informal
	important .... unimportant
meetings and conversations	only one person .... several talk at once

Figure 21.6 Examples of cultural differences

Figure 21.6 and 21.7 illustrate some of the areas where significant differences are likely to be encountered.

Human resource management – the international context

The globalization of the hospitality industry and the development of worldwide groups such as Starwood Lodging and Accor have implications for the quality and effectiveness of HRM within an international context. At one level, there might seem little difference in that employees need to be resourced, trained, developed, managed and the like. However, there are serious and subtle questions for HRM practitioners to address. Cultural issues and national characteristics and regulations have been mentioned above and clearly these need to be considered. Some UK-based hospitality firms with little or no experience of dealing with trade unions have found that their expansion plans take them into countries where hotel and restaurant workers are 100 per cent unionized. In other words, HRM needs to address all the particular factors prevailing on the workforce in each and every country in which the firm operates (see D'Annunzio-Green et al., 2002; also Beardwell et al., 2004).

Forms of greeting	Continental Europeans tend to be more formal than people from the UK or the USA, and may address one another as 'Mr' or 'Mrs' throughout their working lives. First-name terms may be reserved for genuine friends or family. The familiar *tu* in France and its equivalents in other countries may have to be avoided.
	Some continental Europeans tend to shake hands the first time they meet each day and when they finish work.
Meals	In some cultures meals are extremely important; some cultures 'eat to live whilst others live to eat'. Staple elements of diet – e.g. rice, pasta, potatoes – vary between cultures.
	Courses may be in a different order. The French take cheese before dessert. Meals may consist of more courses, each of one item.
	Meals may contain different items. A Nordic breakfast may contain cheeses, hams, salami-type sausage. Asian breakfast may contain curry-like dishes.
	Table lay-ups may be different. The French may eat continental breakfast, using large cups, with no plate on the table. Side plates may not be used at other meals either. The same cutlery may be used throughout a meal.
	Many ingredients have local characteristics which can be important, e.g. the Latins drink much stronger coffee than do Anglo-Saxons.
	Meal times may be different, e.g. southern Europeans tend to eat for a longer period and later than the British.
	Children are not just tolerated but are welcome in most continental restaurants. Children tend to eat meals at the same time as their parents.
Drinks	Attitudes may be very different towards drink: in some cultures it is forbidden, other cultures view alcohol as an accompaniment to a meal, whilst other cultures may see drinking as an end in itself, with status connotations, e.g. a macho thing to do.
	Drinks may be used differently, e.g. port may be used as an aperitif, whisky as a digestif/liqueur.
Accommodation	Some nationalities prefer twin beds to doubles, showers to baths, duvets to blankets.
	Some ethnic groups require the Koran rather than the Bible in the bedroom.
Complaining	Some nationalities complain readily but are satisfied if the cause is rectified. Others, e.g. the British, tend not to complain but do not return.

Figure 21.7 Some examples of cultural differences of interest to the hospitality industry

Such firms need to be more aware of the salary and benefit packages expected by truly mobile international personnel, and need to plan issues not normally part of the host-country operations such as language and culture training, schooling for management's families, taxation and legal aspects. There will be different types of employees with different terms and conditions and situations, such as expatriates, local workers and temporary secondments, and truly global, multi-site organizations will need to develop highly sophisticated succession planning systems in order to monitor and plan the future management of the business (see Goss-Turner, 1993; Chapter 22 in this book).

Further reading and references

Barlett *et al.* (2008) *Transnational Management: Text, Cases and Readings in Cross-Border Management*, 5th edn, New York: McGraw-Hill.

Beardwell, I., Holden, L. and Claydon, T. (2004) *Human Resource Management – A Contemporary Approach*, 4th edn, Harlow: Prentice Hall.

Caligiuri, P., Lepak, D. and Bonache, J. (2010) *Managing the Global Workforce*, Chichester: Wiley.

D'Annunzio-Green, N., Maxwell, G. and Watson, S. (2002) *Human Resource Management – International Perspectives in Hospitality and Tourism*, London: Continuum.

Dibben, P., Klerck, G. and Wood, G. (2011) *Employment Relations: A Critical and International Approach*, London: Chartered Institute of Personnel and Development.

French, R. (2010) *Cross-cultural Management in Work Organisations*, 2nd edn, London: Chartered Institute of Personnel and Development.

Goss-Turner, S. (1993) 'Human resource management', in Jones, P. and Pizam, A. (eds.) *The International Hospitality Industry*, London: Pitman.

Harttig, M. A., Strozik, M. and Mukherjee, A. (2010) 'Global workforce planning', *Benefits and Compensation International*, 40(1): 19–20, 22–23.

Harris, H., Brewster, C. and Sparrow, P. (2003) *International Human Resource Management*, London: Chartered Institute of Personnel and Development.

Hofstede, G. (1980) *Culture's Consequences: International Differences in Work-related Values*, Newbury Park, CA: Sage; 2nd edn, 2001.

Hofstede, G. (1989) 'Organising for cultural diversity', *European Management Journal*, 7(4): 390–397.

Hofstede, G. (1991) *Cultures and Organizations: Software of the Mind*, London: McGraw-Hill.

Hofstede, G. (1994) *Cultures and Organizations: Intercultural Cooperation*, London: HarperCollins.

Hofstede, G., Hofstede, G. J. and Minkov, M. (2010) *Cultures and Organizations, Software of the Mind*, 3rd rev. edn, New York: McGraw-Hill.

Home Office, Border and Immigration Agency (2008) *Guidance for Employers on the Avoidance of Unlawful Discrimination in Employment Practice while Seeking to Prevent Illegal Working*, London: Home Office.

Home Office, Border and Immigration Agency (2010) *Guidance for Employers on Preventing Illegal Working: Asylum Seekers and Refugees*, London: Home Office.

Javidan, M. and Dastmalchian, A. (2009) 'Managerial implications of the GLOBE project: a study of 62 societies', *Asia Pacific Journal of Human Resources*, 47(1): 41.

Jayawardena, C. (2000) 'International hotel manager', *International Journal of Hospitality Management*, 12(1): 67–69.

Lundby, K. and Jolton, J. (2010) *Going Global: Practical Applications and Recommendations for HR and OD Professionals in the Global Workplace*, San Francisco, CA: Jossey Bass.

Mole, D. (1995) *Mind Your Manners*, 2nd edn, London: Industrial Society.

People 1st (2011) *State of the Nation Report 2011, Analysis of labour market trends, skills, education and training within the UK hospitality, leisure, travel and tourism industries*, London: People 1st.

Perlmutter, Howard (1969) 'The tortuous evolution of multinational enterprises', *Columbia Journal of World Business*, (1): 9–18.

Perlmutter, V. H. and Heenan, A. D. (2000) 'How multinational should your top managers be?' *Harvard Business Review*, 1–13.

Sinclair, A. and Robertson-Smith, G. (2008) *Managing Teams across Cultures: How to Manage across Borders, Time Zones and Cultures*, Horsham: Roffey.

Sparrow, P. R. (2006) *International Recruitment, Selection and Assessment*, London: CIPD.

Tayeb, M. H. (2005) *International Human Resource Management: A Multinational Company Perspective*, Oxford: Oxford University Press.

Trompenaars, F. (1998) *Riding the Waves of Culture*, 2nd edn, London: McGraw-Hill.

Members of the UK's Institute of Hospitality can access publications including Management Guides which summarize key information of relevance to hospitality operations (www.instituteofhospitality.org).

Members of the UK's Chartered Institute of Personnel and Development (CIPD) can access a range of materials including Fact Sheets and articles from over 300 online journal titles relevant to HR. CIPD members and *People Management* subscribers can see articles on the People Management website (www.peoplemanagement.co.uk).

Questions

1 Describe, with examples, various ways in which one culture may differ from another. Apply your answer to the hospitality industry.

2 Describe different aspects of the hospitality experience which management need to consider when providing for people from different cultures. Consider first customer needs, then staff needs.

3 Give examples of lack of cultural awareness which you have observed. Choose a particular setting such as at work, on holiday or at college.

4 Describe the measures that you believe would be necessary in order to develop an effective cultural awareness programme for a group of employees with whom you are acquainted. (You may find it useful to refer to Chapters 22 and 23.)

5 Discuss how cultural differences may lead to the need for different approaches to management style.

6 Discuss the proposition that cultural differences may be greater between socio-economic groups within a country than between similar socio-economic groups from different countries.

CASE STUDY QUESTION – see the Lux Hotels case study Appendix 5

In this chapter key issues concerning the management of businesses in a multicultural context have been discussed.

How would you describe Lux Hotels approach, using Perlmutter's categorization? How could this affect recruitment and training of management and staff in the longer term? Would Hofstede's contribution affect the types of management the company will need to recruit?

What are the main issues Lux Hotels needs to consider in its management of its hotels in a number of different countries? You will need to consider ownership, management, staff and customers.

Is the present structure suitable? What about the make-up of senior and hotel managers?

Chapter 22

HRM and multi-site hospitality operations

In numerical and structural terms, the hospitality industry remains to this day an industry of predominantly independently owned enterprises, providing a particular locality with a range of appropriate food, beverage and accommodation services (Lee-Ross, 1999). These businesses are often small, and may be considered family businesses or lifestyle choices regarding entrepreneurship (Lucas, 2004). Many of these businesses stay the same size, whilst others grow and develop, the firm replicating the product or service in other locations further and further afield (Goss-Turner and Jones, 2000). In the past half-century a feature of the national and international industry has been the development of large hospitality chains, many emanating from US post-war prosperity and expansion, with brand extension strategies placing high in public consciousness company names such as Hilton, Sheraton and Kentucky Fried Chicken. It has been estimated, for example, that there are 900,000 restaurant units in the United States, of which almost 300,000 are owned and managed by chain restaurants (DiPietro *et al.*, 2007). These large, multi-site, often multinational corporations have unparalleled profile, and utilize their size and influence in areas such as economies of scale, quality assurance, customer recognition and standardization (Ritchie and Riley, 2004).

The expansion of service organizations such as hospitality businesses, often by replication of a successful brand, has inevitable consequences for the organizational structure, reporting relationships and managerial competencies. In the period after 1945, many such organizations originally adapted the principles of mass production and those of retailing services, consistent with the seminal work of Levitt (1972) and later related by Schmenner (1986) as an industrialization of services. This highly systematic approach involved meticulous control and management of the supply chain from the sourcing of products, to central purchasing and distribution, to the operational elements of standardized menus, service delivery concept and system, pricing, decor and uniforms. This chapter explores HRM and employee development issues and the challenges facing multi-site hospitality organizations as they continue to expand both nationally and internationally in a sector constantly subjected to the merger and takeover impacts of consolidation.

The development of multi-unit organizations

Much of the most pertinent literature on the subject of multi-site management and the service sector was developed by US researchers and writers (see Umbreit, 1989). In view of the point raised above about the origin of many such multi-unit organizations, this is not surprising. Of notable relevance is the work of Olsen *et al.* (1992), who devote considerable attention to the development of multi-unit hospitality firms, including a review of the HRM implications. Their definition of a multi-unit (multi-site) firm is a useful starting point: 'an organization that competes in the industry with more than one unit of like concept or theme'. Olsen *et al.* point to the problems of managing a dispersed operation across many geographical boundaries, and the subsequent challenges associated with quality control, in particular the supervision of the skills and attitudes of service delivery employees. They also raise the issue of the span of control, i.e. the number of unit managers reporting directly to a multi-site manager, their research indicating that this can vary between two and 15. In reflecting on the US restaurant sector more recently, DiPietro *et al.* (2007) estimate that there are about 39,000 multi-site managers for US restaurants alone. There is also reference to the typical hierarchical structure and the position of the multi-unit manager within that structure. Literature on this subject focuses on the first-line area or regional management level, positioned between single-unit management and senior executive responsibility (see Goss-Turner, 1999).

In reviewing the US literature, factors which emerge as significant include the link between HRM development in multi-unit firms and the organizational life cycle considerations of introduction, growth, maturity and decline, a link well established by Sasser *et al.* (1978), when extending the concept of the product life cycle into a service firm life cycle. The implication is that HRM will develop, either reactively or in alignment with business strategy and growth, in the areas of recruitment, selection, training and development, and in compensation and benefits. This concept gains insight when considering the circumstances of a new start-up business and its ensuing developing life cycle. The founding entrepreneur will probably be a dynamic, creative force behind the initial business, and will ensure that the other personnel involved are appropriately talented and enthusiastic, but perhaps like-minded as well. The approach to HRM is likely to be ad hoc and without structure. Growth of the firm, including the opening of more identical concepts elsewhere, is associated with a need to develop more systematic HR approaches, and ultimately consideration of human resource planning, management development and succession planning. In the author's own research this proposition has been largely supported (Goss-Turner, 2002), with personnel documentation and techniques such as organization charts, job descriptions and appraisal systems often a later phase development as the multi-site firm grows in scale.

Implications for HRM and line management

Literature from the UK has focused on strategic and operational implications and service development issues connected with multi-site management, and there have been a number of studies covering the operational systems aspects of the contemporary hospitality industry, and about what hospitality managers actually do at unit level (Lockwood and Guerrier, 1990). The impact of the managerial ideology of empowerment has also been addressed in connection with multi-site firms, analysing the knock-on effects of the delayering of hospitality organization structures and therefore the nature of the roles of the different layers of management, including the impact on the multi-unit manager position. Lashley (1997) has contributed to the understanding of the concept of empowerment within a service industry context, relating particularly to research within the Harvester Restaurants chain. In Harvester, the empowerment of service employees via more self-managing work groups and the redistribution of responsibilities led to a delayering of two managerial levels. The removal of a layer above the regional or area manager and directly below the managing director increased the accountability of the regional management positions. More recently, Ritchie and Riley (2004) further stress the importance of the human capital inherent within the multi-unit manager role and the crucial aspect of organizational knowledge within a multi-unit structure, including a sense of the power of the hierarchy. The theme of human capital, training and of multi-unit manager competences has also been the subject of recent published research by Rivera *et al.* (2008) in the United States.

The implications of empowerment initiatives for the role of middle management is also considered by Simons (1995) who points to the need for robust control systems in order to avoid the danger of control failures due to a more remote management style, as in the situation often observed in delayered, decentralized organizations where the multi-site manager is made responsible for a span of control of 20 units when previously he or she had only 12 direct reporting unit managers.

Simons's framework, directly related here to the multi-unit manager role and the multi-site business, consists of four dimensions. The first dimension concerns the need for diagnostic control systems, exemplified by the multi-unit management responsibility for checking that goals and targets have been achieved effectively and efficiently. The second dimension is the dimension of beliefs systems or core values, such as the strong multi-unit manager influence in disseminating and reinforcing corporate culture or preferred management style. The third dimension is boundary systems, providing clear parameters of the job and, finally, the fourth is interactive control systems like regular face-to-face meetings or on-site business reviews to assess performance, issues and future plans and actions.

The perspectives and implications put forward by Lashley (1997), Simons (1995) and Rivera *et al.* (2008) all impact on the topic of this chapter by assisting in the understanding of the role of the multi-unit manager within the wider managerial hierarchy, particularly focusing on the inherent tensions between the actual job and the range of tasks required, and, as Ritchie and Riley (2004) vividly describe, the resultant 'messiness' of the role.

The role of the multi-unit manager

In reviewing research outputs from the USA and the UK, it is clear that the multi-site or multi-unit manager role is the most influential interface between corporate strategic management and the operational outlets in which the service encounter takes place. This manager, whilst responsible for the individual unit managers across a particular region or brand, is only rarely present at the operation, is necessarily remote and yet is a line manager of the unit manager, and direct control is only occasionally and briefly possible (Jones, 1999). Similarly the multi-unit managers themselves may well be located far from their own peers and superiors. Coordination and collaboration is therefore relatively difficult, as is ensuring that performance is enhanced across a wide range of units (Harrington, 2006).

Goss-Turner and Jones (2000) conclude from their extensive research within multi-unit hospitality firms that there are four key aspects of the first-line multi-unit management level: job scope, organizational congruence, geographic density and unit conformity. Within job scope, i.e. the range of tasks and responsibilities, there was great variance, polarized between those with a very tightly defined set of tasks geared towards inspection and a broader concept within which the manager would have a degree of accountability for development of the business and innovation. International and more mature restaurant chains with global brand significance tended towards the rigorous control aspect, in standardizing the offering and achieving high margins through control. Firms in earlier growth stages and of a less international nature were characterized by a broader range of duties. Interestingly, those with a strongly branded set of products, such as the major pubs groups, although national rather than international, also followed a pattern of ever more narrowly defined job scope.

For international firms, organizational congruence was particularly important, i.e. the extent to which all managerial levels share a common vision and purpose. In global franchised hotel brands there were clear and formal systems of developing management and employees in the corporate culture and values of service inherent in the base company's strategic underpinning. Such international firms are also attempting a congruence of systems (such as information technology, appraisal and management development) and culture (such as values, beliefs and service culture).

Geographic density, i.e. the number of units in an area or region relative to the size of the area, is again a key difference between large, mature multinationals and the developing, less mature nationals. For example, international hotel firms tended to have a low relative density, requiring an even more mobile and experienced international manager to take on the area role.

As for unit conformity, i.e. the extent to which units within an area are identical or not, there was a definite trend towards 'streaming' by brand rather than by geography due to the effectiveness and efficiency gains to be achieved from a regional manager always reviewing identical units. As a result, this multi-unit manager possesses a comprehensive bank of knowledge about the brand, its operational procedures and its product and service delivery standards.

In a study of further HRM implications of these characteristics of multi-site firms, Goss-Turner (1999) concludes that the multi-unit manager role is predominantly an implementer of policy, not a creator of policy. This is largely a function of the role being so clearly placed between the strategy-makers in the boardrooms and the operational front-line unit managers. It is also because all the companies in the research had strategic expansion plans specifically dedicated to the expansion of their already tightly branded concepts, sometimes within strictly controlled global franchises related to international growth potential. As a result such organizational development involving growth, consolidation and brand extension requires the implementation and maintenance of absolute standards. There is therefore a need for inspection, checking and systematic control, and contrary to some people's view of empowerment, the role has not necessarily become more strategic.

From an overall HRM perspective, the aspect of the role which appears to give the multi-unit managers (those interviewed in the research study) the greatest satisfaction is their personal ability to 'make a difference', by motivating unit managers to achieve high performance. Elements of this aspect include also the beneficial outcome of their job in sharing good and bad practice across the area, often trying to combine high levels of brand prescription and company standardization with the need to encourage an equally high level of commitment to the values and philosophy of the company. One hotel company regional manager interviewed during the author's own research study was typical of those managers who saw their job as a combination of the need to implement strategic imperatives with a need to motivate the managers in the units:

> The job entails firstly maintaining the brand – we do have an identity and maintaining that identity in terms of our standards in the customer's mind and in their perception. I also want to stretch the managers as much as I can by getting them to achieve, such as the 'Investors in People' in every hotel, giving them objectives, ensuring they are ambitious over their business plans. But of course you can never take your eye off the profit level, and implementing company policy.

(Hotel Company Regional Manager)

HRM policy issues

In the larger, more complex and mature companies, a move towards more sophisticated human resource practices is evident, in line with the research of Doherty (1998). One national licensed retailer with more than 2,000 outlets had carried out extensive analysis of the multi-site manager role and determined a set of competencies, which formed part of a detailed job profile which itself was a composite of job description, principal tasks, generic business targets and a consideration of key organizational relationships, and progress and review meetings, both internally and externally. The competencies identified were then utilized in an array of HRM procedures, including recruitment and selection criteria, within training and development programmes, and as the basic criteria for performance appraisal systems, ensuring that such managers were assessed closely against a range of results and abilities. Specifically, this company highlighted:

- developing people
- commitment to results and standards
- business acumen
- objective analysis and decision making
- planning and organizing
- maximizing business opportunities
- communicating
- influencing.

The wide range and scope of these managerial competencies and the tasks and activities within which the role-holder displays such competencies are in stark contrast to some companies' approach to multi-unit management. Where standardization is paramount, the multi-unit manager role can be a mere checker/ inspector role, or, if the company culture is dominated by a 'hands-on', almost egalitarian approach, area managers may sometimes be required to cover for absent restaurant managers and unit supervisors. In a typology of the multi-unit manager role, Goss-Turner and Jones (2000) suggest four main approaches (see Figure 22.1). First, there is the 'Archetype' multi-unit management approach; a mature single-brand organization, typified by McDonald's, with strongly branded identical units with tightly defined tasks for area managers, highly suited to international expansion strategies. The area manager would have narrow job scope; the firm, a high degree of organizational congruence with high geographic density so that area managers can visit regularly and control closely. The implications for human resource management are that most multi-unit managers of this type will have had in-depth unit-level experience and be experts on the standards and procedures of the operation. They will be, in the main, inspectors of standards, ensuring consistency and replication of the product and service delivery system.

Second, there is the 'Multi-Brand Manager', with more than one concept, tightly branded, applying identical managerial systems in each brand. While the job scope is still narrow, there is more flexibility and variety as more concepts are involved in mature companies. High congruence is difficult to attain, and geographic density remains high as the firm's structure is predominantly region or area-based,

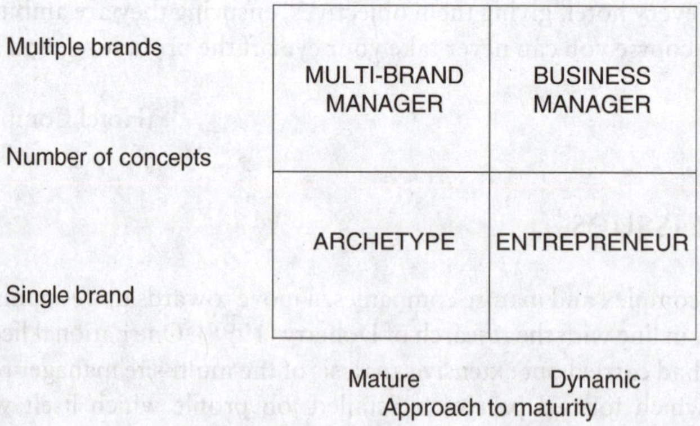

Figure 22.1 Typology of alternative approaches to area management
Source: Goss-Turner and Jones (2000).

predicated on a critical mass of outlets rather than on streamed brands. This approach is difficult to position in the international marketplace. If selecting a manager for this role, there would be a need for an individual less deeply immersed in the detail of one particular brand; more an individual capable of understanding the differences and subtleties of the different brands; more general business management skills, as in an appreciation of merchandizing and consumer behaviour rather than a concentrated focus on one set of standards or operational tasks.

Third, the 'Business Manager', responsible for more than one brand and working within a more dynamic environment, with more opportunity for creative solutions and actions within broad policy guidelines and goals. This approach can be readily applied to international hotel companies for example. The personnel specification with regard to this role would be much wider in its requirement for managerial competencies. There would be a higher calling for large-scale business strategy skills, highly developed communication skills, possibly multicultural experience, and certainly an ability to motivate and direct other senior and experienced managers. A regional manager for an international hotel chain, for example, would be the line manager for perhaps 15 unit general managers who are themselves experienced hotel managers perhaps with international reputations.

Finally, there is the 'Entrepreneur' with each area manager responsible for one concept, tightly branded, but with an autonomy to develop the business, to be innovative where appropriate, and always within the cultural norms of the firm. Organizational congruence is driven by adherence to values and cultural issues, and job scope is relatively broad within a dynamic environment which eschews a global system of control. This approach will tend to be evident within fairly recently founded companies in the early stages of multi-site growth and expansion. The culture and drive behind the organization will still be linked to the personality, philosophy and original concept of the founder. The suitably entrepreneurial area managers will have probably grown up within the company from the start, will be trusted acolytes of the founder and will be trusted implicitly to do the right thing. There will be no need for the paraphernalia of sophisticated HRM systems, and appraisal and performance management will be at most an informal if often extremely frank exchange of opinions and basic comparative performance statistics.

The latitude of regional middle management is also determined by the size and stage of development of the firm's life cycle. It has been found that the larger, more mature companies display a control-oriented, structured approach, while smaller, more youthful, entrepreneurially dynamic firms tend towards a strategy that emphasizes mission, values and culture. Organizational development in recent years is also directly affecting the role, as head office support has in many companies been diminished in downsized and delayered organizations.

In the short term this may mean that the multi-unit managers need a broader range of more general management skills, and indeed it was found in the field research that area managers are considerably more involved with HRM issues and practice than they used to be. Such managers will need more training and development in matters such as recruitment, selection and performance appraisal. Recruitment plans may be affected, with some hospitality and tourism firms perhaps having to recruit more from outside their firm, even the industry. There is evidence from the licensed trade that there are successful multi-unit managers joining the major pubs groups from high-street retailers.

One aspect that will need to be the focus of future research pertains to the longer-term career development and succession planning aspects of multi-site managers. Whilst there may be many more opportunities to become an area manager in the large consolidated branded chains, the decentralization of many such companies is leading to smaller head office support functions. This has a direct impact on future career development prospects, as many area managers in the past have aspired to more specialist, centrally based roles. It is possible that such managers may have to stay in post longer than previously was the case, due to the flatter structure of multi-unit organizations. This clearly has implications for HRM, management development, succession planning and indeed compensation and benefits if motivation is to be maintained.

Training and development challenges

With regard to training and development, the author's research (Goss-Turner, 1999) uncovered two significant challenges at crucial positions within the managerial succession. First, it is imperative that there is more systematic training of unit managers identified as possessing the potential for multi-unit management appointments, particularly in those competencies such as HRM, marketing and financial management which will be needed to a much greater extent in the multi-site role. Add to this the motivational ability required across a large number of units and unit managers in a geographically spread area, and it is clear that the skills of being a top-class unit manager are very different from those required in the area role. Yet many area managers in hospitality companies were identified and promoted because of being highly successful unit managers who experienced little developmental bridging to the new role with its very different set of competencies. Just because an employee is a successful manager of one restaurant does not mean they have the capabilities to be the regional manager of 15 other restaurant managers. The skills are different. These findings have been supported by more recent research in the USA by Rivera *et al.* (2008), who also concluded that involvement with HRM procedures and practice was a key issue and challenge. Indeed, in the restaurant chains investigated, there appeared to be a lack of training in HR basics such as staff training, unit manager development and team-building. They also found that these area managers needed more skills in the areas of finance and control, and were lacking in guidance and development towards higher-level executive skills as they aimed to progress within the company.

The research by DiPietro *et al.* (2007) also revealed interesting combinations of skills and competencies required by multi-unit managers in restaurant chains, and the training and development programmes that would be most compatible. They propose a programme dealing with the following aspects of the role, a set of key success factors for the multi-unit manager:

- unit operations (e.g. labour costs, food costs, staff training)
- standards of performance (e.g. reports, data sets, merchandizing)
- unit finances (e.g. financial interpretation and decisions)
- multi-unit planning (e.g. goal setting, budgeting)
- interpersonal/social duties (e.g. community affairs, developing unit managers)
- unit follow-up meetings (e.g. visiting units, planning logistics of visits)
- human resources (e.g. team-building, cultural issues, values)
- effective leadership (e.g. focus on strategic and operational imperatives).

It has been found that in most multi-site firms, the multi-unit role is one of implementation of standards, and that positions higher up the organization will require additional and enhanced skills in the area of strategic formulation and corporate-level decision making. Some companies in the author's research sample were tackling this issue by introducing executive development programmes for high-potential managers, often utilizing universities and business schools as partners in such development activities. Succession plans must influence management development programmes to ensure that this gap in the training cycle is bridged.

This chapter has reviewed some of the HRM implications of an ongoing phenomenon, namely the continuing development of larger, multi-site firms within an ever more international and branded hospitality industry. It has been established that this has increased the need for, and significance of, a position of multi-site management, immediately above the front-line operations management and between operations and senior/strategic executive levels. As such it has been found to be a very important career development position for many unit managers, but essentially as an implementer of strategy rather than a creator. Further, it has been discussed that the role in many strongly branded chains has the potential to be a largely controlling and checking role, with the proviso that there is still an opportunity for any area or regional manager to exercise their specific skills as a motivator and a coach to unit management. There is still the need to encourage and energize and to gain a high level of commitment to the values and beliefs of the company.

Further reading and references

Collings, D. G. and Scullion, H. (2007) 'Global staffing and the multi-national enterprise', in Storey, J. (ed.) *Human Resource Management: A Critical Text*, 3rd edn, London: Thomson Learning.

DiPietro, R., Murphy, K., Rivera, M. and Muller, C. (2007) 'Multi-unit management key success factors in the casual dining restaurant industry: a case study', *International Journal of Contemporary Hospitality Management*, 19(7): 524–536.

Doherty, L. (1998) 'What makes a successful influential human resource strategy?', *Proceedings of the EuroChrie/IAHMS Conference*, Lausanne, November: 123–131.

Goss-Turner, S. (1999) 'The role of the multi-unit manager in branded hospitality chains', *Human Resource Management Journal*, 9(4): 39–57.

Goss-Turner, S. (2002) 'Multi-site management: HRM implications', in D'Annunzio-Green, N., Maxwell, G. A. and Watson, S. (eds) *Human Resource Management – International Perspectives in Hospitality and Tourism*, London: Continuum.

Goss-Turner, S. and Jones, P. (2000) 'Multi-unit management in service operations: alternative approaches in the UK hospitality industry', *Tourism and Hospitality Research*, 2(1): 51–66.

Harrington, R. J. (2006) 'The moderating effects of size, manager tactics and involvement on strategy implementation in foodservice', *International Journal of Hospitality Management*, 25(3): 373–379.

Jones, P. (1999) 'Multi-unit management: a late twentieth century phenomenon', *International Journal of Contemporary Hospitality Management*, 11(4): 155–164.

Knights, D. and Willmott, H. (eds) (2012) *Introducing Organizational Behaviour and Management*, 2nd edn, Andover: Cengage Learning EMEA.

Lashley, C. (1997) *Empowering Service Excellence*, London: Cassell.

Lee-Ross, D. (1999) *HRM in Tourism and Hospitality*, London: Cassell.

Levitt, T. (1972) 'The production line approach to service', *Harvard Business Review*, September/October: 41–52.

Lockwood, A. and Guerrier, Y. (1990) 'Managers in hospitality: a review of current research', *Progress in Tourism, Recreation and Hospitality Research*, 2: 151–167.

Lucas, R. (2004) *Employment Relations in the Hospitality and Tourism Industries*, London: Routledge.

Olsen, M., Ching-Yick Tse, E. and West, J. J. (1992) *Strategic Management in the Hospitality Industry*, New York: Van Nostrand Reinhold.

Ritchie, B. and Riley, M. (2004) 'The role of the multi-unit manager within the strategy and structure relationship; evidence from the unexpected', *International Journal of Hospitality Management*, 23: 145–161.

Rivera, M., DiPietro, R., Murphy, K. and Muller, C. (2008) 'Multi-unit managers: training needs and competences for casual dining restaurants', *International Journal of Contemporary Hospitality Management*, 20(6): 616–630.

Sasser, W. E., Olsen, R. P. and Wycoff, D. D. (1978) *Management of Service Operations*, Boston, MA: Allyn and Bacon.

Schmenner, R. (1986) 'How can service businesses survive and prosper?', *Sloan Management Review*, Spring: 21–32.

Simons, R. (1995) 'Control in an age of empowerment', *Harvard Business Review*, March/April: 80–88.

Umbreit, W. T. (1989) 'Multi-unit management: managing at a distance', *The Cornell Hotel and Restaurant Administration Quarterly*, 30: 53–59.

Members of the UK's Institute of Hospitality (IoH) can access publications including Management Guides which summarize key information of relevance to hospitality operations (www.instituteofhospitality.org).

Members of the UK's Chartered Institute of Personnel and Development (CIPD) can access a range of materials including Fact Sheets and articles from over 300 online journal titles relevant to HRM. CIPD members and *People Management* subscribers can see articles on the People Management website (www.peoplemanagement.co.uk).

Questions

1 Why has the position of multi-site manager become significant within branded hospitality chains?

2 What is the relationship between management style and the role of the multi-unit manager?

3 What do you understand by job scope, organizational congruence, geographic density and unit conformity?

4 What essential requirements would you include in the personnel specification for a multi-site manager within an international hotel chain?

5 What selection methods would you adopt when assessing the suitability of applicants for a multi-unit manager role in a fast food chain?

6 What would be key elements of a training and development programme for a multi-unit manager?

CASE STUDY QUESTION – see the Lux Hotels case study Appendix 5

How would you utilize the typology of multi-unit management indicated above in Figure 22.1 when advising on the future structure and roles within Lux Hotels?

Chapter 23

Employer branding

Combining certain principles of strategic marketing with the concept and practices of human resource management (HRM) has been an increasingly apparent organizational development in recent years. Television commercials feature 'employees' in the workplace of the organization rather than the traditional advertisement scenarios of well-known actors in rather more exotic locations. Service sector companies ranging from personal computer stores to supermarkets, restaurant chains, hotels and banks have caught on to the notion that 'fronting' the commercials with your employees, and the products and services that they provide, can forge a strong and meaningful marketing relationship with existing and potential customers. Underpinning the notion is the belief that if the customer considers the employees as personified in the advertisement to be supremely socially skilled and in possession of excellent product knowledge, then they will be more inclined to place their custom in such safe, capable and welcoming hands. The employees had better deliver when the customer arrives!

This trend is just one element of a much wider phenomenon that at its conceptual heart harbours the idea that employers need to consider their branding and value proposition not only as far as the customer is concerned but also as far as the existing or potential employee is concerned. Employer branding is attracting much interest in both the HRM and marketing communities, from both an academic and practitioner perspective. In effect, organizations should not only consider customer relationship marketing but employee relationship marketing as well.

The concept of employer branding can be viewed as a natural developmental outcome from the more contemporary policies and practices of HRM. As first outlined in Chapter 2, the modern interpretation and implementation of HRM is founded on a number of key factors which were not as central to prior understandings of personnel management and the management of people, particularly concepts such as strong corporate culture, high commitment and high performance. If the leaders of a service organization are believers in the new form of HRM, they will naturally acknowledge its strategic importance, its role in ensuring the high performance of employees, the need for high commitment from the employees and the supportive coherence of the organization's values and culture. The externalization of that culture and those values is a means of displaying your image as an organization and employer in the shop window of the media. The hospitality industry has had its battles surrounding its image as an employer for many years (Lucas, 2002), and in many ways employer branding is an innovative response to the challenge. Employer branding is predicated on the benefits of organizations marketing themselves towards their workforce as professionally as they market themselves towards their customers. As well as attracting the right customer to your international hotel chain, one who identifies with your standards and values, and remains loyal and committed to the brand, then it is a given that you deploy an equally significant strategy in attracting the right type of employees, who also share your values, remain loyal and committed to the employer. It is a form of classic relationship marketing, a three-way relationship that evolves over time, becoming stronger and more mutually beneficial to the parties concerned, the employer, the employee and the customer. Such a mutuality of interest can only be advantageous to an aspiring hospitality firm of the twenty-first century.

Origins and development of employer branding

The latter half of the twentieth century saw the rapid development of highly prescribed brands across the service sector as a whole and within hospitality in particular. Many of these brands, such as Hilton, Holiday Inn or Pizza Hut, were highly prescribed and standardized, based on a concept of proposing to their markets a clearly articulated set of product, service and value propositions. They were underpinned by an attachment to a strong service culture, designed to possess distinctive attributes in line with their consumer-oriented market research. Branding gave management more control over the product and the nature of the service offer (the blueprint) and, once a proven commercial success, branding became a key strategic parameter, especially in multi-site, replicated operations. Success and expansion led to the most recognizable brand names becoming global phenomena, familiar across developed and developing countries alike. Sophisticated branding attempts to prescribe in great detail the concept, the products, the service standards and the behaviours required of its employees. As such it has the potential for powerful influence over the management approach, the employees, their workplace and its prevailing values and culture (see Zeithaml and Bitner, 2003; De Chernatony and Cottam, 2008). In this way, branding as a whole may be seen as part of a strong corporate and service culture, and the hospitality industry has been in the forefront of services branding and marketing, as can be observed in most UK high streets where the geographical replication of coffee shops, fast food outlets, pub and restaurant chain brands dominate the food and beverage landscape. Employer branding as a developing concept can be said to have its origins within this late twentieth-century environment, bringing together the marketing of a brand to a customer with the need to attract employees to the same brand, with the potential to foster close and loyal relationships between employee and customer within the same brand, described by Sandiford and Seymour (2007) as an 'occupational community'.

As proposed by Allen and Meyer (1990), employee commitment can be attributed to three main elements, and all have linkage to the foundation of employer branding:

- *Affective commitment*: created by an emotional attachment to an organization
- *Continuance commitment*: created by a perception of the risks associated with leaving that organization
- *Normative commitment*: created by a feeling of obligation to the work and to fellow employees.

Strands of each of these elements of commitment may be seen to have resonance with the topic under consideration, a merging of culture and commitment to an organization. Such a merging requires the sharing of purpose and vision, sharing of values and goals, and the feeling of strength and security by involvement and participation within the organization, resulting in a strong desire to stay with and work hard for that organization (see De Chernatony and Cottam, 2008). Here we see the coherence of the employer branding concept with so much that is deemed to be relevant in contemporary HRM in terms of strategy, performance, commitment, culture and the importance of workforce stability.

What is employer branding?

The use of the phrase 'employer branding' can truly be described as a late twentieth-century phenomenon, as it appears to have been first coined, used and defined by Ambler and Barrow of the London Business School in their 1996 publication, *The Employer Brand*. In a paper to the 2010 Eurochrie Hospitality Conference, Gehrels and Looij consider the definitions that have developed over the years as well as consider the application and potential of the concept within the hospitality industry. They define employer branding as:

> the strategy a company could use to differentiate its brand as employer from those of their competitors, with the purpose to ensure the organisation of good applicants, and to maintain talent within the organisation.
>
> (Gehrels and Looij, 2010: 3)

Minchington (2007) supports this and earlier definitions, and the main aspects raised within this chapter, by reference to the need for an interrelationship between the three brands of an organization: the corporate brand, customer brand and employer brand. This integration is critical to the success of the exercise, and the aims of successful outputs from the practice of employer branding in a real and tangible manner, as indicated by Barrow and Mosley (2005: xvii):

> the main role of the employer brand is to provide a coherent framework for management to simplify and focus priorities, increase productivity and improve recruitment, retention and commitment.

This quotation encapsulates many issues discussed throughout this book in terms of the aims of HRM and the particular challenges faced by the hospitality industry such as unacceptably high labour turnover and also the need to retain the most talented and productive employees. Indeed, the equally fashionable concept of talent management, outlined in Chapter 9, has been firmly attached to employer branding as being two connected elements of the drive for attracting and keeping the best workers in a very competitive environment. Here we see the move from the fundamental marketing principle of a customer value proposition to an employee value proposition. This proposition seeks to convince potential employees of the value of joining a particular firm, to understand 'what's in it for me', and to see longer-term benefits of staying with that firm. Christensen Hughes and Rog (2008) suggest that this approach should be embraced by hospitality organizations, as long as it is not superficial, and that there is a coherent HRM review of the component parts of such an employee strategy. They point to the need for a consistent and coherent approach to items such as competitive terms and conditions, training and development opportunities and a workplace culture and climate which encourages and celebrates career development and commitment.

The Chartered Institute of Personnel and Development (CIPD, 2007) has also published papers supporting the adoption of employer branding, outlining just why companies should take it seriously. In a summary of the reasons why organizations should act in this way, the CIPD emphasizes the following benefits:

- being an employer of choice for the employees that you really want to attract
- an effective employer brand has potential employees – and existing employees – shouting 'I'd like/I like that brand on my CV!'
- being able to attract the right employees locally and internationally is vital for organizational success
- helps with retention
- helps build a good, authentic corporate reputation.

These factors can be seen in the following exemplar, expressed as a proposal for website content for the case study company Lux Hotels as in Appendix 5, and based on a number of leading international hotel chains, extracts from publicly accessible corporate/careers websites, the content of which gives an indication of how such organizations try to get a corporate employer brand message across regarding culture and values in order to excite and attract potential employees, exemplifying and illustrating many aspects of employer branding that we have so far considered. In terms of the case study, this example may be adapted to the specific development plans that might be formulated by the Lux Hotels marketing and HRM team:

Lux Hotels: proposal for employer branding policy/website content

What we believe: mission, beliefs and values

At Lux Hotels we've got a number of seriously ambitious goals. We aim to create an organization that is unique, individualistic and stands out from the rest. Our Mission Statement, our Beliefs and Shared Values serve as ever-present guides to remind us of our aim and of our way of behaving with each other and with our customers.

Mission

Our aim is to create the most successful, international hotel company by ensuring that trust and respect for employees and guests are at the forefront of everything we do. We are committed to reviewing the hospitality business with contemporary innovation whilst retaining the values of the traditional gift of hospitality, resulting in a stimulating working environment in which people thrive and yet get a real buzz out of their work.

Core values

- trust in each other
- mutual respect for all
- delight in creativity and innovation
- accountability and responsibility
- success through ethical business behaviour.

We believe that these values, embedded in all that we do and the way we behave, give us a blueprint for actions, so that every day, in actions however small in themselves, we are fulfilling the precepts of our Mission Statement. Ultimately, we want our employees to fulfil their own life missions and aspirations by being a crucial part of the Lux Hotels organization and its future.

Our beliefs

Dedication to the service industry of hospitality, developing a strong service culture and philosophy which gives guidance to what we do and how we do it, to take inner pride in providing excellent service.

People make the difference

International hotels may sometimes look very similar in their physical attributes and facilities, but time and time again customers tell us that it is the quality and helpfulness of the employees that really makes them choose us over our competitors. Customers even say that they can tell that our employees enjoy their work and get real joy out of helping our guests in meeting their needs.

Make every day count

A strong service culture is not just an idealistic dream or an example of management jargon, it is a continuous pattern of interpersonal behaviours and collaborations between the organization, the employees and the customers, founded on a basis of genuine sentiments such as caring, being positive and being helpful. Therefore, every day, every minute gives us the chance to deliver exceptional service and assistance, ensuring that every action, every detail, however small, is thought through and enacted.

Leaders as facilitators

Our managers are not in their positions because they are good at telling employees what to do, but they have achieved their success by being supportive facilitators of the complex task of hospitality, enabling employees to fulfil the mission of the company. Leaders are successful if they give their employees the means to provide the exceptional, world-class service required by our guests.

Business performance and business ethics

The culmination of these values and beliefs must be the reward of success in business as a commercial entity; only then can we develop the company, reinvest in facilities and staffing, and ensure a bright future for all who contribute to that success. However, business success must not come at any price, and a strong ethical, moral foundation to our commercial activity must be adhered to at all times. We must be honest with ourselves, honest with our customers and other associates, and work with integrity and professionalism in everything we accomplish.

Employer branding opportunities

Besides the eloquent words of the message to the employees in the labour market, organizations must also review their employment-related activities as a whole, in order to ensure that there is integration and coherence in the reality of the 'promise' of the message. In other words, companies must make certain that they deliver on the fine words of the marketing and promotional materials. There needs to be a consistency in the treatment and execution of activities across the HR spectrum if employer branding is to be a successful, meaningful and long-lasting strategy, a strategy which ultimately aims to reach the heights of not only employer of choice for a specific company, but also perhaps industry employer of choice for hospitality. The following itemizes some of the activities to be carefully considered and developed in alignment with the message of the employer brand:

- recruitment processes, vacancy advertising, choice of media
- the selection process, criteria for selection
- all documentation and online/website pages (e.g. careers website)
- open days, information packs, social networking sites, podcasts?
- employee handbooks and joining details, welcome packs
- induction and orientation programmes
- all training and development schemes (all employee levels)
- all HRM events, e.g. teambuilding, activities, interfaces with organization
- leadership and management styles and approaches
- all communications with employees including IT, newsletters?
- compensation and benefits strategies, salary slip 'stuffers'?
- physical working environment issues
- all public relations, communication channels
- performance management systems.

This comprehensive approach should not only be considered as the prerogative of large, multinational branded organizations. Employee branding can occur within a single, owner-operated business. There is no reason to ignore the principles underlying marketing just because you have a small hotel with 12 bedrooms and employ only five staff members. Competition for good employees is keen everywhere and your reputation as an employer in a smaller location can be decisive and highly influential in your attracting the best local talent. The opposite is definitely true, as a reputation of being an uncaring, exploitative employer spreads rapidly through a tightly formed community with long-term detrimental outcomes, and can remain fixed for a very long time in the minds of potential recruits and possibly even potential customers.

Whether large or small, the effort and expenditure on different aspects of securing your reputation as an employer through the precepts of employer branding must be seen as an investment and not just a cost. However, it would not be businesslike to ignore the challenge of measuring the benefit of such actions. Indeed, it is important to set up some robust metrics and measurements systems in order to evaluate the return on this particular HR-oriented investment. The CIPD (2007) suggests the following questions when devising and developing a means of assessing that return on investment:

- What is your true cost per hire – including line managers' time spent interviewing? Do you know the costs of recruitment, labour turnover?
- How much are you spending on recruitment consultants/agencies? A strong employer brand will reduce the need to use them.
- What percentage of completed application forms do you receive? The brand should increase this figure, including the unsolicited based on your employer reputation.

- What's your current ratio of offers to acceptances?
- How does your employer brand enable you to tap into new sources, e.g. subsidized training schemes, strong local college and school links, work placements?
- What proportion of starters leave prematurely?

Implications for hospitality

The reasons for the hospitality industry to treat seriously an innovative HRM approach linked to marketing are both long-standing and current. Long-standing because the industry has constantly met with negativity in terms of its reputation as an employer, often perhaps unfairly characterized as autocratic, exploitative and penny-pinching, looking for low skilled people who will accept low skill pay rates. Many people within the industry have worked hard and with integrity to tackle this image, but the disparate nature of the industry makes it very difficult to introduce industry-wide standards. For the enlightened, employer branding offers a solution which truly integrates the purely business-oriented nature of branding, marketing and advertising with the more contemporary approaches to HRM. The components of the 'brand', whether multinational or singularly local, are not superficial statements of intent but are the values and propositions offered to both the customer in one format and to the potential employee in another format.

The more current factors influencing the need to attract and retain the best talent available are tied up with industry competitiveness on both a national and an international scale. Ageing populations in many developed nations eventually make their presence felt directly by there being fewer young people in a crowded employment market place, and hospitality firms need young people in the workforce. Therefore, hospitality firms need to offer such candidates an attractive package of employer brand elements, from basic terms and conditions through to prospects, development, a supportive workplace culture and increasingly a work–life balance that demonstrates the care of the employer, countering the image of 'take it or leave it' management mentalities. In their research for the Eurochrie Hospitality Conference, Gehrels and Looij (2010: 10) feature an extract from an interview with a hospitality firm executive who strongly supported the adoption of employer branding principles:

> While the demand in this market is increasing a shrinking and mobile talent pool will make it more difficult for the hospitality industry to attract and retain the talent when it needs to ensure sustainable growth and profits. Hotel leaders have one thing in common, they have great people and deliver great service, you can't have one without the other. Inquire further and you will see that this doesn't happen by chance. The front end service delivery is supported by superior back end training systems, performance management, recruitment and reward/recognition systems.

Whether large or small, local or global, hospitality businesses are urged to take note of the current and fast-developing concept of employer branding. They need to regard their product and service as a totally integrated package of measures, values and behaviours which aim to fulfil the objectives of the organization, the customer and the employee. The prescription or blueprint of the brand needs to be evaluated in terms of how its component parts can be closely aligned for all concerned. The value proposition is not merely a marketing tool, forging a loyal relationship between brand and customer but is also the basis of a loyal and beneficial relationship between the brand and the labour market, between the brand and the employee.

Further reading and references

Allen, N. J. and Meyer, M. P. (1990) 'The measurement of antecedents of affective, continuance and normative commitment to the organization', *Journal of Occupational Psychology*, 63: 1–8.

Ambler, T. and Barrow, S. (1996) *The Employer Brand*, London: London Business School Press.

Barrow, S. and Mosley, R. (2005) *The Employer Brand*, Chichester: John Wiley.

Christensen Hughes, J. and Rog, E. (2008) 'A strategy for improving employee recruitment, retention and engagement within hospitality organizations', *International Journal of Contemporary Hospitality Management*, 20(7): 743–757.

CIPD (2007) *Employer Branding: The Latest Fad or the Future of HR?*, London: CIPD Publications.

Collings, D. G. and Scullion, H. (2007) 'Global staffing and the multi-national enterprise', in Storey, J. (ed.) *Human Resource Management: A Critical Text*, 3rd edn, London: Thomson Learning.

De Chernatony, L. and Cottam, S. (2008) 'Interactions between organizational cultures and corporate brands', *Journal of Product and Brand Management*, 17(1): 13–24.

Gehrels, S. A. and Looij, J. (2010) 'Employer branding: a new approach for the hospitality industry', paper to Eurochrie Conference, 25–28 October, Amsterdam.

Lucas, R. (2002) 'Fragments of HRM in hospitality? Evidence from the 1998 Workplace Employee Relations Survey', *International Journal of Hospitality Management*, 14(5): 207–212.

Minchington, B. (2007) *Your Employer Brand: Attract, Engage, Retain*, Mile End: Collective Learning.

Sandiford, P. and Seymour, D. (2007) 'The concept of occupational community revisited: analytical and managerial implications in face-to-face service occupations', *Work, Employment & Society*, 21(2): 209–226.

Zeithaml, V. A. and Bitner, M. (2003) *Services Marketing*, 2nd edn, New York: McGraw-Hill.

Members of the UK's Institute of Hospitality (IoH) can access publications including Management Guides which summarize key information of relevance to hospitality operations (www.instituteofhospitality.org).

Members of the UK's Chartered Institute of Personnel and Development (CIPD) can access a range of materials including Fact Sheets and articles from over 300 online journal titles relevant to HRM. CIPD members and *People Management* subscribers can see articles on the People Management website (www.peoplemanagement.co.uk).

Questions

1 What do you understand as the main aims of employer branding?

2 What practical steps would you undertake to review HR policy in terms of setting up an employer brand?

3 Why is employer branding of such potential value to the hospitality industry?

4 How is employer branding aligned to the practices of contemporary HRM?

5 Why is employer branding so much more than a well-designed recruitment advertisement?

CASE STUDY QUESTION – see the Lux Hotels case study Appendix 5

The case study poses the question as to whether or not Lux Hotels should adopt a positive employer branding policy: in terms of Lux Hotels, how would you adapt the exemplar/proposal given earlier in this chapter of employer branding as might be seen on a company website?

Chapter 24

Customer care and quality

Customer care is nothing new. Top class nineteenth-century hotels and twentieth-century transatlantic liners were quite probably attending to their customers far better than most hotel guests are looked after today. What is new, however, is the 'industrialization' or 'systematization' of customer care. As service businesses have become bigger, more of the customers are dealt with by less professional and relatively untrained, often uncommitted staff. These are frequently from the secondary labour market, young and not well versed in social skills. And as competition becomes more severe, the need arises for a systematic approach to ensuring that the target customers receive the quality of service they expect.

Researchers at the University of Manchester Institute of Science and Technology (UMIST) (Lascelles and Dale, 1993) classified organizations into:

- uncommitted – quality initiatives (QI) not yet started
- drifters – QI started 18–36 months ago
- tool pushers – QI started 3–5 years ago
- improvers – QI started 5–8 years ago
- award winners – QI started probably some 10 years ago
- world class – QI started probably more than 10 years ago.

In the very best, the 'world-class' organizations, customer care is clearly a responsibility of every single employee from the most junior to the chief executive. In other organizations, however, customer care may be the responsibility of customer service or training departments, with little direct involvement of senior management. Many of the customer care initiatives of hospitality companies tend to fall into the 'tool pusher' category, at best. One indicator is that their quality initiatives are given titles, rather than being central to the company's policy.

In setting out to provide customers with a defined quality of service it is essential to recognize that the quality of service is influenced by a number of different factors. Some elements of service are only noticed by the customer if the factor is deficient in some way, e.g. slow service, poor room temperature and excessive noise levels. Other factors contribute positively to the customer's experience, such as being recognized by the staff and being addressed by one's name. One can draw parallels with Herzberg's hygiene factors and motivators, which relate to employees' perceptions of their work experience (Herzberg *et al.*, 1959; see Figure 2.5).

There are many different approaches to customer care programmes, with many concentrating on the staff-training element. It is for this reason that customer care and quality are included in this book.

Today the majority of the populations of advanced nations now experience a wide range of service offerings, be they fast food, fine-dining, medical care, leisure or education. And the expectations of these consumers have been heightened, and are constantly raised, by these self-same service offerings. Concomitant with this has been the increasing similarity of many competing products.

In many cases the search for product differentiation, the process by which a provider of a generic product makes the product different from competitors' products, has to be concentrated on the 'people interactions'. The classic example is the air transport industry, in which companies compete on similar routes using similar aircraft. The main way by which such companies set out to gain competitive advantage and increase their market share is either through pricing, which is the case with the budget airlines or, in the non-budget sector, by obtaining the best flight slots and offering better service, such as speedier check-in, better waiting arrangements and better in-flight food and cabin service.

SERVQUAL (Parasuranam *et al.*, 1988) is based on a generic 22-item questionnaire that considers five broad aspects of service quality:

- tangibles (appearance of physical elements)
- reliability (dependability, accurate performance)
- responsiveness (promptness and helpfulness)
- assurance (competence, courtesy, credibility and security)
- empathy (easy access, good communications and customer understanding).

Customers are asked to complete a questionnaire; the first part identifies their expectations and the second part identifies their perceptions of the actual offering. Using a value (Likert) scale the value gap between expectations and perceptions of the offering can be determined.

This process identifies a company's strengths and weaknesses. Different weightings can be given to the various elements. From the results can be derived a list of priorities needing attention through the most appropriate means such as training or investment in equipment.

SERVQUAL goes on to identify five key gaps:

- *Gap 1* – A gap between consumer expectations and management perceptions – managers think customers want one thing whereas the customers may prefer something else.
- *Gap 2* – A gap between management perception and service quality specification. Management may not specify clearly what is needed or they may set unachievable quality standards.
- *Gap 3* – A gap between service quality specifications and service delivery. Simply put, a service provider fails to meet the standards set.
- *Gap 4* – A gap between service delivery and external communications. This may result from expectations being unrealistically raised through intermediaries such as sales offices, agencies or promotional materials.
- *Gap 5* – A gap between perceived service and expected service. This gap is the result of one or more of the previous gaps. Basically the customer does not get what he or she expects.

The SERVQUAL method then goes on to identify a zone of tolerance, which is effectively the zone between what customers expect and what they consider to be the minimum acceptable service level.

Select for attitude – train for skills

In hospitality businesses social skills play a crucial role in the success of the enterprise. Many managers argue that these cannot be easily taught or learned and that the ideal is to concentrate on recruiting and selecting people with the right attitudes to customers. To do this successfully, employers need to develop effective selection skills and some of the industry's leaders now devote considerable resources to training their managers in selection interviewing skills, increasingly referred to as 'talent acquisition'.

Some organizations (e.g. TGIF and Disney) look for the skills of entertainers rather than the more traditional skills associated with restaurants and hotels. Consequently they audition their applicants rather than interview them.

In many cases it is vital that staff have a good understanding of what the customer expects. Some employers consider that the best way of achieving this is to recruit staff who share similar life experiences with their customers. In some cases employers encourage their employees to use their facilities as customers, maybe in other establishments owned by the employer, as part of staff development but also as part of the rewards package.

Some employers set out to develop in staff the awareness that they must 'own' problems that affect customers. This means that they must seek solutions, not look for ways to avoid solving problems. No one should walk past litter in an establishment, even if it is not in their section. No one should leave a telephone ringing if there is no one else ready to answer it. No one should leave a customer with a problem, saying, 'Sorry, this is not my section.' Customers waiting at a reception desk or bar should always be acknowledged even if they cannot be served immediately.

Some forms of training concentrate on teaching the staff certain 'scripts', such as 'Good day, how may I help you?' or teaching staff to use a customer's name or to reply in a particular way to a telephone call. Others may be less prescriptive but may still require certain rituals to be observed. Sheraton for example set a variety of 'Sheraton Guest Satisfaction Standards' (see Figures 24.1 and 24.2).

Radisson Hotels run a 'Yes I Can' programme, which sets out to train staff so that they never say 'no' to a customer. Specific selling skills may also be developed. For example, one of the leading fast food chains trains staff to attempt to 'upsell' one item more than the customer has ordered but never two or more.

Different approaches to customer care

Frances Sacker, of the Industrial Society, in her article 'Customer service training in context' (*Personnel Management*, March 1987) divided training into two main types: the 'evangelical' and the 'exploratory' styles. This appears to be still relevant today. The evangelical style is aimed at creating 'a high degree of excitement and enthusiasm' whereas the exploratory style is concerned with giving individuals 'the opportunity, through discussion, video, on-line etc. to make decisions about their own behaviour and about practical actions they can take to improve their own performance'.

If an employer claims that customer care is crucial to the success of the enterprise then the employer must demonstrate that commitment by developing proper rewards. This could be in the form of bonuses, but many programmes involving rewards appear to use other forms of employee incentive. Several of the

Figure 24.1 A Sheraton Guest Satisfaction Standard

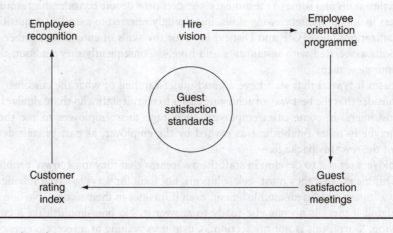

Figure 24.2 The Sheraton customer care cycle

large hotel groups, for example, select the 'employee of the month' from the workforce and reward accordingly. Sometimes these are selected by management, sometimes by customers. Unfortunately, many such schemes are known by the staff to be manipulated – the award going to each department in turn. It could be argued, however, that such approaches to motivation are external or extrinsic to a proper customer care programme. Instead a good programme, which is also concerned with recruiting the right staff, engages the interest of the staff and of itself provides the necessary motivation. Policy behind the Ritz-Carlton motto might illustrate this: 'We are Ladies and Gentlemen serving Ladies and Gentlemen'.

The need for a policy and diagnosis

An increasing number of companies have such mission statements reflecting customer care policies, sometimes displayed in customer areas, e.g. in reception areas, on price lists, brochures and the like. Often customer care plans derive from customer care analysis such as guest comment cards, mystery shoppers and social media comments. Many hospitality companies have regular customer rating processes which provide each unit with its own customer rating index and its rating relative to other similar units within the group. Some companies set out to measure accurately the cost of poor customer care. One measure used by a North American company is the number of abandoned enquiries and what this represents as lost revenue to the company.

Industry-wide initiatives

A good number of hospitality companies participate in quality assurance schemes including the ISO 9000 family of schemes. In addition, a number of hospitality industry-specific initiatives focused on quality also exist. These include external hotel and restaurant rating schemes such as those run by the tourist associations, plus the tourist industry's Welcome Host scheme. The Institute of Hospitality runs the Hospitality Assured scheme (see Appendix 1). In addition the British Hospitality Association runs the 'Excellence through People' scheme which measures operations against five key performance indicators: increases in staff retention; staff satisfaction; productivity; customer service levels; and business profitability.

To date (2012), three main evaluation studies have been carried out to assess the results and achievements of 'Excellence through People'. ETP has already had a considerable impact on the business results of those establishments which have been accredited: 59 per cent have reported increased customer satisfaction and 55 per cent have seen improvements in their image as a local employer. Others have reported increases in overall profitability of up to 100 per cent, skill shortages have reduced by up to 60 per cent, and staff retention levels have increased by 39 per cent. In all, 92 per cent of ETP accredited establishments have indicated they will seek reaccreditation. One study with 200 businesses identified:

- customer satisfaction up 39 per cent (against a target of 20 per cent)
- staff turnover reduced by 13 per cent (against a target for 18 months of 25 per cent)
- absenteeism down in one case by 60 per cent (compared with a target of 10 per cent)
- value added per employee up by over 7 per cent (compared with a target of 5 per cent).

Over 5,000 establishments have been engaged in the scheme and more than 2,650 have been accredited. These include both large and small employers across different sectors of the industry such as Lucknam Park Hotel, Shearings Hotels, Royal Garden Hotel, Pabulum Catering, TLH Leisure Resort, Magpie Café, Rumour Wine Bar and At Your Service Group. (For further information about 'Excellence through People' log onto the website www.bha.org.uk/.../hrs-hotel-excellence-awards)

Further reading and references

Herzberg, F., Mausrer, B. and Snyderman, B. (1959) *The Motivation to Work*, New York: Wiley.

Lascelles, D. and Dale, B. (1993) *The Road to Quality*, Bedford: IFS.

Parasuranam, A., Zeithasml, V. and Berry, L. L. (1988) 'SERVQUAL: a multiple item scale for measuring consumer perceptions of service quality', *Journal of Retailing*, 64(1): 12–40.

Shames, G. and Glover, W. (1989) *World Class Service*, Yarmouth, OH: Intercultural Press.

Teare, R. and Olsen, M. (eds) (1998) *International Hospitality Management*, London: Pitman Publishing.

Members of the UK's Institute of Hospitality can access publications including Management Guides which summarize key information of relevance to hospitality operations (www.instituteofhospitality.org).

Members of the UK's Chartered Institute of Personnel and Development (CIPD) can access a range of materials including Fact Sheets and articles from over 300 online journal titles relevant to HR. CIPD members and *People Management* subscribers can see articles on the People Management website (www.peoplemanagement.co.uk).

Questions

1 Describe the key elements that need to be considered relative to customer care.

2 What constitutes the service offering from a customer care perspective?

3 What can be done to minimize dissatisfaction caused by customers being obliged to wait?

4 Evaluate the effectiveness of the customer care approach of an employer with whom you are familiar.

5 Design a customer care programme for an employer with whom you are familiar.

6 What issues will need to be considered in designing customer care programmes in the future?

CASE STUDY QUESTION – see the Lux Hotels case study Appendix 5

In this chapter key approaches to quality management have been described.

What are Lux Hotels key quality objectives and how can these be achieved? The UK part of the company is already involved in schemes such as Quality Assured and Investors in People. Where do you think the company fits into the UMIST quality classification and why? Can SERVQUAL contribute to managing quality within the company? Within the overall company structure, who is, or should be, most responsible for quality standards?

Chapter 25

Business ethics

In the last few years we have witnessed a serious number of cases that question the ethical behaviour of many of the leaders of business, the public sector, government. In fact, illegal, unethical and corrupt behaviour has occurred in a whole range of different sectors of society ranging from politics, government and business to sport.

This chapter sets out to discuss ethical issues and behaviour mainly within the human resource context because organizational ethics, more than anything else, determine an organization's and its individual employees' behaviour. Managers of organizations function within a complex cultural environment. Key elements within that environment are what cultures consider to be right and wrong and good and bad (Trompenaars 1998; see Chapter 21) – issues at the heart of organizational ethics.

This chapter does not attempt to state what 'good' or 'ethical' behaviour is. This would lead into the realms of philosophy, which would pose such questions as who and what determines what is right and wrong. Instead, this chapter sets out a way of evaluating an enterprise's or an individual's behaviour in business, so that the reader can arrive at his or her own judgements. It also sets out to describe the overall 'ethical' environment created by institutional and organizational codes of practice.

At the international level the UK comes out well in terms of not being involved in business corruption – according to Transparency International (an organization concerned with monitoring international corruption), the UK is in the top six nations involved least in corruption, ahead of Germany (seventh) and France (fifteenth).

In this type of analysis we can look to a number of business tools such as PEST (Political, Economic, Social, Technological) which identify the types of pressures or restraints on companies and individuals ranging from the 'hard', such as anti-corruption legislation, through moderately hard, such as codes of practice concerned with food labelling, through to very soft, i.e. those of a completely voluntary nature which are motivated by altruistic considerations.

At the strictly legal level there is a whole network of laws, both civil and criminal, covering corruption, competition, consumer protection, employment, health and safety. To support the strict legal requirements there may be statutory codes of practice which, whilst not law themselves, may be used as evidence or otherwise of 'due diligence' in legal cases.

There are codes that constitute conditions of membership of some industry federations such as the Federation of Tour Operators and the British Hospitality Association, whose members are required to adhere to a code designed to protect their customers.

At another level there are schemes that may be ethically motivated and voluntary; such as the International Hotels Environmental Initiative and the UK's 'Investors in People' scheme.

Other schemes include good hygiene practices or best practice guides such as the Hospitality Assured and Excellence through People schemes (see Chapter 23) which, if implemented correctly, ensure good management and employment practices.

Many industrial federations now encourage or support 'sustainability'. Stopping the sale of endangered species such as some varieties of tuna is one example. Some, however, are less visible but are probably of even greater importance such as the use of palm oil – responsible for massive deforestation, contributing to global warming and to loss of endangered species.

Many companies including coffee chains support programmes that are environmentally friendly or support disadvantaged communities. The Fair Trade and CAFE movements are examples. Another such issue, of growing significance, is 'food miles'. Many organizations now make the question of 'food miles' an important consideration in their sourcing and purchasing decisions.

On the other hand we have the lobbying industry, the main purpose of which is to promote and protect the business interests of constituent members of certain sectors, often militating against the interests or welfare of some members of the population.

At the professional and management level most professional institutions have their codes of conduct whether they are lawyers, accountants, managers, HR specialists or professional hospitality managers. Each of these can apply sanctions for unprofessional behaviour. An extract from the Code of Conduct of the UK's Institute of Hospitality is contained in Appendix 3.

Most larger organizations are well aware of their corporate social responsibilities (CSR), reporting publically on an annual basis. Joanna Daniels of the Business in the Community (BITC) organization wrote in 2010 that 'in the last five years the thinking around CSR has moved away from being solely about managing social impact, or giving to charity. Now it is focussed on action which firmly integrates responsible business practices into all areas of commercial operations'. BITC is an organization of companies committed to improving the way they manage their resources (their people or the planet). Members range from major multinationals to small independents in emerging economies.

At the geo-political level restraints include the charters and codes of organizations such as the United Nations, the World Trade Organization and the International Labour Organization. In this last case most multinational companies recognize provisions concerning child and forced labour. Adherence to these codes may well be monitored by professional audit companies such as PricewaterhouseCoopers. On the other hand, some multinational companies leave monitoring of the codes to their local contractors who may not be as rigorous as the client company, so abuses do occur.

At the other extreme the consumer is steadily, even remorselessly, becoming much more demanding in terms of value for money but also in terms of sustainability and ethical sourcing of goods and services. Consumer movements range from very 'niche' movements such as the international 'Slow Food' movement, which originated in Italy – its main concerns being that our food should not harm the environment, that animal welfare should be considered, food producers should be paid a fair price and food should, of course, taste good. Another 'niche' movement is the UK's Campaign for Real Ale (CAMRA) which has had a real impact on the quality of beer and pubs. At a much wider level we have the UK's Royal Society for the Prevention of Cruelty to Animals (RSPCA) and its labelling schemes working hard for animal welfare.

Of course the question has to be asked if those who adopt such schemes do so for 'image building' or for the genuine concerns behind the schemes.

The chief executive of one of the world's largest caterers and on-site service providers states that 'sustainability' is now an important issue and is a way of winning business both for his client companies and for his own company (*Caterer and Hotelkeeper*, April 2010). Such views are expressed by a significant number of hospitality companies, recognizing that many potential corporate clients and institutions such as universities now make it policy to spend only with companies that share their 'ethical or sustainability' views.

Ethical issues are of concern to all managers within an enterprise but particularly to the most senior managers because it is they who create and control the whole environment in which their enterprise functions. They also create the pressures on their subordinates to deliver the required results, which can frequently lead to subordinates acting unethically.

Ethical issues are of particular concern to human resource managers because many of the roles of human resource managers are concerned with ensuring that an enterprise functions ethically through the recruitment of the right people, training them in the norms and values of the employer and, particularly, motivating employees in such a way that the employer's ethical position is not compromised.

The definition of ethical behaviour is very difficult, since it depends upon each individual's own perceptions of issues within the broader social/moral context.

As Mole (1990; see Chapter 21) writes, 'There are different degrees of belief as to what constitutes actual wrongdoing. What is illegal need not be unethical and vice versa.' Some will argue that the law defines what the limit of business behaviour is, whereas others argue that the law merely provides a safety net to prevent the worst excesses. Some business people will argue that their sole responsibility is to their shareholders and so long as what they do is no different from what their competitors do then nothing is wrong. At the other extreme are owners and managers who apply very strict ethical standards to everything they do in business, showing consideration for all stakeholders, i.e. owners, managers, employees, customers, suppliers and the wider community.

Recent developments in Europe have seen many organizations include statements of corporate responsibility and ethics within mission statements and annual reports. Furthermore, the public is ever more aware of issues such as ethical or fair trade (the non-exploitation of supplying nations), as it is about financial abuses which have brought the topic of managerial ethics and legality to the forefront. The hospitality sector has seen a massive increase in interest in the sourcing of foods, from debates on organic farming to the humane rearing of beef cattle and chickens to supply the huge fast food market.

Hoffman and Frederick (1995) defined business ethics as 'the study of what is good and right for business' and they suggest three questions: What is the better decision for the business? What is the better decision from a legal point of view? What is the better decision from a moral point of view? This last question, however, raises difficult value judgements.

Seven tests for ethical business behaviour

In order to determine what is moral or good and right, Steven Hall (1992), of the International Institute for Quality and Ethics in Service and Tourism (IIQUEST), devised a number of questions which test a manager's or an organization's ethical behaviour. These seven questions can be applied to all aspects of running a business.

1 Is it legal?
The first question to ask is, 'Is it legal?' Relevant examples in the catering industry include common sharp practices such as short measuring of drinks, substituting products and misleading customers by false descriptions (e.g. 'frozen' for 'fresh'). Overcharging is common as well. How many price lists are hidden so that customers cannot check what a round of drinks should really cost?

2 Does it hurt anyone?
Many business decisions may be legal but they may hurt people. Obviously some actions will hurt the competition – they are designed to do just that. The mere decision to open a unit somewhere is almost bound to hurt the neighbouring competitors. It is an overt action and it could be argued that if the benefits to the consumer through lower prices, better service, etc., outweigh the damage done to a few competing traders then the behaviour is justified. Some other activities, however, may be less ethical. Acquiring others' mailing lists is an example. Spreading damaging false reports through social media

sites such as TripAdvisor is another.Breaching copyright on business products, be they recorded music or computer programs, is another example. In some respects this question 'Does it hurt anyone?' may be more valid than the first question, 'Is it legal?' Some activities may be illegal but may not hurt anyone (the concept of the victimless crime). Serving drinks after hours in a small village pub may hurt no one, but it is illegal.

3 Is it fair?

Whether something is fair or not depends upon a person's own perception of fairness. But probably a good test would be to ask what the other person would think if he or she knew the full facts (see also Question 6). For example, what would customers think if they knew that they were being sold wine, mixers or food that was left by previous customers?

Other aspects of being fair could include how the business is promoted. For example, is the price list clear? Are there hidden extras so that customers spend much more than they may have expected to spend? Unadvertised hotel telephone charges are an example.

4 Am I being honest?

Again, honesty, like fairness, is dependent upon a person's own perception of 'honest behaviour'. Honesty may be defined, among other things, as not being deceitful. It is in this sort of area that there are many ethical problems.

How many business people try to close a sale by falsely boosting the scarcity of something – 'you should really decide now because we only have one room left'; 'someone else has already offered so much for it', etc. Such phrases are built into the normal vocabulary of many people concerned with selling, so that additional deceptions come easily.

5 Can I live with myself?

This question probably poses even more ethical problems than the others. If someone has, over the years, developed a business ethic that encourages sharp practice then, maybe, not only can the person live with him or herself but he or she may actually celebrate the completion of a sharp deal. This question, however, may be of most relevance to senior managers because it is often they who profess all the ethical objectives of their organization and then apply such pressures to achieve other business objectives, such as sales targets, on the middle and junior managers that the latter cannot behave ethically.

6 Would I publicize my decision?

This is probably the best of tests of ethical behaviour. If, for example, cheaper products or substitutes are used, would a business advertise the fact? If the service charge is not distributed to the staff, would this be advertised to the world?

7 What if everyone did it?

The last question is really concerned with what would happen to commerce, maybe an industry or even a whole society, if everyone did the same. Some trades, usually because of the behaviour of a few, over the years have acquired a reputation for dishonesty, making business life more difficult for everyone in those trades. This is the reason that the leading professions and corporations have developed codes of practice. It is through businesses aiming for and achieving a trustworthy level of service that consumers are led to have faith in an industry, trade or profession.

What are the ethical issues?

The questions above highlight the fact that questions of ethics range through fundamental policy issues such as 'should we be in the business we are in?' through to straightforward operational issues such as ensuring that customers are not short-changed, overcharged or served substandard or substitute products. The range of ethical issues includes relationships with all stakeholders:

- customers
- employees and managers
- supplies and suppliers
- sources of finance
- the community.

Customers

As indicated above, most ethical concerns appear to focus on relationships with customers. In many respects this is the easiest area to look at. Questions include the following:

- Are trade descriptions, menus, price lists honest and complete or is only limited information given?
- Are customers told about controversial products, e.g. irradiated foods and genetically modified foods?
- Are prices misleading, with hidden extras?
- Are customers misled about past performance?
- Do staff bonus schemes put customers at risk?
- Is customers' ignorance of their rights exploited?
- Are significant facts hidden, e.g. hidden commissions in contract catering? Punitive cancellation policies?
- Are risks taken with customers' health and safety, e.g. taking risks with food handling, temperatures, fire exits?

Employees and managers

A major area of ethical concern is how employers treat their employees. One major fast food retailer attracted a lot of adverse publicity when it was found that some branches were offering a form of 'zero hour' contracts, i.e. 'You will be present at the place of work (sit down and have a coffee) but you will only be paid when you actually work.'

What about equal opportunities – are staff selected and promoted fairly, or are some candidates passed over because of their gender, race, disability or even age? Is discipline even-handed? There are questions also of job security, dignity and the like. Does an employer try to meet his/her employees' needs in these respects? From the treatment and fairness of young workers to the higher-order considerations of family-friendly policies in attempting to address the so-called work–life balance and any accusation of exploitation, HRM practitioners are faced with ethical as well as regulatory questions (see Legge, 1998; also Lucas, 2004). Woodall and Winstanley (2001) considered that contemporary HRM, with its emphasis on performance management and strategic alignment, is faced with a set of ethical issues, 'In particular, the preoccupation with flexibility, commitment, culture, quality and performance'.

What should be of major concern to senior managers is the fact that, though they may profess ethical principles, they often put such pressure on their middle and junior managers that ethical behaviour becomes difficult and often impossible. Just one example will illustrate this – pizza home-delivery target times have caused serious road accidents and even death. Another factor within the hospitality sector may not lead to such a tragic outcome as this example but nevertheless is worthy of mention. Particularly with regard to front-line customer contact roles, the hospitality sector requires its staff to show certain emotions as part of their job: the smiling welcome, the concerned listener to a customer's problems, the calm response to a vitriolic complaint from an angry, perhaps rude, guest. The need to display such behavioural responses, however, which can conflict with the employee's actual inner feelings, is known as emotional labour, and management need to consider just how much emotional stress and pressure its employees should be required to 'suffer' (see Mann, 1997). 'Burnout' is a term used to describe the state of staff who have experienced serious stress over a period of time.

Robbins (2005) reports that in the USA there is a significant increase in company training schemes which specifically deal with ethical issues. A survey conducted in the late 1990s found that around 75 per cent of the workers in the 1,000 largest US corporations received some level of ethics training. In the UK there has also been an increase in employee awareness of ethical issues and whistleblower protection supported in an attempt to encourage employees to alert external bodies of unethical or illegal practice.

Supplies and suppliers

The seven questions listed above (Hall, 1992) could also be applied to a business's supplies and suppliers. These days, hospitality managers are faced with a range of ethical problems concerning supplies. Should a caterer give a customer what the customer wants in spite of ethical considerations? Some animal products – frogs' legs and sharks' fins, for example – are obtained using very cruel methods. Some methods endanger whole species. Should a caterer offer these or even supply them if asked? More restaurants are now switching to 'line-caught' fish because this method does little damage to fish stocks and their marine environment. Some countries and states in the USA have banned 'foie gras' (fat goose liver) because the method of production is considered to be cruel.

When stationery, furniture, staff uniforms, etc., are bought, are the sources checked out? Are they from sustainable sources or are they contributing, even in a very minor way, to ecological damage? Are cleaning materials, energy sources and other supplies environmentally friendly? How are the suppliers' employees treated? Are they treated ethically?

Sources of finance

Not many business people have a free choice of the sources of finance available. Most smaller and medium-sized businesses will be obliged to use conventional banks. For various reasons they may be locked into one bank. However, where choices can be made about finance, the types of questions to be considered will be concerned with how the banks invest their money and from what sources the banks derive their funds and profits. In 2012 some investors in many different countries expressed concerns over bank senior executive pay and ethically questionable conduct (see High Pay Commission, 2011).

Another source of finance is the taking of credit from suppliers. Are the periods taken as agreed originally or are 'unfair' periods of credit taken? Are smaller suppliers exploited because they cannot afford to lose the business even if credit periods are extended unilaterally?

The community

Finally, every business operates within a community and it has a responsibility to that community. How it meets these responsibilities varies considerably. The community creates a whole range of laws and regulations covering taxation, planning, building, food safety, waste disposal, noise, pollution, fire precautions and licensing. Are these adhered to or are they ignored, putting people's comfort, health and maybe lives at risk?

Ethical, environmental and sustainability issues are increasingly coming to the forefront of business generally and within the hospitality industry as well. The UK Institute of Hospitality and the Chartered Institute of Personnel and Development, along with most other professional bodies, have codes of conduct. At the international level ethics and ethical issues become even more complex. As Mole (1990) writes, 'Values differ from country to country … conventions of behaviour can be misinterpreted ... normal practice can engender mistrust. Faced with such diversity the best course is probably to reserve ethical judgement for one's own behaviour and suspend it when looking at others.'

Further reading and references

Hall, S. (ed.) (1992) *Ethics in Hospitality Management*, New York: Educational Institute of the American Hotel and Motel Association.

High Pay Commission (2011) *Cheques with Balances: Why Tackling High Pay Is in the National Interest*, London: High Pay Commission.

Hoffman, W. M. and Frederick, R. E. (1995) *Business Ethics*, 3rd edn, New York: McGraw-Hill.

Legge, K. (1998) 'The morality of HRM', in Mabey, C., Salaman, G. and Storey, J. (eds) *Strategic Human Resource Management: A Reader*, London: Sage/Open University Press.

Lucas, R. (2004) *Employment Relations in the Hospitality and Tourism Industries*, London: Routledge.

Mann, S. (1997) 'Emotional labour in organizations', *Leadership and Organization Development Journal*, 18(1): 4–12.

Mole, J. (1990) *Mind Your Manners*, London: Industrial Society.

Robbins, S. (2005) *Organizational Behaviour*, 11th edn, Upper Saddle River, NJ: Pearson Education.

Robinson, S. and Dowson, P. (2012) *Business Ethics in Practice*, London: Chartered Institute of Personnel and Development.

Trompenaars, F. (1998) *Riding the Waves of Culture*, 2nd edn, New York: McGraw-Hill.

Woodall, J. and Winstanley, D. (2001) 'The place of ethics in HRM', in Storey, J. (ed.) *Human Resource Management – A Critical Text*, London: Thomson Learning.

Members of the UK's Institute of Hospitality can access publications including Management Guides which summarize key information of relevance to hospitality operations (www.instituteofhospitality.org).

Members of the UK's Chartered Institute of Personnel and Development (CIPD) can access a range of materials including Fact Sheets and articles from over 300 online journal titles relevant to HR. CIPD members and *People Management* subscribers can see articles on the People Management website (www.peoplemanagement.co.uk).

Questions

1 Describe a business's key stakeholders and the ethical considerations which can enter into the relationships between the business and its stakeholders.

2 Evaluate, using examples, Steven Hall's tests for ethical behaviour in business. Are certain issues omitted from his questions?

3 What are the key ethical considerations in employment relationships?

4 Evaluate the ethical behaviour of an employer with which you are familiar using the key stakeholders as a basis.

5 To what extent do public companies' social responsibility statements accord with their actual behaviour?

6 Identify significant organizations concerned with ethics and sustainability influencing the hospitality industry and describe their main aims.

7 Download the mission statement and any related value or ethical statements of a number of leading hospitality companies and discuss. How many stakeholders are addressed in these mission statements?

CASE STUDY QUESTION – see the Lux Hotels case study Appendix 5

In this chapter the question of ethics in business has been addressed.

What is Lux Hotels' position regarding ethics? Does Lux Hotels appear to have an explicit or implicit policy regarding the environment and sustainability?

What should be the company's position concerning the main 'stakeholders', including shareholders, property owners (i.e. the owners of hotels managed by Lux Hotels), customers, staff, suppliers and the community? Now prioritize these.

The Institute of Hospitality's Hospitality Assured for Service Excellence in Business

Introduction

Hospitality Assured is the Standard for Service and Business Excellence in hospitality. It is championed by the Institute of Hospitality and supported by the British Hospitality Association (BHA). Hospitality Assured is the only standard within the hospitality industry that focuses on the customer experience.

The standard is fully endorsed by both the British Quality Foundation and the Quality Scotland Foundation as meeting the criteria in the EFQM Excellence Model, which is owned by the European Foundation for Quality Management (EFQM).

Who can become Hospitality Assured?

Any organization – large or small, single or multi-unit in hospitality, leisure and tourism, with a desire to improve its service to customers and its operational and business excellence – is eligible. There are currently over 130 accredited businesses representing some 3,500 trading outlets and involving more than 50,000 staff. The following sectors are all eligible to participate in Hospitality Assured:

- restaurants and cafés
- hotels and accommodation providers
- colleges and universities
- leisure businesses
- membership and private clubs
- local authorities
- transport
- holiday parks
- pubs, bars and nightclubs

- visitor attractions
- hospitals and care homes
- gambling establishments
- food service and facilities management
- events, meetings and conference centres.

The process for achieving Hospitality Assured recognition is rigorous, but very worthwhile because it takes into account customer opinion and considers all the aspects of service from the customers' point of view. Equally important is the assessment process that provides a series of valuable performance indicators – or benchmarks – against which an organization can continually judge and measure itself.

The Standard for Service and Business Excellence comprises nine steps:

1 customer research
2 the customer promise
3 business planning
4 operational planning & standards of performance
5 resources
6 training and development
7 service delivery
8 service recovery
9 customer satisfaction improvement.

These steps comprise forty-four key requirements of criteria and are all measurable objectives. The standard does not lay down precisely how objectives will be met – they vary from organization to organization, according to that organization's customer promise. For example, a customer promise of a conference centre will be different from that provided by a cruise ship, a pub or a care home.

Why become Hospitality Assured?

Hospitality Assured was created for the industry by the industry and is based on best international practice. 'Accredited' organizations attaining Hospitality Assured status enjoy a number of significant advantages including:

- being seen as one of the very best organizations in the hospitality industry by customers, employees, stakeholders and competitors;
- being able to use powerful business tools and objective external assessment to stimulate and measure performance improvement in service delivery and business excellence;
- being able to benchmark the accredited organization against the best in class;
- the authorized use of the Hospitality Assured mark to promote the accredited organization to existing and new customers;
- demonstrating that the accredited organization is a quality employer;
- for local authorities or contractors, it helps significantly with preparation for 'best value' review by demonstrating 'best value';
- encouraging staff motivation and team building at all levels;
- finding any gaps in service delivery;
- highlighting good practice;
- facilitating target-setting and performance monitoring.

What does the Hospitality Assured process involve?

The Hospitality Assured process provides guidance every step of the way and support is available to businesses undergoing assessment from specially trained Hospitality Assured experts. The process is straightforward and involves the following steps:

1 Contact Hospitality Assured (see details below) to discuss the programme and costs.
2 Purchase the Introduction Pack containing the standard and guidelines as to the evidence required to meet the standard.
3 Carry out a 'self-assessment', a fast and dynamic process to check your organization's own strengths and weaknesses against the standard's nine steps. Prepare for 'External Assessment' – a period of building on strengths and addressing areas for improvement, highlighted by the self-assessment process. Assistance is available from independent trainers specializing in Hospitality Assured during this period.
4 Book an 'External Assessment' – when confident, an organization can request Hospitality Assured to organize a visit from the scheme's assessors who visit the business and score it against the nine steps in the standard and supply a comprehensive report of their findings.
5 Accreditation – is awarded when an organization scores at least 60 per cent against the 'Standard for Service and Business Excellence', with a minimum score of 50 per cent in each of the standard's nine steps.
6 Re-assessment can be done annually to maintain accreditation and assist the business in important benchmarking activity. Alternatively, re-assessment can be done biennially interspersed with an Interim Review. In addition, organizations might opt for 'committed to' status on the basis of annual self-review and subscription. Re-assessment measures positive change and continuous improvement.

Further information

To learn more about Hospitality Assured or obtain a scheme pack, please contact Ann Corrigan, Managing Director, Hospitality Assured at:

Institute of Hospitality,
Trinity Court,
34 West Street Sutton,
Surrey SM1 1SH

Ⓣ +44 (0)20 8661 4900
Ⓕ +44 (0)20 8661 4901
Ⓔ hospitality.assured@instituteofhospitality.org
Ⓦ www.hospitalityassured.com

Further resources

Harmer, J. (2010) 'Thistle achieves hospitality assured accreditation,' *Caterer and Hotelkeeper*, 31 August 2010: www.caterersearch.com/Articles/31/08/2010/334875/Thistle-achieves-Hospitality-Assured-accreditation.htm (accessed 26 March 2012).

Stamford, J. (2011) 'BaxterStorey achieves IoH Premier status,' *Caterer and Hotelkeeper*, 9 November 2011: www.caterersearch.com/Articles/09/11/2011/341001/BaxterStorey-achieves-IoH-Premier-status.htm

Stamford, J. (2009) 'Elior division wins Hospitality Assured status,' *Caterer and Hotelkeeper*, 29 October 2009: www.caterersearch.com/Articles/29/10/2009/330647/Elior-division-wins-Hospitality-Assured-status.htm (accessed 26 March 2012).

Institute of Hospitality, Trinity Court, 34 West Street, Sutton, Surrey SM1 1SH, UK.
Tel: +44 (0)20 8661 4900
Fax: +44 (0)20 8661 4901
Email: library@instituteofhospitality.org
Website: www.instituteofhospitality.org

Appendix 2

The Institute of Hospitality's Business Continuity Planning in Hospitality

Reproduced with the permission of the Institute of Hospitality.

What is business continuity?

Business Continuity involves identifying the key things your business or organisation cannot afford to lose – such as personnel, stock, data, facilities, technology and even brand image – and ensuring that, if a crisis occurs, the business and its services are minimally affected through business continuity management.

Does your hospitality business have the resilience to withstand the impact of a crisis? Consider, for example, the autumn 2009 floods in Cumbria, UK, which cost in excess of £200m. Over 60% of insurance claims were made by businesses.[1] However, having insurance may not be enough because insurers may not cover every type of event.

Figures from the Tourism Industry Emergency Response Group estimate the 7/7 bombings in London may have resulted in a £3m loss to UK tourism. It notes that popular venues such as the Tower of London and Madame Tussauds saw a loss of up to 15% of visitors following 7/7. Many businesses may not be able to survive a significant loss of custom and income.

Who needs a business continuity plan (BCP)?

Although crises may be unexpected they are not usually unforeseen. Most managers understand the types of risk that can affect the running of their business. More importantly, many resources exist to help business owners develop a Business Continuity Plan (BCP) that creates organisational resiliency activities such as risk assessment, contingency planning, systems security, crisis management and recovery planning.

Businesses with regularly reviewed BCPs in place prior to an event are more likely to recover from the impact of an incident. Companies that fail to make contingency plans will find it difficult to sustain the business. For instance, over 600 businesses were affected following the 1996 bombing in Manchester, UK. Within six months 250 of the 600 had gone out of business.[2]

---

[1] http://news.bbc.co.uk/1/hi/uk/4706615.stm [accessed 13 July 2012]
[2] http://www.broxtowe.gov.uk/index.aspx?articleid=608 [accessed 13 July 2012]

Every small, medium or large business needs to have a BCP in place. A plan can ensure the least impact to a business's staff, customers, property, company finances and perhaps even the community at large. BCPs create resilience within an organisation enabling it to maintain a smooth running service whilst continuing to provide its 'deliverables'.

How do I create a BCP?

There are a number of different sources providing information, from basic to detailed, regarding establishing a BCP (see Further Resources). Some are fee-based companies specialising in business continuity management, however, there are also quality free guides and materials for those who wish to put together and manage their own BCP.

The Business Continuity Institute offers an official standard, BS 25999, describing the framework and process for a Business Continuity Manager to use and offering good practice recommendations. It can also be used to assess an organisation's ability to meet regulatory and other requirements. (See: http://www.bsigroup. hk/Assessment-and-certification-services/Management-systems/Standards-and-schemes/BS-25999/)

Some of the key points to consider when assessing risk and creating a BCP are:

- Identify and list potential events that pose a likely threat to the business.
- Analyse how to minimise the risk of these event(s) affecting the business by creating a Business Impact Analysis.
- Start a BCP as soon as possible. Having a draft in place during an emergency is better than having no plan at all.
- Assign roles, implement the BCP and make sure it is regularly revisited and updated as personnel change.

Individually, small to medium enterprises (SMEs) may consider their property less vulnerable to, for example, terrorists or rioters. However, the venue may be part of a crowded place and the risk is increased. For example, a boutique hotel located next to a busy shopping street, plaza or mall is part of a crowed place and will require resources to address these circumstances.

The UK's National Counter Terrorism Security Office (NaCTSO) and the national network of CTSAs can support businesses of all sizes in performing an assessment of a venue's contingency plans. NaCTSO offers a free Crowded Places Vulnerability Self Assessment Tool (VSAT) that informs owners, operators and security managers about the level of a facility's vulnerability to attack.

Another initiative, Project Argus, explores how to prevent, handle and recover from a terrorist attack. A three hour training tool includes a simulation of an attack and can locate a business's weaknesses.

A third option, created in partnership with Facewatch and the Metropolitan Police, is London Hotelwatch. The website provides a completely free and highly flexible communication portal for security information to be shared amongst participating hotel managers. In addition, information about crime is uploaded by the Metropolitan Police on a real time basis and also sent out to users by email.

Hotel operators outside London are encouraged to sign up to Hotelwatch and the plan is to develop the system for the whole of the UK with bespoke portals for cities and hotel groups using the same system e.g. Birmingham Hotelwatch, Holidayinnwatch, Portsmouth Hotelwatch.

BCP in Information Technology (IT)

Rapid changes in technology have resulted in new solutions that may support companies and their BCPs. For example, 'cloud computing' allows businesses to hold data in a 'cloud' rather than in on- or off-site servers or other devices which are susceptible to damage, theft and attack. Should an emergency occur, employees can still access the company's data and files held in the 'cloud' from any computer and location – allowing them to continue working with the least disruption. Learn more about cloud computing and creating a BCP focussed on IT at the UK's Businesslink website.

Ongoing management of business continuity

BCPs should be considered 'living' documents that require regular reviews and updates. According to a UK Cabinet Office publication on Emergency Preparedness, there are seven factors, or the '7 Ps', to consider when managing business continuity:

1   **Programme** – proactively managing the process
2   **People** – roles and responsibilities, awareness and education
3   **Processes** – all organisational processes, including ICT (information and communication technologies)
4   **Premises** – buildings and facilities
5   **Providers** – supply chain, including outsourcing
6   **Profile** – brand, image and reputation
7   **Performance** – benchmarking, evaluation and audit

Source: Business Continuity Institute, 2003

Conclusion

Companies with the foresight to create and incorporate a Business Continuity Plan are helping to ensure their continued existence in an uncertain environment. By preparing for the unexpected with an actively managed BCP, companies have the greatest chance of surviving a catastrophic event.

References

Association of British Insurers (ABI) – Insurance advice advice for protecting businesses: http://www. abi.org.uk/Information/Business/Insurance_Advice_for_Businesses.aspx

Business Continuity Institute (BCI) Access over 75 of the BCI's free-upon-registration webinarscovering all aspects of business continuity from supplychain and London2012 to communications strategies: http://www.thebci.org/index.php?option=com_content&view=article&id=98&Itemid=331

BusinessLink – Cloud computing information. Available from: http://www.businesslink.gov.uk/bdotg/action/layer?topicId=1084685982 [accessed 22 June 2012]

BusinessLink – Support for businesses including a business continuity online planning tool: http://www.businesslink.gov.uk/bdotg/action/layer?r.s=tl&r.l1=1073858799&r.lc=en&r.l2=1081627247&topicId=1074458463 [accessed 22 June 2012]

CBI – *Future proof: preparing your business for a changing climate.* **(2009) Available from:** http://www.ukcip.org.uk/wordpress/wp-content/PDFs/CBI_Futureproof_Preparing-business-for-CC.pdf [accessed 22 June 2012]

London Hotelwatch – Combined resources of Facewatch and London's Metropolitan police, this portal informs hoteliers about incidents and provides current data regarding security issues: http://facewatchcli.destravel-002.vm.brightbox.net/

Project Argus – Training tool incorporating a simulation of a terrorist attack, this resource helps businesses avert, prepare for and respond to events: http://www.nactso.gov.uk/OurServices/Argus.aspx

Vulnerability Self-Assessment Tool (VSAT) – A confidential online assessment determining whether a business's security plans are adequate to address an incident: http://www.nactso.gov.uk/OurServices/VSAT.aspx

Walker, B., Summer 2012. Don't keep security a secret. *Hospitality*, the magazine for hospitality management professionals. Issue 26, 22–25. Available from the Institute of Hospitality.

Institute ebooks

Available on the Institute's website:

- *Auditing for Managers: The Ultimate Risk Management Tool.* (2005) Pickett, K. H. Spencer.; Pickett, Jennifer M. John Wiley & Sons
- *Bioterrorism : A Guide for Facility Managers.* (2005) Gustin, Joseph. Fairmont Press.
- *Bioterrorism and Food Safety 2005. Rasco, Barbara.;* Bledsoe, Gleyn E. CRC Press.
- *Crisis Management in the Food and Drinks Industry: A Practical Approach* {2Nd Ed.} (2005) Doeg, Colin. Springer.
- *Crisis Management in the Tourism Industry.* (2003) Glaesser, Dirk. Butterworth-Heinemann.
- *Making the Most of HACCP: Learning from Other's Experience.* (2001) Mayes, Tony.; Mortimore, Sara. CRC Press.
- *Managing Business Risk: A Practical Guide to Protecting Your Business* {2Nd Ed.}. (2005) Reuvid, Jonathan. Kogan Page.
- *Restoring Tourism Destinations in Crisis: A Strategic Marketing Approach.* (2003) Beirman, David. Allen & Unwin.
- *Risk Issues and Crisis Management: A Casebook of Best Practice* {PR in Practice Series; 3rd Ed.}. (2005) Regester, Michael.; Larkin, Judy. Kogan Page
- *Risky Foods, Safer Choices: Avoiding Food Poisoning.* (2000) Cerexhe, Peter.; Ashton, John
- University of New South Wales Press.
- *The HACCP Food Safety Employee Manual.* (2006) Paster, Tara. John Wiley & Sons.
- *The HACCP Food Safety Training Manual.* (2006) Paster, Tara. John Wiley & Sons.

Further resources

Home Office – counter-terrorism and prevention strategies. www.homeoffice.gov.uk
London Prepared – for any type of business disruption. www.londonprepared.gov.uk
National Counter Terrorism Security Office (NaCTSO) – contributes to the nation's counter terrorism strategy. http://www.nactso.gov.uk/OurServices/VSAT.aspx
UK Resilience, Cabinet Office – emergency preparedness. www.cabinetoffice.gov.uk/ukresilience/

Institute of Hospitality, Trinity Court, 34 West Street, Sutton, Surrey SM1 1SH, UK. Tel: +44 (0)20 8661 4900 Fax: +44 (0)20 8661 4901 Email: library@instituteofhospitality.org Website: www.institute ofhospitality.org

Appendix 3

Extract from the Institute of Hospitality's Code of Conduct

Reproduced with the permission of the Institute of Hospitality.

Members of the Institute will ...

Personally –

i. Regulate their professional affairs to a high standard of integrity and uphold their statutory responsibilities in all respects.
ii. Make proper use of resources available.
iii. When in pursuit of personal ambitions and interests take account of the interest of others.
iv. Maintain their standards of professional competence, knowledge and skill; and
v. Take advantage of opportunities for training and education offered to advance and improve professional standards.

In respect of their employers –

i. Carry out duties and responsibilities conscientiously and with proper regard for the employer's interest.
ii. Apply the lawful policies of the employer obviating corrupt practice, particularly in receiving gifts and benefits.
iii. Disclose immediately and fully to an employer any interest which conflicts with those of the employer.
iv. Consult with and advise the employer on the implementation or adoption of new developments in the profession or industry.
v. Have full regard for the interest of the profession and the public interest in fulfilling obligations to the employer.

In respect of colleagues and subordinates –

i. Help and encourage their professional development through the acquisition of skills, qualifications and training.

ii. Promote good relationships through effective communication and consultation.
iii. Establish their confidence in and respect for himself (the member) and his qualification.
iv. Protect at all times their health, safety and welfare.

In respect of customers, clients and suppliers –

i. Promote the standing, impartiality and good name of Institute of Hospitality.
ii. Establish good, but detached relationships.
iii. Avoid endorsing any product through advertising in a way which impairs Institute of Hospitality's impartiality.
iv. Establish and develop with customers, clients and suppliers a relationship leading to mutual confidence.
v. Protect at all times the health and safety of customers.

Disciplinary procedures

The Articles of the Institute of Hospitality provide for the Executive Council to conduct an enquiry to administer disciplinary action and in the case of an appeal to nominate an arbitrator.

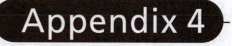

Appendix 4

Training

An abridged version of the publication *How to Get the Best from Your Staff: An Introduction to Staff Training Skills* by Michael J. Boella.

Author's note

This book sets out to cover the basics of staff training. It covers in a simple, step-by-step process, each of the main areas of knowledge and skills required by senior staff, supervisors and managers responsible for training. Because it is a partially programmed text it enables those who do not have the opportunity to attend a course to study and practise the basics. It also helps more senior managers to know just what is expected of their supervisors and staff trainers. Third, it can be used as a refresher for those who may have already attended a staff trainers' course. Finally, for those who themselves run staff training courses this makes a concise, easy-to-use guide and hand-out.

This book is not however to be seen as a substitute for attendance at a proper course.

Acknowledgements

My thanks are due to many people, known and unknown, who over the years have contributed the knowledge, experience and material which have made this short book possible. Regretfully, I cannot acknowledge everyone personally. However, I would like particularly to record my gratitude to the Tack Organization and the Industrial Society whose courses I attended and to the HCITB (Hotel and Catering Industry Training Board) with whom I have collaborated on many occasions.

Introduction

The success of every business depends upon it staff and it has been found that people work most satisfactorily when they have confidence in their employer, in their surroundings and particularly in their own performance of their job.

Obviously no single factor contributes to creating this sense of confidence. But possibly more than anything else, effective induction, that is, the introduction of everything surrounding a person's job, and thorough training in the knowledge and skills necessary to do the job, are responsible for creating the confidence which can lead to a person doing his job in a competent and satisfactory manner. Unfortunately however there are those who feel that systematic training is unnecessary, is too costly, and is beyond their capabilities – or they feel that the ability to train others is something that one is born with. Yet most managers know that a person such as a secretary or a chef, who is skilled in his or her job, is more efficient than an unskilled person. This principle applies equally to the *skill of training* which is distinct from, and additional to, the *job skills* to be passed on. The skilled trainer trains more effectively than the unskilled trainer and, in contrast to the myth that there is not enough time to train, the skilled trainer makes training opportunities throughout the normal working day and will help to create a well-trained employee in a shorter time than an unskilled trainer.

Training others is a skill which can be learned by many normal staff and it makes sound business sense to train key staff, particularly the heads of departments, in this essential skill.

Benefits of training

Training, as with all other activities of an organization, should benefit the organization in the short or long term. These include:

1 Increased customer satisfaction
2 Increased customer demand
3 Better use of time
4 Safer working methods
5 Reduced waste
6 Reduced damage
7 Reduced staff turnover.

Hence – more efficiency.

However, because the staff are the people being trained they should also benefit in some way. These include:

1 Increased efficiency
2 Increased earnings
3 Improved job security
4 Improved job prospects.

Hence – increased job satisfaction and confidence in the job.

Planning training

If you are to train staff efficiently it will need to be properly planned and in order to do this four main elements have to be considered:

1 Who is to do the training?
2 What is to be taught?
3 How is it to be taught?
4 How is it to be judged?

Who is to do the training?

We all know that some people can do a job very efficiently themselves but when it comes to teaching others they are no good at all. This is because to teach others requires certain characteristics which are additional to being able to do the job well.

Anyone who is selected to teach others consequently will need to have certain characteristics. These include:

1. Wish to help others
2. Sympathetic and patient manner
3. Competence in the job
4. Understanding of trainees' needs and problems
5. Systematic approach to work
6. Knowledge and skill of teaching techniques
7. Ability to be self-critical.

From this description it is apparent that most trainers will be more mature people, generally employed at some supervisory level. However, this is not always the case as many craftsmen and even more junior staff make excellent trainers; they enjoy the responsibility and often they are in the best position to train their colleagues, and the task of training others can be a valuable step in developing such people for promotion.

As a principle, however, everyone who has to give some form of instruction or coaching during the normal working day should have or should develop some training skills. This applies particularly to every manager and supervisor. A trainer once trained is going to be able to:

1. Know what performance is expected of the staff
2. Recognize training opportunities and make use of them
3. Make training opportunities
4. Know which tasks and critical points need to be learned by trainees
5. Recognize shortcomings in performance
6. Analyse tasks
7. Plan training
8. Prepare and give instruction
9. Produce training aids
10. Keep records
11. Review training.

What is to be taught?

Training in a business context is concerned with bridging the gap between an individual's capabilities and the employer's requirements. This gap is a *training need*. Put this way it sounds simple but in practice it can be quite difficult. This is because what a person needs to bring to a job is a mixture of:

- General knowledge
- Technical knowledge
- Aptitudes
- Attitudes
- Skills.

Training needs, apart from consisting of knowledge, skills and attitudes, occur at different times in the working life of employees and organizations. For example when:

- A new employee starts
- Changes take place
- Things go wrong.

When a new employee starts

Of course a whole range of things need to be known. You should include items from each of the following:

- Relationships between staff and departments
- Hours and other conditions
- Safety and security practices
- Rules and regulations
- Methods of work.

When changes take place

A person needs training when the following occur:

- Changes in methods, products or standards of performance
- Changes in equipment
- Transfers and promotions.

When things go wrong (remedial training)

A person may need training when any of the following occur:

- Unsatisfactory trading results or standards
- Customer complaints
- Breakages, waste.

What can be taught?

Some things, such as knowledge and skill, can be transferred to most reasonable trainees quite easily given adequate training expertise on the part of the trainer.

Attitudes, on the other hand, are very difficult and in many respects it is better to aim to select people with the attitudes you want rather than to attempt to 'instil' attitudes into unwilling employees. If, for example, a person resents serving others, it is unlikely that you will have the time and psychological expertise to change his attitudes. Much better to avoid recruiting him in the first place. It is apparent therefore that most training should be concerned with transferring knowledge and skills. To do this the trainer will need to examine his own knowledge and skill and break it down so that he is completely aware of what he has to put over.

This process – job analysis – can be vital, because most skilled people take for granted large parts of their own knowledge and skill.

The manager's responsibility

These different activities have to be set in motion and monitored constantly by management. And as with most other management processes it is a cyclical one starting and finishing with the planning stage.

The manager responsible for training must:

1 Set training objectives. To do this, job descriptions may be needed and these will, so far as possible, set standards of performance. For example, if a person is expected to attend to twenty people in an hour, then the trainer should use this standard as his training objective and set progressively more difficult targets during the programme.
2 Select trainers and, where appropriate, he will arrange for them to be trained in training skills. Maybe he should be the first to attend such a course.
3 Delegate training responsibilities.
4 Provide training facilities such as rooms, equipment and training aids.
5 Inform staff of any changes and any training to be given to cope with changes.
6 Show that he really believes in training by participating in it himself.
7 Review the effectiveness of training by checking upon the work of people who have finished their training and occasionally by interviewing some or all of them or having informal chats with them to obtain their views on the training they received.

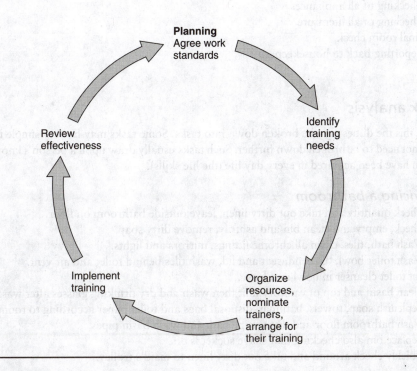

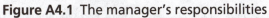

Figure A4.1 The manager's responsibilities

What is to be taught?

What has to be taught?

The types of factors staff may have to learn have been listed. One of the problems, however, of teaching others is that the experienced person automatically (even subconsciously) does many things which the trainee is going to have to learn step-by-step. A good example is the difference between a novice driver, who consciously thinks about each element of driving, and the expert who integrates each element unconsciously into the total driving process. Consequently, to be sure that all points are taught the trainer needs to use a systematic process for listing everything that is going to be taught.

If this is not done, many points, sometimes essential or even vital, may be over-looked in training. The omission will then only be highlighted when the trainee (or ex-trainee) does something wrong – possibly with expensive consequences for the employer. Unfortunately in these circumstances the trainee and not the inadequate training is usually blamed.

Here is a simple job broken down into duties.

A room-maid's duties:

1 Collection of guest departure list, and early morning tea and breakfast lists and keys from head housekeeper's office
2 Service of early morning tea and breakfasts in bedroom
3 Preparation of trolley for servicing rooms
4 Servicing of bedrooms
5 Servicing of bathrooms
6 Checking of all appliances
7 Checking of all literature
8 Final room check
9 Reporting back to housekeeper.

Task analysis

After this the duties may be broken down into tasks. Some tasks may be very simple to learn and they may not need to be broken down further. Such tasks usually draw upon a person's knowledge and skills which have been acquired in every day life (the life skills).

Servicing a bathroom

 1 Check quantity and take out dirty linen, leave outside bathroom on floor.
 2 Check, empty and clean bin and ashtray, remove dirty soap.
 3 Wash bath, tiles, clean all chrome fittings, mirrors and lights.
 4 Wash toilet bowl, 'U' bend, seat and lid, wash tiles behind toilet and air vent.
 5 Put toilet cleanser in bowl and leave.
 6 Clean basin and top of vanitory unit then wash and dry drinking glasses after washing hands.
 7 Replenish soap, towels, bathmat, disposal bags and toilet paper according to room quantities list.
 8 Wash bathroom floor and door, wipe bath and wash basin pipes.
 9 Replace bin also checking that shave socket is off.
10 Quickly check around and take out dirty linen to maid's trolley.

More difficult tasks, however, will need to be analysed into the various steps in order to identify exactly what a person has to learn and what he has to avoid. This is called 'task analysis'.

Task analysis – the main elements

Task analysis consists of:

1 *Listing WHAT is done*   This should be one word or a brief phrase describing each distinct step:
Greet guest
Take glass

2 *Describe HOW the action is performed*   This should be a brief description of how each step is carried out starting with:
by taking …,
by saying …,

3 *Describing CRITICAL points*   This should describe signs which inform the person carrying out the task that it is going well or otherwise. Such points should consist of sentences or phrases such as:
Check that totals cross-cast
See that the sauce has not curdled

4 *Adding any additional points that should be taken into account*, such as security, safety, sales promotion. Note: This is omitted in some task analyses.

Lesson plans

Once the job has been broken down into the key words or phrases which list all the tasks, and once complicated tasks have been broken down into analysed tasks – the next step is to put all this knowledge and skill into a planned training session.

Not only does the trainer have to analyse and then organize what he is to transfer, but also he has to consider how he is going to:

1 Motivate his trainees to learn.
2 Present the knowledge and skill so that it is assimilated.
3 Give his trainees the opportunity to 'cement in' or consolidate the new knowledge and skills.
4 Ensure that what he has been attempting to transfer has been transferred permanently.
5 Motivate his trainees to use what they have learned.

These processes are incorporated into what is generally called a lesson plan. A lesson plan consists of:

- Introduction – motivate to learn
- Development – transfer knowledge
- Consolidation – make it permanent
- Close – motivate to use it.

The introduction

The introduction is concerned primarily with motivating the person to want to learn. It should be used to:

1 Establish a personal contact with trainees.
2 Reduce their nervousness.
3 Overcome any particular worries they may have, such as: when the training finishes, what it covers, what will be expected of them.

What	How	Critical point	Additional information
List each key step or stage, using short phrases starting with words such as:	Describe concisely the method to be used; start sentences with words such as:	Describe the critical signs which indicate that the operation is proceeding satisfactorily or otherwise. Use words which encourage a trainee to use his senses; look for, feel, taste. This column includes elements which involve using the senses in order to make judgements.	Add any additional information which may be necessary for the satisfactory performance of the task or to enhance a normal performance.
write, greet, cut, dispense	by writing by greeting by cutting by dispensing		This column is omitted in some task analyses.
For example, take a glass	For example, by taking a 6 oz Paris goblet by the stem	For example, check that the glass is clean and undamaged	—

Figure A4.2 Task analysis sheet

Unless the introduction is effective the trainee may not be receptive to what is to follow. To help in preparing the introductory phase a useful mnemonic or memory aid has been used by people for many years. It is:

I   interest
N   need
T   title
R   range
O   objective.

Interest

The first thing anyone communicating with others has to do is to attract their attention. This can be done in one of many ways, including:

- Making a personal connection between the trainee and the subject, for example, giving a taste or sample, and giving them useful information or news.
- Telling a funny story.
- Referring to something topical. Referring to (or inventing) something relevant from one's own personal experience.
- Stating something with an apparent contradiction, for example coffee is more important than caviar.
- Asking questions.
- Giving a demonstration or showing something relevant.

Whatever method is used, however, it should be relevant to the trainee and what is being taught.

Need

The need for the training session should be explained. This should be in two parts, from the employer's point of view and the employee's, but it is essential to emphasize why the trainee needs the training and what benefits he or she will receive.

Title

Obviously the trainee will need to know what is to be taught – usually this is incorporated early on and can be linked with one of the other elements of the INTRO.

Range

The trainee needs to know what is to be covered in the training session and sometimes it is equally important, in order to keep his attention or to reduce his anxiety, to tell him what is not to be covered. It is useful to link back to previous training sessions in order to check, to build confidence and to build on known material.

Objective

Finally the trainee needs to know what he will know or what he should be able to do as a result of the session.

While these five separate elements should be in an introduction, they may be combined skilfully into one or two sentences or, if the training is a long course, the introduction could take thirty minutes or more.

Development

The development stage is the main part of any training session and contains everything to be learned during the session. This should be organized so that:

1 Everything is in a logical sequence.
2 The trainer starts with a quick review of what the trainee knows so that the trainee starts from the known – and therefore feels confident – moving on to the new, the unfamiliar, material.
3 Essential material is picked out ensuring that it is covered, and desirable material is identified – to be covered if the time or opportunity presents itself.

The development stage is concerned with transferring the instructor's knowledge and skills to the trainee. It is, however, rather like serving a meal. The food has to be treated in certain ways to make it appetizing and digestible. In the same way any knowledge and skills to be transferred have to be presented so that they interest the trainee and are retained permanently by him.

There are a number of important rules which will help the trainer to prepare and present his material so that this happens, and these are covered in more depth on pages 305–309.

Consolidation and close

Throughout a training session the trainer must use various means of assisting his or her trainee to learn. One major technique is the correct use of questions and this is covered on page 309. It is vital, however, that at the end of a session the trainer:

1 Tests that the training objectives have been achieved by questioning, testing or observing.
2 Reinforces the instruction by recapitulating and questioning so that key points will not be forgotten.

In addition to testing the effectiveness and reinforcing the instruction the instructor should also make quite clear what is now expected of the trainee in work terms and he will also arouse interest in the next session by explaining:

1 What it is about.
2 When it will be.
3 What the objective is.

A useful form for planning a lesson is as shown below.

The learning 'sandwich'

Every piece of instruction should be a sandwich consisting of a slice of motivation; motivating to want to learn; the filling; the main body of the instruction; a slice of motivation; motivating to want to use what has been learned.

How do we learn?

The ability of people to learn is dependent to a great extent upon their reasons for wanting to learn something. If someone is very keen to learn, he will apply himself. On the other hand, if he is not keen to learn, he will almost certainly bring little enthusiasm to the learning process.

Subject:	Aim:	Time:
Preparation and use of a room-maid's trolley	At the end of this session trainees will be able to: 1 Prepare their trolley for use 2 Recognize and know the use of all the contents of the trolley	30 minutes
Key point	**Detail**	**Aids**
Cleanliness of trolley	Emphasize that a clean trolley is necessary in order to ensure that clean linen is not made dirty	The actual items Questions
Linen	Show the different types of linen and how the number of each is arrived at, to include: towels sheets pillow cases	The actual items Questions
Cleaning	Show the different cleaning materials and explain what each is used for, to include: lavatory cleaner bath and basin cleaner floor polish	The actual items Questions

Figure A4.3 Lesson plan

Why do people learn?

Obviously there are many reasons for people wanting to learn and in a work setting these will be closely linked to why people work. If the trainer knows and understands why each individual wants to learn, he or she should be able to use this to motivate the person – and keep his or her interest. To attempt to treat all people in the same way is certainly not the way to being a successful trainer or supervisor. A key supervisory and training skill therefore is to discover what motivates each of his or her subordinates or trainees.

If a generalization is to be made, however, the main reasons are likely to be one or more of the following:

1   To obtain rewards such as pay, promotion, esteem.
2   To avoid punishment such as dismissal, reprimand, loss of esteem.
3   Interest.
4   Curiosity.

How do people learn?

Learning is the process of acquiring knowledge, skills and attitudes. It occurs when knowledge, skills and attitudes are transferred to the learner from other people or situations. The transfer is through five primary senses and is best when as many senses as possible are used – particularly in combination. For example, in teaching a person to cook it is possible merely to give him detailed recipes but the results are not likely to be edible! In addition to the recipes, however, the trainee would watch demonstrations and the results are likely to be an improvement. But to involve the trainee fully so that he sees, hears, smells, touches and tastes, is the best and only effective way of teaching cookery.

We learn:

> 1 per cent with our sense of TASTE
> 1.5 per cent with our sense of TOUCH
> 3.5 per cent with our sense of SMELL
> 11 per cent with our sense of HEARING
> 33 per cent with our sense of SIGHT.

(*Source*: Industrial Audiovisual Association, USA)

The transfer is made more effective by ensuring that:

1   The amount and type of material is suited to the person being trained. Frequent, short sessions are much more effective than infrequent long ones.
2   It is transferred in logical, progressive steps, building on the known.
3   The methods and choice of words used must suit the capabilities of the trainees.

How do we remember?

We remember:

> 10 per cent of what we READ
> 20 per cent of what we HEAR

50 per cent of what we SEE and HEAR
80 per cent of what we SAY
90 per cent of what we SAY and DO simultaneously

(*Source*: Industrial Audiovisual Association, USA)

In addition, trainers must recognize that there are many factors which inhibit a person's ability or desire to learn and consequently a trainee will have difficulty learning if he is:

1 Nervous, tired or frightened.
2 Worried about his or her job, money, family.
3 Distracted by noise, interruptions.
4 Uncomfortable, too cold, too hot.

So far as the training session itself is concerned people will not get the most out of it if they are bored by:

1 The trainer's style, tone and language
2 The length of the session
3 The content.

The rate at which people learn varies from person to person but most people learn in steps – sometimes making rapid progress and sometimes appearing to make very little progress at all. This is quite natural and a good trainer will recognize this and he will know when a trainee is stuck and needs sympathy and help rather than badgering. A trainer's main duty is to build up confidence and this will only be achieved by sympathy and understanding. Criticism and lack of patience reduce confidence and only slow down the learning process.

Question technique

A trainer can make use of questions in three main ways. These are, to test a person's level of attainment (test question), to stimulate a person to 'learn for himself or herself' (a teaching or extension question), and thirdly to generate understanding and exchange of information and attitudes between members of a group by tossing questions and answers back and forth (bonding questions).

Questions may be used principally for:

1 Testing the level of attainment before a 'training' session.
2 Testing the effectiveness of training.
3 Helping people to work out answers for themselves, thus teaching themselves.
4 Encouraging an exchange of knowledge and information, in a group.
5 Obtaining or focusing interest.
6 Maintaining interest.
7 Creating understanding between the group, and between the group and the instructor.

Question structure

Questions generally are more effective when they are 'open-ended'. This encourages a person to think for the answer. Where questions give simple alternatives or anticipate yes or no, less thought is required by the trainee and the question consequently is less effective both in testing and in consolidating learning. Most questions should contain why, where, when, what, who or how.

Questions, particularly teaching questions, should be planned beforehand – and should relate particularly to the 'critical points' identified in the 'task analysis' stage.

Where questions are not answered satisfactorily by the trainee, the trainer must consider first if the question was properly framed and understood. If not the question should be rephrased and put again. If the question still remains unanswered the trainer must consider whether the training he has given is satisfactory or not.

Putting questions (the three Ps)

When questions are put to a group of people this should be done in a way which encourages everyone in the group to participate. This is achieved by:

1 Putting the question – without naming anyone to answer it.
2 Pausing so that everyone thinks about the question and answer.
3 Pointing out who is to answer the question.

Aids to training

Because people learn most easily by using a variety of their senses and their different faculties, trainers should always attempt to support their own instruction with training aids. These include visual aids such as blackboards and film slides and audio aids such as tape recorders. They should only be used to:

- Support but not substitute
- Simplify complex instruction
- Emphasize
- Interest
- Aid memory.

Training aids ideally should be the real thing, but in some cases the equipment or procedures may be too complex for a clear explanation, so a diagram may help. The preparation of training aids should be carefully planned to support the instruction given.

Training aids include:

- Actual equipment or equipment specially modified for training purposes
- Drawings and diagrams
- Films, slides, recordings
- Graphs and charts.

Recently, for various reasons, the need for job descriptions and similar documents has grown considerably with the result that many employers – even small ones – now use such documents as an essential tool of effective management. Unfortunately these documents are rarely used for training purposes although with a little forethought they can be designed to serve the purpose of:

1 Job descriptions
2 Instructor's training programme and checklist
3 Trainee's training programme and checklist
4 Work manual.

Job aids

Many jobs can be made easier with descriptions of the methods or procedures to be employed. Such descriptions may be called job aids.

Job aids can be of value to the experienced worker as a reference, and to the trainee as a learning aid. As such, they can substitute for parts or all of certain training sessions because they enable trainees to teach themselves and they can relieve the trainees from having to attempt to memorize unnecessarily.

Job aids can be used:

1 Where supervision is minimal.
2 Where procedures are changed.
3 Where company standards need to be adhered to.
4 Where mistakes cannot be risked.
5 When memory needs assistance because of the complexity of a procedure, or the infrequency of its use.
6 Where staff may speak limited English but where a drawing or a design will describe what is required.

Job aids include:

1 Diagrams
2 Photographs
3 Price lists, menus
4 Procedural instructions, recipes.

Introducing staff to a new employer

How do people feel?

Most people approach a new job feeling nervous and worried. Sometimes this is quite apparent. In other cases, however, it is well-concealed. But whether it is obvious or not, until people have settled into an organization they will be nervous or worried and this will influence their ability to learn their job – to do it effectively and in particular to get on with their colleagues, supervisors and customers. They will not have the feeling of confidence which is essential to their being able to do a good job.

Success during the first few days in a new job is vital and while most managers admit this less than 10 per cent of managers in some industries actually carry out a formal induction of new employees.

What a job consists of

Induction is not something that takes place on the first morning of a new job, it can be a relatively long process, with some people taking many weeks to settle in. This is because every job has two parts to it. First, there is the work itself and secondly, there are all the peripherals to the job including conditions and social contacts.

People will not be able to cope with the work part of their job unless they understand and are reasonably happy with the surrounding elements. These include:

1 Location and physical layout
2 Conditions of employment and contracts

3 Company and house rules
4 Customers
5 Management, supervision and formal relationship
6 Colleagues and informal relationships.

The induction process is concerned with introducing an employee to all these elements as quickly as possible so that he or she need not worry about them any more. This enables the trainee to concentrate on the work which is the main purpose of the job rather than having to learn and worry about all the elements surrounding the work.

Benefits of induction

The employer benefits from effective induction by:

1 Reducing staff turnover
2 Improving staff efficiency and work standards
3 Improving staff morale.

The employees benefit by:

1 Fitting in and feeling a part of the team.
2 Being accepted as part of the team.
3 Becoming competent and hence confident in the shortest possible time.

Every organization will need to induct its employees in its own particular conditions, rules and methods, so no example can cover all circumstances. However, the checklist below shows the type of subjects that

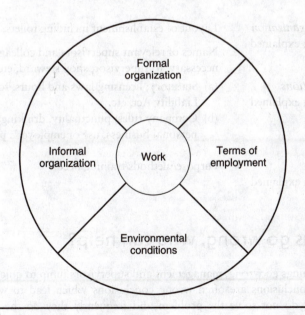

Figure A4.4 The main elements of a job

need to be covered. This, however, shows only the formal aspects of induction, and managers and supervisors should ensure that newcomers are inducted into the informal aspects as well. By definition, however, this can rarely be done by managers or supervisors. Instead, what they need to do is to put a newcomer under the wing of a 'sponsor', that is someone who 'knows the ropes'. This person may well be the newcomer's trainer also.

Checklist for induction programmes:

1	*Documentation* Are the following points covered?	Name/Address/Tel. no. Next of kin/Name/Address/Tel. no. National Insurance no./P45/Bank address
2	*Information* Are the following departments informed?	Wages/Pensions/Insurance/Personnel/Training/etc.
3	*Terms of employment* Are the following explained and understood?	Hours of duty/Meal breaks/Days off/ Method of calculating pay/ Holiday arrangements/Sick leave/Pension scheme. Grievance procedures. Rights regarding trade unions and Staff Association Additional benefits such as Group Insurance rates or other discounts.
4	*History and organization* Are the following explained and understood?	Origin and development of the organization. Present situation/ objectives.
5	*Establishment organization* Are the following explained and understood?	Layout of establishment including toilets, showers, etc. Names of relevant supervisors and colleagues, introduction where necessary, to supervisor, shop steward, etc.
6	*Rules and regulations* Are the following explained and understood?	(a) Statutory; licensing laws and hours, food hygiene, Innkeepers Liability Act, etc. (b) Company rules; punctuality, drinking, smoking, appearance, personal business, use of employer's property, etc.
7	*The job* Are the following explained and understood?	Purpose/methods/training needs

When things go wrong, who can help?

Frequently, when things go wrong, management and supervisors jump to quick conclusions regarding the cause. Quick conclusions are often wrong conclusions which lead to wrong solutions. Wrong solutions obviously do not solve the problem and frequently they do the reverse by aggravating people who recognize what is the real cause and just how ineffective is the solution.

Correcting errors depends upon the correct diagnosis of what causes things to go wrong. The correct procedure for putting things right consists of:

1 Identifying a fault as a variation or departure from a standard of performance which may be either specified verbally, in writing or by custom and practice.
2 Identifying the cause or causes.
3 Identifying the person or persons responsible. The person committing the error may not be at fault, but rather the person who issued the order or trained the person responsible.
4 Deciding what action to take, how to communicate this action and how to motivate the person who may take the new instructions as a criticism.
5 Deciding how to prevent a repetition.

Heads of departments and other senior staff are responsible for the prevention and correction of faults. They should, therefore, pay particular attention during training to 'critical points', that is, the points at which things could go wrong.

This book* is designed to assist managers and heads of departments to understand more clearly the knowledge and skills they need to bring to their responsibility in training their staff. The book, however, cannot substitute for thorough practical and theoretical training in the techniques of training because, as the book itself says, effective training makes use of various methods to transfer and consolidate knowledge and skill. Consequently the best way to become an effective trainer and supervisor, having attended a proper course on the subject, is to practise and to be critical always of one's own performance.

'There are no bad staff, only bad managers'

*How to Get the Best from Your Staff.

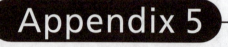

Appendix 5

Lux Hotels
A case study in human resource management in the international context
Mike Boella and Steven Goss-Turner©

Objectives

- To develop the skills and knowledge necessary to make management decisions concerning human resource management policy and practice in an international business context.
- To introduce students to a range of policy options and practices.

> When national chains reach saturation in their home country the only option is to repeat their growth in another country.
>
> (Paul Slattery, Economist Intelligence Unit, 1991)

International management case study: Lux Hotels[*]

Whilst this case study is based on real hotel companies the principles are the same for any company whether in hotels, tourism, travel or even car manufacturing! The case study is concerned with establishing general principles and any student from any discipline should have no problems in understanding and applying the principles developed in the course of this case study.

The way you will learn will be through a case study which is based on a medium-sized international company. First you will aim to analyse and evaluate the present situation in Lux Hotels, which owns a number of hotels in Western and Central Europe.

Following your conclusions you will move on to develop and recommend HR strategy and plans suited to Lux Hotels.

---

[*]Any similarity between this company and any company with a similar name is totally coincidental.

Lux Hotels

Your Chief Executive Officer (CEO) has invited you to join a project team which is to develop strategy together with practices suited to a company which is planning future large-scale expansion through organic growth and acquisition.

LUX HOTELS SA is a UK company. For tax reasons, and on the advice of its auditors, it is registered in Luxembourg, hence its name 'Lux'. Lux has its operational headquarters in the UK.

Lux Hotels operates a total of 60 hotels. Thirty of these are in the UK. The company also has seven hotels in France, four in Belgium, two in Holland, six in Germany, five in Hungary and six in Poland. It has disposed of around ten of the smaller hotels (less than 60 rooms). Five of these are now franchised as Lux Hotels, three to former managers who wished to acquire their own business. The total of hotels is 60, plus the five franchised.

Most of the hotels are typical middle-market three star hotels; some in major city centres, most near busy airports and motorway junctions and a few in rural situations. They range in size from 70 rooms to 350 rooms. The total room stock is 6,000 rooms.

The approximate mix of business in the UK is:

Full rate	10%
Conferences	30%
Corporate discount	24%
Leisure breaks	18%
Tours	16%
Domestic	55%
Europe	27%
North America	11%
Japan	2%
Middle East	1%

Similar figures do not exist for the other countries although efforts are being made to collect them.

All hotels have good 'value for money' restaurants and bars as well as small conference and seminar facilities. Some of the rural hotels have leisure clubs which are open to both the hotel customers and the local community (by annual membership).

Twenty of the properties are owned and 25 are leased by Lux Hotels. The remainder are operated on a management contract for a variety of owners, including insurance companies and banks. Others are operated as franchised 'Express by Holiday Inn' properties (middle-market, Holiday Inn franchised hotels). Three of these ('Express by Holiday Inns') are in France and there is one in each of the other countries, excepting Holland. The company operates five unbranded up-market four star hotels. In addition one large relatively unsuccessful resort hotel is just being developed as a time-share property with Lux Hotels seeking to sell the property to a property investor but maintaining the management of it.

The Express by Holiday Inn franchises have proved particularly profitable with higher occupancy rates and room yields than the Lux Hotels branded hotels.

The five up-market four star hotels are located as follows: one in Paris, two in Holland and two in Germany. These are very profitable, showing a higher profit on average than the Lux Hotels brand and the Express by Holiday Inn properties. The one four star hotel in Paris is managed for private owners. Being in a capital city it achieves a very high occupancy rate, around 85 per cent, and also achieves a high average room rate, of about 85 per cent of the 'rack rate' (standard tariff).

Lux Hotels, as a brand, is perceived as a 'value for money' brand in the same market as Novotel. It does not, however, have the same level of public awareness as the other leading brands. Mr Avago's policy was to be a 'follower' rather than a 'market leader'. He uses Novotel as a 'benchmark' and has recently adopted 'benchmarking' as a method of improving his company's performance. Mr Zandac, his successor as chief executive, is following a similar strategy.

The company has retained its tour operation, from which it developed. It is managed by Mr Schneider. The tour operation consists of organizing coach tours using the company's hotels wherever possible for accommodation, food, etc. The tours are aimed mainly at mid-market, non-specialist type customers interested in sightseeing holidays. The tours are conceived and promoted by the overseas tour operators who also provide the couriers (but not local guides). Demand for this side of the business has been stagnant for the last three years with other holiday products competing strongly. A small number of long-standing contracts have been lost to other hotel operators who have better multinational coverage. Mr Avago is thinking of developing his own tour operator and travel agency subsidiary. In the meantime he is in discussions with some low-cost airlines.

A significant part of the inclusive tour demand is met by the company's own 16 coaches which are modern vehicles (average of about 50 seats), replaced every four years; four a year. The remainder of the demand is met by chartering other companies' coaches. A team of freelance guides and couriers is used where necessary.

Mr Avago believes that there is good potential to grow the tour operation side of the company, particularly towards central Europe, but is being led by Mr Zandac to concentrate on developing the hotel side.

Lux Hotels is perceived as a 'soft' brand which enables the company to either build new or to acquire suitably located hotels. Mr Avago occasionally targets particular hotels in order to achieve suitable geographical coverage and therefore may pay over the normal market price in order to enhance the Lux network.

All hotels have good 'value for money' restaurants and bars as well as conference and seminar facilities. Ten of the hotels have leisure clubs which are open to both the hotel customers and the local community. This is proving to be a useful additional source of revenue and profit in the hotels concerned.

The company has a central reservation system located in the head office, which is in one of the hotels near Oxford. Mr Avago expects all managers to 'network' intensively in the community in order to attract local demand relatively cheaply. This includes membership of organizations such as 'Lions'. In addition he expects all hotels to work closely with the local artistic community, giving artists, artisans and craft sector businesses free display space in public rooms, corridors and guestrooms. Most hotels also have to run music events (e.g. jazz brunches) using local musicians. He also expects managers to identify schools where local business people and community leaders are most likely to send their children and to develop close working relationships with such schools and colleges. Each hotel also has to adopt and support a local charity.

The head office management team consists of *Mr Avago* (63), president, ex-property speculator who, with his family, owns about 30 per cent of the shares of the company. He has retired from day-to-day management of the company, having promoted Mr Zandac to be chief executive.

Mr Avago remains totally committed to the company and loyal to the staff who have helped him develop the company, which has developed from one hotel 16 years ago and one coach 20 years ago. Mr Avago speaks only English.

His son, *Pierre Avago* (27), has recently joined the company as an assistant to Mr Zandac. Pierre studied hotel management at Lausanne Hotel School and Cornell University in the United States, and has since worked in a hotel company in the USA, a position acquired through a friend of his father's. It is intimated that longer term Pierre will take over management of the company's hotels in Central Europe. Some company personnel and external commentators suspect that he is being prepared to take over the CEO's role one day.

Mrs Avago plays an active role in the company, looking after much of the interior design and major housekeeping purchases.

The CEO is *Mr Zandac* (36), who previously worked with Pannonia Hotels in Budapest as a regional director. Before that he worked for three years with Accor in Moscow; he was also responsible for new developments planned in Russia. Before that he worked as assistant manager in a smaller hotel in St Petersburg. He speaks five languages including French, English, Russian and German.

Mr Zandac has some problems because of the strong Avago family influence. A number of posts throughout the company are held by Avago family members and long-serving staff still feel able to refer directly to Mr Avago or to another member of the family. On occasions Avago family members or friends are put forward for jobs.

Mr James (46) was until recently the company's marketing director but as the acquisitions abroad increased, Mr Zandac made Mr James General Manager of all UK properties. Prior to joining Lux Hotels, Mr James was marketing director at Hilton International Hotels in London, with a responsibility for Hilton elsewhere in England. He joined Lux Hotels six years ago. He speaks French and English.

Lux Hotels is now looking for a new marketing director and it is being proposed by Mr Avago that Pierre Avago take on the job, with Mr James having overall responsibility for group marketing as well as his responsibility for managing the 30 UK properties.

The company's marketing strategy and practices are developing effectively, with a centralized hotel reservation service, and yield management systems increasingly being adopted very efficiently. Occupancy rates have improved (around 65 per cent overall). Purchasing of high cost and high volume items (e.g. kitchen equipment, computers, in-room entertainment, alcohols, etc.) is largely centrally controlled.

Mr Schneider oversees the coach operation. He is this operation's original manager and indeed its first coach driver. He is also the longest-serving member of the main board of directors, after Mr Avago himself.

In charge of administration is *Mrs Tellman*, Mr Avago's niece. She is the only woman in the senior management team. Her responsibilities include Human Resource (HR) administration which is concerned mainly with issuing contracts to the more senior appointments and ensuring that employment law is not contravened. Other administration includes such things as applications for planning, various types of licences, purchasing, payroll, VAT, etc. and is handled through a highly centralized head office which employs 40 full-time (equivalent) staff. Labour turnover in head office is relatively low, around 10 per cent. The head office is located in one of the hotels near Oxford. This administrative support function serves only the UK. It is not clear to whom Mrs Tellman reports.

In all other countries administration is left to the local hotel managers with any coordination left to Mr Zandac, to whom all the 'out-of-UK' managers report directly. All the managers of the largest hotels (12 hotels with more than 200 rooms) have been promoted from other Lux hotels and all are British.

Food and beverage policy is left largely to individual hotel managers – the one overall policy being that every Lux Hotels outlet must offer menus priced at €18 for lunch and €22 for dinner. The Express by Holiday Inns and the four star hotels are excluded from this policy. Food and beverage purchasing is left largely to the hotel managers excepting for alcohols and major equipment purchases which are negotiated centrally.

Rooms design is left largely to Mrs Avago – consulting with individual managers. There is little strong branding – Mr and Mrs Avago preferring that local culture is reflected in design and décor.

Mr Charles (54), a Frenchman, is the director of Human Resources. He worked for Marriott Hotels in London for some years, first in food and beverage. He is mainly concerned with hotel general managers; arranging recruitment, transfers and negotiating managers' pay, bonuses and employee benefits on an individual basis. Outside the UK, hotel managers are responsible for the total control of their hotels including salary increases, promotions within the hotel, etc., within the agreed annual budget. There is no overall remuneration policy. There is no formal training scheme – the company believing that the best managers are developed from within through job rotation, transfers and promotions. Management meetings and conferences are organized on a 'needs' basis, i.e. there are no formal, regular conferences or seminars. Vacancies are not disseminated throughout the company.

The one exception to this approach is the British division of the company. The company has a very high standard of Human Resource Management (HRM) practice, reflected in the fact that it has previously acquired the Investors in People (IiP) accreditation. IiP is a demanding standard of HRM and is only granted to companies meeting certain HRM criteria. Labour turnover in these UK hotels is much lower than in the rest of Lux Hotels and is lower than the average for UK hotel companies. The company has a small talent management programme working with hotel schools and universities and has regular staff training and communication sessions. It sets out to offer conditions that put it in the top 25 per cent of British hotel companies. This group of hotels has a group HRM manager, *Miss Ripley*.

Wage costs, including social security charges, as a percentage of revenue are as shown in the table.

	Lux Hotels	National average for all hotels
Belgium	34%	32.7%
Germany	35%	34%
France	29%	30%
Hungary	24%	21.4%
Poland	25%	26.5%
UK	28%	27%
Overall	30%	28.5%

Some of the key issues to be addressed by the project team

There are serious differences across our properties in standards of service caused largely by:

- different attitudes to work, to loyalty, to commitment and to responsibilities to the 'team'; head office functions are clearly divided, competitive with one another rather than cooperative
- a recent employee satisfaction survey resulted in 56 per cent satisfaction against a benchmark of 68 per cent, varying across countries (cf. McDonald's: 91 per cent of staff say they are treated with respect and 82 per cent think they have a reasonable workload)
- different attitudes to work, to women working, to family-friendly policies
- high levels of labour turnover in some hotels, departments and categories particularly amongst ethnic minorities
- very varied levels of absenteeism
- reported high levels of stress, particularly in larger city centre hotels
- different conditions of employment e.g. some hotels (and countries) have fixed salaries, some have the service charge added to pay, whilst others rely heavily on tips; some hotels offer free accommodation to staff, others do not
- differences in contracts and job security

- UK employees are covered by a private company pension and private health insurance scheme, whereas in other countries only the state system applies
- a relatively high number of tribunal cases
- different role of trade unions, e.g. in Germany quite influential, in France very aggressive, in the UK no role at all
- of the 60 unit managers, 57 are men, the top 12 being of British origin
- there is no company-wide attitude/policy towards corruption – each manager deals with the situation according to the local culture – there is no 'ethics' statement
- different management hierarchy structures, e.g. France and Germany very formal with several layers of management and supervision; UK relatively relaxed, informal and flat
- there is no company-wide policy on 'outsourcing', each manager making his or her own decisions
- there is no company-wide policy regarding staff involvement or consultation
- management–staff relationships are driven by a concern with targets, e.g. occupancy rates, labour costs, restaurant and bar profits.

There are few requests to develop careers by moving from one country to another, excepting that a significant number of staff in all countries are asking to go to the UK, with the main reason being to learn English.

Another reason might be that it is known within the company that the British hotels had received a number of awards including Investors in People (IiP) and Excellence through People. They had also been nominated for a Catey award, a prestigious award granted by the *Caterer and Hotelkeeper* magazine.

Some of the women (mainly younger ones) who have transferred to other countries have encountered unexpected difficulties due to quite different attitudes to 'gender roles'.

Labour turnover, absenteeism and retention rates are not measured in the company. All recruitment, except at general manager level, is dependent upon the use of local recruitment sources such as government or private agencies, or an informal 'word-of-mouth' system. There is no company-wide diffusion of job opportunities.

The HRM project

The CEO, Mr Zandac, has passed you the following note:

> I am asking you to join a project team to advise me on how we can create a team of management and employees who feel loyal and committed to Lux Hotels. Currently we have a reasonably dedicated team in the UK but there is no corporate spirit such as I know exists in companies such as Marriott.
>
> We have had problems in persuading well-qualified managers, and other qualified staff as well, to accept transfers to other countries in which we need to have managers who know the Lux Hotels company culture, aims and practices.
>
> In the circumstances I have decided to form a small team of our own operational managers to look into the possibilities.

The Challenge:

We have to develop a Human Resource policy, strategy and supporting practices in order that we can achieve the following key strategic and marketing objectives, i.e.:

- We want to increase our hotel and room stock by about 10 per cent each year for the foreseeable future.
- We want to increase our proportion of four star properties because of their higher profitability.

- We want to enter one new national market each year.
- We have to improve year on year our profit contribution (REVPAR) per room.

We also need answers to the following questions:

- Is our present organization structure suitable for the future?
- Do we want our employees to be sufficiently loyal to the company so that around 75 per cent of all middle and senior managers are developed from within the company?
- Do we want all staff to perceive that they have lifelong careers with Lux Hotels? Could we meet such an expectation? If so, what do we need to do?
- What role, if any, do we want trade unions to have in Lux Hotels?
- To what extent can we, or should we, develop more flexible approaches to staffing our hotels, e.g. through more outsourcing (including some administrative work to less expensive labour markets, e.g. Morocco, Tunisia, India), subcontracting and the use of short-term contracts and agency staff?
- Finally should we adopt a positive 'employer branding' policy as exemplified by many other international hotel chains?

Please produce a comprehensive proposal which can be considered at the next Board of Directors' meeting.

If you have any queries about this case study please contact: mike.boella@gmail.com

Index